Managing Economic Development in Asia

From Economic Miracle to Financial Crisis

EDITED BY
KUOTSAI TOM LIOU

PRAEGER

Westport, Connecticut
London

Library of Congress Cataloging-in-Publication Data

Managing economic development in Asia : from economic miracle to financial crisis /
  edited by Kuotsai Tom Liou.
    p. cm.
  Includes bibliographical references and index.
  ISBN 0–275–96429–9 (alk. paper)
    1. Asia—Economic policy—1945– 2. Asia—Economic conditions—1945– I. Liou,
  Kuotsai Tom.
  HC412.M3378 2002
  338.95—dc21   2001034615

British Library Cataloguing in Publication Data is available.

Library of Congress Catalog Card Number: 2001034615
ISBN: 0–275–96429–9

First published in 2002

Praeger Publishers, 88 Post Road West, Westport, CT 06881
An imprint of Greenwood Publishing Group, Inc.
www.praeger.com

Printed in the United States of America

∞

The paper used in this book complies with the
Permanent Paper Standard issued by the National
Information Standards Organization (Z39.48–1984).

10 9 8 7 6 5 4 3 2 1

Contents

Preface

For the last several decades, economic development in Asia has been considered a miracle by many researchers of economic development. Many Asian economies, especially the eight high-performing Asian economies (HPAEs), have produced outstanding records in many aspects of economic development. For example, they have achieved high and sustained economic growth rates on the one hand, and low and declining levels of income inequality on the other. Researchers of economic development have published many articles, books, and professional reports to examine the successful development experience in Asia, identify major factors contributing to the development, and discuss general development models. These findings are important for both theoretical development and policy considerations.

One of the major theoretical and policy issues discussed has to do with the argument between the neoclassical approach and the statist approach. While the neoclassical approach emphasizes the important role of market and private enterprises in the process of development, the statist approach focuses on the role of the state in developing and implementing industrial policies to promote economic development. The arguments are especially related to the appropriate role of government in managing economic development, including such issues as the strategic public policies emphasized, the support of institutional development, and the contributions of public management systems.

The recent financial crisis in East and Southeast Asia has further stimulated researchers' interest in the Asian development experience. Many of them again questioned the implications of the statist development model. They are especially concerned about the inappropriate intervention of the government in the financial market, the lack of effective regulation and supervision of the banking system, and the unethical and illegal activities conducted by public officials. In addition, they are also interested in understanding the impact of the crisis on the different Asian economies and the policy options adopted to deal with the crisis and to restore the financial order.

As a researcher of public management and policy, I have been interested in studying the issue of economic development from a comprehensive and an interdisciplinary approach. I decided to edit a book on Asian economic development approximately three years ago after I finished the writing of two books: a single-authored book, *Managing Economic Reforms in Post-Mao China* (Praeger, 1998) and an edited book, *Handbook of Economic Development* (1998). During the preparation process, I realized the important role of government in managing economic development and the lack of interdisciplinary studies on Asian economic development. The purpose of this book is to examine many theoretical and policy issues that are related to the past economic development and the recent financial crisis.

It is a pleasure to acknowledge the many people who provided important support and assistance during the process of editing this book. My colleagues at the University of Central Florida provided the intellectual and institutional assistance in the writing, presentation, and publication of my studies. I appreciate the patience of many authors during the review and selection process. I thank Cynthia Harris, my editor at Praeger, for her professional assistance. I am especially grateful for the assistance of my graduate research assistant, Aaron Streimish, during the production process. Finally, strong support from my family has been critical in finishing this book. My parents have always supported me in my career development. My wife, Susan, has spent a lot of time taking care of three children (Alan, Anna, and Alex) and other family business, which allowed me to concentrate on my research. I owe all to their love and encouragement.

Chapter 1

Political Development, Administrative Capacity, and the Challenge to the Developmental State Model Posed by the 1997–1998 Financial Crisis in East and Southeast Asia

Cal Clark

Political development is often conceptualized as possessing two distinct dimensions: (1) democracy or popular participation and (2) administrative capacity or the ability to formulate and implement effective policies. The dominant interpretation of the East (and, more recently, Southeast) Asian "economic miracle" of the 1980s and 1990s focused on strong and autonomous developmental states, which led economic transformations and prevented dominant interests in a society from engaging in rent-seeking activity (Amsden, 1989; Hofheinz and Calder, 1982; Johnson, 1982; Wade, 1990; White, 1988). Thus, the growth of the administrative capacity of these regimes through developing a skilled corps of administrators and technocrats was assumed to play a key role in their rapid economic development. Consequently, political development in the region was widely viewed as being based on these nations' administrative capacities rather than on their progress toward democracy, which was generally fairly limited until quite recently (Clark, 1999).

The recent economic crisis in East and Southeast Asia has stimulated considerable criticism of the developmental state model, especially from the neoclassical perspective that public officials will almost inevitably distort an economy when they intervene in the pursuit of political goals. Robert Wade (1998) has rather sarcastically labeled this the "Death Throes of Asian State Capitalism" perspective. According to Robison and Rosser (1998, 1594), "With governments under intense pressure to accept change, IMF (International Monetary Fund) policy-makers and other liberals (i.e., neoclassicists) saw the crisis as a blessing in disguise and an opportunity to sweep away long-standing market distortions and practices of state intervention." Certainly, the state has played a major role in almost all East and Southeast Asian economies (Chan, 1993; Clark and Roy, 1997; Fallows, 1994; Hofheinz and Calder, 1982). Thus, just as "East Asian dynamism" (Chan, 1993) seemingly validated the developmental state model not so long ago, the "Asian flu" of 1997–1998 brings into sharp question the image of well-developed and functioning administrative structures in the "Asian tigers." Critics of the developmental state reacted to the Asian flu, however, by advocating laissez-faire policies much more than further democratization.

Yet, a closer examination of the crisis yields a much more nuanced set of conclusions. First, although it is easy to find government "policy failure," "market failure" contributed quite significantly to the crisis as well. Second, even in terms of "government failure," the demise or stillbirth of developmental states was probably much more to blame than the creation of competent bureaucracies. Finally, the nature of state structures varied greatly among the victims of the Asian flu, suggesting that more than a simultaneous crisis of too much "big government" in the region was at work here. Taken together, these conclusions suggest a need to rethink what we mean by political development and to move beyond the simplistic dichotomy between state and market in devising development strategies.

These arguments are developed in the following sequence. The first section provides an overview of the East and Southeast Asian economic crisis and argues that the central cause lay in the failure of national financial systems (as most critics of the developmental state believe). However, in strong contrast to the neoclassical critique, economic liberalization clearly exacerbated these financial problems. The next two sections then present, respectively, the central components in the model of the developmental state and a comparison of how the major countries in capitalist East and Southeast Asia conform to the model. As will be seen, these countries varied considerably in how closely they approximated a developmental state, and the strongest developmental states (Japan and South Korea) have seemingly degenerated considerably over time. Thus, it is at least arguable that strong and autonomous developmental states would have curtailed, if not prevented, the financial failures that spawned the crisis. Finally, the conclusion considers the implications of the Asian flu for statist theory and for views about political development in Asia.

THE ASIAN FLU

To those not paying attention to Southeast Asia or international capital flows, the crisis began almost innocuously when Thailand's government announced on July 2, 1997 that it would (could) no longer support the value of the Thai baht that had been pegged to the U.S. dollar. The consequences, however, were both immediate and dramatic. The baht plummeted, leading to a rapid outflow of foreign capital; the combination of

Table 1.1
The Crash of the Asian Tigers

	Change in Exchange Rate with U.S. $ June–Dec. 1997	Change in Stock Market Index June–Dec. 1997	Real GDP Growth		
			1996	1997	1998
Indonesia	−44.4%	−44.6%	8.0%	5.0%	−13.9%
Thailand	−48.7%	−29.3%	5.5%	−0.4%	−8.0%
South Korea	−47.7%	−49.5%	7.1%	5.5%	−5.3%
Malaysia	−35.0%	−44.8%	8.6%	7.8%	−8.1%
Philippines	−33.9%	−33.5%	5.7%	5.1%	−1.9%
Hong Kong	0.0%	−29.4%	4.9%	5.3%	−5.7%
Singapore	−15.0%	−23.0%	6.9%	7.8%	−0.8%
Taiwan	−14.8%	−9.3%	5.7%	6.9%	3.7%

Sources: Economist (1999a), 100; Goldstein (1998), 2–3.

capital flight and the falling exchange rate wreaked havoc on the stock market. The economic crisis quickly spread from Thailand to its neighbors in Southeast Asia (Indonesia, Malaysia, and to a somewhat lesser extent the Philippines), then jumped to South Korea in Northeast Asia, and finally threatened such distant "developing markets" as Russia and Brazil (Arndt and Hill, 1999; Friedman, 1999; Goldstein, 1999; Wade, 1998). Table 1.1 summarizes the devastation that occurred among the eight "tigers" in Southeast and East Asia, almost all of which went from high-growth to recessionary trajectories in a matter of months. The countries are broken into two groups of four: the top group suffered a massive impact from the crisis, while the Asian flu was considerably milder within the second group. Within each group, the nations are listed in a rough ranking of how adversely they were affected: Indonesia, Thailand, South Korea, and Malaysia in the first group; the Philippines, Hong Kong, Singapore, and Taiwan in the second. (Whether the Philippines belongs in the first or second group is, admittedly, somewhat ambiguous.)

By December 31, the value of the national currencies of Indonesia, Malaysia, the Philippines, South Korea, and Thailand had dropped by approximately 35 percent–45 percent against the U.S. dollar. (Only the Indonesia rupiah continued this downward trend in 1998.) The stock market collapse was equally sharp, as stocks tumbled by about 25 percent–50 percent in all these countries except Taiwan (before stabilizing in early 1998). The impact on economic growth was a little more delayed. For 1997 as a whole, all except Thailand had robust gross domestic product (GDP) growth in the 5 percent–8 percent range; even Thailand's economy only declined slightly by 0.4 percent. In 1998, however, the growth figures were reversed. Indonesia approached economic implosion (which stimulated the political explosion of forcing President Suharto from office) with a growth rate of −14 percent; the Malaysian and Thai economies shrank by 8 percent; there were strong recessions in Hong Kong and South Korea with GDP declines of about 5.5 percent; and only Taiwan experienced a positive rate of growth. When Japan's prolonged economic stagnation and recession of the 1990s is added to the picture, therefore, the transformation of a regional economic "miracle" into a "crisis" is complete.

Perhaps surprisingly, however, the crisis clearly bottomed out in the middle of 1998, at least in terms of the aggregate statistics in Table 1.2. This certainly implies that the region experienced a "phoenix factor," although it is hard to estimate how much of the damage to the poor in these societies (Booth, 1999) has been repaired. GDP growth and especially industrial growth resumed in the middle of 1998 and appeared to be, if anything, accelerating in 1999 and the first half of 2000, although the patterns for stock values and exchange rates were somewhat different. Initially, the recovery of the East and Southeast Asian stock markets was little short of amazing. During the first half of 1999, stock markets in seven of the eight tigers rose 30 percent–50 percent; the other tiger was Indonesia where the stock market nearly doubled. As a result, stock market indices throughout the region almost recovered their disastrous declines during the second half of 1997. Between the middle of 1999 and the middle of 2000, however, stock values either remained stagnant (Malaysia, Hong Kong, Singapore, and Taiwan) or fell appreciably (Indonesia, Thailand, South Korea, and the Philippines). Exchange rates had rebounded as well by mid-1999, although their recovery did not go as far toward reaching pre-crisis levels as the stock market "miracle." However, these rates proved to be more stable than the stock markets, for only three countries (Indonesia, Thailand, and the Philippines) had their currencies lose value appreciably between July 1999 and July 2000. Actually, these devalued currencies almost certainly played a key role in the strong recoveries of the "real" economies by making the region's exports much more competitive in cost terms. In addition, exports, consumer spending, and investment have all increased considerably throughout the region, suggesting that the recovery is well under way ("Economies," 1999). Interestingly, Malaysia, which spurned Western advice and aid by clamping on capital controls (Felker, 1999) does not appear to be that much different from the rest of the tigers in "shuffling forward" (Mertens, 1999).

At the most proximate level, the Asian flu crisis can be explained as resulting from a series of interlinked "external misalignments" involving exchange rates, exports, current account balances, and an overreliance on short-term debt (see the data in Table 1.3). The first step in this chain, as modeled in Figure 1.1, is that the currencies of the tigers had become over-

Table 1.2
Indicators of Economic Recovery

	Growth Rate Spring 1998–Spring 1999		Growth Rate Spring 1999–Spring 2000		Change in Stock Market			Exchange Rate with U.S. $			
	GDP	Industry	GDP	Industry	Jan.–July 1999	July 1997–July 1999	July 1997–July 2000	July 1997	July 1998	July 1999	July 2000
Indonesia	1.8%	0.1%	3.2%	34.8%	97.3%	-8.2%	-29.4%	2,500	15,200	6,740	9,375
Thailand	–	7.2%	5.2%	4.2%	42.7%	-2.1%	-38.8%	24.7	41.3	32.3	39.6
S. Korea	4.6%	21.8%	12.8%	20.0%	83.5%	35.0%	11.4%	909	1,333	1,172	1,117
Malaysia	-1.3%	5.4%	11.7%	18.6%	43.2%	-22.1%	-24.1%	2.53	4.18	3.80	3.8
Philippines	1.2%	1.8%	3.4%	-4.0%	34.4%	-7.2%	-45.2%	26.4	41.4	38.3	43.8
Hong Kong	-3.4%	-9.8%	14.3%	-2.7%	41.7%	-6.2%	8.4%	7.75	7.75	7.66	7.80
Singapore	1.2%	4.8%	9.1%	20.0%	49.7%	6.4%	4.6%	1.43	1.71	1.70	1.74
Taiwan	4.3%	10.8%	7.9%	8.6%	31.7%	-6.2%	-6.8%	27.8	34.4	32.4	30.8

Sources: Economist (1999b), 100; *Economist* (2000), 100; Goldstein (1998), 2–3; Robinson and Rosser (1998), 1594.

Table 1.3
Indicators of External Misalignments

	IMF Estimated Currency Overvaluation June 1997	Export Growth		Current Account Balance % of GDP 1996	Short-Term Debt % of Total Debt June 1997
		1995	1996		
Indonesia	4.2%	13.4%	9.7%	–3.3%	24%
Thailand	6.7%	23.1%	0.5%	–7.9%	46%
South Korea	–7.6%	30.3%	3.7%	–4.9%	67%
Malaysia	9.3%	20.3%	6.5%	–4.9%	39%
Philippines	11.9%	28.7%	18.7%	–4.7%	19%
Hong Kong	22.0%	14.8%	4.0%	–1.3%	–
Singapore	13.5%	13.7%	5.3%	15.7%	–
Taiwan	–5.5%	20.3%	3.8%	4.0%	–

Source: Goldstein (1998), 11, 15.

valued by 1996–1997. Most of these currencies had been pegged to the U.S. dollar and followed the dollar upward as it appreciated in the mid-1990s. As simple economic theory tells us, an overvalued currency is incompatible with the export-driven growth strategies that the Asian tigers were following. Moreover, this appreciation and overvaluation occurred at precisely the time the tigers' exports were coming under pressure from other important factors, such as global overcapacity in many of their key industries and the rapid industrialization of China with its very low-cost labor.

Consequently, there was a substantial slowdown in export growth which hurt the current account balances and foreign reserves of these nations. This weakness, in turn, created expectations that the currencies would fall, which led to speculative attacks against them by foreign currency traders and speculators. The governments involved thus faced a Hobson's choice. If they devalued their currencies, they might well set off the twin financial crises described in Figure 1.2. Conversely, if they defended the currency, they would use up their dwindling foreign reserves, thereby making themselves more vulnerable to another attack whose likelihood increased with their growing vulnerability (Garnaut, 1999; Goldstein, 1998; Taylor, 1998; Wade, 1998).

A significant devaluation would not just alter the terms of trade (making exports cheaper and imports more expensive) but also threatened to set off a financial crisis along the two distinct dimensions sketched in Figure 1.2 because of the great inflow of foreign capital during the 1990s. This had resulted from the combination of financial liberalization under U.S./IMF pressure with the attractiveness of rapidly growing economies that provided

Figure 1.1
External Imbalances and Pressure to Devaluate

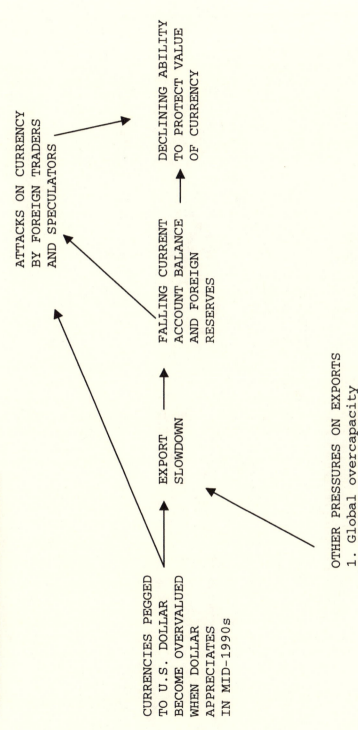

Figure 1.2
The Dual Destructiveness of Devaluation

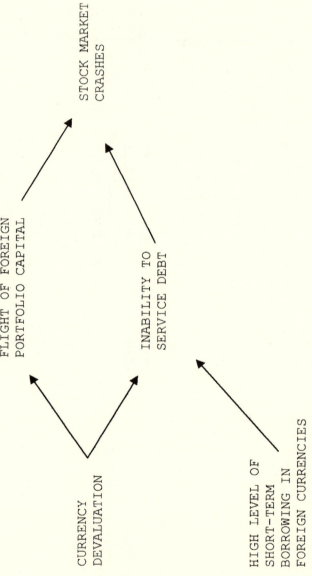

CURRENCY
DEVALUATION

FLIGHT OF FOREIGN
PORTFOLIO CAPITAL

INABILITY TO
SERVICE DEBT

HIGH LEVEL OF
SHORT-TERM
BORROWING IN
FOREIGN CURRENCIES

STOCK MARKET
CRASHES

a high return on capital. Along one dimension, devaluation would proportionately reduce the value of foreign portfolio capital, so that these investments rested on faith in currency stability. Thus, the threat and then the fact of devaluation set off massive capital flight which, in turn, resulted in the stock market crashes described in Table 1.1. Along the other, by the mid-1990s a comparatively high degree of the foreign debt in these countries was in the form of short-term borrowing (see Table 1.3), much of it denominated in foreign currencies. Substantial devaluation, therefore, would greatly increase the "real" debt burdens of the financial institutions and corporations that had assumed this debt, in many cases making it practically impossible for them to repay it (Garnaut, 1999; Goldstein, 1998; Taylor, 1998).

The model sketched in Figures 1.1 and 1.2 seems logical and certainly accords well with popular perceptions of the Asian flu. In particular, it seems to fit the Thai case perfectly. In terms of the dynamics in Figure 1.1, Thailand was able to fight off several speculative attacks against the baht in 1996–1997 but depleted its foreign reserves in so doing (Lauridsen, 1998; Suchitra, 1999). Once it admitted defeat in early July, it set off the dual destructiveness of Figure 1.2 as foreign capital fled and many financial institutions and companies faced unsustainable debt burdens. Once Thailand showed that, indeed, "the bottom could fall out," the process was repeated elsewhere in developing economies with similar characteristics where the calling in of foreign loans and the flight of foreign capital occurred much earlier in the cycle (Taylor, 1998; Wagner, 1998). That is, once "contagion" commenced, the financial implosions in Figure 1.2 became the cause, not the result, of these governments' inability to handle their external economic dislocations—which, obviously, made it much harder to deal with the crisis.

Yet, the data in Table 1.3 also suggest that a little caution should be in order before this "external misalignment" interpretation is fully accepted. At the aggregate level, the data fit the model: six of the eight tigers had overvalued currencies; all experienced considerable drops in export growth—three (South Korea, Taiwan, and Thailand) of over 80 percent; six had negative current accounts balances, with Thailand being by far the worst off; and short-term debt was atypically high in the region (although missing data make this conclusion somewhat tentative). The individual relationships among these variables do not tell such a consistent story, however. First, only three countries had currency that was overvalued by more than 10 percent (Hong Kong, Singapore, and the Philippines), and none of these was among the worst hit by the crisis. Moreover, almost all the currencies (Hong Kong excepted) collapsed by three times or more their estimated overvaluation (compare Tables 1.1 and 1.3), indicating that the crisis involved far more than a correction in misaligned currencies. Second, the correlation between currency overvaluation and export collapse appears almost nonexistent. For example, the two nations (South Korea and Taiwan) with undervalued currencies, which should stimulate exports, shared the dubious distinction with Thailand of having the largest export collapses in 1996. Thus, something besides currency misalignment (such as the two factors included in Figure 1.2) was the major driving force in the ubiquitous drop in the tigers' export dynamism.

Third, the data on the balance in current accounts as a percentage of GDP in the fourth column of Table 1.3 are, at first glance, consistent with the model. There is a strong association between the size of a country's negative balance relative to the economy and the severity of its subsequent crisis; and all of the hardest-hit nations, plus the Philippines, were close to the current account balance of −5 percent of GDP that sparked the Mexican debt crisis of 1982 (Taylor, 1998). Yet, even here, one can question the "misalignment model" since the slightly overvalued currencies and recent export slowdowns are far from sufficient in themselves to explain this emerging crisis in the current account balance. A far better explanation comes from the high level of short-term borrowing in the worst hit countries. Thus, the prime misalignment appears to have been in the East Asian debt structures, but this turns our attention to the question of why an influx of foreign capital into rapidly growing "miracle" economies led to crisis and collapse rather than expanded dynamism.

The conventional image of debt crises in developing nations is certainly one of "government failure." According to this laissez-faire logic, incompetent governments borrow extravagantly to finance some combination of social services or unproductive development projects or the bank accounts of corrupt politicians; liberal monetary and fiscal policies fan the fires of inflation; consequently, sooner or later the debt on these unproductive uses can no longer be serviced, setting off the debt crisis. Thus, all would be well if governments would allow the "magic of the marketplace" to operate. This scenario did not hold in East and Southeast Asia, however. The crisis was preceded not by an increase in governmental intervention but by the liberalization, under pressure from the United States and the IMF (what Wade, 1998, calls the "Wall Street–Treasury–IMF Complex"), of both the domestic financial systems and international capital flows in most of the tigers. In fact, the Asian flu represented the first international economic crisis in the postwar era where both the lenders and the creditors were overwhelmingly in the private sector.

Thus, the "usual suspects" of the neoclassicists seem to be most remarkable by their absence. Rather, as diagrammed in Figure 1.3, the strong influx of foreign capital that occurred during the early and mid-1990s sparked the transformation of the tigers' "Confucian capitalism" to what might be called "rat hole capitalism" in honor of the huge financial losses that it generated. The cycle was set off as Western pressure to open these economies increased after they were increasingly seen as lucrative invest-

Figure 1.3
The Degeneration from "Confucian" to "Rat Hole" Capitalism

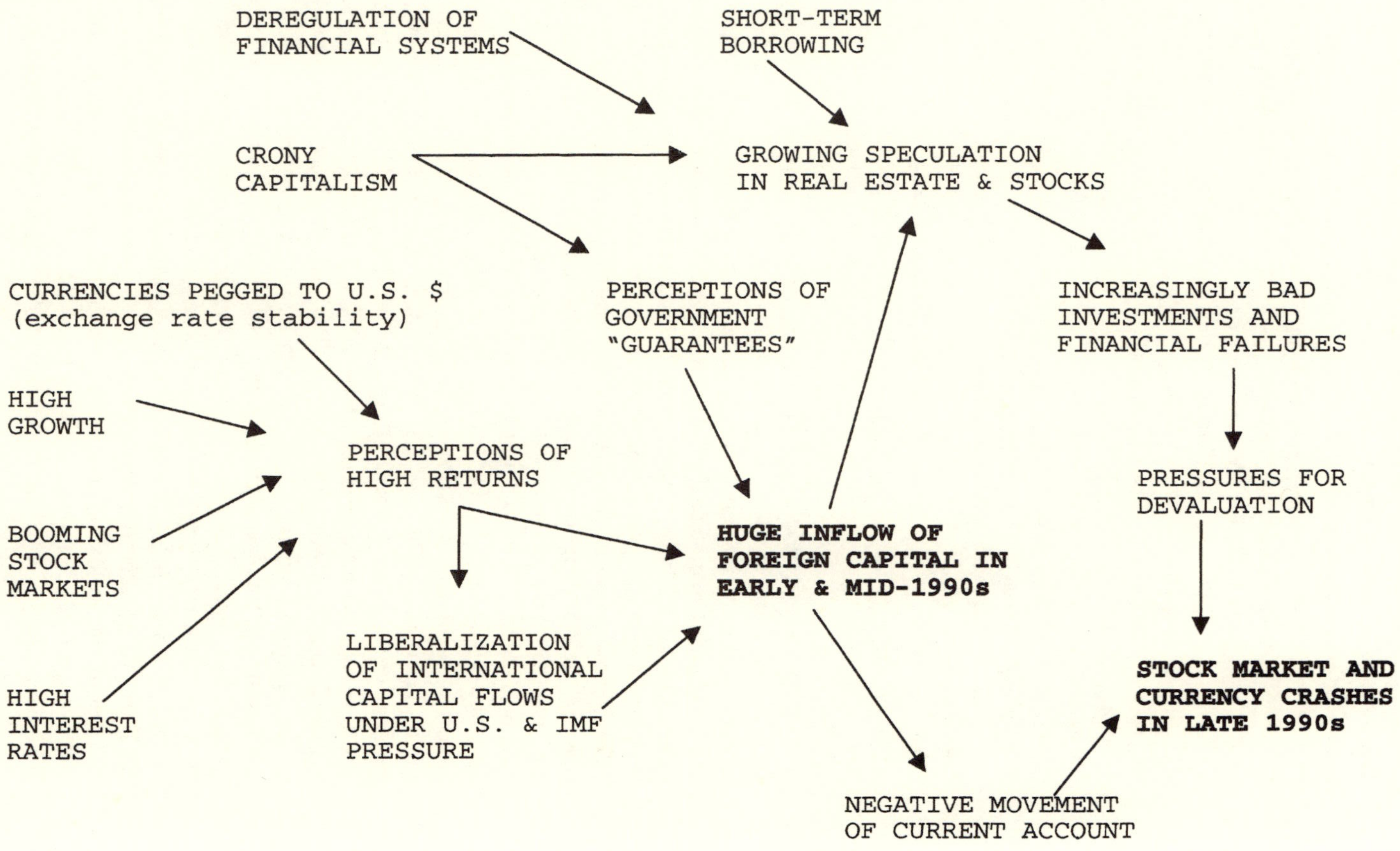

DEREGULATION OF
FINANCIAL SYSTEMS

SHORT-TERM
BORROWING

CRONY
CAPITALISM

GROWING SPECULATION
IN REAL ESTATE & STOCKS

PERCEPTIONS OF
GOVERNMENT
"GUARANTEES"

INCREASINGLY BAD
INVESTMENTS AND
FINANCIAL FAILURES

PRESSURES FOR
DEVALUATION

CURRENCIES PEGGED TO U.S. $
(exchange rate stability)

PERCEPTIONS OF
HIGH RETURNS

HIGH
GROWTH

BOOMING
STOCK
MARKETS

HIGH
INTEREST
RATES

LIBERALIZATION
OF INTERNATIONAL
CAPITAL FLOWS
UNDER U.S. & IMF
PRESSURE

HUGE INFLOW OF
FOREIGN CAPITAL IN
EARLY & MID-1990s

NEGATIVE MOVEMENT
OF CURRENT ACCOUNT

STOCK MARKET AND
CURRENCY CRASHES
IN LATE 1990s

Table 1.4
Indicators of Financial Degeneration

	Foreign Investment as % of GDP 1997	Estimated Bank Lending to Property Sector End of 1997	Goldman-Sachs Estimates of Nonperforming Loans	
			Actual % of Total, 1997	Peak % of Total, 1998–1999
Indonesia	64%	25%–30%	9%	> 25%
Thailand	57%	30%–40%	18%	> 25%
South Korea	34%	15%–25%	14%	> 25%
Malaysia	77%	30%–40%	6%	12%–25%
Philippines	58%	15%–20%	3%	10%–15%
Hong Kong	18%	40%–55%	2%	> 8%
Singapore	13%	30%–40%	2%	> 8%
Taiwan	10%	–	–	–

Sources: Goldstein (1998), 8, 10; Wagner (1998), 602–603.

ment opportunities for a variety of reasons: their sustained records of high growth, booming stock markets, high interest rates, and currencies pegged to the U.S. dollar (which was believed to ensure the exchange rate stability vital for investment security). Even the reputation that many of the countries had for "crony capitalism" was not a detriment for investment because it gave rise to the perception that the governments would bail out their "crony" financial institutions and corporations should disaster strike.

Once their international capital regimes were liberalized, a huge flood of foreign capital therefore poured into East and Southeast Asia. By 1997, for instance, Table 1.4 shows that foreign capital had skyrocketed to well over half of GDP in Thailand (57 percent), the Philippines (58 percent), Indonesia (64 percent), and Malaysia (77 percent). In 1996 alone, international bank claims on Indonesia, Thailand, South Korea, and Malaysia jumped by nearly a quarter from $202 to $248 billion; in Thailand credit to the private sector as a percentage of GDP tripled from 39 percent to 123 percent between 1992 and 1996 alone (Taylor, 1998). Yet, as the indicators of financial problems in Table 1.4 imply, this huge surge of capital, rather than financing increased productivity and growth, set off the dynamics that ultimately triggered the crisis. First, just the logic of national accounting statistics indicates that the inflow of foreign capital will push the current account balance in a negative direction, which, in turn, usually sets off pressures to devalue the currency.

Second, the influx of such a large amount of capital meant that there soon was too much money chasing the productive investment opportunities that even the tiger economies could offer. This situation, when compounded by the concomitant deregulations of the national financial systems and the less savory aspects of corruption and crony capitalism that existed throughout much of the region, led to growing speculation, particularly in real estate and stocks. For example, Table 1.4 shows that by the end of 1997 bank lending to the property sector was high throughout the region, although this by itself need not be a problem as evidenced by the high level of real estate loans in such fairly healthy economies as Hong Kong and Singapore. A very high percentage of these bank loans were short-term with maturities of a year or less—70 percent in Thailand and South Korea, 62 percent in Indonesia, and 47 percent in Malaysia in mid-1996. Moreover, much of the collateral for these loans was in the form of real estate and stocks whose value was becoming increasingly questionable.

This quickly set off a vicious cycle of growing financial failures (see the data on nonperforming loans in Table 1.4). This increased the pressure for devaluation which, as modeled in Figure 1.2, undermined the ability of domestic financial institutions and corporations to service their debt which, in turn, set off a new round of the downward cycle (Cole and Slade, 1999; Goldstein, 1998; Taylor, 1998; Wade, 1998; Wagner, 1998). "Market failure," therefore, seems just as much to blame, if not more so, than "government failure." Private financial institutions and corporations freely entered into transactions that led to disaster. If this be capitalism, it would seem to be the Marxist version that capitalism contains the seeds of its own destruction! The reason for this market failure, however, is almost universally attributed to government failure in the form of a failure to regulate local financial markets effectively (Goldstein, 1998; Knight, 1998; Norton, 1998; Robison and Rosser, 1998; Taylor, 1998; Wade, 1998). Since the major task of a developmental state is using the powers of government to lead and shape national development projects, the East Asian flu can be taken as *prima facie* evidence for the failure of developmental states in East and Southeast Asia. However, this failure does not indicate the need to replace the statist model with laissez-faire logic so much as it raises the question of how to reconstitute or create effective developmental states in Asia.

THE LOGIC OF THE DEVELOPMENTAL STATE

The model of the developmental state rests on two assumptions concerning the processes of development in the Third World. First, most developing nations are at such a disadvantage in terms of their position in the world economy that market forces themselves preclude significant industrial growth. Second, states in at least some of these nations possess the power to overcome the barriers facing "late developers." These two assumptions reflect what might respectively be termed the *demand* for and *supply* of state economic leadership in the political economies of developing nations. (For more detailed discussions of the developmental state model, see Alam, 1989; Amsden, 1989; Chan et al., 1998; Evans et al., 1985; Johnson, 1982; Moon and Prasad, 1994; Onis, 1991; Wade, 1990; White, 1988.)

In terms of demand, there is widespread agreement on several fundamental prerequisites for development that are extremely hard for the private sector in developing nations to attain on its own. First, there needs to be a basic stock of investment capital. Second, even given adequate financial resources, human skills are essential, both for entrepreneurship and for at least a minimally skilled workforce (whose skill requirements escalate quickly as a nation moves up the international product cycle). Finally, development activities in the Third World (generally sooner rather than later) come into competition or conflict with foreign corporations and/or countries that wield considerable market power. Thus, an ability to deal with external forces must be created as well.

Even accepting the first stage of the statist argument—that there is a demand for state developmental activities—a second stage in the line of logic is needed to justify the presumption that there is a "supply" of such economic policy help available for economies attempting to industrialize. According to the statist paradigm, "strong and autonomous developmental states" are able to meet this challenge. As suggested by the outline of such a state in Figure 1.4, each of three institutional characteristics—strength, autonomy, and developmental commitment—must be present if a government hopes to supply the developmental support that its society and business community may "demand."

According to this model, developmental states are viewed as "strong" in the sense that they can effectively implement their policies. This capability, in turn, is based on two subdimensions or factors. First, the policies must be accepted by the broader society because of some combination of personal benefit and self-interest, belief that the government is acting legitimately, and fear of the repressive might of the regime. Second, the policies themselves must be well designed and appropriate. Here, some of the important conditions include the existence of a well-educated bureaucracy and the absence of debilitating political infighting.

The second characteristic of "autonomy" means that state officials can act independently of pressures from social groups, especially "dominant classes" who try to use their influence to prevent change that would threaten their vested interests (Rueschemeyer and Evans, 1985). This can occur when the bureaucracy is both protected and respected by a strong executive leader who, to use the words of Chalmers Johnson (1982), chooses to reign but not rule. As a result of such a situation, economic decision makers within the government are able to take a long-term perspective on national interest, resist pressures for rent-seeking, and make

Figure 1.4
Structural Characteristics of a Developmental State

State Strength

1. Strong capability to implement policies
   a. coercive authority
   b. popular acceptance and legitimacy
2. Capacity for making and implementing decisions
   a. leading role for bureaucracy staffed by expert technocrats
   b. state structure extensive enough for requisite actions

State Autonomy

1. Protection by strong leader who "reigns," not "rules"
2. Independence from both dominant and subordinate classes

Strong Commitment to Development

1. Prevents domination by other priorities
   a. not predation
   b. not bureaucratic and patronage politics
   c. not exclusively military security
2. Takes long-term view of national interest
3. Resists rent-seeking behavior
4. Makes investments for long-term payoffs and structural transformations that would not occur under short-term market pressures

---

long-term investments that might not be justified by short-term market logic.

Third, of course, a strong and autonomous state must be fundamentally committed to treating development as a high priority rather than distributing patronage to political clients, preserving the status quo in society, providing a social welfare net for the population, forwarding the national interest through militarism, engaging in "predation" (Evans, 1995) to line the pockets of its leaders, or any other potential objective. Without such a developmental commitment, a state will use its capabilities for something else, while without strength and autonomy a state will not be able to deliver on any developmental commitments it might have.

Moon and Prasad (1994, 362–363) nicely summarize this stereotype of the East Asian developmental states:

Executive dominance allows political leaders to create and expand spaces for bureaucratic rule. Bureaucratic agencies in the East Asian developmental states are highly structured and competently staffed. . . . The organization is composed of highly capable individuals screened and recruited through cut-throat open competition. They are analytically adept, and technically competent. Bureaucrats in the developmental states are also united in purpose, and show an unusually high degree of congruence with organizational and national goals. Such unity of purpose minimizes bureaucratic in-fighting and enhances inter-agency consensus and coordination. Furthermore, meritocratic practices originating from the Confucian tradition and elite social status prevent public bureaucrats from being "captured" by rent-seeking social groups.

It is also valuable to take a closer look at the more micro policies and activities that are attributed to developmental states. According to the theory of the developmental state, government technocracies can perform a valuable leading role for several central tasks in the national development project. As illustrated in Figure 1.5, these tasks encompass three different types of government activities.

The first group of activities involves the creation and maintenance of a sound business environment without which a market economy could not operate. Most of these, incidentally, are accepted as necessary by neoclassical economists. Such governmental functions include maintaining political order (including holding political corruption and "squeeze" on businesses within acceptable bounds), creating a stable legal order for market relationships, using macroeconomic (fiscal and monetary) policy to curb inflation and dampen the business cycle, and financing expensive physical infrastructure projects (e.g., highways, railroads, harbors, and airports) that are vital for commerce and business expansion. In addition, another policy falling under this rubric may be termed "state *de*-activism" in the economy, such as the privatization of state corporations and market liberalization, which is a common method for moving from import-substitution to export-led growth (Balassa, 1981; Balassa et al., 1989). More broadly along these lines, the state can minimize the drain of resources away from the private sector by limiting the size of government and "unproductive" activities, such as military spending and welfare programs, and bureaucracy in general. Here, of course, there is something of a paradox if we equate strong government with big government.

Direct state activism in the economy represents the second category in Figure 1.5 and constitutes the core of what is usually termed a developmental state. These policy areas create the fundamental divide between the statist approach and neoclassical assumptions that governments simply cannot perform such functions effectively and efficiently. Statists, in sharp contrast, advocate more stimulative macroeconomic policies than are necessary for stability in the expectation that they can generate a virtuous cycle of self-reinforcing growth. More fundamentally, statists also believe that a government in a "late industrializer" should take a leading role in financial mobilization and allocation to ensure that it is effectively used and directed

Figure 1.5
State Roles in Development

Creating a Conducive Business Environment

1. Maintain Political Order
2. Create and Maintain Legal Order Underlying Private Property and Market Relations
3. Maintain Macroeconomic Stability
   —Monetary and Fiscal Policies
4. Provide Physical Infrastructure
5. Sponsor Market Liberalization after Import-Substitution Controls and Privatize State Enterprises
6. Minimize Drain on Private Resources
   —Limit Size of State, Unnecessary Defense Spending, and Huge Welfare Programs/ bureaucracy

State Economic Activism

1. Macroeconomic Stimulation
   —Monetary and Fiscal Policies
2. Control and Channel Finance into Vital Sectors
3. Industrial Policy
   —Target Key Industries
   —Force High Performance Standards on Industry
   —Promote Basic Structural Transformations of Economy
   —Economic Planning
4. Trade Policy
   —Protection for Import-Substitution Industrialization
   —Divert Protectionism of Trading Partners
5. Regulate Multinational Corporations (MNCs)
   —Recruit Foreign Capital
   —Prevent De-nationalization of Economy
   —Channel Foreign Capital and Technology into Key Sectors
6. State Entrepreneurship
   —State Corporations in Key Industries
   —Partnerships of State with Foreign and Local Capital
7. Policy Incentives for General Structural Transformation

State Social Activism

1. Provide Human Capital Infrastructure
   —Education
2. Anti-Poverty Redistributional Policies
   —Spending for Health, Nutrition, and Other Social Services
3. Safety and Environmental Protection
4. Protect Population from Economic Power of Business Class

into targeted "sunrise" sectors. Control over finance, in turn, is the first step toward an activist industrial policy since the provision of capital represents one of the prime tools for targeting an industry (along with tax relief, other types of subsidies, R&D assistance, creating actual state enterprises, and trade protection). In addition to providing assistance to selected industries, these tools can also be used to enforce performance standards on particular industries and firms. Finally, statists also want governments in the developing world to take a strong role in negotiating with foreign corporations and countries. Trade policy is important, especially with rising protectionism in the industrial world. In addition, statists have a somewhat ambiguous view of foreign capital, viewing it as a source both of valuable funds and technology and of fierce and perhaps unfair competition to local industries. Consequently, they advocate state controls over MNCs to ensure that they contribute to the national development project, rather than simply exploiting local resources. More broadly, the state can move beyond policies toward single industries by promoting general structural transformations (e.g., from import-substitution to the export of light industrial goods, from light industry to heavy industry, etc.) and can create systems for large-scale economic planning (Amsden, 1989; Evans et al., 1985; Johnson, 1982; Wade, 1990; Woo, 1991).

A third dimension emerges from the work of scholars committed to the "basic human needs" approach who urge what might be called "social" activism, in addition to economic activism. This can be justified on normative grounds alone—that is, development is not really occurring unless the bulk of the population in a country benefits from economic growth. However, the growing emphasis on human capital as an important source of growth suggests that the creation of an educated and healthy society may actually promote growth in the long term. Recent comparative analysis, for example, does indeed suggest that investment in human capital has a positive long-term effect on economic performance (Clark and Roy, 1997; Moon, 1991; Moon and Dixon, 1992).

THE MANY ROADS TO ASIAN DYNAMISM AND ASIAN DISLOCATIONS

Popular perceptions (and the data presented in Tables 1.5 and 1.6) view Asia's vaunted economic dynamism as occurring in a series of waves as first one country or set of nations "took off" (Rostow, 1960) on sustained trajectories of rapid industrialization and growth: first Japan in the 1950s; then the East Asian tigers (Hong Kong, Singapore, South Korea, and Taiwan in the 1960s); then the Southeast Asian tigers by the late 1970s (Indonesia, Malaysia, and Thailand but not the Philippines, which was languishing under Marcos's "crony capitalism"); then China and the major nations of South Asia (Bangladesh, India, Pakistan, and Sri Lanka) by the

Table 1.5
Indicators of Asia's Economic Development

	GNP per Capita 1997	GNP per Capita (Parity Purchasing Power) 1997	Rank in World	Manu-facturing % of GDP		Agri-culture % of GDP	
				1980	1997	1980	1997
Developed Asia							
Japan	$37,850	$23,640	6	29%	25%	4%	2%
East Asian Tigers							
Hong Kong	$25,280	$25,540	4	24%	7%	1%	0%
Singapore	$32,940	$29,000	1	29%	26%	1%	0%
South Korea	$10,550	$13,550	24	28%	26%	15%	6 %
Taiwan	$11,600*	–	–	36%	29%*	8%	4%*
Southeast Asia							
Indonesia	$1,110	$3,470	67	13%	25%	24%	16%
Malaysia	$4,680	$10,920	29	21%	34%	22%	13%
Philippines	$1,220	$3,670	63	26%	22%	25%	20%
Thailand	$2,800	$6,590	41	22%	29%	23%	11%
Communist Tiger							
China	$860	$3,570	65	41%	40%	30%	20%
South Asia							
Bangladesh	$270	$1,050	106	11%	9%	50%	30%
India	$390	$1,650	92	18%	19%	38%	27%
Pakistan	$490	$1,590	94	16%	17%	30%	26%
Sri Lanka	$800	$2,460	75	18%	17%	28%	22%
World Average	**$5,130**	**$6,330**	–	**24%**	–	**7%**	–

*1994.
Sources: *Taiwan Statistical Data Book* (1995), 1–2; World Bank (1999), 190–191, 212–213.

1990s; and finally the post–Marcos Philippines by the early 1990s. Har-kening back to a theory that originated in interwar Japan, some (but not all) scholars and observers have observed a pattern of "flying geese" starting with Japan and then fanning back through each successive wave of industrializers (Bernard and Ravenhill, 1995; Chan, 1993; Clark and Roy, 1997; Cumings, 1984; Fallows, 1994; Gereffi and Wyman, 1990; Hobday, 1995; Hofheinz and Calder, 1982; Jomo, 1997; Ravenhill, 1995; World Bank, 1993).

Tables 1.5 and 1.6, respectively, present data on the development levels and on the economic and social performance of these Asian nations. They

Table 1.6
Indicators of Asian Nations' Economic and Social Performance

	GNP Growth		Industrial Growth		Infant Mortality 1996	Consumption per Capita Growth 1980–1996	Adult Literacy 1995	
	1980–1990	1990–1997	1980–1990	1990–1997			Male	Female
Developed Asia								
Japan	4.0%	1.4%	4.2%	0.2%	4	2.9%	99%	99%
East Asian Tigers								
Hong Kong	6.9%	5.3%	—	—	4	5.3%	96%	88%
Singapore	6.6%	8.5%	5.4%	9.1%	4	4.9%	96%	86%
South Korea	9.5%	7.2%	12.1%	7.5%	9	7.1%	99%	97%
Taiwan	7.9%	6.5%*	6.3%	4.5%*	5*	7.0%*	94%*	94%*
Southeast Asia								
Indonesia	6.1%	7.5%	6.9%	10.2%	44	4.3%	90%	78%
Malaysia	5.2%	8.7%	7.2%	11.2%	11	3.3%	89%	78%
Philippines	1.0%	3.3%	-0.9%	3.7%	37	0.8%	95%	94%
Thailand	7.6%	7.5%	9.9%	10.3%	34	5.6%	96%	92%
Communist Tiger								
China	10.2%	11.9%	11.1%	16.3%	33	7.7%	90%	73%
South Asia								
Bangladesh	4.3%	4.5%	4.9%	6.8%	77	0.0%	49%	26%
India	5.8%	5.9%	7.1%	7.1%	65	2.3%	65%	38%
Pakistan	6.3%	4.4%	7.3%	5.5%	88	1.5%	50%	24%
Sri Lanka	4.2%	4.9%	4.6%	6.5%	15	2.6%	93%	87%
World Average	**2.9%**	**2.5%**	**2.8%**	**—**	**54**	**2.9%**	**79%**	**62%**

*1990–1994, 1980–1994, or 1994 for Taiwan (for which adult literacy is not broken down by gender).
Sources: *Taiwan Statistical Data Book* (1995), 1–2, 11, 46; World Bank (1999), 192–193, 202–203, 210–211.

certainly vary tremendously by development level. Japan, Hong Kong, and Singapore now rank among the richest countries in the world in terms of both GNP per capita and GNP per capita adjusted for "parity purchasing power." (The latter probably provides the most accurate measure of national affluence compared to the U.S. figure of $28,740.) Taiwan and South Korea technically meet the World Bank's definition of high-income countries, although their GNP per capitas are still well below the $20,000 typical in the developed world. The four Southeast Asian countries are all well into the range of "middle-income" countries, with Malaysia well ahead of the other three. In actual GNP per capita, China and Sri Lanka are at the bottom of the middle-income group, but in terms of "real" purchasing power China has caught up with Indonesia and the Philippines and Sri Lanka is fairly close behind. Finally, the other three South Asian nations remain among the low-income countries, with Bangladesh a step-level behind the other two, especially in regard to its small manufacturing sector. In structural terms, the data on manufacturing's and agriculture's share of the total economy indicate that Japan and the East Asian tigers are already moving in a postindustrial direction, while Southeast Asia is in the middle of its manufacturing buildup and South Asia is completing the transformation away from agriculturally dominated economies. (China's heavy industry focus under communism created a departure from the normal pattern of economic sequencing.)

Despite these huge developmental differences, the data on overall economic (GNP) and industrial growth from 1980 through 1997 show extremely high economic performance throughout the region. (The only exceptions are Japan in the 1990s and the Philippines until the early 1990s.) China had the highest growth rate in the world during this period (10 percent for 1980–1990 and 12 percent for 1990–1997). Both the East Asian and Southeast Asian (the Philippines excepted) tigers were extremely dynamic too, as all but Hong Kong (at slightly over 6 percent) averaged over 7 percent annual growth for the 18 years under consideration. In comparison, the South Asian growth rates of 4.5 percent to 6.5 percent might seem less impressive, but they are well above the world average and well above these countries' previous records. Moreover, in almost every instance, industrial growth was higher than GNP growth, indicating that a positive economic transformation is underway throughout the region. As might be expected, the social performance of these countries (i.e., the levels of literacy and infant mortality) are strongly correlated with GNP per capita, and economic growth tended to be transferred into consumption growth disproportionately less in the poorer nations. Still, Sri Lanka, China, and Malaysia deserve substantial credit for having much better social outcomes than would be expected given their levels of affluence.

Given the spread of East Asian export dynamism to Southeast Asia, China, and South Asia during the 1980s, it might seem reasonable to suppose that other nations in the region had finally learned from East Asia's model of "Confucian capitalism," developed first by Japan and then, presumably, applied by the East Asian tigers. Since these nations formed the empirical base for the model of the developmental state outlined in the previous section, it was easy to conclude that "Asian dynamism" represented a better way of organizing capitalism than the Anglo-American laissez-faire approach—which probably explains the eagerness of some in the West to interpret the Asian flu as the "Death Throes of Asian State Capitalism" (Wade, 1998).

In particular, the power and leadership of the skilled technocracies in the East Asian tigers were widely given credit for charting a course of industrial development and upgrading that moved their nations through several fundamental transitions from agriculture to labor-intensive light industry to heavy industry to advanced high-tech production. Such state elites, moreover, did not intervene in the economy to distort markets and protect monopoly rents. Rather, after short periods of "infant industry" protection, they pursued "market-conforming" strategies and promoted exports and integration into the world economy, in contrast to the "import-substitution" strategy of industrialization followed in most other parts of the Third World. These developmental states were able to implement such "industrial policies" because the state assumed control of the national financial systems, thereby gaining the power to direct investment into "sunrise industries," and developed close working relationships with the business community. State power was also used to control and channel the activities of foreign multinational corporations (MNCs), as well as to prevent traditional elites and vested interests from holding back change, as well as suppressing labor activism to hold down wage costs (Amsden, 1989; Fallows, 1994; Johnson, 1982; Prestowitz, 1988; Wade, 1990; Woo, 1991).

The brief summaries of the Asian political economies in the first two columns of Figure 1.6, however, cast considerable doubt on such an interpretation of a spread of developmental statism for several reasons. As the crude ratings of national economic and social performance in Table 1.6 showed, the developmental states in capitalist East Asia have been quite successful in promoting "growth with equity"; that is, they have good records in both the economic and social realms. Yet, other types of regimes have displayed considerable success as well. Moreover, whatever else may be included among the causes and consequences of the recent economic transformations in other parts of Asia, leadership by a strong developmental state was not one of their characteristics. Even the successful developmental states in East Asia appear to be deteriorating.

In Southeast Asia, the state structures tended to be somewhat weaker and more open to social, especially business, pressures. The results in both economic and social terms were generally better than in South Asia, but few if any analysts give much credit to state leadership. Rather, there were more clientelistic links between business and top leaders which were more marked by payoffs for doing business rather than positive state support. The "crony capitalism" of the Marcos regime marked an extreme example, which, unfortunately, was later replicated elsewhere in Southeast Asia, with the worst excesses occurring in Indonesia (Case, 1997; MacIntyre, 1994; Robison and Rosser, 1998). Perhaps more tellingly for testing the developmental state model, the transformation of these economies from import-substitution to export-orientation did not involve state-directed development policies à la Japan, South Korea, and Singapore (Jomo, 1997). In direct contrast, economic reform in these countries, as in China and South Asia (Bhagwati, 1993; Clark and Roy, 1997), was based primarily on market and trade liberalization, that is, the *withdrawal*, not the intensification, of state controls (Haggard and Kaufman, 1995; MacIntyre, 1994).

Even East Asia, furthermore, is not totally consistent with the argument that a strong developmental state comes close to being a necessary and sufficient condition for strong economic performance since the role of developmental states varies considerably among these five political economies. Two of the East Asian countries, Japan and South Korea, have archetypical developmental states that implemented strong industrial policies supporting the push of large domestic corporations to become "national champions" in most of the world's leading industries (Amsden, 1989; Fields, 1995; Hart, 1992; Johnson, 1982; Jones and Sakong, 1980; Mardon and Paik, 1992; Okimoto, 1989; Woo, 1991). Yet, even in Japan, many industrial sectors do not conform to the developmental state model, either because business provided the primary leadership (sometimes directly ignoring government "guidance") or because business–government relations were primarily clientelistic (Calder, 1993; Friedman, 1988).

Furthermore, as indicated in the second column of Figure 1.6, both of these developmental states appear to be heading toward an eclipse. In Korea, democratization and the developmental state's very success in creating strong conglomerates or *chaebol* have clearly undercut the autonomy and leadership power of the technocracy (Chang, 1998; Hahm and Plein, 1997; Moon and Prasad, 1994). Japan appears to be suffering from a variety of ills deleterious to its vaunted developmental state: political gridlock in the domestic arena, a state bureaucracy now primarily concerned with protecting its power over the economy, and gross corruption in business–government relations (Calder, 1993; Clark and Roy, 1997).

The other East Asian dragons, furthermore, have significantly different types of political economies. Singapore also has a strong developmental state, but it has pursued a strategy almost opposite to the economic nationalism of Japan and Korea by relying on growth-through-invitation-to-multinational corporations (MNCs) (Mirza, 1986; Rodan, 1989). In the mid-1980s, for example, MNCs accounted for 26 percent of GDP, 41 per-

Figure 1.6
State and Development in Asia

	Primary State Economic Role	Recent Change in Economic System	Current Regime	Major Postwar Type	Pye's Political Culture Type
East Asia					
Japan	Effective developmental state based on business-government cooperation	Growing bureaucracy and corruption undercut developmental state	Consolidated Democracy	Consolidated Democracy	Confucian Feudal
South Korea	Effective developmental state with strong government leadership	*Chaebol* power and democracy undercut developmental state	New Democracy	Military Rightist Authoritarian	Confucian Feudal
Singapore	Strong developmental state: recruit MNCs and state corps	No	Semi-Democracy	Semi-Democracy	Confucian Patriarchal
Taiwan	Developmental state in heavy industry and regulate MNCs, but just created conducive environment for small "guerrilla capitalists"	Major movement of low-tech manufacturers to China	New Democracy	Rightist Authoritarian	Confucian Patriarchal and Heterodox
Hong Kong	Laissez-faire emphasis on trade and small business	Major movement of low-tech manufactures to China; increasingly, *guanxi* capitalism	PRC "Protectorate"	British Colonial	Confucian Heterodox

Southeast Asia					
Philippines	From crony capitalism to macroeconomic stabilization	No	New Democracy	Semi-Democracy	Clientelistic
Malaysia Thailand Indonesia	Some development policies but no strong state à la East Asia	Market liberalization in switch from import substitution to export-based industrialization	Semi-Democracy	Authoritarian or Semi-Democracy	Clientelistic
South Asia					
India	Strong state control over economy for industrializing led to inefficiency and waste	Significant liberalization reforms	Consolidated Democracy	Consolidated Democracy	Caste-Bureaucratic
Pakistan Bangladesh	Statist economy like India's	Significantly less reform than in India	Semi-Democracy	Military Rightist Authoritarian	Caste-Bureaucratic
Sri Lanka	Initially, statist economy and large social programs	Market liberalization in 1980s	Consolidated Democracy	Consolidated Democracy	Caste-Bureaucratic
Communist					
China	Command economy, heavy industrial push	Market liberalization and *guanxi* capitalism in 1980s	Communist Authoritarian	Communist Authoritarian	Confucian Patriarchal and Heterodox

cent of investment, 63 percent of industrial output, and 72 percent of exports in Singapore (Mirza, 1986). In stark contrast, Hong Kong has had what may be the closest approximation to a laissez-faire economy in the world (Krause, 1988; Lam and Lee, 1992; Rabushka, 1979; Wong, 1988). Taiwan occupies something of a middle position. It has been touted as a very successful developmental state (Amsden, 1985; Gold, 1986; Haggard, 1990; Wade, 1990) because state policy instituted the major structural shifts in the economy, did a remarkable job of channeling foreign capital into a few key sectors (e.g., electronics), and exercised strong control over the formal financial system and a fairly large state corporation sector until quite recently. Yet, much of Taiwan's (like Hong Kong's) dynamism, especially in the key export sector, comes from small-scale firms with few ties to the government (Fields, 1995; Greenhalgh, 1988; Kuo, 1995; Lam and Clark, 1994; Lam and Lee, 1992; Skoggard, 1996).

If the developmental state per se does not provide a complete explanation for Asia's economic dynamism, are there other explanatory factors that should be investigated? Given the recent wave of democratization in East Asia (Diamond and Plattner, 1998; Friedman, 1994), democracy itself might be a crucial component of the Asian political economies. Columns 3 and 4 in Figure 1.6, therefore, provide a tentative ranking of each country's current regime and dominant type of regime for the postwar period to help an exploration of how regime type and political development might (or might not) influence economic structures and performance. This typology is based on categories in fairly wide usage (Diamond et al., 1989; Huntington, 1991): (1) "consolidated democracies" in which democratic practices and organizations have become strongly institutionalized; (2) "new democracies" where democratic institutions do not appear to have yet become fully consolidated and, thus, may be subject to challenge and reversal; (3) "semi-democracies" where elections coexist with political restrictions severe enough to render the label of full democracy unwarranted; and (4) authoritarian regimes of varying ideological hues.

A priori, democracy could have very different effects on economic policy. On the one hand, popular power could be expected to check the abuses of "predatory" authoritarian states. On the other, democratic pressures could undermine a state's ability to implement strategic economic policy or could create pressures to override broader economic strategies in order to give economic favors to the politically well connected. Unfortunately, the data in Figure 1.6 show democracy to be far more associated with policy perversions than with policy reforms in Asia. Both the "consolidated democracies" (India and Japan) display policy gridlock and government support for anticompetitive business practices. Furthermore, democratization does not seem to have resulted in much change in the clientelistic nature of business–government relations in Southeast Asia (e.g., Hutchcroft, 1994, argues that the Aquino government brought little change to the "booty capitalism" of the Philippines). Moreover, democratization actually seems to be associated with growing corruption and business abuses in South Korea and Taiwan (C. H. Chang, 1996; H. J. Chang, 1998; Chu, 1994; Kuo, 1998; Moon and Prasad, 1994).

Yet, democratic government should not be scorned either for two very important reasons. First, there is no reason to conclude that Asian democracies performed worse than the region's more authoritarian regimes regarding crony capitalism. If democratization boosted the power of corrupt politicians and their business allies in Thailand (Lauridsen, 1998; Robison and Rosser, 1998), as well as in South Korea and Taiwan, these countries' records are no worse than those of many more authoritarian regimes in Asia. Indonesia and Malaysia were just as capable of creating corrupt government–business networks that contributed to their economic implosions in 1997–1998 (Gomez and Jomo, 1997; Robison and Rosser, 1998); China's "*guanxi* (personal relations) capitalism" most probably surpasses Southeast Asia's crony capitalism in gross corruption (Kristof and Wu-Dunn, 1994; Tinari and Lam, 1991; Vogel, 1989); and it should not be forgotten that it was the Marcos dictatorship that brought the phrase "crony capitalism" to Southeast Asia in the first place.

It is here that Mancur Olson's (1982) theory of "distributional coalitions" appears most applicable. According to Olson, stable democracies generate strong interest groups over time which use their political power to distort the economy for their own advantage, in reality reaping monopoly rents. For example, Japan's ministries now seem less concerned with promoting development and structural transformation than with holding back market liberalization which would threaten their power over the economy (Calder, 1993). Yet, there is little reason to think that such a process might not occur in other settings as well. In fact, authoritarian regimes have less to worry about in terms of public reaction if they turn to crony capitalism. Thus, Lee Kuan Yew's very "clean" regime in Singapore should probably be considered an aberration, while Sukarno's Indonesia represents the more probable path for nondemocratic administrations.

Second, the data reported in Table 1.7 might come as quite a surprise to anyone who accepted the neoclassical image of "government failure" as the principal factor giving rise to the Asian flu. The stereotype here is that profligate liberal governments bring on their own financial woes. Yet, the Asian governments do not appear to have committed these sins. None has a particularly large central government (except perhaps Taiwan since the early 1990s) as measured by the ratio of its revenues and expenditures to gross domestic product—the United States (which has the smallest government in Europe and North America) and Brazil (as a more or less typical "emerging market") are used as comparators. Moreover, the East Asian tigers and the Southeast Asian countries generally run budget surpluses; and while the nations in South Asia habitually run sizable deficits, they

Table 1.7
Indicators of Asia's Avoidance of Big and Liberal Government

	Central Govt. Revenues 1996	Central Govt. Spending 1996	Social Services % of Budget 1996	Inflation Rate 1990– 1997	Gross Savings % of GDP 1997
Developed Asia					
Japan	14.5%*	15.8%*	–	0.6%	30%
East Asia Tigers					
Hong Kong	–	–	–	6.7%	31%
Singapore	25.9%	15.9%	39.7%	2.9%	51%
South Korea	21.3%	18.8%	34.3%	5.3 %	34%
Taiwan	30.9%*	30.0%*	–	3.8%*	27%*
Southeast Asia					
Indonesia	17.0%	14.7%	39.0%	8.5%	31%
Malaysia	25.0%	22.0%	42.5%	4.4%	44%
Philippines	18.5%	18.0%	26.0%	8.7%	16%
Thailand	18.5%	16.1%	38.1%	5.0%	35%
Communist Tiger					
China	5.6%	–	–	11.6%	40%
South Asia					
Bangladesh	–	–	–	4.7%	2%
India	13.7%	16.2%	–	9.4%	22%
Pakistan	19.4%	23.2%	–	11.4%	14%
Sri Lanka	19.0%	27.4%	–	9.9%	18%
Comparators					
Brazil	25.8%	33.1%	40.5%	475.2%	18%
United States	20.8%	22.3%	53.1%	2.4%	16%
World Average	–	–	–	–	22%

*1992 for Japan; 1994 and 1990–1994 for Taiwan.
Sources: Taiwan Statistical Data Book (1995), 1, 3, 157, 161; World Bank (1999), 210–211, 214–217.

come from the part of Asia that turned out to be immune to the Asian flu. None devotes an atypically high percentage of their budgets to social spending. The fiscal and monetary sins of liberal governments are also supposed to promote inflation and discourage savings and productive investment. Yet, inflation is moderate throughout Asia (especially compared to the rampant inflation rates of many developing countries), and savings rates are very high in all the East and Southeast nations except the Philippines and are respectable in South Asia except in poverty-stricken Bangladesh. Thus, in several important respects, government performance in Asia appears to be quite good, even by neoclassical standards.

Another important variable used to explain a nation's economic performance is its political culture. Many area studies specialists have long argued that a nation's governmental institutions and economic performance are decisively shaped by its underlying political culture. Indeed, the sophisticated typology of Asian political cultures developed by Lucian Pye (1985) that is summarized in the last column of Figure 1.6 appears to be quite congruent with the overall national political economies in Asia and with the regional variations among them.

The Confucian tradition is the only one that stresses a positive role for an enlightened state bureaucracy. Correspondingly, the Confucian nations of East Asia are the only ones that have had successful developmental states. In addition, the feudal Confucianism of Japan and Korea, which is based on long traditions of large nonkinship groups fighting and working together, has seemingly facilitated cooperation between large-scale business and governmental organizations, while the economic dynamism in most of the Chinese dragons (Hong Kong, Taiwan, and most recently China) derives from the "guerrilla capitalism" (Lam and Lee, 1992) of highly entrepreneurial small-scale firms, reflecting what Pye (1988) has called a "heterodox counterculture" to official Chinese patriarchal Confucianism. Similarly, the clientelistic cultures of Southeast Asia seemingly have created a much different nature of government–business relations that are far from conducive to developmental state activities. Finally, the caste-bureaucratic culture of India and South Asia appears to be especially destructive of effective state action and leadership. The caste system smothers the need for individual achievement and separates religious and political leadership, with the latter being quite amoral and "pragmatic" (i.e., given to patronage politics). This is quite consistent with the region's record for statist economies which are not particularly effective in promoting either economic growth or social equity. (Clark and Chan, 1995, develop this model of the economic impact of political culture in Asia in much more detail.)

As an illustration of how culture can be woven into a complex model of the evolving East Asian political economies, Figure 1.7 sketches how Japan's "Feudal Confucian" culture has seemingly promoted several economic and political institutions that varied in their effectiveness over time. Feudal Confucianism, as noted above, seems quite congruent with the creation and maintenance of effective large-scale organizations. In postwar Japan, both the developmental state and the Japanese conglomerates (*keiretsu*) which evolved evidently reflect this culture. A combination of the "flexible production" that Japanese organization created and the "industrial policy" developed by business–government collaboration, then, undergirded the "economic miracle" that had made Japan an economic

Figure 1.7
The Twisting Vine of Culture and Competitiveness in Japan's Political Economy

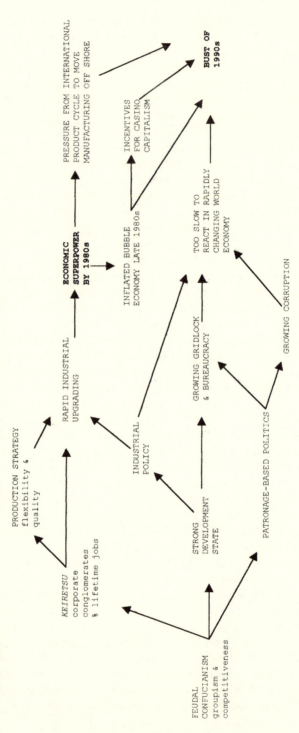

superpower by the late 1980s (Gerlach, 1992; Johnson, 1982; Okimoto, 1989; Prestowitz, 1988; Vogel, 1979; Womack et al., 1990). The impact of Feudal Confucianism on the polity was seemingly less positive because it produced a patronage-based politics in which favors were exchanged for large campaign contributions, not so differently from the clientelistic systems in Southeast Asia. However, as Kent Calder (1988) perceptively argued, this "spoils system" did not detract from Japan's economic competitiveness because it was limited to "nontradables" (i.e., construction, retailing, and agriculture), while corporate leaders and elite technocrats implemented successful industrial and trade policies for manufacturing. As Figure 1.7 sketches, however, this system broke down in the early 1990s for several reasons. Japan's successful development strategies generated a huge trade surplus that ultimately pumped up an inflated "bubble economy" of overvalued stock and land prices; Japan's "patronage" economy both undercut overall competitiveness and exacerbated trade disputes; the technocratic elite became less "developmental" and more of a "distributional coalition"; and the combination of all these factors created political and policy gridlock. (Calder, 1993, provides a good overview of these changing forces in Japan's political economy.)

Both the overall analysis in this section and the Japanese case sketched in Figure 1.7 should instill a good deal of humility in anyone trying to explain East Asian economic performance with *any* overarching theory since all the candidates emerge as far too simplistic. The many variations that exist among the political and economic characteristics of Asian nations demonstrate that there are "many roads" toward both "economic dynamism" and "economic degeneration." Both developmental states and the "magic of the marketplace" have contributed to Asian dynamism and economic prosperity; yet, perversions of both state and market clearly exacerbated the Asian flu. The effects of democratization on economic structure and performance appear to be quite variable as well. Finally, although the cultural model helps us to understand many of the differences among Asian political economies, it utterly fails to explain the increasingly prevalent regionwide phenomena, such as rapid economic growth throughout Asia during 1980–1997 or the Asian flu of the East and Southeast Asian tigers in 1997–1998.

IMPLICATIONS FOR CONCEPTS OF POLITICAL DEVELOPMENT

This chapter has argued that the growth of administrative competence was central to the creation of effective developmental states in Japan, South Korea, Singapore, and, to a lesser extent, Taiwan. In contrast, the financial crises of the 1990s occurred after two important transformations of the Japanese and Korean developmental states. First, government control over investment funds and business behavior eroded and, second, the key ministries (at least in Japan) degenerated from elite leaders of national development projects to bureaucratic empire-builders primarily concerned with maintaining control over the domestic economy. Together, these trends resulted in the casino capitalism, rent-seeking behavior, and counterproductive regulation that spawned the crisis. The more clientelistic regimes in Southeast Asia ignored the technocratic parts of these administrations that had been built up (Case, 1997; Gomez and Jomo, 1997; Kuo, 1995; Lauridsen, 1998) and, consequently, moved much more quickly to this degenerate state of government–business relations. In Taiwan, ironically, the very mild nature of the crisis can probably be attributed to the "underdeveloped" financial system—a rigid and bureaucratic formal system and a highly entrepreneurial "curb" market, which by a weird coincidence produced "prosperity from countervailing perversities" (Clark, 1997, 166). This greatly constrained the opportunities for the excess of highly leveraged casino capitalism. In addition, the Taiwan example, points out a "dogs that didn't bark" situation that should be highly embarrassing to both neoclassicists *and* statists. This is that the parts of Asia that escaped the flu (China and South Asia) are marked both by grossly distorted markets and by states whose "developmental" credentials are quite tattered.

Taken together, these conclusions imply that, in contrast to neoclassical orthodoxy, administrative capacity and state leadership are important variables for economic success. Just as importantly, however, strong state leadership does not necessarily guarantee success; even governments with high administrative capacity can degenerate à la Olson's (1982) theory of institutional decay. This, in turn, implies an "institutional indeterminancy in developmental effectiveness" (Clark and Roy, 1997, 165). Such "indeterminancy" can be interpreted either positively or negatively. A pessimist would conclude that "nothing is guaranteed to work" and that "what works today probably won't work tomorrow," thereby challenging the very idea that political development can serve as the foundation for economic progress.

A much more positive interpretation is possible, however, which suggests that the two dimensions of political development (i.e., democracy and administrative capacity) may be more compatible and mutually reinforcing than many approaches to Asian political economy normally assume. Several conceptions of the developmental state in East Asia were built on the idea that administrative competence was the key factor in political development and, based on the theory of Samuel Huntington (1968), that democratization could actually undercut state capacity by overloading it with political demands. Thus, Asian authoritarianism could be seen as an important component of a developmental state which protected its technocratic policy makers from popular pressures (Cumings, 1984; Hofheinz and Calder, 1982; Zeigler, 1988). The findings presented here about crony capitalism in Southeast Asia, *guanxi* capitalism in China, the degeneration of developmental states in Japan and Korea, and the economically deadening effects of bureaucratic statism in South Asia all militate against a blind reliance on state leadership, authoritarian leaders' willingness to defer to technocratic elites, or even technocratic elites not falling prey to bureaucratic *malaise* and rent-seeking. A healthier skepticism about the state, therefore, might suggest a turn to democracy as a mechanism for holding the political elites accountable for self-seeking behaviors and for allowing the appropriate utilization of technocratic capabilities in the promotion of national development projects.

REFERENCES

Alam, M. S. (1989). *Governments and Markets in Economic Development Strategies: Lessons from Korea, Taiwan, and Japan.* New York: Praeger.

Amsden, A. H. (1985). "The State and Taiwan's Economic Development." In P. B. Evans, D. Rueschemeyer, and T. Skocpol, eds., *Bringing the State Back In.* New York: Cambridge University Press, pp. 78–104.

Amsden, A. H. (1989). *Asia's Next Giant: South Korea and Late Industrialization.* New York: Oxford University Press.

Arndt, H. W., and H. Hill, eds. (1999). *Southeast Asia's Economic Crisis: Origins, Lessons, and a Way Forward.* New York: St. Martin's Press.

Balassa, B. (1981). *The Newly Industrializing Countries in the World Economy.* New York: Pergamon.

Balassa, B., G. M. Bueno, P. P. Kuczynski, and M. H. Simonsen. (1989). *Toward Renewed Economic Growth in Latin America.* Washington, DC: Institute of International Economics.

Bernard, M., and J. Ravenhill. (1995). "Beyond Flying Geese and Product Cycles: Regionalization, Hierarchy, and the Industrialization of East Asia." *World Politics* 47: 171–209.

Bhagwati, J. N. (1993). *India in Transition: Freeing the Economy.* Oxford: Clarendon.

Booth, A. (1999). "The Impact of the Crisis on Poverty and Equity." In H. W. Arndt and H. Hill, eds., *Southeast Asia's Economic Crisis: Origins, Lessons, and a Way Forward.* New York: St. Martin's Press, pp. 128–141.

Calder, K. (1988). *Crisis and Compensation: Public Policy and Political Stability in Japan, 1949–1986.* Princeton, NJ: Princeton University Press.

Calder, K. (1993). *Strategic Capitalism: Private Business and Public Purpose in Japanese Industrial Finance.* Princeton, NJ: Princeton University Press.

Case, W. (1997). "Pseudo-Democracy in Southeast Asia: Uncovering State Leaders and the Business Connection." Paper presented at the 17th World Congress of the International Political Science Association, Seoul.

Chan, S. (1993). *East Asian Dynamism: Growth, Order, and Security in the Pacific Region,* 2nd ed. Boulder, CO: Westview Press.

Chan, S., C. Clark, and D. Lam, eds. (1998). *Beyond the Developmental State: East Asia's Political Economies Reconsidered.* London: Macmillan.

Chang, C. H. (1996). "The Limits of Statism in Taiwan: The Distortions of Policies Ignoring Small Enterprise Dynamism." *American Asian Review* 14: 71–96.

Chang, H. J. (1998). "Korea: The Misunderstood Crisis." *World Development* 26: 1555–1561.

Chu, Y. H. (1994). "The Realignment of State-Business Relations and Regime Transition in Taiwan." In A. MacIntyre, ed., *Business and Government in Industrializing East and Southeast Asia*. Sydney: Allen & Unwin, pp. 113–141.

Clark, C. (1997). "Taiwan's Financial System: Prosperity from Countervailing Perversities?" In R. D. Bingham and E. W. Hill, eds., *Global Perspectives on Economic Development: Government and Business Finance*. New Brunswick, NJ: CUPR Press of Rutgers University, pp. 116–165.

Clark, C. (1999). "Modernization, Democracy, and the Developmental State in Asia: A Virtuous Cycle or Unraveling Strands?" In C. Jillson and J. Hollifield, eds., *Pathways to Democracy: The Political Economy of Democratic Transitions*. London: Routledge.

Clark, C., and S. Chan. (1995). "MNCs and Developmentalism: Domestic Structures as an Explanation for East Asian Dynamism." In T. Risse-Kappen, ed., *Bringing Transnational Relations Back In: Non-State Actors, Domestic Structures, and International Institutions*. Cambridge: Cambridge University Press, pp. 112–145.

Clark, C., and K. C. Roy. (1997). *Comparing Development Patterns in Asia*. Boulder, CO: Lynne Rienner.

Cole, D. C., and B. F. Slade. (1999). "The Crisis and Financial Sector Reform." In H. W. Arndt and H. Hill, eds., *Southeast Asia's Economic Crisis: Origins, Lessons, and a Way Forward*. New York: St. Martin's Press, pp. 107–118.

Cumings, B. (1984). "The Origins and Development of the Northeast Asia Political Economy: Industrial Sectors, Product Cycles, and Political Consequences." *International Organization* 38: 1–40.

Diamond, L., J. J. Linz, and S. M. Lipset, eds. (1989). *Democracy in Developing Countries*. 4 vols. Boulder, CO: Lynne Rienner.

Diamond, L., and M. F. Plattner, eds. (1998). *Democracy in East Asia*. Baltimore, MD: Johns Hopkins University Press.

"Economies: Cause and Effect." (1999). *Far Eastern Economic Review*, July 1, pp. 38–41.

The Economist. (1999a). "Emerging Market Indicators." May 1, p. 100.

The Economist. (1999b). "Emerging Market Indicators." July 10, p. 100.

The Economist. (2000). "Emerging Market Indicators." July 8, p. 100.

Evans, P. (1995). *Embedded Autonomy: States and Industrial Transformation*. Princeton, NJ: Princeton University Press.

Evans, P. B., D. Rueschemeyer, and T. Skocpol, eds. (1985). *Bringing the State Back In*. Cambridge: Cambridge University Press.

Fallows, J. M. (1994). *Looking at the Sun: The Rise of the New East Asian Economic and Political System*. New York: Pantheon.

Felker, G. (1999). "Malaysia in 1998: A Cornered Tiger Bears Its Claws." *Asian Survey* 39(1): 43–54.

Fields, K. J. (1995). *Enterprise and the State in Korea and Taiwan*. Ithaca, NY: Cornell University Press.

Friedman, D. (1988). *The Misunderstood Miracle: Industrial Development and Political Change in Japan*. Ithaca, NY: Cornell University Press.

Friedman, E., ed. (1994). *The Politics of Democratization: Generalizing East Asian Experiences*. Boulder, CO: Westview Press.

Friedman, T. L. (1999). *The Lexus and the Olive Tree: Understanding Globalization*. New York: Random House.

Garnaut, R. (1999). "Exchange Rates and the East Asian Crisis." In H. W. Arndt and H. Hill, eds., *Southeast Asia's Economic Crisis: Origins, Lessons, and a Way Forward*. New York: St. Martin's Press, pp. 93–106.

Gereffi, G., and D. Wyman, eds. (1990). *Manufacturing Miracles: Paths of Industrialization in Latin America and East Asia*. Princeton, NJ: Princeton University Press.

Gerlach, M. L. (1992). *Alliance Capitalism: The Social Organization of Japanese Business*. Berkeley: University of California Press.

Gold, T. B. (1986). *State and Society in the Taiwan Miracle*. Armonk, NY: M. E. Sharpe.

Goldstein, M. (1998). *The Asian Financial Crisis: Causes, Cures, and Systemic Implications*. Washington, DC: Institute for International Economics.

Gomez, E. T., and K. S. Jomo. (1997). *Malaysia's Political Economy: Politics, Patronage, and Profits*. Cambridge: Cambridge University Press.

Greenhalgh, S. (1988). "Families and Networks in Taiwan's Economic Development." In E. A. Winckler and S. Greenhalgh, eds., *Contending Approaches to the Political Economy of Taiwan*. Armonk, NY: M. E. Sharpe, pp. 224–245.

Haggard, S. (1990). *Pathways from the Periphery: The Politics of Growth in the Newly Industrializing Countries*. Ithaca, NY: Cornell University Press.

Haggard, S., and R. R. Kaufman. (1995). *The Political Economy of Democratic Transitions*. Princeton, NJ: Princeton University Press.

Hahm, S. D., and L. C. Plein. (1997). *After Development: The Transformation of the Korean Presidency and Bureaucracy*. Washington, DC: Georgetown University Press.

Hart, J. A. (1992). *Rival Capitalists: International Competitiveness in the United States, Japan, and Western Europe*. Ithaca, NY: Cornell University Press.

Hobday, M. (1995). *Innovation in East Asia: The Challenge to Japan*. Aldershot, UK: Edward Elgar.

Hofheinz, R., Jr., and K. E. Calder. (1982). *The Eastasia Edge*. New York: Basic Books.

Huntington, S. P. (1968). *Political Order in Changing Societies*. New Haven, CT: Yale University Press.

Huntington, S. P. (1991). *The Third Wave: Democratization in the Late Twentieth Century*. Norman: University of Oklahoma Press.

Hutchcroft, P. (1994). "Booty Capitalism: Business–Government Relations in the Philippines." In A. MacIntyre, ed., *Business and Government in Industrializing East and Southeast Asia*. Sydney: Allen & Unwin, pp. 216–243.

Johnson, C. A. (1982). *MITI and the Japanese Miracle: The Growth of Industrial Policy, 1925–1975*. Stanford, CA: Stanford University Press.

Jomo, K. S. (1997). *Misunderstood Miracle: Industrial Policy and Economic De-*

velopment in Thailand, Malaysia and Indonesia. Boulder, CO: Westview Press.

Jones, L., and I. Sakong. (1980). *Government, Business, and Entrepreneurship in Economic Development: The Korean Case.* Cambridge, MA: Harvard University Press.

Knight, M. (1998). "Developing Countries and the Globalization of Financial Markets." *World Development* 26: 1185–1200.

Krause, L. B. (1988). "Hong Kong and Singapore: Twins or Kissing Cousins?" *Economic Development and Cultural Change* 36: S11–S43.

Kristof, N. D., and S. WuDunn. (1994). *China Wakes: The Struggle for a Soul of a Rising Power.* New York: Times Books.

Kuo, C. T. (1995). *Global Competitiveness and Industrial Growth in Taiwan and the Philippines.* Pittsburgh: University of Pittsburgh Press.

Kuo, C. T. (1998). "Private Governance in Taiwan." In S. Chan, C. Clark, and D. Lam, eds., *Beyond the Developmental State: East Asia's Political Economies Reconsidered.* London: Macmillan, pp. 84–95.

Lam, D.K.K., and C. Clark. (1994). "Beyond the Developmental State: The Cultural Roots of 'Guerrilla Capitalism' in Taiwan." *Governance* 7: 412–430.

Lam, D.K.K., and I. Lee. (1992). "Guerrilla Capitalism and the Limits of Statist Theory." In C. Clark and S. Chan, eds., *The Evolving Pacific Basin in the Global Political Economy: Domestic and International Linkages.* Boulder, CO: Lynne Rienner, pp. 107–124.

Lardy, N. R. (1998). *China's Unfinished Economic Revolution.* Washington, DC: Brookings Institution.

Lauridsen, L. S. (1998). "The Financial Crisis in Thailand: Causes, Conduct, and Consequences." *World Development* 26: 1575–1591.

MacIntyre, A., ed. (1994). *Business and Government in Industrializing East and Southeast Asia.* Sydney: Allen & Unwin.

Mardon, R., and W. K. Paik. (1992). "The State, Foreign Investment, and Sustaining Industrial Growth in South Korea and Thailand." In C. Clark and S. Chan, eds., *The Evolving Pacific Basin in the Global Political Economy: Domestic and International Linkages.* Boulder, CO: Lynne Rienner, pp. 147–168.

Mertens, B. (1999). "Shuffling Forward." *Asian Business* 35(4): 32–36.

Mirza, H. (1986). *Multinationals and the Growth of the Singapore Economy.* New York: St. Martin's Press.

Moon, B. E. (1991). *The Political Economy of Basic Human Needs.* Ithaca, NY: Cornell University Press.

Moon, B. E., and W. J. Dixon. (1992). "Basic Needs and Growth-Welfare Trade-offs." *International Studies Quarterly* 36: 191–212.

Moon, C. I., and R. Prasad. (1994). "Beyond the Developmental State: Networks, Politics, and Institutions." *Governance* 7: 360–386.

Naughton, B. (1995). *Growing Out of the Plan: Chinese Economic Reform, 1978–1993.* New York: Cambridge University Press.

Norton, J. J. (1998). "The Korean Financial Crisis, Reform and Positive Transformation: Is a Second 'Han River Miracle' Possible?" *Global Economic Review* 27: 3–36.

Okimoto, D. I. (1989). *Between MITI and the Market: Japanese Industrial Policy for High Technology.* Stanford, CA: Stanford University Press.

Olson, M., Jr. (1982). *The Rise and Fall of Nations: Economic Growth, Stagflation, and Social Rigidities.* New Haven, CT: Yale University Press.

Onis, Z. (1991). "The Logic of the Developmentalist State." *Comparative Politics* 24: 109–121.

Prestowitz, C. V., Jr. (1988). *Trading Places: How We Allowed Japan to Take the Lead.* New York: Basic Books.

Pye, L. W. (1985). *Asian Power and Politics: The Cultural Dimensions of Authority.* Cambridge, MA: Harvard University Press.

Pye, L. W. (1988). *The Mandarin and the Cadre: China's Political Cultures.* Ann Arbor: University of Michigan Press.

Rabushka, A. (1979). *Hong Kong: A Study in Economic Freedom.* Chicago: University of Chicago Press.

Ravenhill, J., ed. (1995). *The Political Economy of East Asia.* 2 vols. Aldershot, UK: Edward Elgar.

Robison, R., and A. Rosser. (1998). "Contesting Reform: Indonesia's New Order and the IMF." *World Development* 26: 1593–1609.

Rodan, G. (1989). *The Political Economy of Singapore's Industrialization: National, State and International Capital.* New York: St. Martin's Press.

Rostow, W. W. (1960). *The Stages of Economic Growth: A Non-Communist Manifesto.* Cambridge: Cambridge University Press.

Rudolph, L. I., and S. H. Rudolph. (1987). *In Pursuit of Lakshmi: The Political Economy of the Indian State.* Chicago: University of Chicago Press.

Rueschemeyer, D., and P. B. Evans. (1985). "The State and Economic Transformation: Toward an Analysis of the Conditions Underlying Effective Intervention." In P. B. Evans, D. Rueschemeyer, and T. Skocpol, eds., *Bringing the State Back In.* New York: Cambridge University Press, pp. 44–77.

Skoggard, I. A. (1996). *The Indigenous Dynamic in Taiwan's Postwar Development: The Religious and Historical Roots of Entrepreneurship.* Armonk, NY: M. E. Sharpe.

Suchitra, P. (1999). "Thailand in 1998: A False Sense of Recovery." *Asian Survey* 3(1): 80–88.

Taiwan Statistical Data Book. (1995). Taipei: Council for Economic Planning and Development.

Taylor, L. (1998). "Lax Public Sector, Destabilizing Private Sector: Origins of Capital Market Crises." Paper presented at the Fifth International Conference on Development and Future Studies, Central Michigan University.

Tinari, F. D., and D.K.K. Lam. (1991). "China's Resistance to Economic Reforms." *Contemporary Policy Issues* 9: 82–92.

Vogel, E. F. (1979). *Japan as Number One.* Cambridge, MA: Harvard University Press.

Vogel, E. F. (1989). *One Step Ahead in China: Guangdong under Reform.* Cambridge, MA: Harvard University Press.

Wade, R. (1990). *Governing the Market: Economic Theory and the Role of Government in East Asian Industrialization.* Princeton, NJ: Princeton University Press.

Wade, R. (1998). "The Asian Debt-and-Development Crisis of 1997–?" *World Development* 26: 1535–1553.

Wagner, H. (1998). " 'Invisible Hands': Who Paid the Bill and Who Made a Bargain in the Asian Financial Meltdown?" *Journal of East Asian Affairs* 12: 599–619.

White, G., ed. (1988). *Developmental States in East Asia*. New York: St. Martin's Press.

Womack, J. P., D. T. Jones, and D. Roos. (1990). *The Machine that Changed the World: The Story of Lean Production*. New York: Macmillan.

Wong, S. L. (1988). *Emigrant Entrepreneurs: Shanghai Industrialists in Hong Kong*. Hong Kong: Oxford University Press.

Woo, J. E. (1991). *Race to the Swift: State and Finance in Korean Industrialization*. New York: Columbia University Press.

World Bank. (1993). *The East Asian Miracle: Economic Growth and Public Policy*. New York: Oxford University Press.

World Bank. (1999). *World Development Report, 1997/98*. New York: Oxford University Press.

Zeigler, H. (1988). *Pluralism, Corporatism, and Confucianism: Political Association and Conflict Resolution in the United States, Europe, and Taiwan*. Philadelphia: Temple University Press.

Chapter 2

Japan's Economic Crisis: The Role of Government

Edward W. Schwerin

INTRODUCTION

Only a decade ago Japan appeared to be an economic powerhouse destined to dominate international finance and trade, and the United States seemed to be in economic decline. American commentators and policy makers were deeply concerned about the threat that the dynamic Japanese economy posed to the United States and the other Western industrial democracies. Numerous books and articles analyzed the lessons of the Japanese economic model and corporate management style, and suggested strategies for either adapting the Japanese approach to the American system, or combating the threat of Japanese economic strength and its global preeminence in consumer electronics and other industries. But in the last few years that assessment has changed considerably.

In 1990 the Japanese asset price bubble of the 1980s burst, and the Japanese economy first slowed down, then stagnated, and finally slid into recession and deflation. Western experts are no longer concerned about the threat of Japanese economic competition, but now they warn about the possible dangers of contagion from Japan's economic crisis. It is difficult to imagine that this is the same economy known throughout the world as the Japanese "miracle." What went wrong? Who or what is to blame? Was the Japanese miracle really a myth? Did something change in the last decade that has fundamentally altered Japanese economic performance? How long will it take for Japan to escape from its present economic difficulties?

In this chapter I begin with a brief discussion of Japan's economic transformation following World War II and the development of the Japanese model of economic development that appeared to be miraculous to other

Asian countries and threatening to the United States and Europe. I then discuss the development of the "bubble economy," the bursting of the bubble, and the economic stagnation that followed. Next, I consider the probable causes of the Japanese recession and deflation and possible policy prescriptions. With regard to policy responses and possible solutions, I consider what has been tried and the resultant levels of success or lack thereof, and what might still be done and the likelihood of success.

THE JAPANESE MIRACLE

Japan's transformation from a devastated and occupied nation in 1945 to a prosperous and powerful nation in the 1990s is one of the most remarkable stories of the twentieth century. Japan's economy was devastated by the war. At the end of World War II, Japan's industry, infrastructure, and major cities had been destroyed by Allied bombing. Unemployment and homelessness had reached epidemic proportions, and it was difficult to feed people and provide basic services. But the reconstruction of Japan after 1945 was rapid. Economic recovery was a key objective and entrepreneurial activity was encouraged with emphasis on new technologies. By 1950, aided by the Korean War, Japan had embarked on a period of accelerated economic growth. Growth rates averaged an extraordinary 10 percent a year from 1950 to 1973, until slowed drastically by the first oil shock in 1973. In 1974 Japan suffered negative growth for the first time since World War II. Annual growth between 1974 and 1991 was 4.4 percent, less than half the rate of the previous 20 years (Weinstein, 1999).

By the early 1970s, however, after nearly 25 years of almost 10 percent annual growth, Japan had become the world's second largest capitalist economy, and by 1980 Japan became the largest creditor nation in the world. By 1993 Japan's citizens enjoyed an average income of $31,450, far exceeding that of the average American ($24,138) (Reid and Bluestein, 1995, 21). By 1995 the per capita GDP of Japan was 3,830,700 yen (approximately $40,726 U.S. dollars) while the per capita GDP of the United States was $26,438. (Mak et al., 1998; Yoshikawa, 1995).

What factors explain Japan's phenomenal economic success? Differing explanations include the following: Japan's dedicated and highly educated workforce and its highly competitive private sector, the national character of the Japanese, and the effort Japanese industry put into product design and development. Initially, Japan was helped by a global economic system that encouraged exports by keeping the yen cheap against other currencies. Japan also invested heavily in new plants and equipment during the 1950s, laying the foundation for later economic growth. The energy crisis of the early 1970s slowed that growth, but it encouraged Japan to conserve energy and develop new fuel- and labor-efficient technology, which in turn lowered the breakeven points of Japanese industry.

Japan was helped by its low defense budget, which was made possible during the Cold War by the protection afforded Japan by the U.S. "nuclear umbrella." Where as much of the U.S. investments in R&D during the Cold War went into the military, the bulk of the Japanese R&D budget went into industry, with emphasis on greater automation. The Japanese economy was aided by the high levels of household savings, much of which was invested and helped economic development (see Argy and Stern, 1997; Unger and Blackburn, 1993).

THE ROLE OF THE GOVERNMENT IN ECONOMIC DEVELOPMENT

Another key factor credited for Japan's economic success is the close relationship between government and business, which has allowed Japanese companies to borrow funds and has protected established industry from competition while encouraging the growth of new industries.

The Japanese government played a strong activist role in economic development. It promoted the goals of rapid industrialization and catching up with the Western industrial democracies. The Japanese used the power of the state to encourage or curtail investment and competition according to "industrial policy" and to the short- and long-range plans prepared by government ministries. Tariffs, quotas, and other import barriers were used to shelter infant industries, and selective allocation of scarce foreign exchange allowed favored corporations to import the raw materials and technology they needed to thrive and grow while supplies of imports were denied to others. Government funds were provided for certain key industries such as steel in the 1950s and automobiles in the 1960s. Led by the highly professional bureaucracy which was inherited from prewar imperial Japan, Japanese economic policy making became a highly coordinated and reciprocal process in which key decisions were made with input from the three elements of the so-called iron triangle: career bureaucrats, top politicians primarily from the Liberal Democratic Party (LDP), and influential business leaders.

Among the most distinctive aspects of the Japanese state are the links between government and industry, specifically the relationship between top politicians, leading bureaucrats, and big business executives. Of the two groups of government decision makers, the bureaucrats dominate because most of the legislation is in fact drafted by the bureaucrats rather than by Diet members, and so the bureaucrats, not politicians, generally have set the policies that have made Japan an economic success story. The bureaucrats were influential in part because they were so highly regarded by the public. The civil service traditionally has been the most prestigious of all careers and has consequently attracted the best and the brightest from Japan's top universities (see Drucker, 1998).

At about age 51 most of the bureaucrats retire from the civil service but not from professional life. They engage in what the Japanese call *amakudari* (literally, descent from heaven), and they retire to second careers in either business or partisan politics. The former bureaucrats have been at the heart of policy-making power within the LDP. Even more important perhaps are the ex-civil servants who are found at or near the top of all the major corporations. The individual ministries have broad areas of responsibility and clear lines of authority. The Ministry of International Trade and Industry (MITI) is in charge of virtually all microeconomic policy, including foreign trade, resource management, the development of new technology, and much of commerce. The Ministry of Finance (MOF) has equally far-reaching control over the treasury and macroeconomic policy.

Japanese big business is organized in groups called *keiretsu*, which employ about one-third of the Japanese workforce and have until recently offered lifetime employment. These groups include a large number of interconnected businesses that share management resources and markets. Together they plan new business ideas and do much of the needed research and development. Although these groups do not dominate the entire economy, they are generally the firms that have spearheaded Japanese development and set the tone for much of the economy.

In short, the Japanese state is based on a highly integrated elite and one party (the LDP) that ruled for 38 years until 1993, providing continuity in personnel and policy. The bureaucratic presence in both business and partisan politics is powerful, and the bureaucrats themselves are highly unified in terms of their policy goals and self-definitions, which facilitates highly coordinated and coherent policy making.

In a seminal book entitled *MITI and the Japanese Miracle* (1982), American political scientist Chalmers Johnson argued that this alliance between government and business constituted a unique "Japanese model" of capitalism, which was the key to understanding Japan's extraordinary economic success. Johnson called the Japanese approach the "developmental state," and he contended that it was the leadership of a small elite group of economic bureaucrats who were able to develop long-range coordinated economic plans that made it possible to achieve a higher level of economic development more rapidly than was possible using the neoclassical free market model favored by the Western capitalist nations. The industrial policy characteristic of the "developmental state" approach provided an alternative to the market-oriented approach the Western economists proposed for Asian developing economies. Indeed, this new Japanese model appeared to be more effective than the market-oriented models, and it appeared to threaten even the U.S. dominance of the world economy. (For a cogent critique of Johnson and an alternative interpretation, see Calder's study *Strategic Capitalism*, 1993.)

IMPLICATIONS OF JAPAN'S ECONOMIC SUCCESS

During the 1970s and 1980s, the growth of Japan's economic power created unease in the United States. As Japan began to project its economic power abroad, the United States and other Western states were particularly alarmed by the high level of investment by Japanese companies in private sector research and development, acquisition of foreign competitor firms, and purchase of prime real estate in the United States and Europe. When the Japanese purchased most of the hotels in Waikiki Beach, Hawaii, Rockefeller Center in New York City, Columbia movie studios in California, and other highly visible and valuable properties, many Americans became alarmed that the Japanese were "buying out" America.

Spectacular increases in Japan's exports and overall economic performance during the 1960s and 1970s, which were soon followed by other Asian countries, posed especially formidable challenges to the United States and the West (Destler, 1995). Japan's rising trade surplus was reflected in a growing trade deficit in the United States. In the 1980s there was a sense that America was in decline, and the trade deficit was seen as a sign of national weakness. Japan was viewed as the preeminent neomercantilist power and was thus the target of America's protectionist ire. The continuing trade imbalance between Japan and the United States reinforced the belief that Japan's trade policies were detrimental to the United States' commercial interests, and Japan became the scapegoat for American economic problems. For their part, the Japanese accused their American critics of being "Japan-bashers" (see Fallows, 1994; Prestowitz, 1989; for a contrasting view, see Bergsten and Noland, 1993; Emmott, 1994; Weinstein, 1999).

While Japan's economic success presented a challenge to the West, it provided a powerful and influential model for other East Asian developing economies and an inspiration for Asian leaders. The Japanese model did not provide a detailed blueprint for economic development, but it set forth a style of development characterized by government intervention in the economy and an export strategy as the primary vehicle for promoting economic growth. Japanese economists suggested the "flying geese" theory for East Asian development, in which Japan would be the lead goose and other Asian countries would follow according to their levels of technological and economic development (Freedman, 1998; Garran, 1998, 48).

THE JAPANESE BUBBLE ECONOMY AND ITS
AFTERMATH: THE END OF THE MIRACLE

In the early 1970s, Japan's economy slowed significantly. In addition to the oil shock of 1973, there were other problems in the economy. The economy was overheated, inflation was increasing, and Japan's long-term growth potential began to fall. During Japan's earlier period of industrial buildup, high rates of capital investment enabled the increasingly efficient use of Japan's highly educated workforce, but each additional new investment meant less of an increase in economic activity. Having caught up with the West technologically, Japan's growth rate slowed significantly (see Garran, 1998; Weinstein, 1998).

As labor productivity increased, wages also increased, and Japan lost its comparative advantage in labor-intensive industry. But because it was politically difficult to allow large-scale unemployment and bankruptcies, the Japanese government acted to protect inefficient sectors from both foreign and domestic competition through webs of regulations and subsidies. The long-term result was overinvestment and declining productivity growth in the protected sectors, which in turn brought down the productivity of the Japanese economy as a whole. Thus, Japan developed what Robert Garran calls the "dual economy syndrome," which is characterized by "an efficient, competitive export sector, increasingly dragged down by an inefficient, corrupt and costly domestic sector" (1998, 4; see also Tomio, 1998b, 18). In the late 1980s this productivity deficit was hidden by the "bubble economy," as economic growth increased rapidly once again as a result of large-scale financial speculation.

THE BUBBLE BURSTS

Many of the root causes of the financial crisis in the 1990s can be attributed to the policies developed in the 1980s. In the early 1980s, the high budget deficits of the Reagan administration, combined with high interest rates, made the United States an attractive place to invest. Foreign investors had to buy dollars to enter the U.S. market and were willing to pay for the privilege of earning high rates of return. This drove the value of the dollar to very high levels relative to the currencies of its major trading partners. The strong dollar made foreign goods and assets cheaper, but it also made it very difficult for U.S. producers to export and to compete against foreign products in the domestic market, resulting in a very high U.S. trade deficit.

After the 1985 Plaza Accord, the dollar began to fall in value relative to the yen. From about 260 yen/$1 in February 1985, it had dropped below the 200 yen/$1 mark by early January 1986, and then it continued to fall. With the strengthening of the yen Japan's exports became more expensive. With declining exports, Japanese policy makers feared recession; therefore, they acted to lower interest rates four times during 1986 hoping to provide an incentive to consumer spending and investment, as well as making the yen less attractive relative to other currencies and putting a stop to its rapid rise. As a result, most prices stabilized, and investment was increasingly stimulated, with much of the money going into the purchase of domestic assets such as stocks and real estate. In addition to domestic investment, the strength of the yen meant that overseas assets were becoming bargains for Japanese investors. As a result of speculative investment, the Nikkei stock index tripled between the end of 1985 and the end of 1989, land prices in major Japanese cities increased by 126 percent, and Japanese overseas investment in the United States, Asia, and Europe expanded rapidly (see Cargill et al., 1997; Naoyuki, 1999, 12; Tateishi, 1998, 24; Williams, 1994).

Japanese companies easily raised money through new stock issues or from banks at low or negative real interest rates. The money was used for large-scale investments in fixed capital, which resulted in overinvestment, thus adding to Japan's existing productivity problems. Companies also became heavily involved in speculation, and as the value of stocks and real estate rose, so did the value of companies holding those assets. As their value rose, they were able to use their assets as collateral for raising more money to buy more stocks and real estate. This process generated an upward economic spiral, known as the "bubble" economy. As major corporations were able to obtain funds more cheaply by issuing equities and bonds, they moved away from their traditional dependence on bank lending. Therefore, banks that had traditionally been conservative in their lending policies were forced to move their loan portfolios into riskier areas, and soon they were lending money for highly speculative purposes (see Lincoln, 1998).

By 1989 Japanese policy makers, nervous about the speculative boom and the sustainability of the rapid asset price increases, acted decisively to cut off the supply of easy money and to try and prevent the boom rising to even more dizzying heights. The Bank of Japan raised interest rates in 1989 and 1990, and the bubble burst. Stock prices responded almost immediately, and the Nikkei stock index dropped from its peak of nearly 39,000 yen at the close of 1989 to 20,221 yen by October 1, 1990 (see Sakamaki, 1998, 21–23).

Another two years passed before the full effects of the interest rate hikes fully hit home in the real economy, with tumbling real estate and share prices and a slump in industrial output. Although at first it seemed that Japan was suffering another cyclical downturn and that it would soon regain its composure, the longer the slump continued the more it became clear that Japan's problems were deeper than the familiar ups and downs of economic cycles. The country that had spawned the Asian miracle and had become the world's second largest economy was in deep trouble, and Japan's economic malaise throughout the 1990s was a significant factor behind the East Asian financial crisis (see Goldstein, 1998; Posen, 1998).

The end of the bubble economy placed Japan's financial system under immense strain, with the hangover of enormous debts from the collapse of asset prices leaving many institutions technically insolvent. These events severely eroded the confidence of both business and consumers in the economy, generating a self-perpetuating cycle of slow growth. The MOF was heavily criticized for its role in creating and bursting the bubble, for not guiding the banking industry through the turmoil of nonperforming loans, and for trying to maintain the "convoy" system that perpetuated the banking crisis (see Ito and Melvin, 1999). American economist Edward Lincoln blames the bubble economy and its mismanagement on reckless speculation, shocking examples of indiscretion and malfeasance, and scandals about "illegal dealings between financial institutions, politicians, bureaucrats, and the involvement of organized crime" (Lincoln, 1998, 59–60).

THE POST-BUBBLE ECONOMY

After the bubble burst, it appeared at first that little serious damage had been done to the economy, but in 1991 bankruptcies began to increase in number and magnitude, and land prices began to fall as demand cooled. Thus, nonperforming loans accumulated in the Japanese banking system. Banks tried to conceal the large amount of nonperforming loans, hoping that the economy would begin to grow again and that the problem would be solved. Overall economic growth had slowed considerably by 1992, land prices continued to decline, and the problem of nonperforming loans became a major media focus. A credit crunch arose, as banks were constrained by their burdens of bad loans from new lending. A vicious cycle developed in which firms that were unable to obtain new credit could not pay their debt service, which increased the banks' burdens of nonperforming loans, which in turn reduced their ability to lend money to the companies that might need it. The credit crunch has continued since then, despite government policies to try to fix the problem (see Reijiro, 1998, 24; Rohwer, 1998, 124–125).

Since 1992, Japan has experienced rising unemployment, economic stagnation, financial crisis, recession, deflation, panic, loss of consumer and business confidence in the economy, and political upheaval (see Keizo, 1998, 12–14; Sakae, 1998, 32). The Tokyo stock market has lost about two-thirds of its peak value since the end of 1989; commercial and residential land prices have dropped both in the major cities and nationwide every year since 1992; economic growth rates from 1992 to 1997 averaged under 1.4 percent; and the economy actually shrank in fiscal year 1997 and again in 1998. In 1993 defections from the LDP caused it to lose its Lower House majority, since then, Japan has been governed by a series of governments whose instability has led to policy inertia (Garran 1998; Posen 1998).

For most of the 1990s, Japan suffered from deflation, an economic affliction unfamiliar since the 1930s. *The Economist* cautioned that "It's conceivable that the world may be in for a new period of global deflation (meaning falling consumer prices) for the first time since the 1930s"

("Could It Happen Again," 1999, 19) and that "Japan has been flirting with deflation for several years, but the complaint may be catching." Furthermore, *The Economist* argued that Japan "is on the brink of a vicious deflationary spiral, with falling prices swelling companies' real debts and keeping real interest rates high" and that Japan's nominal GDP fell by 3.4 percent in the year to the third quarter of 1998 (p. 22; see also Sakae, 1998, 33).

During the late 1990s, the actions taken by the Japanese government to revive the stagnant economy were not effective; nor did they prevent Japan from sliding further into a recession. One of the major reasons for these failures was the lack of strong political leadership. This problem was especially apparent during the brief administration of Yoshiro Mori, when public dissatisfaction rose rapidly as Japan's economic condition further worsened (see Helweg, 2000). In April of last year, in response to the declining economic situation, the Mori administration approved a $35.3 billion public works package, the largest economic stimulus package issued in the past decade. At the same time, Mori's administration did little to revise protectionist policies in sectors such as construction, retail, small business, and agriculture. These sectors have traditionally been closely linked with the LDP, and they have strongly opposed any radical economic restructuring measures that might negatively affect them.

Mori argued that boosting the information technology (IT) sector would greatly facilitate the recovery of Japan's economy. Instead of supporting radical economic restructuring, he proposed that the government should focus on sponsoring IT-related economic revitalization and projects aimed at making Japan the world's leading IT nation. This approach did not produce the desired economic impact, and as Japan continued its economic downturn it became the leading indebted nation among the G-7 countries, with current debt exceeding 130 percent of its GDP. Mori's failure to take appropriate actions to deal with Japan's serious economic problems, and his other political missteps, led to a widespread public dissatisfaction and dismal opinion-poll scores, as people denounced Mori and the LDP style politics he represented. Under these pressures the deeply unpopular Mori resigned as prime minister in April 2001 (see "Can't Get Started," 2001, 12).

Four candidates contended for president of the LDP, a post that virtually guarantees the premiership. The former Minister of Health and Welfare Koizumi Junichiro overwhelmed his opponents, attracting the support of rank-and-file LDP members by advocating sweeping party reform and radical economic reforms. Koizumi's campaign slogan was, "change the LDP, change Japan." Koizumi became Japan's ninth prime minister in 10 years, and he now faces the difficult task of implementing his promised reforms.

As Koizumi and his cabinet assumed power, the Japanese economy was facing another recession and Koizumi advocated drastic structural reforms as a necessary solution to the problem. His suggested reforms included an immediate cleaning-up of the banking sector that would require the Japanese banks to dispose of as much as $88.53 billion of the bad loans within two years. Among the other biggest problems facing the new administration are high unemployment, high public savings, and large debt that has to be trimmed in order for the Japanese economy to recover. According to projections in his proposed reform package, the revival of the Japanese economy and cleaning up of the banking sector would be achieved within a two-to three-year period (see "Japan's Economy: Chronic Sickness," 2001, 71–74).

But the effectiveness and likelihood for success of his proposed economic reforms will depend on a complex combination of economic, political, and social factors both inside and outside Japan. First, the present global economic decline will complicate the implementation of structural reforms. At this time, both the United States and Europe are caught up in an unusual simultaneous economic slump, and the recent increases in oil prices in the world market have added to the worsening global economic conditions. Internally, as a result of the present economic uncertainty and a growing number of layoffs by major corporations, consumer confidence in Japan has reached a low point. Consequently, while public spending has been rapidly decreasing, the public savings rate in Japan has continued to increase, further decreasing domestic demand and increasing deflation (see "A Global Game of Dominoes," 2001, 22–24).

On July 29, Junichiro Koizumi won another momentous victory in the election for the upper house of Parliament. The LDP candidates overwhelmed their opposition, claiming 64 of the 121 seats that were contested in the Upper House ballot. Koizumi, the most popular leader since World War II, has taken his election victory as a mandate to pursue his reforms aimed at restoring Japan's economic and social vitality (see "Japan's Great Hope," 2001, 11).

But implementing real reform will mean fighting the vested interests that have been the mainstays of LDP support. The LDP old guard has recently muted its criticism of reform in order to exploit Koizumi's popular appeal, but now that the LDP had been victorious in the election, they can be expected to show their gratitude by sharply opposing his economic and political reform agenda. Having used the prime minister to their advantage, they will now resume their resistance to radical reforms. The voters who are now backing Koizumi may desert him if his program stalls because of opposition from the LDP old guard. In order to succeed in this battle, Koizumi will have to genuinely believe in reform and be willing to fight for it, but while his determination is essential, it is not in itself sufficient to change Japan. Koizumi's program will not succeed unless the Japanese people are ready and willing to support real reform. After experiencing a decade of economic stagnation and recession as well as continuous government mismanagement, the Japanese public says it now wants radical change, but the public's willingness to actually endure the drastic pain that radical and lengthy reform will necessitate is untested and may not be long lasting.

Additional factors complicate the prospects for reform. Since Mr. Koizumi took office in April, the economic news, hardly good, has grown even worse. The economy is declining drastically again. Figures released on July 30 show that industrial production shrank at an annualized rate of 15 percent in the second quarter of this year. The economy as a whole having shrunk in the first quarter now seems almost certain to shrink again in the second. That would officially put Japan back in recession, for the fourth time in only 10 years. Recession is worsening the mess in the banking system by adding to the bad-debt burden. It also makes prices fall even faster. Falling prices make the real value of debt grow, adding further to the banks' miseries. In addition, the day after Mr. Koizumi's victory, the stock market fell to a new, 16-year low. At this level, the banks are closer to a crisis. Unemployment is rising rapidly, so consumers are likely to cut back even more, and that will lead to additional cuts in production, and even more unemployment, and further declines in prices. Unfortunately, many economists agree that Mr. Koizumi's ideas may accelerate the slide into recession, deepening the downturn and perhaps resulting in an economic depression. That possibility would make his economic and political goals much harder to achieve (see "The Voters Give Koisumi a Chance. Will the LDP?" 2001, 21–23).

Clearly, the road to Japan's economic revival will not be easy or smooth. On the positive side, the popularity of Prime Minister Koizumi and his team enhances the opportunities for success. Koizumi appears to be a new kind of leader and his energy and charisma helped him to gain wide support for his political program during the elections. On the other hand, however, the obstacles he faces internally and with the global economy are formidable, and if Koizumi is not successful in implementing serious reforms at this time, it is difficult to see any other possibility for radical change in the near future.

POLICY ANALYSIS AND POLICY PRESCRIPTIONS

What went wrong with Japan's economy, and who is to blame? The appropriate policy prescriptions for getting Japan's economy back on track are closely linked to policy analysis judgments over whether Japan's problems are cyclical or have more deep-seated structural features. However, analysts have not reached consensus on the diagnosis of causes for the economic crisis and for policy prescriptions. During the early 1990s the typical view was that Japan was in a cyclical downturn and would soon recover. But the economic upturn has not yet occurred. Numerous Japanese and Western academics and policy makers have offered their diagnosis of

Japan's economic problems and have proposed a variety of policy prescriptions.

Shinpo Seiji, director general of the Research Bureau of the Economic Planning Agency, defends the government's policies of fiscal consolidation and discounts the "fiscal deflation" thesis offered by government critics. His explanation for "Japan's anemic growth" (1998) includes four factors: (1) the aftermath of the "bubble" period has worked to dampen economic recovery because the need to repay debts incurred during the "bubble" years has caused both consumers and business firms to be cautious with respect to new consumption and investment; (2) cyclical factors; (3) the shift of manufacturing production overseas; and (4) "the greater than expected backlash that followed the huge surge in demand in the latter half of fiscal 1996 prior to the consumption tax hike" (16).

Seiji's prescription includes using public funds to stabilize the financial system, eliminating bad debt, consolidating financial institutions, and making a thorough review of the tax and regulatory system with a view to stimulating real estate transactions. To prevent a hollowing out of industry and finance, Seiji suggests making Japan a more attractive market for industrial activity by lowering corporate and security taxes. Finally, he proposes decisive reforms of the economic system, led by deregulation such as the Big Bang package.

But not everyone agrees that the timing is right for the Big Bang reforms. Sakamoto Sakae, economic news editor at the Jiri Press news agency, quotes a former minister of finance official who says that it is "impossible to solve financial institutions' problems simultaneously with 'Big Bang' reforms to deregulate, internationalize and securitize the financial system based on rules of being free, fair and global." Given the existing economic conditions, the "former official calls for a suspension or postponement of the 'Big Bang,' saying that 'resolving the financial crisis and going ahead with the 'Big Bang' while the economy is in deflation, frankly speaking, poses a dilemma' " (1998, 33). Sakae points out that economists are increasingly pessimistic about the future and some of them believe that the Japanese economy "passed the stages of depression and deflation, and has taken a plunge into panic" (1998, 32).

In contrast, Nagatani Keizo, an economist, argues that Japan's "current trouble is nothing extraordinary. It is no cause for a national panic" (1998, 14). Keizo predicts that the Japanese economy will founder for a few more years and that personal taxes will rise, job prospects will worsen, and social unrest will increase. He concludes that there is no quick and easy way out of the current economic stagnation. But the worst result of the economic situation, according to Keizo, is that the "Japanese have lost themselves" (1998, 14). He argues that the Japanese are undergoing a crisis of self-confidence and that "It is imperative that they regain composure, take stock of what they are made of and how they came to be where they are, and then to take a hard look at where they want to go from there" (1998, 14). He says that the Japanese have lost faith in their own system and tend to overrate Western ways and economic models. He suggests that current reform campaigns are too rash and that the Big Bang might decimate Japan's financial industry. A consensus-based society like Japan, Keizo says, needs more time than Western societies to reform and that in the process they should not scrap Japanese economic models built on the principle of equity or coexistence for the sake of efficiency and competition. He concludes that "a global free market offers little assurance of success either theoretically or empirically," and since "Japanese can never be Americans," the "Japanese must deal with problems as best they can, given their national gifts" (1998, 14).

Hashiyama Reijiro, a professor of management information at Teikyo University, agrees with Keizo that the Japanese people have lost confidence. He claims that this is the real reason that individual consumption has begun to stagnate. But he disagrees strongly with Keizo about the need to maintain traditional Japanese models and values. Indeed, Reijiro argues that "The key to Japan's economic recovery is not in piecemeal adjustments but in the radical reform of government administration and finances, coupled with structural change in the relationship between government and the private sector" (1998, 24). Reijiro is concerned that the reforms will not succeed because of resistance from the bureaucrats and conservative politicians. He points out that the MOF lacks the courage to let unhealthy banks fail and that it continues to pour huge amounts of capital into unnecessary and inefficient public works projects (1998).

In *Tigers Tamed: The End of the Asian Miracle* (1998), economic and political writer Robert Garran, points out that Japan's postwar economic miracle seemed to demonstrate a Japanese alternative model of development that improved upon the Western laissez-faire model of capitalism. This challenged the traditional "neoclassical" modernization model for developing economies promoted by the United States and other Western industrial nations, and it appeared to provide, especially for Asian nations, a blueprint for faster economic growth, using Asian values. Garran contends that both Japan's economic crisis and the 1997 Asian financial crisis reveal that the "miracle is a myth" (1998, 2) and that the model is deeply flawed by cronyism and corruption, poor infrastructure, lack of transparency in decision making, poor governance, weakness of financial institutions, insufficient accountability, and absence of the rule of law. He acknowledges that some elements of the Japanese model might have been appropriate to the period from about 1950 until 1973 when Japan's economic growth averaged an extraordinary 10 percent a year. By the early 1970s, however, having caught up with the West technologically, Japan's growth rate slowed down and slipped behind that of the West. The model's inflexibility became a drag on innovation and other flaws became increasingly dysfunctional (see also Madsen, 1998).

Garran does not believe that change will come easily in Japan because the vested interests against reform are formidable, political leadership is weak, the bureaucratic ability to manage the financial system is limited, and Japan seems "unable or unwilling to repair its financial system and resuscitate its economy" (73). Garran's view of Japan's economic prospects is generally pessimistic. He states that "Japan is beset by gloom inside and outside, by a failure of leadership, by weak economic growth. . . . Changes will come, but slowly and Japan will likely never regain the heady optimism of the late 1980s bubble. Japan is caught between the growing burden of an aging population and the demands, from inside and out, that it apply more budget stimulus to try and solve the immediate problem of its economic slump. Whatever balance is found between these opposing demands, the best prognosis is that Japan will muddle through; and the worst that failure to tackle some of the deeper structural problems will spark another crisis" (196–197).

Edward L. Lincoln, senior fellow in foreign policy studies at the Brookings Institution and former economic advisor to the American ambassador to Japan, is also highly pessimistic about "Japan's financial mess" (1998). While the problems of the 1990s started with the bursting of the stock market and real estate bubble, Lincoln blames the government for the financial excesses and stagnation that followed. He charges that despite government pronouncements about deregulation and economic stimulation packages, little will be done because Japanese bureaucrats and politicians are in deep denial about Japan's economic problems, and they continue to have a strong faith in the Japanese style of capitalism. According to Lincoln, the bureaucrats and politicians "do not comprehend the extent of reforms necessary to restore the nation to economic health." Furthermore, "they regard their current problems as a passing incident with no fundamental implications for the existing system" (1998, 57–58). In addition, the Japanese public does not strongly support deregulation because it associates economic reform with unemployment and instability in their personal lives.

Lincoln cites a lengthy catalog of other problems that plague the Japanese financial system, including the dogmatically conservative attitudes of government officials toward macroeconomic policy that are delaying recovery, numerous scandals that expose ethical and illegal behavior in the financial sector, ingrained resistance to reform, governmental distrust of private markets, reckless speculation, cronyism and malfeasance, illegal dealings between financial institutions, politicians, and bureaucrats, and the involvement of organized crime. While Lincoln does not expect Japan to undergo an outright financial collapse, he does believe that it will just muddle along with substandard growth and an unstable financial sector for the foreseeable future. In "The Return of Depression Economics" (1999) and other recent writings, Paul Krugman, a well-known American economist, contends that Japan is suffering something like the economic situation of the United States during the 1930s in which a highly productive industrial society stumbles into a financial crisis and has not been able to get restarted. Although nobody quite knows what went wrong, Krugman points to problems in the banking system that hasn't come to terms with bad debts, and the service sector that is overregulated and lacks competition. Krugman also blames the "once-fabled Ministry of Finance," which "has consistently raised taxes whenever the country has shown signs of recovery, seemingly determined to keep the economy depressed" (1998, 43). Krugman contends that Japan is now caught in the "dreaded 'liquidity trap' in which monetary policy finds itself 'pushing on a string.' Attempts to expand the economy by easing credit fail because banks and consumers alike prefer holding safe, liquid cash to investing in risky, less-liquid bonds and stocks" (1999, 66). Krugman believes that fiscal policy, tax cuts, and bank reform are probably not enough to get Japan out of its slump. Therefore, Krugman proposes an unconventional policy solution, "managed inflation." He argues that the central bank has to "credibly promise to be irresponsible." He proposes that Japan should actively seek a target of 3 or 4 percent inflation to counter deflationary pressures (1999, 74). In this dire situation the central bank ought to promise to pump enough money into the economy to create expectations of future inflation. Only then will consumers start spending the money they have been hoarding. While Krugman believes that his solution is based on sound economic theory and will work, he admits that it is highly unlikely that the central bank will try to implement it because the idea of fighting deflation by promising inflation sounds crazy to bankers who have spent their whole careers preaching the evils of inflation.

Adam S. Posen, an American economist, presents one of the most detailed analyses of Japan's economic decline and the most specific program for restoring the economy. According to Posen, growth has not returned to Japan because Japanese macroeconomic policy has followed a mistaken course and the appropriate policies have not been tried. Posen argues that "The stagnation of Japan in the 1990s was anything but inevitable, and it was misguided macroeconomic austerity and financial laissez-faire—not lack of return on investment or political deadlock—that caused it. In the 1990s, Japanese economic policy makers were presented with the opportunity to fight the last war, the demand-shock-caused depression of the 1930s, and they chose to adopt the strategy that lost the war. As a result, growth in Japan could have been much higher in the 1990s than it was," (2). Posen contends that, "Today's policy should be one of active macroeconomic expansion to restore that attainable rate of higher growth. The longer that Japanese policymakers leave their economy in decline, the more attainable wealth they forego" (1998, 4; see also Weinstein, 1999).

In Posen's recommended program for economic recovery, the goal is to restore growth on a sustainable basis, and the primary purpose is to change Japanese savers' and investors' confidence by convincingly restoring expectations of above-potential growth and price stability and by removing the incentives to excessive savings, which perpetuate the downturn. The three legs of the program include fiscal expansion, monetary stabilization of price expectations, and financial reform. According to Posen, fiscal expansion should include fiscal stimulus, permanent tax cuts, and use of short-term government debt to fund deficits. He suggests a fiscal stimulus of 4 percent of GDP, arguing that "unless the economy is stimulated above potential growth of 2 to 2.5 percent per year, unemployment will continue to rise and capacity utilization will continue to drop. Confidence, and with it consumption and investment, will erode further" (1998, 8).

Posen favors permanent tax cuts over temporary cuts because they are more likely to be spent and to affect consumer planning. He also suggests that "income tax cuts are better than consumption tax cuts because income tax cuts get money directly to the salarymen, whose rise in precautionary savings is the main problem" (1998, 8). But he stipulates that either form of permanent tax cut is preferable to more public works spending (which has been favored by the LDP and construction companies) because tax cuts reduce distortions in the economy and induce future cuts in public spending.

Posen proposes monetary stabilization of price expectations against both deflation and inflation. He argues that in order for both Japanese households to spend and Japanese businesses to invest, they need to have faith in the stability of the purchasing power of their currency. This is also a prerequisite to any lasting revival of Japanese asset prices. Therefore, in order to offset the threat of deflation without setting off an inflationary spiral, the Bank of Japan should announce an inflation target of 3 percent. Posen maintains that "such an anchored and transparent monetary policy offers almost all of the advantages of simply inflating by 'turning on the presses' without any of its destabilizing risks" (1998, 9).

Business professors Michael Porter and Hirotaka Takeuchi offer somewhat different policy prescriptions for "fixing what really ails Japan." While they agree that stimulating the economy and restoring the flow of capital are necessary steps, they contend that macroeconomic measures will not do enough because what ails Japan is deeply rooted in the microeconomics of how Japan competes and in Japan's flawed economic model. Their analysis and prescriptions are based on a major empirical study of both Japan's government model and its model of corporate success. These models have had a profound impact on other Asian countries. As a result of Japan's postwar economic miracle and the boasts of some Japanese policy makers that they had invented a new model of capitalism superior to the Anglo-Saxon model of capitalism, many Asian countries tried to clone the Japanese model or at least adapt it to their cultures and circumstances.

Porter and Takeuchi charge that the Japanese government's mistrust of competition causes it to intervene in the economy in ways that actually harm Japan's prosperity and productivity, and that corporations' mistaken approach to competition undermines profitability. Therefore, they conclude that fixing what ails Japan will require no less than fundamental changes in both government and corporate practices. Porter and Takeuchi studied 18 industries representing all sectors of the Japanese economy from the 1940s to the 1990s. Previous studies had focused primarily on successful industries, but Porter and Takeuchi also studied the failures and uncompetitive industries. Based on case studies and statistical analysis, they stated that the "government model played little if any role in the successful industries," but "Among the failures the government model prevailed." They concluded that, "If anything the Japanese government model is a cause of failure, not of success" (1999, 71).

Although they concluded that the Japanese corporate model had some merit, especially with regard to operational effectiveness, most corporations were weak in the area of broad, innovative competitive strategy. The few notable exceptions included a handful of successful but maverick companies like Honda, Sony, and Nintendo. These companies prospered in spite of government policies, not because of them. Japanese government policies limit competition in many ways, and Porter and Takeuchi argue that this is harmful because "vigorous rivalry is the only path to economic vitality," driving innovation and continuous improvement in productivity (1999, 74). They point out that, in their study, in virtually all of the Japanese failure cases, rivalry was constrained, often by government impediments.

Given the deep, underlying problems associated with both the government and corporate model, Porter and Takeuchi state that only fundamental microeconomic changes will solve Japan's economic ills. The biggest lesson from Japan's economic failures, according to Porter and Takeuchi, is that the government must abandon its anticompetitive policies, including cartels, subsidies, government guidance, and regulatory barriers to competition. Japan must remove barriers to imports and embrace free trade. Inefficient, fragmented, and noncompetitive domestic sectors such as retailing, financial services, health care, and housing must be allowed to compete and fail if necessary, without government subsidies and protection. New government policies must promote greater transparency and accountability in the financial sector and remove guarantees that encourage moral hazard investing.

Business must change the way it competes and catch up in information technology, the Internet, office productivity, marketing, and other traditionally weak areas. Companies must develop more competitive strategies, focus on profitability as the only reliable measure of sound strategy, restructure companies to "enhance autonomy, foster innovation, speed up decision-making, and improve accountability . . . and take steps to improve governance" (1999, 81). Porter and Takeuchi also suggest that Japanese companies need to change their internal incentive structures which penalize mistakes but do not reward successes, and they must abandon their egalitarian, seniority-driven models, for compensation linked to performance and entrepreneurship. Porter and Takeuchi conclude that it is "time for Japan to reinvent itself once more, based on a deeper understanding of the strengths and limitations of its approach and a new, more sophisticated way of competing" (1999, 81). But they do provide neither a detailed program for implementation nor a timetable for completion of these fundamental reforms of the government and corporate models.

In *The Lexus and the Olive Tree*, his widely read book on globalization, Thomas Friedman, foreign affairs columnist for *The New York Times*, contends that while Japan's economy has a free market element, it was always a lot more communist than capitalist in that throughout the Cold War it was dominated by a single party, the LDP, and the state was run by a nomenklatura, an elite bureaucracy, much as Russia and China were. Japan also had a docile media and a deeply conforming population. Friedman argues that "if Japan is to avoid permanent stagnation, the communist segment of the Japanese economy is going to have to be 'privatized' just like China's and Russia's. Inefficient firms and banks are going to have to be taken out and shot and their dead capital transferred to more efficient firms." He indicates that he has "no doubt that Japan can be a formidable economic power again, but only after it goes through some painful social, political and cultural adjustments. . . . Will Japan eventually adapt? It must. But not without turmoil" (1999, 334–335).

According to Friedman, economic success in the post–Cold War globalization era will only come to countries (including Japan) that are willing to don the "Golden Straitjacket," which means privatizing enterprises, balancing budgets, lowering tariffs, removing restrictions on foreign investment, and eliminating subsidies for companies, installing recognized auditing and accounting standards, strong financial market regulation, and equitable bankruptcy procedures. Embracing globalization means replacing cronyism with a culture of transparency. In short, the only route to economic growth is to confirm to a political-economic model with U.S.-style institutions.

GOVERNMENT POLICY RESPONSES AND PROSPECTS FOR SUCCESS

Japan's policy makers have considered and tried a variety of solutions, including macroeconomic policy, resolution of bad loans, structural reforms, and deregulation, but so far none has been sufficient to fix the problems. In 1991, a year after the last of the interest rate hikes that had burst the bubble, the Bank of Japan began lowering interest rates. Indeed, by 1995, short-term money market rates were under 0.5 percent, an extraordinarily low figure. In the fall of 1998, these rates dropped to under 0.2 percent. While loose money policies certainly dampened the crisis, their impact has been limited (Posen, 1998, 6–7).

In 1996 the Hashimoto government announced a "Big Bang" package of financial reforms aimed at tackling the weaknesses in the financial system. This plan to deregulate and liberalize the financial sectors meant an end to the "convoy" system of no failure and regulatory practice that had guided Japanese financial markets since the end of World War II. The Big Bang plan represented a repudiation of the Japanese postwar model of managed economic development in favor of a more market-oriented model.

According to the MOF, the intent of Big Bang was to make the Japanese financial systems "fair, free, and global." The goal was to lower the barriers between different kinds of financial institutions. There were three main objectives. First, the Big Bang aimed at making the Japanese market more efficient and internationalized. As the market became more active and competitive, it was expected that users, such as Japanese corporations and retail consumers, would be beneficiaries. Second, the Japanese institutions, with competitive pressures from foreign institutions, would have to become more efficient. Third, deregulated markets would help deflect the political pressures on the MOF coming from special interest groups.

The Japanese government also tried mobilizing fiscal policy by raising spending or lowering taxes to deal with weak demand. The use of deficit spending, particularly in 1994–1996, created concern for many fiscally conservative policy makers. They argued that because of the rapid aging of Japanese society it was crucial to consolidate public finances rather than rely on bonds that would have to be paid off by a declining workforce in the future. By 1996, many influential fiscal conservatives in the MOF and the LDP came to the conclusion that deficit spending was not fixing the problems of the economy. Despite surprisingly high economic growth in 1996, these policy makers acted to reverse fiscal policy (see Posen, 1998).

In 1997 the national consumption tax increased from 3 percent to 5 percent, several temporary tax cuts were allowed to lapse, national health insurance premiums were raised, and public works spending was scaled back. The economic effects of these contradictory measures demonstrated that deficit spending had indeed had positive effects on the economy—the economy went into a nosedive with real growth in GDP contracting by 0.7 percent for the fiscal year, the first negative growth rate for a full year since 1974 (see Madsen, 1998, 51; Seiji, 1998, 15). The government did an about-face by December 1997 and offered large-scale new spending. By the end of November 1998, the Japanese Diet prepared to pass a new fiscal stimulus package, officially valued at over 17 trillion yen (see Weinstein, 1998, 8).

The MOF has traditionally been reluctant to let any bank actually go out of business, and the implied guarantee that no bank would be allowed to fail had become a central pillar, ensuring the stability of the financial sector. But that policy has become untenable because many problem banks are in such bad shape that other banks are reluctant to attempt to bail them out. The problems in the financial sector are so pervasive that there are not enough healthy banks to absorb all the problem banks. Moreover, increased competition from non-Japanese banks has taken away enough of the MOF's discretionary powers that it has lost its ability to provide sufficient incentives for even the healthiest banks to take on major new obligations (see Naoyuki, 1999, 13). In the 1990s, the process of financial liberalization accelerated. Japan's banking sector began to have to compete with foreign institutions and to keep up with rapid technological innovations. While financial liberalization may free up the most competitive institutions to profit from their greater efficiency and innovativeness, it also threatens the existence of many weaker institutions.

CONCLUSIONS

At this point in time it is unclear how Japan's economy will unfold in the near future. Will the new Koizumi administration be able to implement and maintain the radical reforms it deems necessary to get the Japanese economy back on track? If the Koizumi reforms are implemented will they bring about the desired changes or create additional economic dilemmas? Will globalization and other pressures stimulate Japan to reinvent itself once more, or will it fail to meet the challenge? Is it possible to construct both optimistic and pessimistic scenarios for Japan's future?

In the optimistic view, Koizumi and Japanese elected politicians, elite bureaucrats, and business leaders may lead an economic resurgence by implementing some combination of the policy prescriptions discussed above. Japan may resume strong economic growth, although at a lower level than during the 1950s and 1960s, and take its place again as the economic and political leader in the Asia-Pacific region. Japan would then be in a position to contribute to the political and economic stability of other East Asian nations.

In a more pessimistic scenario, the Japanese crisis could worsen. If financial reforms are resisted or fail to solve Japan's economic problems, Japan may continue to muddle along with slow economic growth, changing gradually, but not fast enough to help solve its problems. Or Japan's recession and deflation could be transformed to a full-blown depression. Japan might hollow out as talented citizens and the best business firms fled the country. Japan might then go into an economic decline that would last for the foreseeable future. If China were also to suffer an economic melt-down, the shock waves would buffet the other world economies, including the United States and Europe, and perhaps produce a global depression.

The divergence of thinking on whether Japan will rise again in the near future is nicely illustrated by two contrary articles appearing in a recent issue of *Foreign Affairs*. M. Diane Helweg's article, "Japan: A Rising Sun?" (2000) optimistically predicts that business innovation will drive Japan's economic revolution. Aurelia George Mulgan's (2000) focuses on the extraordinary connection between the government and business sectors and somewhat more pessimistically concludes that recent reforms will not overcome the drag of self-serving politicians.

Helweg believes that Japan is undergoing an economic revolution led by the wave of small, creative, high-tech companies that are building Japan's version of Silicon Valley. She contends that the government's lackluster economic stewardship is no longer of any consequence in Japan because the government is not driving the emerging economic revolution. According to Helweg, business is now the driving force. She argues that "today's structural reforms in the Japanese financial system are quietly setting the stage for an economic revolution" and that "Japan's revolutionary path will utterly transform it from the state-run industrial powerhouse of the twentieth century toward an innovation-driven globalized economy of the twenty-first" (26).

Despite Helweg's optimism, she admits that Japan's economic revolution will not succeed without a fight because there is a great deal of resistance to reforms in Japan. It is also problematic that the reforms are neither comprehensive nor universal, and they "have been implemented piece-meal—offering too little, too late" (37). Helweg acknowledges other serious problems, including ineffective corporate restructuring plans, bureaucratic resistance to reforms by the MOF, and "high personal savings coupled with low consumer spending, leaving Japan in an interminable deflationary spiral" (37). Perhaps most problematic is that "the enormous fiscal stimulus packages of the 1990's that the government implemented to break this deflation produced nightmarish budget deficits" (37). In addition, Helweg admits that the LDP is lagging on political reform. Indeed, after considering the many obstacles to reform and economic revolution that Helweg presents, it is somewhat difficult to understand her optimism about the prospects for an economic revolution that will transform Japan in the next few years.

In "Japan: A Setting Sun?" Aurelia George Mulgan contends that "Reform peaked in 1998 when Tokyo moved to rescue the financial system from imminent collapse, cut regulations, and revitalize industry" (40). In 1998, Japan's economy was locked in recession, and the threat of deflation became apparent. Japan's political and business elite finally realized that strong measures were needed to get the economy back on track. The government acknowledged the need for a radical structural reform of the economy and a comprehensive overhaul of Japan's banking system. Some major banks like Sanyo Securities, Takushoku Bank, and Yamachi Securities were allowed to fail, and other large banks merged, including the Sumitomo Sakura and the Asaki-Tokai-Samwa bank mergers. Japanese companies began to voluntarily restructure and to focus on the most profitable areas of their business. Traditional employee guarantees of lifetime job security and seniority-based pay in big companies began to deteriorate. According to Mulgan, "Just when the momentum for reform appeared unstoppable, the government's revival strategy began to lean too heavily on fiscal stimuli, pushing Japan into a spending rut" (40). Between 1992 and 1999, the Japanese government launched nine mammoth stimulus packages totaling $1.2 trillion which created massive public debt.

Once the Japanese economy began to show some signs of recovery, the sense of urgency for reform began to ease up and the momentum for change lessened. Mulgan argues that political appointments and a succession of policy developments since late-1999 clearly demonstrates that the antireform forces within the government are gaining the upper hand. The LDP was never a true advocate of radical reform, and now it appears to be blocking efforts for deregulation on all fronts.

Mulgan claims that "Japan is facing a crisis of governance. Not only do politicians pander to special interests, but vested interests are institutionalized in the very structures of governance" (47). The special interests that provide the major support for the LDP such as the farmers, small business, and construction industry oppose both deregulation and economic liberalization. Bureaucrats have a vested interest in resisting deregulation because systems of regulation require that corporations maintain good relationships with the bureaucrats who regulate them. Thus, the corporations are motivated to offer bureaucrats lucrative post-retirement positions and to provide all kinds of inducements such as golf club memberships, interest-free loans, and travel benefits. For these reasons, the push for reform is being derailed by the bureaucrats and LDP politicians.

As a consequence, public trust in the Japanese government is all but gone, and most Japanese harbor grave doubts about whether much needed reforms will be implemented. Mulgan argues that, "This pessimism is holding back consumer spending and undermining Japan's shaky economic recovery," and therefore, "the structure of vested interests . . . needs to be dismantled" (51). Economic recovery would require that Japanese politicians give up many benefits of the status quo, but they are not likely to do so without a fight. Therefore, Japan may be on the brink of structure decline. The underlying economic problems remain, but the vested interests of bureaucrats, politicians, and LDP supporters are derailing the radical reforms that are vital to developing the self-sustained growth necessary for Japan's future economic recovery. If Mulgan's analysis is correct Mr. Koizumi will have to be both bold and lucky to prevail in the turbulent world of Japanese politics, and to implement his reform agenda.

While the Japanese and Asian economic crises are important, they are not unique. These types of crises are occurring with increasing frequency as the globalization process spreads and increases the world's economic, financial, and technological integration. Globalization appears to be an inevitable process, and while it promises opportunities for increasing economic growth, it also increases the risks of financial crisis. As the expansion of financial markets and networks becomes truly global, governments must learn to deal with currency crises, both in terms of prevention and response. Accurately diagnosing the causes of the Japanese economic crisis, assessing the viability of the proposed policy prescriptions, and the most efficacious role for government in economic development, can be crucial for deriving valuable lessons relevant to future economic crises.

REFERENCES

Abe, S. (1999). "China's Economic Influence on Japan." East-West Center Conference paper, University of Hawaii, January.

Akira, A. (1998). "The Big Bang Blueprint." *Look Japan* (July): 14–16.

Argy, V. E., and L. Stein. (1997). *The Japanese Economy*. New York: New York University Press.

Bergsten, C. F., and M. Noland. (1993). *Reconcilable Differences? The United States–Japan Economic Conflict*. Washington, DC: Institute for International Economics.

Blomstrom, M., B. Gangnes, and S. J. La Croix, eds. (2001). *Japan's New Economy: Continuity and Change in the Twenty-First Century*. New York: Oxford University Press.

Bremner, B. (1998a). "Japan: Wanted a New Economic Model." *Business Week*, November 30, pp. 45–48.

Bremner, B. (1998b). "This Is Going to Happen, MITI's Yosana Pledges Reform." *Business Week*, December 7, pp. 106–107.

Calder, K. (1993). *Strategic Capitalism*. Princeton, NJ: Princeton University Press.

"Can't Get Started." (2001). *The Economist*, April 12, p. 12.

Cargill, T., M. M. Hutchison, and T. Ito. (1997). *The Political Economy of Japanese Monetary Policy*. Cambridge, MA: MIT Press.

"Could It Happen Again." (1999). *The Economist*, February 20, pp. 19–22.

Destler, I. M. (1995). *American Trade Politics*, 3rd ed. Washington, DC: Institute for International Economics.

Drucker, P. (1998). "Defending Japanese Bureaucrats." *Foreign Affairs* (September–October): 68–80.

Ely, B. (1999). "Is Creditor Better Than Debtor?" *Wall Street Journal*, January 11, p. A22.

Emmott, W. (1991). *The Sun Also Sets: The Limits to Japan's Economic Power*. New York: Touchstone Books.

Emmott, W. (1994). *Japanophobia: The Myth of the Invincible Japanese*. New York: Times Books.

Fallows, J. (1994) *Looking at the Sun: The Rise of the New East Asian Economic and Political System*. New York: Pantheon Books.

Fox, J. (1998). "Why Japan Won't Budge." *Fortune*, September 7, pp. 82–83.

Freedman, C., ed. (1998). *Japanese Economic Policy Reconsidered*. Cheltenham, UK: Edward Elgar.

Friedman, T. (1998). "Pay Attention to Japan Before Catastrophe Demands It." *Sun Sentinel*, April 9, p. 23A.

Friedman, T. (1999). *The Lexus and the Olive Tree*. New York: Farrar, Straus, & Giroux.

Fulford, B. (1999a). "The Bouncing Yen." *Forbes*, January 25, p. 55.

Fulford, B. (1999b). "Japan's Cement Shoes." *Forbes*, February 8, pp. 82–83.

Funabashi, Y. (1998). "Tokyo's Depression Diplomacy." *Foreign Affairs* 77(6) (November–December): 27–36.

Garran, R. (1998). *Tigers Tamed: The End of the Asian Miracle*. Honolulu: University of Hawaii Press.

Garten, J. E. (1999). "Lessons for the Next Financial Crisis." *Foreign Affairs* 78(2) (March–April): 76–92.

Gibney, F. (1998). *Unlocking the Bureaucrat's Kingdom: Deregulation and the Japanese Economy*. Washington, DC: Brookings Institution Press.

"A Global Game of Dominoes." (2001). *The Economist*, August 25, pp. 22–24.

Globerman, S., and A. Kokko. (1999). "A New Millennium for Japanese–North American Economic Relations." East-West Center Conference paper, University of Hawaii, January.

Haggard, S. (1999). "The Debate from East Asia." *APSA-CP Newsletter* (Winter): 14–16.

Haggard, S. (2000). *The Political Economy of the Asian Financial Crisis*. Washington, DC: Institute for International Economics.

Helweg, D. M. (2000). "Japan: A Rising Sun?" *Foreign Affairs* 79(4) (July–August): 26–39.

Ito, T. (1992). *The Japanese Economy*, Cambridge, MA: MIT Press.

Ito, T., and A. Krueger, eds. (1996). *Financial Deregulation and Integration in East Asia*. Chicago: University of Chicago Press.

Ito, T., and M. Melvin. (1999). "The Political Economy of Japan's Big Bang." East-West Center Conference paper, University of Hawaii, January.

"Japan's Economy: Chronic Sickness." (2001). *The Economist*, June 2, pp. 71–74.

"Japan's Great Hope." (2001). *The Economist*, August 4, p. 11.

"Japan's Other Debt Crisis." (1998). *The Economist*, December 12, pp. 71–72.

Johnson, C. (1982). *MITI and the Japanese Miracle: The Growth of Industrial Policy, 1925–1975*. Stanford, CA: Stanford University Press.

Johnson, C. (1996). *Japan: Who Governs? The Rise of the Developmental State*. New York: W. W. Norton.

Katy, R. (1998). *Japan: The System That Soured*. Armonk, NY: M. E. Sharpe.

Keizo, N. (1998). "Japan's Sagging Credibility: A Crisis of Self Confidence." *Look Japan* (March): 12–13.

Kenji, A. (1999). "We Can Rebuild Them." *Look Japan* (January): 22–23.

Kojima, A. (1999). "Getting to the Bottom of Japan's Economic Blues." *Japan Echo* 26(1) (February): 15–17.

Krugman, P. (1998). "America the Boastful." *Foreign Affairs* (May–June): 32–45.

Krugman, P. (1999). "The Return of Depression Economics." *Foreign Affairs* 78(1) (January–February): 56–74.

Kunio, N. (1999). "First Step Toward Recovery: Emergency Economic Package Targets 2000." *Look Japan* (February): 12–13.

La Croix, S. J. (1999). "Regulatory Reform in Japan: The Road Ahead." East-West Center conference paper, University of Hawaii, January.

Lincoln, E. (1990). *Japan's Unequal Trade*. Washington, DC: Brookings Institute.

Lincoln, E. (1998). "Japan's Financial Mess." *Foreign Affairs* 77(3): 57–66.

Madsen, R. A. (1998). "Expect No Help from Japan." *World Policy Journal* 15(3) (Fall): 50–55.

Mak, J. et al., eds. (1998). *Japan: Why It Works, Why It Doesn't*. Honolulu: University of Hawaii Press.

Makino, N. (1999). "Four Crises Confronting Japan." *Japan Echo* 26(1) (February): 13–14.

Mason, A., and N. Ogawa. (1999). "Population and Japan's Economic Outlook." East-West Center conference paper, University of Hawaii, January.

Montes, M. F. (1998). "Global Lessons of the Economic Crisis in Asia." *Asia Pacific Issues* (Honolulu, HI: East-West Center) (March): 35.

Mulgan, A. G. (2000). "Japan: A Setting Sun?" *Foreign Affairs* 79(4) (July–August): 40–52.

Nakanishi, T. (1999). "The Country That Can't Make Up Its Mind." *Japan Echo* 26(1) (February): 9–12.

Naoyuki, Y. (1999). "Toward Financial Stabilization." *Look Japan* (January): 12–13.

Neff, R. (1998). "A Major Roadblock to Reform: The U.S." *Business Week*, November 30, p. 71.

Nishiyama, C. (1999). "An Emergency Declaration for Japan." *Japan Echo* 26(1) (February): 18–22.

Okabe, M., ed. (1995). *The Structure of the Japanese Economy: Changes on the Domestic and International Fronts*. New York: St. Martin's Press.

Osamu, N. (1998). "On the Eve of the 21st Century: A Strange Political Landscape." *Journal of Japanese Trade & Industry* (November–December): 40–43.

Pempel, T. J. (1986). "Japan: The Dilemmas of Success." New York: Foreign Policy Association/Headline Series.

Porter, M. E., and H. Takeuchi. (1999). "Fixing What Really Ails Japan." *Foreign Affairs* 7(3) (May/June): 66–81.

Posen, A. S. (1998). Restoring Japan's Economic Growth. Washington, DC: Institute for International Economics.

Prestowitz, C. (1989). *Trading Places: How We Are Giving Our Future to Japan and How to Retain It*. New York: Basic Books.

Pyle, K., ed. (1997). *The Trade Crisis: How Will Japan Respond?* Seattle, WA: Society for Japanese Studies.

Reid, T. R., and P. Bluestein. (1995). "What a Difference a Half Century Makes." *Washington Post National Weekly Edition* 12 (August 21–27): 21.

Reijiro, H. (1998). "Revolution Number Four." *Look Japan* (October): 24.

Rohwer, J. (1998). "Yikes! Japan's Bank Debt Bomb is Scarier Than You Think." *Fortune*, November 9, pp. 124–126.

Sakae, S. (1998). "Will Japan's Deflation Be Prolonged." *Journal of Japanese Trade & Industry* (September–October): 32–33.

Sakamaki, S. (1998). "The Road to Ruin." *Time* (November 9): 20–22.

Sato, R., R. Ramachandran, and H. Hori, eds. (1996). *Organization, Performance, and Equity: Perspectives on the Japanese Economy.* Boston: Kluwer Academic Publishers.

Satoshi, H. (1998). "Is Japan That Financially Unsound as Data Suggests?" *Asia 21* (November): 26–28.

Seiji, S. (1998). "Japan's Anemic Growth: Diagnosis and Cure." *Look Japan* (May): 15–17.

Sheridan, K. (1993). *Governing the Japanese Economy.* Cambridge, MA: Polity Press.

Tadashi, N. (1998). "Near Future Scenarios." *Look Japan* (June): 12–15.

Tamamoto, M. (1998). "The Privilege of Choosing: The Fallout from Japan's Financial Crisis." *World Policy Journal* 15(3) (Fall): 25–31.

Tateishi, T. (1998). "The Plaza Accord Saved America from Fiscal Downfall." *Asia 21* (November): 23–24.

Teruhiko, M. (1999). "Staring at the Sun." *Look Japan* (January): 3.

Tomio, T. (1998a). "Japanese Industrial Policy." *Journal of Japanese Trade & Industry* 4 (July/August): 8–15.

Tomio, T. (1998b). "Japan's Economy—Analysis of the Recent Situation and Future Perspectives." *Journal of Japanese Trade & Industry* (November–December): 16–18.

Unger, D., and P. Blackburn, eds. (1993). *Japan's Emerging Global Role.* Boulder, CO: Lynne Rienner.

Valery, N. (1999). "Japan's Unhappy Introspection." The World In 1999 (Special Issue). *The Economist.*

Vogel, St. (1998). "Why Can't Japan Reform?" *Look Japan* (December): 13.

"The Voters Give Koisumi a Chance. Will the LDP?" (2001) *The Economist*, August 4, pp. 21–23.

Wade, R. (1999). "A Clash of Capitalisms." *APSA-CP Newsletter* (Winter): 23–26.

Weinberg, Neil. (1998). "Opiate of the Masses." *Forbes*, November 16, pp. 202–206.

Weinstein, D. E. (1999). "How Bad Is the Japanese Crisis? Macroeconomic and Structural Perspectives." East-West Center Conference paper, University of Hawaii, January.

Williams, D. (1994). *Japan: Beyond the End of History.* London: Routledge.

Yamamura, K., and Y. Yasukichi, eds. (1987). *The Political Economy of Japan.* Stanford, CA: Stanford University Press.

Yoshikatsu, T. (1998a). "Largest-Ever Package to Boost Domestic Demand." *Look Japan* (July): 12–13.

Yoshikatsu, T. (1998b). "Pipelines Clogged." *Look Japan* (October): 22–23.

Yoshikawa, H. (1995). *Macroeconomics and the Japanese Economy.* New York: Oxford University Press.

Zielenziger, M. (1999). "Strong Yen Is Hurting Japan." *The Miami Herald*, January 12, p. 1C.

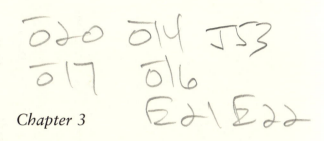

Chapter 3

Managing the Singapore Economy

Chew Soon Beng and Rosalind Chew

OVERVIEW

Singapore, a nation of immigrants, obtained self-government from Britain in 1959. The country had no banking or industrial experience, and its economy relied on entrepot trade. At that time, labor unrest was quite prevalent, causing high unemployment and engendering living conditions that were very poor. Today, Singapore is regarded as one of Asia's newly industrializing economies, and it has sustained a rate of economic growth of about 8 percent annually over the past three decades. Interest in management of the Singapore economy has increased, for among all the Asian countries it has been least affected by the recent currency turmoil in the region.

Table 3.1 presents the key indicators of the Singapore economy for the period 1980–1999. It reveals that Singapore has been able to achieve high GDP growth rate without experiencing high inflation.[1] Furthermore, although the unemployment rate remained around 3 percent for the period under consideration, foreign labor accounted for more than 20 percent of total employment. The Singapore dollar also appreciated against the U.S. dollar for the same period. With the onset of the currency turmoil, the Singapore dollar has depreciated against the U.S. dollar during 1999. However, unlike some of the other currencies which have depreciated by as much as 35 percent since June 1997, the Singapore dollar has only depreciated by less than 10 percent.

The present study focuses on the impact of macroeconomic policy instruments on the individual worker. An essential feature of macroeconomic management in any country involves the adoption of appropriate labor

Table 3.1
Key Indicators of the Singapore Economy, 1980–1999 (selected years)

Indicators	1980	1990	1995	1996	1997	1998	1999	Average Annual Rate, 1970–1995
GDP growth rate	9.3	8.6	8.8	6.9	7.8	0.4	5.4	7.70
Inflation rate (cpi)	8.1	3.4	1.7	1.4	2.0	-0.3	0.0	3.40
Unemployment rate	3.9	1.7	2.7	2.0	1.8	2.3	3.3	3.26
Foreign reserves (S$ million)	13,758	48,521	97,337	107,750	119,617	124,584	128,457	41,046
Exchange rate (S$/U.S.$)	2.14	1.81	1.42	1.41	1.48	1.67	1.69	2.09

Source: Ministry of Trade and Industry, *Economic Survey of Singapore*, various years.

Table 3.2
CPF Contribution Rates, 1980–1999 (selected years)

| Effective Date | Rates of Contribution | | Ordinary Account | Special Account | Medicare Account | Total (%) |
	Employer	Employee				
1980	20.5	18.0	32	6.5	–	38.5
1984	25.0	25.0	40	4.0	6	50.0
1985	25.0	25.0	40	4.0	6	50.0
1986	10.0	25.0	25	4.0	6	35.0
1990	17.5	22.5	32	2.0	6	40.0
1995	20.0	20.0	30	4.0	6	40.0
1996	20.0	20.0	30	4.0	6	40.0
1997	20.0	20.0	30	4.0	6	40.0
1998	20.0	20.0	30	4.0	6	40.0
1999	10.0	20.0	24	0	6	30.0

Source: Central Provident Fund Board, *CPF Annual Reports*, various years.

market policies. This is because the labor market can affect both the cause and the outcome of major economic problems. For instance, unsound economic policies can lead to a loss of competitiveness, which will in turn lead to a higher unemployment rate. At the same time, because unsound labor market policies can cause workers to become choosy over jobs, giving rise to high reservation wages, this will also erode the competitiveness of the country. The first section examines the impact of the Central Provident Fund scheme on workers' incentive to work, while the second section discusses its impact on government budget policies. The remaining sections discuss the labor market policies of Singapore with regard to wage determination; attempt to evaluate the impact of these policies on the strength of the Singapore dollar and its competitiveness; and present some conclusions.

THE CENTRAL PROVIDENT FUND SCHEME

The Central Provident Fund (CPF) scheme was set up in 1959 as the main social security scheme for plan retired workers in Singapore. The CPF is a compulsory saving plan for all employees under which, an employee with a monthly pay of, for example, S$1,000 must contribute 20 percent of his pay to his CPF account, if the employers' CPF contribution rate is 20 percent. At the same time, his employer is also required by law to contribute an amount equal to 20 percent of his pay toward the same account. Thus, every month, the employee has CPF savings of S$400, and his take home pay will be S$800. CPF contributions are tax exempt. The cost of employing this worker therefore amounts to S$1,200. Table 3.2 gives the

CPF contribution rates for the period 1980–1999. In 1984, for instance, the employer and employee each contributed 25 percent.

Singapore workers' CPF savings therefore represent 40 percent of their salary, if employers' and employees' CPF contribution rates are 20 percent each. CPF members can only withdraw their CPF balances at the age of 55, which was the mandatory retirement age in Singapore until it was raised to 60 in 1993 and to 62 in 1997. Given this high rate, it is easy to understand why the self-employed do not want to take part in the CPF scheme.

CPF members can withdraw their CPF balances under one of the following conditions: They have attained the age of 55; they have decided to emigrate; or they are certified to be physically or mentally unable to work. It should be noted, however, that CPF members are permitted to use a portion of their CPF balances for investment purposes.

CPF balances are allocated into three accounts: the Ordinary Account, the Special Account, and the Medisave Account. Of the total CPF contribution, 80 percent is allocated to the Ordinary Account, 8 percent to the Special Account, and 12 percent to the Medisave Account.

The CPF balances in the Special Account can be used only for old age and special contingencies. The balances in the Ordinary Account may be used for the purchase of housing as well as to buy stock and shares approved by the CPF board. Most Singaporeans use their CPF balances to purchase residential property. Consequently, more than 90 percent of households in Singapore own their own homes, making Singapore among the few countries with a high level of homeownership.

The objective of the Medisave Account is to enable members to meet medical contingencies. Members may use the CPF balances in their account to pay hospitalization expenses.

The Impact on Work and Skill Level

The CPF scheme, as noted, is a compulsory saving scheme. The level of saving depends on the worker's wages, which in turn depend on his continued active participation in the labor market. If he changes his place of employment, the CPF scheme will continue with the new employer, for the CPF scheme is a national saving scheme.[2]

The CPF scheme encourages workers to work hard. It also provides an incentive for them to take training seriously because a worker's pay depends on his skills, which he can acquire through training. If a worker is suddenly retrenched in Singapore, he is not allowed to withdraw his CPF balances to maintain his lifestyle. He will be told to get another job. He should have no problem in getting a job because the unemployment rate in Singapore is about 2 to 3 percent, and foreign labor accounts for about 20 percent of total employment.

Table 3.3
CPF Investment in Government Stocks, 1981–1998 (S$ billion, selected years)

Year	Investment in Government Stocks	Advance Deposit with MAS	Total	Members' Balance	Total as % of Members' Balance
1981	9.0	2.9	11.9	12.2	97.5
1982	9.8	5.4	15.2	15.7	96.8
1983	14.9	4.2	19.1	19.5	97.9
1984	14.5	7.5	21.9	22.7	96.5
1985	13.6	12.0	35.6	26.8	95.5
1986	13.6	13.4	27.0	29.9	90.3
1987	28.6	1.2	29.8	31.5	94.6
1988	30.1	2.2	32.3	33.5	96.4
1989	32.1	3.7	35.8	37.0	96.8
1990	32.1	8.2	40.3	41.8	96.4
1995	45.1	20.5	65.6	66.0	99.4
1996	51.6	20.4	72.0	72.6	99.2
1997	57.1	22.1	79.2	79.7	99.4
1998	59.6	25.0	84.6	85.3	99.2

Source: Central Provident Fund Board, *CPF Annual Reports*, various years.

The CPF scheme is different from the unemployment benefits scheme that can be found in some developed countries. The unemployment benefits scheme is subject to inherent disadvantages. First, it inevitably encourages workers to be unemployed to take advantage of their investment in the scheme. Second, such a scheme raises the reservation wage rate, which will erode the country's competitiveness. Third, the unemployment scheme is likely to run into deficit conditions, which must be financed by raising tax revenue. This implies that income tax rates will be high, which discourages people from working for more income. The CPF scheme, on the other hand, is a fully funded scheme that encourages workers to give their best in the labor market and does not need the government to subsidize it.

Impact on Funding for Government

CPF members earn interest on their CPF balances, though the rate of interest on these balances has always been lower than the market rate of interest. However, Singaporeans do not resent the low rate of interest because the CPF balances have been employed for economic development. The CPF board has deposits with the Monetary Authority of Singapore (MAS), which is the de facto central bank of Singapore. The share of both CPF investments in government stocks and advance deposits with MAS has been more than 95 percent (see Table 3.3). This provides the government

Table 3.4
Capital Formation, Saving, and Capital Inflow at Current Market Prices, 1980–1998 (selected years)

Year	Gross Domestic Capital Formation		Gross National Saving		Net Capital Inflow	
	$M	% of GDP	$M	% of GDP	$M	% of GDP
1980	10,991.1	45.3	7,641.8	31.5	3,349.3	13.8
1985	16,510.2	47.0	15,954.2	45.4	555.8	1.6
1990	24,245.5	38.7	28,504.3	45.5	−4,258.8	−6.8
1995	39,328.3	32.6	60,720.1	50.3	−21,391.8	−17.7
1996	46,170.0	35.3	66,734.6	51.0	−20,564.6	−15.7
1997	53,422.3	37.4	75,144.7	52.5	−21,722.4	−15.2
1998	47,355.7	39.1	76,834.4	63.4	−29,478.7	−24.3

Sources: Ministry of Trade and Industry, *Economic Survey of Singapore* and *Yearbook of Statistics*, various years.

with a steady source of cheap funds that can be used to finance housing and infrastructure projects.

Table 3.4 presents the capital formation, savings, and capital inflows during 1980–1999. Capital formation must be financed by either domestic saving or capital inflow, or both. In the case of Singapore, the CPF scheme enabled the share of national saving in GDP to rise from 31.5 percent in 1980 to 50.3 percent in 1995. Singapore has experienced an outflow of capital since 1990. This is due to Singapore's desire to develop its external wing since 1990; consequently, firms in this country, especially the government-linked companies, have been encouraged to invest abroad.

Impact on Macroeconomic Management

Singapore registered a negative GDP growth rate of 1.8 percent in 1985, for the first time in more than two decades. Three reasons have been cited for the recession: the collapse of the construction sector, falling prices of primary products which hurt the Malaysian and Indonesian economies, and high labor costs in Singapore.[3] The only way Singapore could recover quickly was to reduce labor costs. However, reducing wages was not an option because wages were determined by market forces; moreover, reducing wages would affect the standard of living. Fortunately for Singapore, labor costs could be lowered by reducing employers' CPF contribution rate; still this amounted to a wage cut. However, such a reduction in employers' CPF rate does not directly affect their standard of living, inasmuch as take-home pay remains unchanged. In any case, no workers or trade unions would accept any wage cut without some persuasion.

Figure 3.1
CPF Contribution Rates

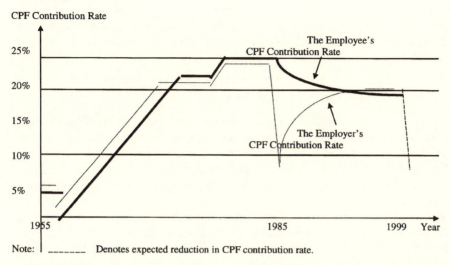

Note: ┊ _ _ _ _ _ _ Denotes expected reduction in CPF contribution rate.

To overcome this problem, the government, trade unions, and management met to discuss the problem in late 1985. At that time Singapore had two options:

1. Let market forces adjust gradually, which implied that unemployment would rise and wages would fall over a period of about three years, after which Singapore could recover. During this process, however, some Singaporeans would face hardship. Moreover, Singapore might not stay ahead of its competitors in certain knowledge-intensive industries.
2. Reduce labor cost drastically by reducing the employers' CPF contribution rate by 15 percent (see Figure 3.1). This means that every Singaporean would make a sacrifice of the same extent, which would enable the country to recover quickly.

It is fortunate for Singapore that, under the National Wages Council, the industrial relations climate in the country has been cordial. Therefore, it was easy to persuade workers and trade unions to accept the CPF rate cut.[4] This austere measure was softened by the government's promise to restore the employer's CPF contribution rate when the recession was over. The adoption of this option enabled the Singapore economy to grow at 1.6 percent in 1986 and to experience full recovery in 1987 with 7.8 percent.[5]

The quick recovery marks a milestone in the industrial relations history of Singapore, signifying the concerted effort of workers, unions, employers, and the government to reach a quick decision to solve a national problem.

Despite this successful experience, the government believes that the CPF scheme as a major instrument to control labor costs should only be used as a last resort, for it is basically a saving plan. For this reason and also because a 25 percent contribution rate for both employee and employer is regarded as unsustainable, the government has decided that the long-term contribution rate for both employee and employer should be 20 percent (see Figure 3.1).

Impact on Government Budget Policy

The basic objective of the CPF scheme is to ensure that Singaporeans save for housing, medical expenses, and old age. Singaporeans are able to save as long as they work, and jobs are plentiful in Singapore because Singapore's industrial relations system is employment-driven.[6] It is thanks to the CPF scheme, that its homeownership is one of the highest in the world.

The CPF's main impact is seen in the amount of government spending on welfare. This amount is minimal in Singapore. In fact, Table 3.5 shows that the government is able to generate a budget surplus year after year. A government with a continuous annual budget surplus is able to think, plan, and implement long-term strategies for the country because it has the funds to do so. Consequently, the government has been able to invest in both physical and human capital formation, such as on education and infrastructure. Since 1995, more than 60 percent of the cohort of the secondary school graduates (equivalent to Cambridge O-levels) go on to a three-year polytechnic or a two-year junior college program. Most of the students graduating from junior colleges proceed to the two local universities, and most of the graduates of the polytechnics end up pursuing university programs on a part-time basis within 10 years.

As the same time, a government with a budget surplus also has more resources to address short-term problems. For instance, to cope with the 1985 recession, the government adopted an expansionary fiscal policy without resorting to internal or external borrowing. Table 3.6 shows that the share of the public sector in national saving was 45 percent in 1980. To help overcome the recession in 1985, the government wisely undertook various projects to stimulate the economy. Afterward, the public sector share declined to around 11 percent in 1995. Table 3.6 also shows that CPF balances have been an important source of savings.

INDUSTRIAL RELATIONS IN SINGAPORE

The People's Action Party (PAP) has been the ruling party in Singapore since 1959, when Singapore gained its self-government status from Britain. Historical events had forged a close working relationship between the PAP and the National Trades Union Congress, which since 1963 have been

Table 3.5
Government Operating Revenue and Expenditure, 1990, 1995, 1998 (S$ million)

Operating Revenue/Expenditure	1990	1995	1998
Operating expenditure[1]	7,062	10,884	14,236
Security	3,405	5,246	7,190
Social and Community Services	2,604	2,834	5,254
Education	1,742	2,678	3,327
Health	457	685	934
Environment	189	274	319
Public Housing	45	164	167
Others	171	319	507
Economic Services	428	688	976
National Development	246	357	236
Communications	31	76	318
Trade and Industry	127	214	335
Labor	25	41	88
General Services	367	720	816
Pensions	257	109	–
Development expenditure	4,220	4,671	10,557
Operating revenue[2]	13,102	24,782	28,213
Tax revenue	10,534	19,579	22,154
Income tax	4,908	8,768	10,966
Corporate and individual tax	4,396	8,138	9,798
Contributions by Statutory Boards	512	628	1,168
Assets taxes	1,111	1,839	1,850
Taxes on motor vehicles[3]	1,338	1,817	1,548
Customs and excise duties	1,306	1,597	1,612
Betting taxes	522	982	1,267
Stamp duty	655	1,364	1,081
Goods and Services tax[4]	–	1,647	1,689
Others	695	1,565	2,143
Fees and charges	1,499	3,665	3,355
Other receipts[5]	1,070	1,538	2,704

[1]Expenditure on manpower, other operating expenditures (excluding expenses on investment and agency fees on land sales), grants-in-aid, and pensions (up to first quarter 1995).
[2]Receipts coedited to the consolidated revenue account, development fund account, and sinking fund account, but excludes investment income and capital receipts.
[3]Additional registration fees, road tax, special tax on heavy-oil engines, passenger vehicles, seating fees, and non-motor vehicle licenses, but exclude import duties on motor vehicles that are classified under customs and excise duties.
[4]Implemented in 1994.
[5]Exclude repayment of direct loans and advances but include interest on loans previously classified under investment income.
Source: Ministry of Trade and Industry, *Economic Survey of Singapore*, 1998.

Table 3.6
Savings by Public and Private Sector ($ million), 1990–1998 (selected years)

Year	GNS	Public Sector Savings	Private Sector Savings	
			Total	CPF
1980	8,282.0	3,407.0	4,875.0	2,295.9
1985	16,543.4	11,052.0	5,491.4	5,993.4
1990	29,961.7	12,774.7	17,187.0	7,174.2
1995	60,556.5	25,199.1	35,357.5	15,536.1
1996	66,734.6	na	na	na
1997	75,144.7	na	na	na
1998	76,834.4	na	na	na

Notes: Public sector savings = current surplus in consolidated accounts of the public sector; na = not available.
Source: Central Provident Fund Board, *CPF Annual Reports*, various years.

working closely as partners in nation-building.[7] Indeed, Singapore's industrial relations regime can be regarded as employment-driven, as shown by the operations of the National Wages Council (NWC) and the Skills Development Fund (SDF).

The NWC was set up as an advisory body to the government in 1972 with the objective of ensuring that workers receive an equitable share of the country's prosperity without triggering a wage-price spiral. It is a tripartite organization consisting of representatives of the government, the National Trades Union Congress (NTUC), and employers. Effectively, its role has been to recommend wage guidelines for the country.[8]

Every year around April, the NWC would meet and discuss employment conditions in Singapore, and in July each year, the NWC would issue guidelines for wage increases for the next 6 to 12 months. Although wage guidelines are not mandatory, the NWC recommendations generally have been adopted by firms in Singapore. Table 3.7 lists the NWC wage guidelines for 1972–1997.

The basic underlying principle of the NWC wage guidelines is that wage growth should not exceed productivity growth. Hence, in arriving at the wage guidelines for each year, the NWC takes into account factors such as the tightness of the labor market, balance of payments, export growth, productivity, and inflation.

Through the operation of the NWC, Singapore has enjoyed harmonious industrial relations over the years. It is precisely for this reason that the government was able to convince the trade unions and workers to accept the wage cut policies that were necessary to combat recession in 1985–1986.

Another important tripartite committee in Singapore is the SDF.[9] It was

Table 3.7
NWC Wage Recommendations, 1972–1997

NWC Year			NWC Wage Guidelines
1972	Interim	(i)	Option I: 13th month payment + Bonus
		(ii)	Option II: 13th month payment + Annual Wage Adjustments of 6% (without offsetting of annual increments)
1973			9% (with varying rates of offsetting depending on salary)
1974	Interim	(i)	Flat rate increase of $25 (not subjected to CPF contribution)
		(ii)	$40 + 6% (inclusive of the $25 interim wage supplement, without offsetting of annual increments)
1975			6% (with full offsetting of annual increments provided that employees on incremental scales received a minimum increase of 3% after off-setting, while employees at the maximum of their pay scales were to receive a wage increase of 3%)
1976			7% (with full offsetting of all forms of increases in remuneration on a group basis)
1977			6% (with full offsetting of all forms of increases in remuneration on a group basis)
1978			$12 + 6% (with full offsetting of all forms of increases in remuneration on a group basis)
1979			$32 + 7% (with full offsetting of all forms of increases in remuneration on a group basis)
1980	1st tier:		$33 + 7.5% (with full offsetting of all forms of increases on a group basis)
	2nd tier:		Additional 3% of the group monthly wage bill of June 1980 to be distributed only among above average employees
1981	1st tier:		$32 + 6%–10% (with full offsetting of all forms of increases on a group basis)
	2nd tier:		Additional 2% of the group monthly wage bill of June 1981 to be distributed only among above average employees
1982			$18.50 + 2.5%–6.5% (with full offsetting of all forms of increases on a group basis)
1983			$10 + 2%–6% (with full offsetting of all forms of increases on a group basis)
1984			$27 + 4%–8% (with full offsetting of all forms of increases on a group basis)
1985			3%–7% (with full offsetting of all forms of increases on a group basis)

Table 3.7 (continued)

NWC Year	NWC Guidelines
1986	Wage freeze, coupled with a 15% point cut in employers' CPF contribution
1987	Wage restraint, reduction of 1984 NWC wage increase by 30%
1988	Moderate wage increase in 2 parts, a basic wage increase and a variable bonus, taking into account increase in employer's CPF rate by 2% and reduction in employee's CPF rate by 1%
1989	Reasonable wage increase in 2 parts, a basic wage increase and a variable bonus, taking into account increase in employer's CPF rate by 3%
1990	A basic wage increase not exceeding productivity growth and a generous variable bonus, depending on company profitability and performance, taking into account increase in employer's CPF rate by 1½%
1991	A basic wage increase not exceeding productivity growth and a variable bonus smaller than in 1990, depending on co. profitability and performance, taking into account employer's CPF rate increase of 1%
1992	A basic wage increase not exceeding productivity growth and a moderate variable bonus in line with the expected slower economic growth, taking into account increase in employer's CPF rate by ½%
1993	A basic wage increase not exceeding productivity growth and a variable payment which should reflect company performance, with companies which have done exceptionally well paying special bonuses
1994	A basic wage increase not exceeding productivity growth and a variable payment which should closely reflect company performance, with companies which have done exceptionally well paying a one-off special bonuses
1995	Total wage increase reflecting the performance of the economy, and the built-in wage increase lagging behind productivity growth. The variable component, which should reflect the performance of the economy, should consititute about 20% of total annual wages. Companies which have done exceptionally well should pay an additional one-off special bonus.
1996	Total wage increase reflecting the performance of the economy, and the built-in wage increase, which should also include a dollar quantum to benefit lower income employees, lagging behind productivity growth. The

Table 3.7 (continued)

NWC Year	NWC Guidelines
	variable component, which should reflect the performance of the economy, should consititute about 20% of total annual wages. Companies which have done exceptionally well should pay an additional one-off special bonus.
1997	Moderation of the wage increase taking into consideration the intense global competition and the projected slower economic growth for the year, and the built-in wage increase lagging behind productivity growth. The variable component, which should reflect the performance of the economy, should consititute about 20% of total annual wages. Companies which have done exceptionally well should pay an additional one-off special bonus.
1998	Initial recommendation of wage restraint to reflect the slowing down of the economy, with built-in wage increases lower than productivity growth rates, and variable payments reflecting the performance of individual companies, supplemented by non-wage cost-cutting measures.
	Subsequent recommendations to achieve a reduction in overall wage costs of 15%, issued in November 1998 owing to the deterioration of the regional economic crisis and Singapore's declining economic performance. Thus, total wages to be cut by 5% to 8% compared to 1997, in addition to a 10% cut in the employers' CPF contributions as recommended by the Committee on Singapore's Competitiveness, with a moderation of the wage cut for lower income employees by implementing a deeper cut for the higher income executives.
1999	Continued wage restraint, with a mid-year bonus to be given by companies with satisfactory or better performance, while those with good prospects or which have done exceptionally well to reward workers with a wage increase largely in the form of a monthly variable component. The introduction of the monthly variable component will further enhance the flexible wage system and increase the responsiveness of companies and the economy to changing business conditions.
2000	Wage increases to reflect the recovery of the economy, together with a restoration of 2% to the employers' CPF contribution rate, with companies which are profitable to reward workers with a bonus payment, and those which have done exceptionally well to include a special bonus to workers as well.

Source: NWC Chairman's letters to the Prime Minister, 1972–2000.

set up in 1978 in order to deal with the impact of high labor turnover on training. This is because the tight labor market in Singapore resulted in a high incidence of job-hopping. Attempts to bring in foreign workers did not reduce labor turnover. Consequently, firms in Singapore, were reluctant to train workers for they were likely to leave for another company after training. Because this specter of staff poaching was always present, the level of training was less than socially optimal.

All firms are required by law under the SDF regulations to pay an SDF levy equal to 1 percent of the total wage bill of employees who earn less than S$1,000 per month. Firms that employ skilled workers are thus exempted from the SDF levy.[10] However, regardless of whether they contribute to SDF, all firms in Singapore are eligible to apply to the SDF for subsidies for the training of their employees. Applications for training subsidies take the following procedure: (1) The company submits to the SDF a training plan; (2) upon acceptance of the training plan, the SDF grants a subsidy ranging from 30 percent to 70 percent of total training costs, depending on the peculiarities of each case. To encourage corporate responsibility for employee training, the subsidy never covers the full amount of training costs.

Under this system, companies that do not provide training for workers will receive no benefits from the Fund, even if they have made contributions to the SDF. The SDF levy is therefore a sunk cost to every firm that employs unskilled or semiskilled workers. The number of training places has increased significantly, from 151,509 in 1987 to 530,755 in 1998 (see Table 3.8).

The SDF scheme is characterized by one significant weakness, which is that, under the scheme, small firms end up subsidizing large firms in training. This is because small firms generally are unable to afford the release of manpower for training. At the same time, a greater proportion of low-wage workers are employed in small firms. Moreover, small firms are not as efficient in submitting a written report on manpower training as big firms and multinational corporations (MNCs) which have training managers to handle such reports. Complaints of this peculiarity have directed the SDF's attention to this issue since 1987. Consequently, as Table 3.8 shows, the number of places for small firms has also become significant.[11]

THE LABOR MARKET POLICIES OF SINGAPORE

In a labor market transaction, a worker and an employer would enter into an agreement under which the worker would work for the employer according to agreed terms of employment. The terms of employment cover two categories of issues: visible and invisible terms of employment. Visible terms of employment consist of wages, wage increases, number of working hours, job duties and titles, fringe benefits, and so on. Invisible terms of

Table 3.8
SDF Principal Statistics on Training Grant, 1987–1998 (selected years)

Category	1987	1990	1995	1998
Applications:				
No. of applications received	15,713	32,156	52,417	53,368
No. of applications approved	13,880	30,018	43,839	44,564
No. of companies with approved applications	4,430	8,828	9,883	10,898
Training Places:				
No. of training places	151,509	405,621	461,651	530,755
No. of training places for workers (i.e., employees who have "A" level qualifications and below)	124,090	346,562	371,971	421,681
No. of training places for small companies	–	–	63,720	81,364
No of training places for workers aged 40 and above	–	–	71,495	132,260
No. of training places for BEST* and WISE*	–	–	35,789	33,620
No. of training places for FAST FORWARD (pilot phase)	–	–	NA	NA
Grant Commitment ($ million):				
Commitment for training grants (including Training Needs Analysis Consultancy Grant Scheme)	37.0	71.4	62.2	84.8
Commitment for BEST/WISE	–	–	5.2	3.6
Total Commitment ($ million)	44.7	90.5	67.6	88.4

* = total number enrolled including noncitizens.
FAST FORWARD pilot phase ended in December 1993. Figures from January 1994 onward
    have been included under the Training Grant Scheme.
BEST = Basic Education for Skills Training.
WISE = Worker Improvement through Secondary Education.
Source: *National Productivity Board Annual Report*, various years.

employment refer to occupation hazards, safety conditions of the workplace, the environmental impact of the workplace, and the like.

The Singapore government does not generally interfere with the visible
terms of employment agreed upon in a contract. For instance, there is no
minimum wage law in Singapore. Moreover, even though there is an Employment Act in force, the philosophy of the government is that the worker
should decide whether the job is good enough for him. If the worker feels
that the pay is too low or the working hours are too long, then the worker
should not accept the job.

The Employment Act is rather comprehensive. It spells out the rights,
obligations, and duties of employers and employees as well as the basic

terms and conditions of employment. Most Singaporean workers are educated enough to know the contents of the Employment Act. In any case, in a labor-deficit economy, employers do not have much luck in short-changing workers.

On the other hand, the government is concerned about the invisible terms of employment agreed upon in a labor contract. This is because workers themselves cannot determine whether the workplace is safe for them until it is too late. Hence, the Employment Act states that an employee can quit without notice if he is asked, for instance, to work under conditions where he is exposed to lead-dust or fumes without protection from lead poisoning.

The Singapore Factories Act is one of the most stringent in the world. It spells out the rights and responsibilities of employers or occupiers of factories and other working places regarding the health, safety, and welfare of persons working therein. For instance, to ensure cleanliness, dirt and refuse must be removed daily by a suitable method from workrooms, staircases, and passages. The floor of every workroom must be washed or swept once a week. The inside walls and ceilings of a factory must be washed once a year and either repainted and revarnished every seven years or white-washed or color-washed every year.

To ensure workers' safety, for example, every flywheel or moving part of a prime mover or any other machinery must be fenced, unless it can be safely used without being so fenced. Every factory with more than 25 workers must have on-site first-aid personnel trained in first aid treatment. A workplace with more than 500 workers must have a first-aid room where injured workers can be treated. If workers are exposed to toxic or corrosive substances, the factory must have facilities for emergency treatment, including suitable facilities for quick drenching and flushing of eyes and body within the work areas.

Although these laws make the cost of doing business in Singapore rather high, as people are its only resource, the country must protect this resource. With its high cost of doing business, only high value-added firms find it profitable to invest in Singapore. However, the country has reached a stage where it needs to be selective with foreign investment in order to retain its competitiveness.

There is a small informal sector in Singapore in which workers work without being protected by the Employment Act or covered by the CPF scheme. For instance, Singaporeans who undertake house-cleaning jobs for people are in general paid $250 a month by working for a family three mornings on a weekly basis. These workers could work for four families a week, which would provide them with a total income of $1,200 a month.

At the same time, close to 100,000 households in Singapore employ live-in foreign maids. The pay of such foreign maids ranges from $250 to $350 a month, but the cost of employing foreign maids is more than double this amount because the government imposes a foreign worker levy of $345 a

Figure 3.2
Singapore's Competitiveness Structure

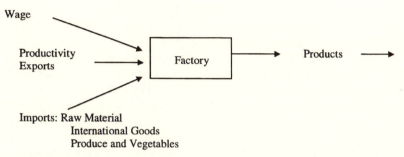

month on the employment of each foreign maid. This levy has a dual effect: it dampens the demand for foreign maids, and it protects the interest of low-income Singaporeans whose employment prospects may be jeopardized by the availability of foreign maids.

To sum up, the labor market in Singapore is allowed to operate freely to achieve a maximum level of employment. While there is no minimum wage law, it may be argued that the foreign worker levy serves as a form of minimum wage law in Singapore.

THE THREE COMPETITIVENESS POLICIES

Being a small country with a land size of 647.8 km² without any natural resources, Singapore has to import nearly all products, including rice and vegetables. Given this constraint, the people have to strive to maintain their country's competitiveness.

The workings of the Singapore economy can be illustrated with reference to how a manufacturing enterprise operates (see Figure 3.2). A factory can produce a good quality product at a low cost if it can find the right combination of workers, raw materials, and equipment. Since Singapore's products are generally produced for the export market, an appreciation of the Singapore dollar vis-à-vis the U.S. dollar makes Singapore's exports more expensive. Therefore, an appreciated Singapore dollar discourages exports, and a weaker Singapore dollar increases exports. At the same time, since Singapore is a city-state that imports all raw materials, equipment, and food, its import costs would be lower with a strong Singapore dollar. This implies that a strong Singapore dollar can moderate imported inflation in the country. Thus, changes in exchange rates do not necessarily exert a significant negative impact on the competitiveness of Singapore's manufacturing operations.

Nevertheless, the government has managed to move toward a gradual appreciation of the Singapore dollar (see Table 3.1). This indeed is Singapore's first principle for economic competitiveness—that is, to maintain the stability of its currency value so as to promote itself as a financial center, which is one of its comparative advantages.[12]

Even though the gradual appreciation of the Singapore dollar has had a marginally negative impact on exports of manufactured products due to the imported value-added components in the production process, the government continues to look for ways to help the manufacturing sector compete. One of these ways is the adoption of the second principle, that wage growth cannot exceed productivity growth. For instance, if productivity growth is 5 percent, the rate of wage growth cannot exceed 5 percent. Hence, there must be a mechanism to influence wage expectations. This is precisely the job of the NWC, which has ensured that its wage recommendations enable wage growth to take place without exceeding productivity growth and hence ensure output growth without inflation.

In many countries, wage rates increase in line with living costs. Trade unions and workers would ask for higher wages in compensation for higher costs of living. The adoption of the second principle above also implies that the cost of living in Singapore must be contained; otherwise, the NWC would have a difficult task in conforming to the principle of wage growth not exceeding productivity growth. This has indeed taken place in Singapore because the Singapore dollar has appreciated against all major currencies (see Table 3.1); as a result, imported inflation is kept low.

To Singaporeans, wage growth not exceeding productivity growth is acceptable only if that productivity growth has been substantial. This is because there would be no wage growth if productivity growth were zero, which would also mean that there would be no improvement in the standard of living. The third principle for economic competitiveness, therefore, is that a concerted effort must be made to raise productivity. As pointed out earlier, the SDF has been very active in providing incentives for firms to train their workers. At the same time, the CPF scheme has also provided the inducement for workers to attend training programs, for it would mean that they would acquire the ability to generate more CPF savings. Equally significant is the fact that the labor movement in Singapore has placed an increasing emphasis on training. Thus, unions in negotiation with management are nowadays insisting that the management allocate 4 percent of the wage bill for the training of workers. The labor movement has also initiated two nationwide training schemes, known as BEST (Basic Education for Skills Training) and WISE (Worker Improvement through Secondary Education). These two programs aim to train older workers who are not proficient in English and mathematics.

It should be emphasized that the strength of the Singapore dollar is decided not by the MAS but by the overall performance of the economy. The health of the Singapore economy is attributable to a combination of the following factors: the worker's positive attitude toward work, the CPF

Figure 3.3
Determination of Singapore–U.S. Exchange Rate

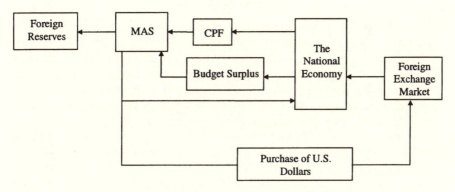

scheme which ensures social stability, a continuous budget surplus, and a balance-of-payments surplus.

As Figure 3.3 shows, the CPF board receives a large amount of CPF contributions from workers and firms every year. These large sums are managed by the MAS, which also manages the surplus government budget. Through the MAS, a substantial portion of the CPF funds is used to buy government bonds. Each year, Singapore also chalks up a balance-of-payments surplus. Under these circumstances, there is a strong tendency for the Singapore dollar to appreciate against the U.S. dollar.

The MAS buys a large amount of U.S. dollars each year using Singapore dollars, so that the returns from the CPF and the budget surplus can be transferred back to various economic agents. This helps to keep the exchange rate stable and prevents a dramatic appreciation of the Singapore dollar. Without such purchases of the U.S. dollar, the appreciation of the Singapore dollar would have been much larger, and this would have significantly reduced the competitiveness of the manufacturing sector. Thus, Singapore has been able to accumulate a large amount of foreign reserves (see Table 3.1).

The two underlying forces accounting for the strength of the Singapore dollar are the competitiveness of manufacturing in the export market and the prices of imported food. With strong export performance, if the prices of imported foodstuffs are to be lower, one would expect the Singapore dollar to be stronger.

THE CURRENT CURRENCY TURMOIL IN EAST ASIA

The current currency turmoil in East Asia is still unfolding, with the impact still being felt in the region and expected to affect other regions as well. Table 3.9 shows how the regional currency and stock markets have

Table 3.9
Impact of Currency Turmoil in East Asia, July–November 1997

Country	Exchange Rate 1996 Dec. 31	Exchange Rate 1998 Aug. 31	Stock Market Index 1996 Sept. 4	Stock Market Index 1998 Sept. 2	Property Stock Market Index 1996 Dec. 31	Property Stock Market Index 1997 Dec. 31	GDP Growth Rate 1997	GDP Growth Rate 1998	GDP Growth Rate 1999
Indonesia	2,360	11,200	546.0	329.6 (60%)	143	40 (28%)	4.7	-4.5 (-15.5)	3.0 (-0.6)
Malaysia	2.53	4.18	1,105.4	294.6 (26.7%)	294	64 (21.8%)	7.8	2.0 (-6.8)	4.0 (0.6)
Philippines	26.3	43.8	3,197.6	1,197.8 (37.5%)	119	59 (49.6%)	5.8	3.0 (1.6)	5.0 (3.2)
Thailand	25.6	41.9	1,049.7	207.6 (19.8%)	99	7 (7.1%)	-0.4	-3.2 (-7.3)	1.8 (1.1)
Korea	845	1,350	791.6	314.4 (39.7%)	–	–	5.9	-1.0 (-4.9)	2.9 (2.1)
Taiwan	27.5	34.8	6,228.8	6,471.7 (104%)	55	55 (100%)	6.8 6.8	6.3 (4.9)	6.4 (5.1)
Hong Kong	7.73	7.75	11,077.0	7,355.7 (66.4%)	1,682	941 (55.9%)	5.2	2.6 (-0.9)	3.3 (1.7)
Singapore	1.4	1.77	2,094.5	827.9 (39.5%)	648	357 (55.1%)	7.8	4.0 (0.9)	6.0 (2.9)
China	8.3	8.3	849.5	1,209.2 (142%)	na	na	8.8	8.0 (6.7)	8.5 (7.2)
Mexico (1995 Crisis)	na	na	na	na	na	na	-6.2 (1995)		

Sources: The forecasts for 1997, 1998, and 1999 were made by the Pacific Economic Cooperation Council, using data until September 1997. The figures within parentheses are forecast figures from the *Economist* poll (July 1998).

been affected by the currency crisis. As we will explain in this section, Singapore is the least affected among the countries in the Association of Southeast Asian Nations (ASEAN).

The typical development strategy of East Asian countries has been to rely on foreign investment to develop their manufacturing sector for the purpose of export. With political stability and relatively low wages as the initial conditions, this strategy of relying on foreign investment has paid off. Hence, the exports of these countries grew rapidly. At the same time, not only were the saving rates of these countries high, but the governments and the people of these countries placed a premium on education and training. Hence, these countries enjoyed low inflation and high GDP growth rates, which in turn attracted more foreign investment.

Over time, the currencies of these countries also appreciated against the U.S. dollar. This further attracted more investment, much of which, however, went into stock markets, property markets, and the financing of infrastructure projects, therefore causing the escalation of stock prices and property prices. This was the situation in East Asia in the 1980s and 1990s. All countries enjoyed currency appreciation and high GDP growth rates during this period.

Thus, on the surface, all East Asian countries were apparently doing well economically. However, the undercurrent economic forces were very different for two groups of countries: Singapore, Hong Kong, and Taiwan in one group and Thailand, Malaysia, and Indonesia in the other. The countries in the first group have large foreign reserves, enjoy budget surpluses and current account surpluses, and have almost zero external debt. The economic health of these countries is very good. With such strong economic fundamentals, their economic success is sustainable.

The countries in the second group have a huge external debt and current account deficit. These problems were hidden by strong economic growth. In the early 1990s, these countries enjoyed huge capital inflows. Unfortunately, most resources were channeled into property and infrastructure projects. These projects worsened the current account. The situation continued until 1995. Indeed, the problems of huge external debt and serious current account were highlighted by various sources, but the capital inflows continued because these governments were determined to maintain the strong exchange rates. The impact was a greater boom of the property and stock markets and initiation of more grand projects.

Eventually, the bubble burst, first in Thailand on July 2, 1997. Thailand could not maintain the Thai baht against the U.S. dollar. With the depreciation of the Thai baht, foreign capital quickly withdrew, and the stock market collapsed rapidly. This in turn compounded the weakening of the Thai baht. As is well known, shares and properties are used as collateral. Banks started to call back loans, which aggravated the stock and property markets, making the Thai baht even weaker. To make matters worse, loans were made on the basis of political and personal factors rather than on an economic basis or market factors; this kind of arrangement is not transparent. In such a situation, the nonperforming loans compounded the problems.

The same thing happened to Malaysia and Indonesia, and Singapore suffered as a result. However, Singapore is the least affected because of its huge foreign reserves, almost zero external debt, and current account surplus. Currency speculators therefore could not press the panic button on the Singapore dollar.

Thailand and Indonesia have accepted the International Monetary Fund's rescue package in order to qualify for IMF loans to bail their countries out of the crisis. The essence of the IMF package consists of trimming the current account deficit and reforming the financial market. Many features of the IMF package have been actually consistent with Singapore's macroeconomic policies.

Nevertheless, the Singapore economy may suffer further from the currency turmoil because of the following two factors. First, the Singapore dollar has significantly appreciated against regional currencies, especially the Malaysian ringgit, as a result of the currency crisis. This will hurt Singapore's exports. It is expected that the Singapore dollar will depreciate against the U.S. dollar as a result. Second, the weak economies of Malaysia and Indonesia will hurt the Singapore economy, because all three economies are interdependent. Thus, the lesson is that the health of an economy does not depend solely on its own macroeconomic policies, but also on the macroeconomic policies of the region.

CRISIS MANAGEMENT

In order to enjoy strong economic growth, Singapore must continue to maintain the same policies it has adopted in the past, such as a high savings rate and strong commitment to education and training. In other words, voters in Singapore must continue to vote for a government that will implement such policies. Since the young make up the largest number of voters, youth's attitude to such values as hard work and thriftiness is critical to the election of such a government in the future. It is very heartening that Chew, Leu, and Tan (1998), in a recent survey of high school and university students on how they perceive the value of hard work and education find that young Singaporeans still believe in hard work and education.

Nevertheless, due to poor regional demand and high wage cost, many firms in Singapore have started retrenching workers, and many more are in the process of doing so. The government has no choice but to cope with the economic problem.

The government has taken actions to address the following issues: First, the major issue facing Singapore is that it has about 400,000 unskilled workers whose skills may not be better than those of workers in Malaysia and China; yet they command a higher salary. Singapore must therefore continue to utilize SDF funds to train and retrain older workers before they are retrenched. The government, as well as the labor movement, has been working very hard to encourage older workers to participate in continual upgrading. The labor movement initiated two programs to enable these workers to learn English and mathematics, which are necessary for up-grading. In collective bargaining, the trade unions would request that 4 percent of the total payroll be allocated for the training of staff.

Second, Singapore has suffered from the currency turmoil and will continue to suffer for the reasons stated earlier. However, it can take advantage of the falling prices of assets and weak currencies to invest in the region. Singapore is expected to be able to take advantage to do so as the government-linked enterprises have sufficient financial resources for investment overseas. Such investment may also help to restore confidence in the region. In today's economic environment, no country can enjoy prosperity until most countries in the region do.

Third, East Asia as a whole is expected to ride out this crisis and to resume normal growth within two to three years, as strong economic fundamentals such as a high savings rate and investment in education are still present. But East Asia should take steps to gradually reform the financial sector and make the banking industry more transparent. The banking sector in Singapore is considered to be the best in the region in terms of transparency. Singapore is therefore taking the lead in this area by setting up three committees: the Stock Exchange of Singapore review committee, the corporate financing issues committee, and the commercial banking disclosure standards committee. The work of these three committees is expected to help restore confidence in the region's banking sector.

More importantly, Singapore must implement policies to trim wage costs. Indeed, many of its firms have reduced wages and bonuses, and many other firms are in the process of doing so. The government has made it quite clear that favors cutting the CPF employers' contribution rate by 10 percent (see Figure 3.1). It is reported that a reduction of the CPF rate by about 5 to 10 percent will reduce the labor cost of firms by about $4 billion annually (*The Straits Times*, September 10, 1998). At the same time, the government is willing to devote more resources for training and to reduce government charges and levies to lower business cost. The government is prepared to operate a budget deficit during this difficult period.

Figure 3.4 shows how Singapore is coping with the crisis. Point X represents a situation in which there is high GDP growth, budget surplus, and high labor cost, and collective bargaining is at the plant level. However, in the present difficult times, Singapore is likely to move from X to Y, where Y represents low GDP growth rate, budget deficit, low labor cost, and higher level of collective bargaining. It went through this kind of adjust-

Figure 3.4
Crisis Management

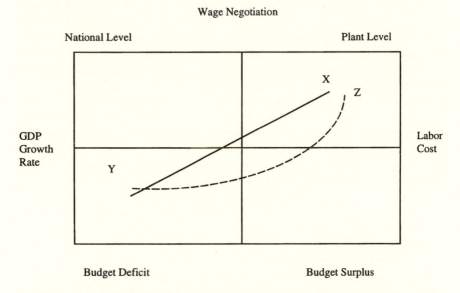

ment before in 1986. During that time, it took about nine months to move from X to Y and about three years to move from Y to Z. This time, it will probably take nine months to move from X to Y and perhaps slightly longer to move from Y to Z. That Singapore is able to change its economic policy so quickly is due mainly to the excellent industrial relations in Singapore, which the government and the labor movement have carefully nurtured.

CONCLUSION

For a small open economy, Singapore has been able to activate many mechanisms to cope with changes in external demand. In this chapter, we highlight the fact that Singapore's social security system, that is, the CPF system, is based on self-reliance and reliance on government welfare. This has accounted for low unemployment in the country and has also provided tremendous incentive for workers to adopt good work attitudes and an inclination toward life-long learning. The CPF system has contributed to the government's accumulation of a budget surplus, enabling it to promote the training of workers during recessions. The years of strong budget surpluses have also helped the government to operate a budget deficit during the recession years so that firms need not have to pay unduly high taxes and tariff at such times.

The most important feature of the CPF system is that it allows Singapore to lower labor costs without excessive lowering of wages as in the 1985–1986 recession and 1998–1999 crisis. Nevertheless, because a reduction in the employer's CPF contribution rate is still unpopular, implementing such unpleasant policies requires goodwill among the government, trade unions, and the workers. At the same time, the National Wages Council will also moderate workers' wage expectations in line with the state of the economy.

Hence, Singapore's ability to cope with any crisis lies within various mechanisms such as the CPF, SDF, and NWC. As shown in Figure 3.4, during good times, all parties are better off. However, should a recession occur due to a shock in external demand, for instance, the various mechanisms will operate to reduce labor costs and restore the growth of the Singapore economy.

NOTES

1. See Lim (1988), Tan et al. (1996), and Krause et al. (1987) for a discussion of the Singapore economy.
2. See Lim et al. (1986) for an excellent study on the CPF.
3. See Lim et al. (1988).
4. See Chew (1996).
5. For details, see Lim and Associates (1988).
6. See Chew and Chew (1995) for a discussion on employment-driven industrial relations system.
7. See Chew and Chew (1995) for a discussion on Singapore industrial relations strategies.
8. See Chew (1996) for a discussion on the NWC.
9. See Lim (1980) for the origin of SDF.
10. See Chng et al. (1986) for a discussion on skills training in Singapore.
11. See Chew (1988) for a discussion of this issue.
12. See Teh and Shanmugaratnam (1992) and Kapur (1981) for a systematic discussion of Singapore's exchange rate policy.

REFERENCES

Chew, Rosalind. (1996). *Wage Policies in Singapore: A Key to Competitiveness.* International Labor Organization, vol. 4, Asian Pacific Project on Tripartism. Ilo, Bangkok, Thailand.

Chew Soon Beng. (1988). *Small Firms in Singapore.* Singapore: Oxford University Press.

Chew Soon Beng, and Rosalind Chew. (1991). *The Singapore Worker: A Profile.* Singapore: Oxford University Press.

Chew Soon Beng, and Rosalind Chew. (1995). *Employment-Driven Industrial Relations Regimes: The Case of Singapore.* Aldershot, UK: Avebury.

Chew Soon Beng, and Rosalind Chew. (1996). *Employment-Driven Industrial Relations Regimes: The Singapore Experience.* Aldershot, UK: Avebury.

Chew Soon Beng, Mike Leu, and Tan Kim Heng. (1998). *Values and Lifestyles of Young Singaporeans.* Singapore: Prentice Hall.

Chia Siow Yue. (1986). "The Economic Development of Singapore: A Selective Survey of the Literature." In B. K. Kapur, ed., *Singapore Studies: Critical Surveys of the Humanities and Social Sciences.* Singapore: Singapore University Press, pp. 183–242.

Chng Meng Kng, Linda Low, Tay Boon Nga, and Amina Tyabji. (1986). *Technology and Skills in Singapore.* Singapore: Institute of Southeast Asian Studies.

Goh Keng Swee. (1972). *The Economics of Modernization and Other Essays.* Singapore: Asia Pacific Press.

Goh Keng Swee. (1995). *Wealth of East Asian Nations.* Singapore: Federal Publications.

Hughes, H., and You Poh Seng, eds. (1987). *Foreign Investment and Industrialization in Singapore.* Canberra: Australian National University Press.

Krause, L., Koh Ai Tee, and Lee (Tsao) Yuan. (1987). *The Singapore Economy Reconsidered.* Singapore: Institute of Southeast Asian Studies.

Kapur, B. K. (1981). "Exchange Rate Flexibility and Monetary Policy." In *Papers in Monetary Economics.* Singapore: Singapore University Press.

Kapur, B. K. (1983). "A Short Term Analytical Model of the Singapore Economy." *Journal of Development Economics* 12(3) (June 1983): 355–377.

Lim Chong Yah. (1980). *Economic Development in Singapore.* Singapore: Federal Publications.

Lim Chong Yah. (1984). *Economic Restructuring in Singapore.* Singapore: Federal Publications.

Lim Chong Yah. (1996). "The Trinity Growth Theory: The Ascendency of Asia and the Decline of the West." *Accounting and Business Review* 3(2) (July): 175–199.

Lim Chong Yah et al. (1986). "Report of the Central Provident Fund Study Group." *Singapore Economic Review* 31(1) (April). Special Issue.

Lim Chong Yah and P. Lloyd. (1986). *Singapore: Resources and Growth.* Singapore: Oxford University Press.

Lim Chong Yah and Associates. (1988). *Policy Options for the Singapore Economy.* Singapore: McGraw-Hill.

Lim Chong Yah, ed. (1996). *Economic Policy Management in Singapore.* Singapore: Addison-Wesley.

Low Aik Meng and Cao Yong. (1996). "The Singapore System Taxation and 1994 Taxation Reform." In Tan Teck Meng, Low Aik Meng, and Chew Soon Beng, eds., *Development Experience of Singapore.* India: Allied Publishers, pp. 171–187.

Tan Chwee Huat. (1975). "The Public Enterprises as a Development Strategy: The Case of Singapore." *Annals of Public and Cooperative Economy* (January): 61–85.

Tan Khee Giap and Chen Kang. (1996). "A Quarterly Macroeconometric Model of Singapore: A Rational Expectation Approach with Disequilibrium Money." In Lim Chong Yah, ed., *Economic Policy Management in Singapore.* Singapore: Addison-Wesley, pp. 397–418.

Tan Teck Meng, Low Aik Meng, and Chew Soon Beng, eds. (1996). *Development Experience of Singapore.* India: Allied Publishers.

Tan Teck Meng and Chew Soon Beng, eds. (1997). *Affordable Healthcare*. Singapore: Prentice Hall.

Teh Kok Peng and T. Shanmugaratnam. (1992). "Exchange Rate Policy: Philosophy and Conduct over the Past Decade." In Linda Low and Toh Mun Heng, eds., *Public Policies in Singapore: Changes in the 80s and Future Signposts*. Singapore: Times Academic Press, pp. 285–314.

The Straits Times, September 10, 1998.

You Poh Seng and Lim Chong Yah, eds. (1984). *Singapore: Twenty-Five Years of Development*. Singapore: Nan Yang Xing Zhou Lianhe Zaobao.

Chapter 4

Financial Crisis and Policy Reform: The South Korean Experience

Roy W. Shin and Yeon-Seob Ha

A CHANGING ECONOMIC ENVIRONMENT

In the mid-1990s, the rules underlying Asian economic growth changed considerably. What did not change, however, was the behavior of the financial players surfing the boom. The most important change concerned the steady appreciation of the U.S. dollar and the yen's depreciation since 1995. As an immediate result, the exchange rate of the East Asian currencies pegged to the dollar rose correspondingly whereby the emerging Asian nations' export lost its price competitiveness in the world market. The export driving engine began to splutter as their exports increasingly ran into trouble, while their import expenditures rose because imports had become comparatively cheap. As a result, the countries' current account balance deteriorated in an alarming fashion. Adding to the financial problems were difficulties in the corporate sector and concerns about its competitiveness. Major conglomerates had undertaken ambitious expansion and diversification drives in the 1990s, with borrowed funds from South Korean commercial and merchant banks. Given their poor credit culture and the lack of adequate risk analysis and management, banks relied mainly on collateral in the allocation of credit, and relatively little attention was paid to the earnings performance and cash flow generation, or the corporation's ability to pay.

South Korea's financial crisis is further compounded by lack of oversight in the financial sector. Following a long period of government control over the financial system, liberalization measures in the late 1980s and the 1990s were not followed up by such related support measures as rules governing the supervisory and disclosure framework. The extent of supervision over banks and financial institutions focused mostly on compliance with rules rather than on assuring the soundness and proper management of individual financial institutions. The situation that South Korea faces under the IMF bailout plan is similar to the one that many Asian countries are now experiencing and will be the focus of this study. As national economies are globalized and as nations compete within a multinational trade framework, South Korea has to turn away from inward-looking and protectionist policies to an open economy and liberal trade regime. In addition, the twin forces of democratization and economic liberalization are forcing change on South Korean domestic policy fronts.

Change involves the issues of administrative reform and structural adjustment. The former focuses on institutional development that is responsive to the people (e.g., democratization, decentralization, and economy and efficiency in government). The latter is concerned about "getting prices right" by creating open and transparent markets (e.g., deregulation, financial liberalization, industrial restructuring, etc.). Accordingly, the process of designing strategies will differ in the two domains (Klitgaard, 1995, 238). This study views the 1997 financial crisis not as an end but as the beginning of a new reform era for strategies that contribute to sustainable economic development.

This chapter is divided into two parts. The first part deals with a study of the parallel existence, and dynamic interaction, of politics and economics which characterizes the South Korean political economy, and it examines the nature of the financial crisis and the IMF bailout plan. The second part focuses primarily on regulatory reform that will further structural adjustments for stabilization and growth under the new government led by President Kim Dae-Jung. This is followed by an attempt to evaluate the reform programs to date. There is much debate in the literature on how reforms should be sequenced (OECD, 1997, 33–34). The South Korean situation gives a window into a "reform" environment. This study analyzes South Korea's approach to structuring reform: how reforms can be sequenced and how important sequencing is. The strategy chosen was to adopt the optimal sequencing from both political and economic perspectives. Politically, it is to maximize the political momentum of reform. From an economic point of view, it is to reduce transition costs and to achieve the objectives of policy reform.

A CRISIS IN SOUTH KOREA'S POLITICAL ECONOMY

Structural Problems in the Economy

The South Korean economy is going through painful structural adjustments that are necessary to stimulate economic growth. Many factors have made the current restructuring process particularly painful. On the domestic side, several internal structural problems, notably in the financial and labor markets, had to be faced. The government supported *chaebol* (conglomerates) expansion and often directed them into specific lines of business; at the same time, the government failed to implement effective deregulation throughout the economy. Sins of both commission and omission were responsible for continued high increases in the costs of production, including wages, interest rates, and rents. The continued decline in South Korea's overall competitiveness may be attributed to the failure to address these issues.

Another important structural problem is the weak financial structure of South Korea's chaebol and the banking system. Past experience with the government's bailout policies had generated expectations throughout the markets that the government would not stand by and allow the chaebol to go under. In such an environment, the chaebol tended to make aggressive investment decisions without careful analysis of the associated returns and risks, and the financial institutions had little incentive to look into the financial soundness of those companies. As a result, their financial structures became excessively leveraged. The policy of aggressiveness worked well as long as the economy and export expanded and the return on new investment exceeded the cost of capital. In recent years, however, the debt/equity ratios of chaebol continued to rise due to declining demand and falling prices for South Korean exports—particularly in semiconductors, chemicals, shipbuilding, and steel markets. The low profitability led to heavy borrowing in the last few years from both domestic and foreign sources. Following the devaluation of the Thai baht, the increasing nervousness of the markets drew attention not only to the weakness of many conglomerates like Hanbo Iron and Steel, but also the banks closely related to the business groups.

The South Korean government recognized the problems. Piecemeal, ad hoc reform efforts had been made without paying much attention to sequencing reforms and coordinating the implementation schedule. For example, the National Assembly passed a reform proposal aimed at enhancing labor market flexibility. A package of financial liberalization programs was also introduced in the early 1990s. However, the politically compromised reform measures were too weak, and the pace of reform was also too slow. In addition to weak measures, the chief economic minister (the deputy prime minister) was replaced seven times during the Kim Young-Sam government, making it almost impossible for the economic ministries to pursue a coherent policy and to coordinate needed policy adjustments.

South Korea's bank failures and the ensuing foreign exchange crisis are unique in that they were not attributable to weakness in the real side of the economy. It appears that South Korea's banking system collapsed due to the foreign creditors' loss of confidence as the structural flaws in the financial system came to surface in the course of democratization and globalization. This situation was compounded by the contagion effect emanating from the financial crises in the Southeast Asian countries and Japan.

Asian Contagion Effect

Competitive currency devaluations that occurred in Thailand and Indonesia in 1997 did not achieve what was intended because countries in the region are trying to export more goods than the world could absorb at prevailing prices. As the problem of excess export capacity is being handed from one country to another like a hot potato, each handoff has led to a currency crisis, higher interest rates, devaluation, and exposed banking system weaknesses. Although the region's economies were characterized by soft exports and slowing economies, the difference has been that localized symptoms laid bare severe macroeconomic illness.

In January 1997, the medium-sized Thai property firm Somprasong Land defaulted on $80 million worth of convertible Eurobonds. It first focused attention on how overbuilt the Bangkok property market was, how overextended property developers and finance houses were, and how much private foreign debt was actually due to be paid in 1997. In other words, the uncontrolled influx of foreign capital was channeled into the real estate market for speculative investments, following financial market deregulation in many Pacific Rim countries. Around the same time, Hanbo Iron and Steel of South Korea failed after binging on overexpansion. Next door, Tokyo bailed out the troubled Nippon Credit Bank in April but the same month let Nissan Life become the first Japanese life insurer to fail since World War II. These were the early rumblings of turmoil. Speculators began hammering the baht (Thai currency) in the early spring of 1997. The Bank of Thailand at first beat them back, but the attacks kept coming. In July, after spending tens of billions of dollars, mostly on forward currency contracts, the Thai government admitted defeat and floated the baht. The currency lost 20 percent of its value to the U.S. dollar in less than a week. The Malaysian ringgit, Indonesian rupiah, and Philippine peso soon followed downward.

The question can be raised; why did something that had started as merely a bad exchange rate dream turn into a full-blown nightmare? Many Southeast Asian economies had pegged their currencies at least loosely to the U.S. dollar. Undeniably, the dollar peg of these currencies has brought significant economic benefit to the countries concerned. The very fact that the stability of the currencies' exchange rate was guaranteed in this way has had the effect of strengthening international trust not only in these currencies but also in their economies, for the absence of any exchange rate risk was likely to lure foreign investors. But the links started to look unreasonable once it became clear that high currency account shortfalls, inflation, and asset bubbles left many economies out of sync with America's economic fundamentals. That gave speculators the incentive to keep up the pressure. Furthermore, Asian financial institutions and companies had borrowed massively overseas to take advantage of relatively low interest rates. As local currencies fell, the borrowers bought more dollars, seeking to hedge against further devaluation, swelling foreign obligations further. Meanwhile, too much of the borrowed money had been misdirected—into unsalable property or uneconomic factories, for instance—by cronyism, corruption, and plain bad business. The initial government policy response to all this (almost everywhere but in Malaysia) was to raise interest rates as a way to protect local currencies. However, tight credit only aggravated the burgeoning slump and pushed debt-ridden companies to the edge.

In South Korea, the domino effects that started with the Hanbo group (steel) spread to other large firms like Kia (auto), while banks and politicians dithered over the bankruptcy rescue plan. Policy options left politicians and policy makers with two equally unpalatable choices: either to support a government rescue, which would further incur public debts, or to lay off a lot of workers, which might fuel social unrest. As the so-called Kia crisis dragged on, the economy suffered along with it, alerting major international credit-rating firms and financial institutions of future trouble in South Korea. Germany's Bayerische Landesbank, Westdeutsche Landesbank, and Dresdner Bank with loans to South Korean businesses exceeding $10 billion (as of the end of 1997) are the nation's second largest foreign creditor after Japan. They are followed by such American banks as J.P. Morgan, Chase Manhattan, and Citicorp. In times of economic crisis, the prospect of capital flight leaves policy makers with a lose–lose choice. Either they must raise interest rates sky-high to defend their exchange rate, thus harming the domestic economy, or they must let their exchange rate collapse, which will be equally detrimental. Capital outflows deprive them of the ability to stimulate the economy through lower interest rates. South Korea's economic downturn soon led to a sharp depreciation of the won (South Korean currency) and soaring market interest rates, bringing an overall paralysis in the financial sector.

The problem worsened as major global stock markets simultaneously plunged in the aftermath of the Southeast Asian currency crisis. International financial institutions began to slash South Korea's credit rating, further putting the clamps on the flow of funds into and out of the country. As the situation continued to deteriorate, the South Korean government turned to the IMF to intervene and bail out its credit crunch in the winter of 1997. Amid the turmoil engulfing Asia, the countries involved, and their currency "pegs," have found themselves at the core of the global financial system. The event demonstrates the multiplying and deepening linkages among national markets created by the mobility of capital and foreign direct investment (Julius, 1990, 93).

Table 4.1
South Korea's External Obligations ($ billion)

	End of 1996	End of Sept. 1997	End of Nov. 1997	Dec. 20, 1997
(a) Foreign Debt (World Bank):	**107.9**	**119.8**	**116.1**	**118.6**
1. Domestic Financial Institutions	69.9	75.0	70.8	64.4
(Head office)	(53.9)	(54.9)	(50.0)	(43.4)
(Foreign Bank Branches)*	(16.0)	(20.1)	(20.8)	(21.0)
2. Private Enterprises	35.6	47.2	43.4	43.2
3. Public Sector	2.4	2.1	2.0	11.0
(b) Additions:	**52.9**	**50.9**	**40.7**	**34.4**
1. Offshore Borrowings**	21.2	22.7	20.9	18.9
2. Overseas Branches***	31.7	28.2	19.8	5.5
(a) + (b) Gross External Obligations (IMF)	**160.8**	**170.7**	**156.8**	**153.0**

*Amount borrowed abroad by the branches of foreign banks in South Korea.
**Amount borrowed and used abroad by the head offices of South Korean banks.
***Amount borrowed and used abroad by the overseas branches of South Korean banks.
The debt volume at the end of November 1997 breaks down to $92.2 billion, or 58.8 percent of the total or short-term loans maturing in less than a year and $64.7 billion, or 41.2 percent of long-term loans with maturity of more than one year.
The net foreign debt, or the gross debt minus the nation's foreign assets, is estimated at $55.5 billion at the end of November 1997, according to the Ministry.
Source: Official figures announced by the Ministry of Finance and Economy and the International Monetary Fund.

What is portrayed here may be a defining characteristic of the new high-tech financial system. The new more sophisticated financial markets seem to punish errant government policy behavior far more profoundly than in the past. Moreover, the South Korean government's attempts to pull together an integrated foreign exchange information system had failed in computing cross-border flows of private companies' foreign debts in the age of increasingly liberalized capital markets. According to the report released by the Ministry of Finance and Economy (1998, 5), "it is realistically impossible for the government to trace all private-sector foreign exchange dealings, due to the sheer size of the South Korean economy and the rapid pace of capital-market liberalization." This abnormal situation is, of course, rooted in the heyday of economic development during the 1960s and 1970s, when the government heavily intervened in bank management to guide fund allocation in favor of development. This can be seen in Table 4.1. As a result, South Korean banks have had little incentive to modernize the financial system. The fact that the offshore borrowing of private enterprises far exceeds that of the public sector has committed the government to design an integrated currency information system. The government has recently commissioned a foreign consulting firm to develop a model to correctly compile the size and maturities of external liabilities.

THE IMF'S RESPONSE TO THE SOUTH KOREAN CRISIS

The crisis unfolded against the backdrop of three decades of outstanding economic performance in South Korea, and the difficulties that the country now faces are not primarily the result of macroeconomic imbalances. Rather, they stem from weaknesses in its financial system and, to some extent, governance. A combination of inadequate financial sector supervision, poor risk management, and the maintenance of a relatively fixed exchange rate led banks and conglomerates to borrow large amounts of foreign capital, much of it short-term.

The bailout plan calls for sweeping changes in South Korea's political economy—the state-guided capitalism, and the IMF conditions have hastened the inevitable reform that South Korea found difficult to implement before. This element of being forced to reform under the IMF bailout scheme is what makes the current situation so radically different from others. Unlike debt in the Latin American crisis of the 1980s and the current Indonesian crisis, which were mainly sovereign, South Korea's current debt problems involve primarily private lenders and borrowers. Unlike troubled Thailand or Indonesia, the South Korean government has vigorously pursued and has enacted the necessary legislation in order to implement the IMF-imposed retrenchment policy and structural reforms by enlisting the support of the major actors (i.e., business, labor, and government) who have a stake in reconstituting the economy.

First, let us examine the IMF-imposed retrenchment policy. The macroeconomic objective of the IMF program is to establish the conditions for an early return of market confidence and a recovery toward potential in 1999. Hence, the government's program is built around: (1) a strong macroeconomic framework designed to continue the orderly adjustment in the external currency account; build up international reserves; and contain inflationary pressures, involving a tighter monetary stance and significant adjustment; (2) a comprehensive strategy to restructure and recapitalize the financial sector, and make it more transparent, market-oriented, and better supervised; and (3) measures to reduce the high degree of reliance of corporations and financial institutions on short-term debt and allow a better diversification of risk in the country (IMF, 1997, 5–6).

The successful outcome of the short-term debt negotiations, which has substantially lifted South Korea's short-term external liquidity constraint, will allow the country's long-term external credit fundamentals to reassert themselves. As part of the IMF's $57 billion bailout, the IMF had insisted on high interest rates to boost the value of the South Korean currency, the won.

MANAGING THE ECONOMY: INSTITUTIONAL REFORM

Any effort to understand the origins of the economic policies in South Korea must start with a review of the institutional conditions in which these policies were formulated. South Korea is the most dramatic case of an undeveloped country turning itself into an industrial powerhouse in a mere third of a century. South Korea's drive to catch up with the industrial countries started in the early 1960s under the military government of Park Chung-Hee. Following the model of Japan and the pioneering example of Taiwan, Park adopted an aggressive strategy of export promotion. This involved an initial devaluation and liberalization of trade in inputs needed to produce exports, and subsequently a switch to a crawling peg in order to keep the exchange rate competitive despite the continuing high rate of inflation.

The government remained an active player in the allocation of resources, using the banking system to channel policy-directed loans to the targeted industries. Trade liberalization was highly selective. In fact, major trade policy reform did not come back onto the agenda until the 1980s. In the meantime, the government sustained a strong commitment to education, which contributed to a continuous upgrading in the quality of the labor-intensive products South Korea was capable of exporting. Following the installation of a new military government under Chun Doo-Hwan in 1980, the government moved with alacrity not only to stabilize the economy but also to initiate a series of liberalizing reforms, in concert with the government's stabilization plan to slow down the economy and accelerating inflation. The government launched a new round of trade liberalization and moved incrementally to liberalize the financial system.

As the country moved closer toward political democratization in 1987, the new government continued the basic outward-oriented strategy pursued by its military predecessors and began to accelerate the liberalization of trade. Then came the functioning democratic state when South Korea elected its first civilian President Kim Young-Sam in 1992, and his civilian government was succeeded by the long-time champion of democracy, President Kim Dae-Jung in 1998. Today South Korea is a viable, functioning democracy, but it faces the daunting challenge of overcoming a financial crisis that hit the country in 1997.

Administrative reform in South Korea can be divided into four stages: (1) the initial stage of economic development beginning in the 1960s, during which the institutional basis for South Korea's export-oriented industrialization was laid through the strengthening of executive leadership in policy design and implementation. The first phase of this period was marked by economic mobilization and export activity, followed by stabilization and structural adjustments in the early 1980s; (2) the second period of economic growth and stabilization (1987–1992) was characterized by the period of economic liberalization and the political transition toward democratization; (3) the third period was defined by democratic transformation and gradual liberalization programs (1993–1997); and (4) the fourth period constitutes the present retrenchment and restructuring stage under the IMF plan which began in late 1997. The new government has embarked on bold policy initiatives that include comprehensive structural reforms.

The Period of Institutional Development for Export-Oriented Economic Growth

Throughout the 1960s and 1970s, outward-looking policies for trade and industry were essential for the country's development. Critical to their success, however, was a set of institutional mechanisms that support the alliance of business and government in the effort to export. The Park Chung-Hee government, which had seized power through a military coup in May 1961, pursued economic development as a means of gaining popular support and legitimizing its authoritarian rule. More importantly, the fundamental and administrative features of South Korean bureaucratic development were crystallized during the initial phase of the military government's first Five-Year Economic Development Plan. Park's military government came to rely on professionalism, efficiency, and technocratic advice. As a result, the new alliance between the military and technocrats had evolved, and this period witnessed the burgeoning bureaucracy.

The Presidential Office became the central locus of policy formulation and innovations. President Park and his in-house policy advisors were deeply involved in the economic policy-making process and provided detailed guidance on broad policy directions (Luedde-Neurath, 1988, 94). The most important institutional innovation was the creation of the Economic Planning Board (EPB) in June 1961. The EPB took over planning responsibility from the Ministry of Reconstruction, which played a key role in the post–Korean War era, and took over budgetary functions by absorbing the Bureau of the Budget from the Ministry of Finance. The EPB also undertook the collection of national statistics by transferring the Bureau of Statistics out of the Ministry of Home Affairs. The EPB combined and concentrated various enclaves of economic and planning activities that previously had been scattered. Furthermore, in 1963 the head of the EPB was elevated to the status of deputy prime minister. The elevated position of the EPB brought about the newly added but important function: the authority to coordinate all the economic and budgetary policies as well as their activities emanating from various economic-related ministries or agencies in the South Korean bureaucracy (Haggard, 1990, 64–65). Therefore, the EPB emerged as the most powerful economic policy-making organ in the South Korean bureaucracy.

The EPB used the banking system as one of its principal instruments of development policy, setting low interest rates and directing loans to government target industries. Moreover, the EPB was granted control over the flow of foreign loans, foreign direct investment, and the transfer of technology. By controlling the inflow of foreign capital (including the screening of foreign investment applications and the provision of government guarantees to foreign loans), the EPB served as an intermediator between foreign capital and domestic capital. This intermediary role of the EPB enabled it to monitor and control specific investment decisions of the private sector.

Another noteworthy institutional innovation was the establishment of the Office of National Tax Administration in February 1966. The existence of a substantial gap between tax law and actual tax collection in South Korea generally reflected inefficient tax structures, and collected taxes were often small fractions of what those structures should have yielded. The policy stance taken to increase tax collections was not to raise tax rates but simply to strengthen tax enforcement measures. The ramification of this policy decision is significant to note here. The government not only used the power of tax investigation beyond the scope of its original intent, but also selectively conducted tax audits on individual firms as a policy tool to steer businesses toward objectives consistent with the national economic priorities (Ha, 1993, 75–76).

The commitment of political leadership to the export-oriented strategy was such that the major thrust of administrative reform in the 1960s was to centralize decision-making power in the executive branch and to introduce modern administrative procedures and techniques. In essence, this initiative unified all economic agents in South Korea in a common undertaking, and in the process it forged a partnership of business, banks, and government. The implementation of export-oriented industrialization strategy relied on a system of incentives: one for providing policy-directed loans and tariff-free access to the imported intermediate inputs used in export production; the other for allowing continuous access to bank loans for the needed capital for export activity (Amsden, 1989, 143). In short, the EPB functioned as an institutional mechanism that allowed the government to gain an overview of the economy as a whole, and acted as a regulator of the whole industrialization process.

Although the basic organizational structures and administrative procedures remained basically intact until the 1980s, a change in the locus of economic policy making took place when the South Korean government pushed the development of the heavy and chemical industries in the 1970s. South Korea's big push reflected the government's strategy to upgrade its industrial structure. It was also partly a response to the rapid deterioration of its international environment, following the "oil shock." The increased level of government involvement in the sector-specific industrialization of the 1970s marks another defining characteristic of the development process in South Korea. But the very policy initiatives underpinning the industrial deepening program resulted in a serious economic crisis at the end of the 1970s. Chronic overcapacity and underutilization caused by excessive competition and overinvestment in the heavy and chemical industrial sector led to high inflation and foreign debts.

The Search for Efficiency and Stabilization

The 1980s signaled a major policy shift in the development strategy. The basic purpose of economic policy was to create an institutional environment under which market forces could play a larger role in the allocation of resources and thereby improve the overall efficiency. Economic liberalization programs were designed to create a competitive domestic economic environment, to liberalize financial institutions, and to introduce foreign direct investment, thus representing a shift away from the industrial targeting system and injecting the elements of competition. The shift toward a market-oriented economic management characterizes the Chun Doo-Hwan authoritarian government (1980–1987). With the shift in the development strategy, the role of the government changed from "controller" of the economy to "rule-setter" in the economy.

As greater reliance on market mechanisms became the central tenet of economic management, the role of the EPB also changed, reflecting a radical departure from the interventionist regime era. They focused more on information-gathering, budgeting, and planning functions. In line with the Chun administration's emphasis on "efficiency" in government, the major direction of administrative reform in much of the 1980s was to shrink the public sector. The government reorganization plan in October 1981 was a major attempt to revamp the government operations. The October reform reduced the size of 41 bureaus and 135 divisions in the government bureaucracy and resulted in the 11.8 percent cutback in personnel from the middle management rank or above (Chung and Jun, 1991, 46–47). However, Chun's cutback reform was shortlived, and his government could not curb the voracity of expansionary forces in the bureaucracy. Some observers here argued that the so-called regime-level politics was a driving force behind the reform strategy (Arnold, 1995; 408). By pursuing the popular sentiment of the "small government" idea, the Chun government simply hoped to overcome Chun's unpopular image as the former military general. His reform effort fell far short of its stated objective: to increase administrative efficiency. The major thrust of the reform may best be described as cutback reform rather than innovative reform.

Administrative reforms under the governments of Presidents Park and

Chun had been mainly those of changes of government structures. Changes included the consolidation of organizational functions and the streamlining of inefficient operations while the centralized bureaucracy remained intact. Within these structural constraints, the regime type would oscillate within relatively narrow parameters without bringing about increased productivity and improved efficiency. In short, executive reorganization had been a means of reform that was related to an evolving mode of executive governance.

Political Democratization and Administrative Innovation

After almost three decades of authoritarian rule, the politico-economic context of South Korea's public administration began to change in the late 1980s. In 1987, President Rho Tae-Woo was elected by direct popular vote, and he was replaced by Kim Young-Sam who became South Korea's first civilian elected president (1993–1998). Along with democratization and economic development, South Korea has evolved toward a pluralistic society, and its economy has developed into a highly sophisticated one. Whereas participatory patterns of behavior have been widely accepted among the general populace, many institutional and structural conditions of democratization have not been solidified.

The primary goals of the Presidential Commission for Administrative Innovation are threefold: (1) to establish service- and people-oriented government, (2) to create a responsive and efficient administration, and (3) to accomplish a small, corruption-free, and professionally competent government. The strategies for better governance required a fundamental institutional transformation. The first phase of this transformation (1993–1994) was to develop and cultivate a new civic culture, shifting away from the bureaucratic domination in the policy formulation. It called for citizen participation at the grass-roots level and people-oriented attitudes on the part of the bureaucrats. The second phase concentrated on policy measures to strengthen South Korea's economic competitiveness in the global marketplace and to improve "the quality of life." Accordingly, the government considered deregulation and financial liberalization measures as the key elements in the reform.

Deregulation was conceived as a necessary step toward a corruption-free government. It was believed that government-led economic growth inevitably resulted in a symbiotic relationship between the state and big business. The complicated web of government regulations with overlapping jurisdictions not only stifled private initiatives and foreign investment but also resulted in the arbitrary use of power by enlarging the scope of bureaucratic discretion. President Kim Young-Sam stressed the importance of globalization, and his administration urged the bureaucrats and the citizenry alike to adopt global perspectives by supporting an overseas training program and a foreign language program. To meet these challenges, the agenda of governments at all levels included such economic development items as free trade agreements, global environmental agreements, and immigration issues that were mostly of the transnational nature.

The Kim Young-Sam administration emphasized people-oriented policy initiatives with an emphasis on the improvement of the quality and convenience of public services by simplifying administrative procedures. The hallmark of his government reorganization was a merger of the two most powerful ministries, namely, the Economic Planning Board (EPB) and the Ministry of Finance, into a single unit, renamed the Ministry of Finance and Economy. The merger was originally intended to downgrade the EPB's role by transferring the policy coordinating responsibility from the EPB to the Office of Prime Minister. However, under the presidential system in South Korea, the Office of Prime Minister does not enjoy much authority in the overall process of policy making and policy implementation. Therefore, the real power of policy formulation and coordination resides in the presidential staff. To make matters worse, there was no agency to supervise and coordinate all reform activities. Under this circumstance, one could not expect the design and implementation of comprehensive and consistent reform proposals.

The very success of the country's industrial policy altered the basic features of South Korean society. Both the Rho and Kim governments' reform efforts were a response to the rapidly changing environment. The major goals of their reforms included democratization of administrative procedures and political decentralization, small and efficient government, restructuring of government-business relations, market-oriented economic management, and performance-oriented management. To grapple with the challenges, the Administrative Reform Commission under President Rho Tae-Woo attempted to democratize the governmental processes. Thus, the Commission focused on streamlining government structures and rearranging administrative portfolios of various agencies, whereas President Kim Young-Sam's Reform Commission on Administrative Innovations directed its efforts at providing the quality of service with a "citizen first" focus and implementing deregulation.

To be sure, the general trend has been toward increasing the liberalization of the South Korean economy since the 1980s. For instance, credit policy in South Korea has experienced four distinct phases. In the 1960s it was directed toward export-oriented industries. In the 1970s it increasingly pursued industrial policy targeting specific industries like the heavy and chemical industries. However, the successes and failures of industrial policy induced a change in strategy, and in the 1980s the government became involved in the restructuring of industrial and financial sectors, focusing not only on picking winners, but also on phasing out losers. In the 1990s credit policy was redirected toward functional activities such as research and development efforts as well as paying greater attention to small and medium-sized companies (Vittas and Cho, 1996, 287–288). Thus, in contrast to the overregulated, highly distorted economies, the South Korean economy has been characterized by diminishing intervention in most spheres of economic activity, and the degree of distortion is considerably less. But a highly centralized system of government could not respond in a timely fashion to the competing demands of pluralism and democratization in South Korea.

The Retrenchment Stage: The IMF Era

The current financial crisis clearly demonstrates the government's inability to manage effectively the complex and sophisticated South Korean economy. South Korea's administrative reform was far from improving managerial competence and reinventing government. It focused primarily on the rearrangement of government structures. Without reforming the bureaucratic practices and strengthening administrative capabilities, one cannot expect the creation of an "efficient" government. The inauguration of President Kim Dae-Jung (hereafter called D. J. Kim) on February 25, 1998 marks South Korea's first transfer of power from the ruling party to the opposition. The new government of President D. J. Kim has taken two major policy initiatives: one on the comprehensive structural reform of the South Korean economy to recapture momentum toward sustainable economic development, and the other on furthering democratic governance.

South Korea has been undergoing the decentralization process since 1993. Obviously, the national economic woes become more than an obstacle in the process of transferring power to local authorities. It is premature to speculate about the ultimate consequences of restructuring government, but the various challenges the nation faces make "regulatory reform" imperative, and the South Korean people believe that it must succeed—both as a support for decentralization to pay greater attention to public preferences when setting priorities, and as the motivation for converting the capabilities of a bureaucracy stuck in the regulatory mode to a new economy able to adapt to change and remain competitive in global markets.

As part of the institutional adjustment and reform measures, a government downsizing plan proposed by then President-elect D. J. Kim was submitted to the special session of the National Assembly convened in February 1998. D. J. Kim's renewed demand for a drastic government reorganization bill became bogged down in the legislative process, and the compromised reform bill was far from the envisioned "small and efficient" government plan. The reorganization bill has revamped the government structure by reducing the number of cabinet ministries to 17 from 21, and the number of civil servants has been reduced to 120,000 at the end of the year 2000. The reduction represents a cut of about 25 percent from the prior year's number. This figure accounts for 11.7 percent of central and local government employees excluding police and teachers. In the first wave, 24,000 positions had been phased out by the end of 1998 (Transition Committee, 1997, 56).

The downsizing quota is to be met by an early retirement incentive package and amended law that lowers the retirement age (by one year) for civil servants. In concert with its efforts to slim down the public sector, the D. J. Kim government will also pursue active privatization of remaining state-owned enterprises such as railroads, the postal service, and telecommunications. D. J. Kim has also suggested that the legislative and judicial branches of the South Korean government follow the 10 percent manpower reduction guidelines. These gut-wrenching measures reflect the president's commitment to the equal sharing of the IMF-imposed retrenchment burdens among the government, business, and labor. They represent more than just the personnel reshuffling and rearrangement of agency portfolios.

REFORM STRATEGIES UNDER THE NEW GOVERNMENT (PRESIDENT D. J. KIM)

The "emergency economy" task force, part of the transition committee formed by then President-elect D. J. Kim, recognized that government-supplied rations are no recipe for the wealth of nations. They have developed new strategies to deal with global markets for capital and with the flood tides of private funds that over the past decade have helped produce both the huge rise in Asian prosperity and the recent plunge. Its foreign debt totals some $153 billion, most of which is owed by private sector borrowers to private Japanese, European, and American banks. The debt restructuring negotiations between South Korea and a dozen or more international banks reached an agreement in New York in January 1998 to roll over the maturity of South Korean commercial banks' short-term debts ($24 billion) due early this year by one to three years under the government's payment guarantees.

Opportunities for genuine reform come rarely, and often only when crises and external pressures make clear the cost of inaction. The IMF bailout resulting from a financial crisis provided the newly elected president of South Korea with an opportunity for comprehensive reform. When D. J. Kim was elected president in December 1997, he lost no time in announcing that he would abide by the commitment of the government to the IMF. President D. J. Kim moved swiftly onto the reform agenda for his government during the transition period between the presidential election in December 1997 and his inauguration in February 1998. Policy responses have been designed to halt a downward spiral and to restore confidence in the economy. They are directed at improving the macro/microeconomic and institutional fundamentals, including establishing an effective regulatory system, improving corporate governance, and enhancing transparency in the government and the economy.

The Political Process of Reform

New realities are being taken on board because South Korea recently became the recipient of the IMF's biggest-ever rescue package, totaling $57 billion. Rather than simply hurl their country into the arms of IMF bureaucrats and hope for salvation, the crisis has provided President D. J. Kim with the perfect opportunity to implement the radical changes needed that were long overdue. The president opted for maximizing the political momentum of reform created by the financial crisis and IMF conditions.

As indicated, President D. J. Kim had moved swiftly and decisively to lay the foundation for comprehensive reform during the transition period. There was much debate on how reform could be sequenced and how critical each linkage was. Its success could lie in building national consensus for difficult policy choices and administrative reforms in both the private and public sectors. Prior to his inauguration, President D. J. Kim carefully constituted his transition team, drawn from academia, prominent citizens, business, labor, government, journalists, and politicians, and charged them to map out reform measures to cope with the IMF conditions. The transition team served as a legitimate forum for societal stakeholders to take the lead in advising both the new government and the public of the imperative reform. The president had also chosen a strategy for comprehensive reform that was based on a complete and transparent package of reforms designed to achieve specific goals on a well-defined timetable. The transition team was organized into five key task force groups, each group working on restructuring the formula for a policy area or single sector. They were (1) the "economic emergency task force" for dealing with the currency crisis and short-term external liabilities; (2) the "financial liberalization and regulatory reform" covering capital markets, foreign investments, banking, and bankruptcy laws; (3) "industrial restructuring" which includes chaebol reform; (4) "labor market reform"; and (5) public sector reform.

The transition team, acting as a kind of a deliberative body, held numerous public hearings, examined the issues, and discussed the various proposals. When they reached an accord on each of the proposals, the reform legislation was drafted for approval by the president-elect. Undoubtedly, producing an integrated package of reforms facilitates the balancing of multiple policy objectives and interests. There was a high degree of consensus and cooperation between the new president and the outgoing administration as to the reform agenda and its timetable for the enactment of the major reform legislation. The special session of the South Korean

National Assembly was called to take up the reform measures in the month of February 1998. Having enacted the overwhelming part of the key reform legislation and the government revamping, he now faces the challenges of implementation.

CRISIS MANAGEMENT AND POLICY REFORM

Although the recent financial crisis in South Korea was precipitated by the contagion effect spreading from Pacific Basin countries, the country's economic woes were compounded by the structural problems that have accumulated over a long period of time. The problematic factors that the affected countries have in common are (1) the weakness of central banks and commercial banks; (2) the over-reliance of those nations on banks as opposed to debt-to-equity markets; and (3) "excessive leverage" (Greenspan, 1998). This reliance on short-term, international bank borrowing may turn out be the Achilles' heel of an international financial system that is subject to wide variations in financial confidence.

The thrust of major legislative reform measures was aimed at bringing about far-reaching structural adjustments. The centerpiece of the programs has been the comprehensive reform of South Korea's financial system. As for the governance issues that may also have contributed to the crisis, the reform of the financial system is buttressed by measures designed to improve the efficiency of markets and break the close links between chaebol and government, coupled with increased transparency as regards information on external reserves and liabilities in both the banking and corporate sectors.

The reform efforts have been undergirded by the action taken on December 30, 1997, by the South Korean National Assembly. It passed 19 pieces of legislation that are needed to carry out some of the IMF-imposed reform programs. The key amendments consist of (1) establishing an independent central bank with the primary goal of controlling inflation; (2) creating a consolidated supervisory body with jurisdiction over all financial institutions and operational independence; and (3) mandating companies to report audited and consolidated financial statements (National Assembly, 1997, 1–9).

It is ironic that many of the problems South Korea faces have arisen not because government did too much but because it did too little. For instance, poorly managed financial liberalization lifted some restrictions on bank lending before putting in place a sound regulatory framework. Insufficient financial regulation and implicit or explicit government guarantees, as well as misguided exchange rate and monetary policies, each played an important role in creating the incentives that led to the particular character of external financing and internal misallocation of resources. Very high debt-to-equity ratios being rooted in private sector financial decisions is indicative of the chaebol's overreliance on banks as opposed to private capital markets. These factors have made the South Korean economy vulnerable to a sudden withdrawal of confidence, resulting in a mass exodus of foreign capital. The pace of regulatory reform with respect to the financial sector, industrial restructuring, economic deregulation, and the labor market had been extremely slow under the Kim Young-Sam government. Sometimes a major policy initiative was blocked by political paralysis. For instance, an effort to reform the labor market laws dealing with the issue of redundancies was stuck in neutral due to strong opposition from the unions. Labor unions fought to preserve labor market regulation to the advantage of those already employed.

Chaebol Reform: Increasing Corporate Transparency and Accountability

Under half a century of authoritarian political system and state-led capitalism, business and political collusion became prevalent, and the government controlled finance to channel limited credit to the well connected. The South Korean financial nexus can best be characterized by the tripartite relationship between government, business, and financial institutions. During the drive to high growth, the primary objective of chaebol was growth maximization (i.e., gaining market share) rather than profit maximization. The chaebol strategy often was to expand at top speed to attain a critical mass, at which the government would be unable to allow insolvency or bankruptcy. Fuel for massive expansion was provided by high leverage or heavy dependence on debt financing. Firms played the game of brinkmanship, relying on the government with its power to grant policy loans and thus to rescue them from bankruptcy. In fact, the nonperforming assets of the commercial banks had grown so huge that the government lacked the political leverage to allow some firms to go bankrupt. Accordingly, to avert the immediate financial collapse of insolvent firms, it provided ad hoc relief loans and spent money to bail out failing enterprises (Kim, 1994, 54).

South Korean firms typically have high financial leverage, reaching as high as an 80 percent debt to total assets ratio. When the economy and corporate earnings grow, financial leverage has positive effects on firms, but with an economic slowdown, the leverage becomes a burden. This is exactly what happened in some of the South Korean chaebol recently. In a market system, as firms borrow more money, the cost of debt increases because of greater financial risk. This higher cost of debt puts a limit on the amount of borrowing, and additional debts become "junk" bonds with higher promised return but also a higher risk of default.

In order to increase the competitiveness and transparency of the chaebol, policy design by the "emergency economy" task force included reforming the family-run structure of the business giants as a top priority. The "emergency economy" task force has reaffirmed its policy stance in that transparency is the key to gaining international credibility and market confidence. To that end, the implementation of a combined financial statement system in business groups is essential, notwithstanding strong resistance by large conglomerates because firms fear that their weaknesses would be exposed. Although consolidated financial statements are more commonly used in other countries, including the United States, they would not be sufficient for local business corporations. South Korean firms are not centered around a "holdings" system. Rather, they depend heavily on the various family ties and their firms, which have actual power in running a company. In no case should owners control businesses in an arbitrary way or manipulate accounting to siphon off corporate money for personal purposes. Legislation has now been enacted to ensure that minority shareholders can take legal action against shady management practices.

The restructuring design must also concern itself with the issue of corporate governance. It should disband the so-called offices of the chaebol group chairmen through which most chaebol owners (their family members holding no legal titles within their business empires) have been orchestrating the operation of all subsidiaries in their wide-ranging net of businesses. Furthermore, the chaebol's current business practice of cross-debt guarantees among affiliated firms, which allowed overextension, must be abolished. Policy reform calls for external auditors with more legal power to monitor corporate management in a transparent way. Moreover, the ancillary business units of chaebol need to be restructured along their core business lines. These recommended measures were submitted to then President-elect D. J. Kim, and he has strongly endorsed them.

When President-elect D. J. Kim met the heads of the top 30 conglomerates, he unveiled a new chaebol policy. The policy envisioned three aspects. First, chaebol will be barred from extending cross-payment guarantees among subsidiaries. Second, each chaebol is required to submit a recapitalization plan or debt reduction plan when they borrow fresh loans from banks. Banks will encourage industrialists to recycle their wealth into productive corporate investment. Unless chaebol abide by the rule, banks will immediately call in outstanding loans. Third, all chaebol must prepare consolidated financial statements that record all intersubsidiary cash flow, sales, and subsidies. This will prevent companies from inflating sales or assets, deflating debts, or hiding dubious bookkeeping practices. Pursuant to these policies, the government plans to reduce the amount of tax-deductible interest payments on debt-ridden firms and to introduce penalty provisions on excessive loans and cross-payment guarantees. In a related development, policy makers decided to permit banks to engage in "loan-for-equity" deals for cash-short small and medium-sized companies. In other words, banks can convert corporate loans into equity as part of the steps to help the firms resolve financial burdens ("Appointment of Lee Hun-Jai," 1998).

Financial Liberalization

The South Korean financial structure reflects a system in which state control has been pervasive throughout the banking system. From the government perspective, it was more convenient to utilize financial policy instruments rather than fiscal policy tools in the early stage of development in the 1960s and the early 1970s when the nation's taxable capacity was rather limited. From a bank's perspective, the government's intervention in the financial sector has been a double-edged sword, providing protection as well as control. On the control side, it has influenced all aspects of banking operations, ranging from directing policy loans to lending rates lower than market rates to appointing top officials. On the other hand, the government's safety net against banks' insolvency; the central bank's low interest rate credit to banks; and payment of interest on reserve deposits with the central bank to keep a semblance of profitability at a minimum acceptable level are some of the benefits derived. In essence, the government had attempted to balance the advantages of competition (greater efficiency) with the perceived disadvantages (loss of discretionary power and growing nonperforming assets).

This strategy has been successful in raising and maintaining the average annual growth of the national economy at a rate close to double digits, but it entailed costs and inefficiency, leading to less stable financial institutions. The costs were borne primarily by banks and depositors; managerial efficiency and quality of services were compromised; and the banks accumulated huge amounts of nonperforming loans. With strong intervention in credit allocation, the government could grant or withhold the means of growth, cheap credit, thus ensuring that financial resources went to the preferred or strategic sectors under the economic development plan. The government used its control of the banking system to exert strong leverage on the behavior of firms (Cho and Kim, 1995, 17). Since controls were such that most loan decisions were determined by the government, banks have been deficient in a variety of skills, especially in the areas of risk assessment, credit monitoring, and management of assets and liabilities, which are necessary to their viability in a market environment (Caprio, 1994, 59). The banks were not able to carry out their inherent function to evaluate and to review the efficiency and soundness of investment projects. As a result, the financial institutions chalked up a rather poor growth performance as against the real economy.

The South Korean financial system can also be characterized by a dualistic structure, consisting of a highly controlled formal part and an uncontrolled informal part. The controlled or regulated part gave the government the means to channel large blocks of longer-term domestic and foreign financing to the export industries, whereas the uncontrolled—the curb market—facilitated efficient reallocation of finance to meet critical short-term needs. It meant that the small and medium-sized business firms could not satisfy their demand for funds through regular banking channels, but they relied heavily on the curb market with freely determined interest rates. The distortive credit allocations increased social costs in terms of creating a dualistic financial structure, retarding the nation's financial development, and weakening the internal structure of South Korean firms (Shin, 1990, 80–81). The banking industry as a whole suffered from a lack of competition and incentives.

As part of structural adjustments to improve allocative efficiency in the real sector, the Kim Young-Sam government carried out two reform efforts. They called for major reforms in the policy and institutional framework of the economy that foster openness and financial soundness. On the institutional front, the Kim Young-Sam administration dismantled the Economic Planning Board—an elite technocratic group—which had orchestrated and directed the nation's economic development strategies in an insulated political setting since the Park government—and revamped its activities under the Ministry of Finance and Economy. This change was intended to allow greater participation and openness in the policy-making process in concert with the spirit of democratization. As the political and economic decision-making circle was widened, it became increasingly difficult to coordinate policy measures among "economic" agents of the bureaucracy. The centrifugal tendencies in the bureaucratic atmosphere compounded the inter-ministerial "turf" wars. A lack of coherent economic and fiscal policies resulted in the oscillation between growth and welfare-oriented policy measures.

On the financial side, President Kim Young-Sam moved toward reforming the financial sector. He instituted a controversial "real-name deposit" system in the banking laws in concert with his campaign pledge on the fundamental financial policy reform in 1993. Under the real-name financial transaction system, the depositors were required to hold financial accounts under their true names. The practice of holding financial accounts under false names is now banned. The false-name financial system was a byproduct of the development-oriented regime under the authoritarian President Park Chung-Hee in 1961. A key strategic element in Park's economic development plan was the control of the financial sector. Its goal was to support the state-sponsored activities of investment and production. Under the Park regime, the government kept interest rates artificially low so that it could assist the government-targeted industries for economic growth and development. However, the low interest rates led to lower domestic savings. As corporate demand for cheap bank loans exceeded the available bank credit, the false-name system was introduced to attract savings by inducing money from even dubious sources to be deposited in false-name accounts. The "real-name" financial system implemented under the Kim Young-Sam government was a systematic effort to root out the corruption and activities of the "underground economy." Despite steps to increase openness, there was a legal and institutional vacuum. Supervision of banks and other financial institutions was inadequate.

Restructuring the Banking System

President D. J. Kim believes that the independence of financial sectors from government influence is one of the most urgent tasks for restoring confidence in South Korea's economy. Accordingly, the complete deregulation will allow the nation's financial institutions to manage their own affairs free from government interference. For South Korea to restore strong growth and enter into the next stage of development, the underlying causes of the crisis must be addressed. These include an unsound financial system with a poor regulatory and supervisory framework, excessive government intervention, high chaebol leverage, and weak corporate governance.

The first priority is recapitalizing and restructuring troubled financial institutions. The government has actively facilitated the processes of liquidation, consolidation, and mergers and acquisitions of several financial institutions. During the credit crunch, South Korea's merchant banks were the first to be affected by the crisis, and they experienced severe liquidity constraints and solvency problems. For instance, the government has taken significant steps to consolidate the merchant banking sector. Out of the pre-crisis number of 30 merchant banks, the 14 that remain are under close watch by the Financial Supervisory Commission (FSC). It is a new, fully integrated financial supervision body that oversees all financial activities, established in April 1998. The large banks like the South Korea First Bank and Seoul Bank were insolvent when the crisis broke, they were taken over by the government and are being offered for sale.

The focus of the restructuring and recapitalization is on the banks that failed to meet the 8 percent capital adequacy standards at the end of 1997. The removal of government control does not mean abandoning prudential regulation and adequate supervision of banks and nonbank financial institutions (NBFIs). Since the banking industry is different from the steel and auto industry because of the externalities associated with the payment system and government-guaranteed deposits, complete laissez-faire is not feasible (Caprio and Summers, 1993, 21–22). A degree of regulation and supervision is inescapable because of consumer protection, moral hazard, and systemic risk (Harris and Pigott, 1997, 34). Although the restructuring process is about to enter the final phase, it will take years for those institutions to upgrade staff and train them into such contemporary management practices as risk assessment and credit monitoring.

The lessons from financial reform experiences in recent years suggest that it is imperative that the process of financial reform be accompanied by close supervision of the banks and NBFIs to prevent fraud and circumvention of sound banking practices (OECD, 1994, 14). To that end, the government has taken several measures to ensure the FSC's operational independence and to strengthen regulation and supervision of banks. Full disclosure of connected lending (i.e., intersubsidiary loan guarantees) will be required, and limits on large exposures and bankruptcy laws have been tightened (Financial Supervisory Commission, 1998) because the existent supervisory and disclosure framework has mostly focused on compliance with rules rather than on assuring the soundness and proper management of financial institutions.

Incentives for Foreign Direct Investment

Although foreign direct investments in South Korea more than doubled over the 1996–1997 period, surpassing South Korean firms' overseas investments for the first time since 1990 (Ministry of Finance and Economy, 1998, 36), the Korea International Trade Association (KITA) has urged the presidential transition team to adopt a more positive attitude toward foreign investment and further liberalization by recognizing the importance of its role in the economy. The KITA recommended major changes in the current regulations on foreign investment and also asked the government to set up a separate agency to provide a "one-stop service" for potential foreign investors. The trade body noted that South Korea should follow in the steps of such countries as Great Britain, Ireland, and Malaysia which collectively hold 40 percent of Europe's total foreign investment by offering incentives such as financing benefits and tax breaks (Transition Committee, 1998).

President D. J. Kim's policy in this respect also reflects free market principles. Accordingly, his government intends to drastically enhance the nation's investment climate by improving administrative services and easing regulations. In concert with the new capital market liberalization policy, the government has fully opened the financial and capital markets by allowing the foreign equity ownership ceilings in the nation's stock market listed firms to rise from 55 percent by the end of 1997 to 100 percent by the end of 1998. His policy further ensures foreign investors to launch operations in South Korea on an equal footing with local enterprises. He recognizes that increasing the flow of foreign funds into South Korea is not only key to the settlement of the ongoing foreign exchange crisis but also a good business strategy for the transfer of technology. One such step is to recognize the provision of advanced technology by foreign firms as a type of investment. This measure will not only facilitate the introduction of foreign technology but also help with domestic firms by alleviating their burden to pay royalties to foreign partners. Accordingly, in the special session the South Korean National Assembly has revised the law on the establishment of free trade zones in order to grant tax incentives and special administrative services (e.g., paperwork reduction) to help foreign firms obtain permission to operate in South Korea.

The policy initiative taken by the Ministry of Information and Communication (MIC) represents the overall thrust of the South Korean government's fresh approach toward reforms. The MIC is poised to implement a set of measures to attract direct foreign investment in the domestic information technology (IT) industry. The ministry's move is aimed at acquiring advanced technology and know-how from abroad. Other plans promoted by the ministry include provision of funds to joint R&D projects between South Korean and foreign firms; expansion of tax breaks to foreign investments in selected high-tech areas; and equal treatment of foreign firms participating in domestic R&D projects as nationals. In addition, the MIC has embarked on a strategic plan to create the so-called Software Promotion Zone and to promote South Korea as a base for the Northeast Asian region by giving priority to joint ventures between South Korean and foreign software firms.

The recently liberalized capital market has drastically eased restrictions on foreign equity ownership ceilings and thus will subject many heavily debt-ridden financial and industrial enterprises to bankruptcies, mergers, swaps, and acquisitions. In this context, the government is already pushing to sell two of the nation's insolvent banks—Korea First Bank and Seoul Bank—to foreign institutions. It is believed that the foreign takeovers will provide domestic enterprises with opportunities to learn at first hand the management practices of the market economy, to upgrade services, and to increase competitiveness through direct competition with foreign rivals at home.

The past paradigm in South Korea was for banks to mobilize savings whose allocation was largely made at government behest. The government is now committed to developing a larger role for bond and equity markets to broaden the financial system. This will shift some risks away from the banking system. To be prudent, the government plans to upgrade bond and equity market infrastructure by supporting a strong credit rating agency industry and improving the disclosure requirements and dissemination of financial information by corporations.

The net effect of deregulation and the reform forces unleashed by the IMF bailout has been in the direction of rapid financial liberalization. Increasingly active foreign capital flows under the newly enacted acquisition and merger laws, the free floating exchange rate system, and the simplified foreign investment laws reflect the new policy environment.

The Labor Market Reform

As far as the dynamics of the South Korean labor market is concerned, the labor market went through the Lewisian turning point, moving from an abundant labor supply to a scarce labor supply, especially during the last three decades of rapid economic development (Lewis, 1984, 127). This labor market transition tended to increase labor mobility among firms and industries, resulting in an efficient allocation of human resources. Such a labor market transformation has several implications: the traditional style of authoritarian management is no longer effective in motivating the new workforce; wages have to be adjusted constantly to keep pace with the prevailing wages in the labor market; and workers' demands for participation in workplace decision making through collective bargaining institutions have to be accommodated.

Prior to political democratization in 1987, South Korea's labor market was principally designed to pursue an export-oriented, low wage policy, coupled with suppression of trade union activity. The new industrial relations system negotiated under the Rho government in the late 1980s has brought a sweeping liberalization of the trade union movement in South Korea. At no time in South Korea's industrial history had so many labor disputes taken place with so little government interference as in the summer of 1987. Employers were making concessions to an unprecedented degree because they could no longer look to the government for help. The most rigid labor market law governing the layoff plan came into existence during this period. The fact that there can be no layoffs without the consent of labor unions or without court approval became the major impediment to attracting foreign investment. Foreign investors have been very reluctant to come to South Korea unless they are given the legal right for layoffs.

In the wake of crisis, the social policy agenda comprised two main elements: (1) increasing the flexibility of the labor market to facilitate economic restructuring, and (2) strengthening the social safety nets to mitigate the impact of the crisis on the vulnerable. The tripartite task force in the presidential transition committee was to devise a burden-sharing "social contract" in the ongoing restructuring process. The landmark accord reached by representatives from labor, business, and the government paved the way for the National Assembly to act on one of the most controversial bits of legislation, allowing corporate layoffs during its special session. Labor leaders have accepted layoffs in return for greater labor freedom of action. Under the revised labor law, companies will be allowed to lay off workers in case of merger, acquisition, and corporate restructuring. It also requires a 60-day notice on layoffs. Trade unions are also given the right to engage in political activities and to legalize teachers' unions that had been outlawed. The government has also pledged to increase the employment stability fund (otherwise known as the unemployment fund). The enactment of the Labor Standards Act in 1998 to permit layoffs was a necessary step toward greater flexibility in the labor market.

With the enactment of relevant laws in 1998, flexible labor market policy has become a reality in order to greatly facilitate foreign direct investment into South Korea. In the process of massive economic restructuring, many heavily debt-ridden enterprises will be driven into bankruptcy or be taken over by foreign investors. Mass layoffs have already taken place. The best way to reduce the unemployment rate is to revive the economy. Since few South Korean firms are able to buy insolvent or bankrupt factories, the country must entice foreign companies to buy and operate them. But the new law is expected to facilitate business efforts to streamline their operations as well. Large conglomerates are trying job-sharing programs, reducing working hours, and redeploying staff to different assignments in a bid to minimize the side effects of massive labor layoffs.

The Privatization Process

Privatization covers a wide spectrum of different policies currently being pursued by governments around the world affecting state-owned enterprises and government monopolies. It embraces a range of alternative means by which the state enterprise sector is exposed to market forces. Methods or forms of privatization are many. The approach to state-owned enterprise (SOE) reform has evolved over time in South Korea. Until 1992, reforming SOEs largely meant the rehabilitation and restructuring of individual SOEs. Since then, a major shift has been taken toward a sectorwide approach to SOE reform, with greater emphasis placed on improving competitiveness and efficiency. In general, the shift reflects the increasing emphasis on the role of the overall policy and institutional environment in the adjustment process at the macro level. As applied to the public sector, it implies that the root causes of their poor performance lie to a large extent, in their distorted incentive structure, inappropriate institutional setup, and overextended role in economic activities.

The new president's transition team has set the direction on streamlining government-invested corporations and other public entities. The government under President D. J. Kim would not only hasten the divestiture process but has expanded the scope of privatization. Its aim is to make bloated public enterprises small, efficient, and competitive through full-scale privatization, and mergers between public entities where they have similar business functions. The annual budget for these 537 state-controlled organizations total 162 trillion won with payrolls of 410,000 employees. The task force has recommended a reduction of government employees either through a lowered retirement age by one full year or through layoffs.

In the first phase of implementation, the reform drive will focus on heightening the transparency of SOE's budget and on improving management efficiency by terminating the time-honored practice of appointing politicians, retired army generals, and high government officials. All these entities will be responsible for their own performance by reducing state subsidies drastically. Mergers of government-funded research institutes will be carried out. A synergistic effect is expected from the merger between Korea Housing Corporation and Korea Land Corporation. Much of the same is anticipated from the merger of Korea Petroleum Development Corporation and Korea Oil Pipeline Company. In some instances such as Korea Telecom, the managerial rights of public enterprises are expected to be held by the government through a proposed Korean Investment Corporation with the intent of attracting foreign investments.

In the second phase, most of such giant public corporations as Korea Tobacco and Ginseng, Korea Gas Corporation, Korea Electric Power, Korea Heavy Industries, the Korea Railway, and POSCO (the country's largest steel maker) will be sold off ahead of the original schedule of year 2002. In essence, the new president's task force recommended privatizing all but the national railroad and postal services. The task force proposals are very specific. The above exceptions are based on national needs (i.e., the result of needs analysis study) for a particular enterprise output and its strategic importance to other actors in the economy.

The ultimate goals of most privatization schemes are to incorporate some private sector management disciplines, particularly competition and efficiency, and to reduce the size of government and its deficit. At their simplest level, the goals represent the introduction of competition into the public sector by relinquishing part of the government controls. At the other end of the spectrum, privatization means the transfer of assets from state-owned enterprises to private companies or individual investors. As is the case for the financial reform, it is essential that structural and regulatory reforms be appropriately sequenced so that privatized companies operate in an environment conducive to competition. A set of competition laws and a range of industry-specific rules governing pricing and service quality are needed. The new laws and rules must be set in order to protect consumers from potential misuse of monopoly power in infrastructure sectors and to assure investors of the commercial opportunity.

THE OVERALL TRENDS

December 2000 marks three years since the government officially requested a financial bailout from the IMF. Since then, the restructuring efforts have yielded fruit, nurturing economy out of its life support and making it more adept to handle externalities. The government has pledged to privatize huge and inefficient corporations, such as Korea Electric Power, Korea Tobacco and Ginseng Corporation, and Korea Telecom. Despite modest progress in the public sector reform, the reform effort has been stymied by labor circles which oppose the privatization plan. As far as the corporate sector is concerned, it is far from being out of the woods yet.

The corporate sector is still too high relative to other countries. The debt-to-equity and interest coverage ratios (the company's ability to repay debt with earnings) have to be reduced. As companies move to focus on their core competencies, the sale or spinoff of affiliates as independent business units will become an increasingly important dimension of future corporate direction, as recently demonstrated by the restructuring plans of the nation's largest chaebol, Hyundai Group.

With regard to financial restructuring, the government has taken steps to create viable banks based on forward-looking criteria for loan classification requirements, including loans to companies in workout programs. Now it is up to the banks, under the supervision of the Financial Supervision Service, to exercise continued vigilance and ensure the preservation of asset quality.

Restructuring has forced the government, financial institutions, and corporations to rethink their basic conceptions of economic growth, as the moral hazard created by implicit guarantees and the "too big to fail" principle has been replaced by strengthened market discipline and sound economic principles. Furthermore, the South Korean government must press ahead with the reform agenda by stages. Because of unprecedented democratic and relaxed government control over the labor unions, the union movement is gaining momentum to protect the interest of workforces. Thus, labor market reform is imperative to ensure sustainable labor productivity, for this will reduce inflationary pressures and the unemployment rate in the long run. The public urged labor market trade unions to cease their opposition to the restructuring efforts because it would not be in their best interests to prolong a weak corporate sector. South Korea has set a framework for a market economy in terms of laws, regulations, and institutions. Required are changes in behavior and mindsets.

CONCLUSION

Changes in the global economy have significantly altered the context in which the South Korean economy operates. It is a transition from a fast growing economy whose development was guided and commanded by an elite corps of economic technocrats to a market economy. The price of reform is formidable in terms of the credit crunch, business failures, mass unemployment, and rising prices. The new D. J. Kim government has launched the most comprehensive structural reform and government restructuring in order to overcome the current economic woes. The government recognizes that many traditional policy instruments such as command-and-control regulations are simply not effective and are inappropriate. The policy makers have learned that inflexible and detailed regulations often conflict with other priorities, such as the need for competitive and innovative economies.

With the political leadership's strong commitment to structural reform, the government is trying to establish a new order of rule by the free market. There are many "interlocking wheels" of economic transformation. Therefore, the government likely wants to broaden the measures beyond the structural adjustments and the macroeconomic and institutional features discussed here. For example, efforts to improve education and to support agricultural research and development are critical for overall economic growth and stability. Beginning with a revamped institutional framework, reforms have changed the basic orientation of the economic environment in South Korea toward a more transparent, market-oriented, and globalized paradigm.

We have attempted to evaluate the efforts of policy reforms. The study has focused on the dynamics of the reform process that contribute to the policy and institutional changes. Since the South Korean economy is on the road to full recovery, the role of and scope of government intervention should be reappraised with a view toward fostering greater reliance on the market economy. Other (country) experiences note that an ad hoc approach or a gradual approach to reform tends to loss of proper perspectives on the part of bureaucrats and to a series of claims and counterclaims on the part of major stakeholders. Most significantly, the thrust of reform often gets stalled due to policy and institutional gaps. South Korea's comprehensive reform strategy demonstrates, however, how important "sequencing" reform is to create sound policy environments and to support a package of measures that lead to better outcomes.

NOTE

This chapter represents a revision of the earlier work by Ray W. Shin and Yeon-Seob Ha, "Political Economy of Policy Reform in Korea," published in *Policy Studies Review* 16(2) (Summer 1999): 65–97.

REFERENCES

Amsden, Alice H. (1989). *Asia's Next Giant: South Korea and Late Industrialization*. New York: Oxford University Press, p. 143.

"Appointment of Lee Hun-Jai." (1998). *Korea Herald*, March 7.

Arnold, Peri E. (1995). "Reform's Changing Role." *Public Administration Review* 55(5): 408.

Caprio, Gerard, Jr. (1994). "Banking on Financial Reform? A Case of Sensitive Dependence on Initial Conditions." In Gerard Caprio, Jr., Izak Atiyas, and Michael Hutchison, eds., *Financial Reform Theory and Experience*. Cambridge: Cambridge University Press, p. 59.

Caprio, Gerard, Jr., and Lawrence H. Summers. (1993). *Finance and Its Reform: Beyond Laissez-Faire*. World Bank Policy Research Paper No. 1171. Washington, DC: World Bank.

Cho, Yoon-Je, and Joon-Kyung Kim. (1995). *Credit Policies and the Industrialization of Korea*. World Bank Discussion Paper No. 286. Washington, DC: World Bank.

Chung, Chung-Kil, and Jong S. Jun. (1991). "The Irony of Cutback Reform: The Korean Experience during a Period of Turbulent Transition." *International Review of Administrative Sciences* 57(1): 46–47.

Financial Supervisory Commission (FSC). (1998). *The Report: November 9*. Seoul: FSC.

Greenspan, Alan. (1998). Congressional Testimony before the House Banking Committee, January 30, 1998. *Wall Street Journal*, February 2.

Ha, Yen-Seob. (1993). "State Intervention, Fiscal Policy, and Industrialization in Korea." In Kwang-Woong Kim and Yong-Duck Jung, eds., *Korean Public Administration and Policy in Transition*. Seoul: KAPA, pp. 55–56.

Haggard, Stephan. (1990). *Pathways from the Periphery*. Ithaca, NY: Cornell University Press, pp. 64–65.

Harris, L. Stephen, and Charles H. Pigott. (1997). "Regulatory Reform in the Financial Services Industry: Where Have We Been? Where Are We Going?" *Financial Market Trends* (June):34.

International Monetary Fund (IMF). (1997). "Request for Stand-by Arrangement." In *IMF Document: Report 1*. Washington, DC: IMF.

Julius, DeAnne. (1990). *Global Companies and Public Policy*. London: Royal Institute of International Affairs.

Kim, Yoon-Hyung. (1994). "An Introduction to the Korean Model of Political Economy." In Lee-Jay Cho and Yoon-Hyung Kim, eds., *Korea's Political Economy*. Boulder, CO: Westview Press, p. 117.

Klitgaard, Robert. (1995). "Comment on Incentives, Rules of the Game, and Development, by Elinor Ostrom." In Michael Bruno and Boris Pleskovic, eds., *Annual World Bank Conference on Development Economics*. Washington, DC: World Bank, p. 238.

Korea International Trade Association (KITA). (1998). *KITA Weekly*, February 2.

Lewis, Arthur W. (1984). "Development Economics in the 1950s." In Gerald M. Meir and Dudley Seers, eds., *Pioneers in Development*. Oxford: Oxford University Press, p. 127.

Luedde-Neurath, Richard. (1988). "State Intervention and Export-Oriented Development in Korea." In Gordon White, ed., *Developmental States in East Asia*. New York: St. Martin's Press, p. 94.

Ministry of Finance and Economy. (1998). "Financial Crisis." Report prepared for the presidential transitional team, Seoul, February 5, p. 5.

National Assembly of Korea. (1997). *The Annual Assembly Record*. Seoul: National Assembly of Korea.

Organization for Economic Cooperation and Development (OECD) Report. (1994). *Assessing Structural Reform: Lessons for the Future*. Paris: OECD.

Organization for Economic Cooperation and Development (OECD) Report. (1997). *Regulatory Reform*. Paris: OECD.

Shin, Roy W. (1990). "The Paradox of Privatization: The Case of Korean Commercial Banks." *International Review of Administrative Sciences* 56(1): 80–81.

Transition Committee (The New President's). (1998). *Report* (also known as *The White Paper*). Seoul: Government of Korea.

Vittas, Dimitri, and Yoon-Je Cho. (1996). "Credit Policies: Lessons from Japan and Korea." *Research Observer* 11(2) (Washington, DC: World Bank): 287–288.

Chapter 5

Managing Economic Development in Taiwan

Kuotsai Tom Liou

INTRODUCTION

Economic development in Taiwan in the postwar period has been recognized as one of the few success stories among many developing countries. For the past five decades, Taiwan has achieved one of the highest and most sustained growth rates worldwide in gross national product (GNP) and in international trades. In addition, Taiwan has also performed very well (better than many industrializing countries and several developed countries) in its efforts to control inflation and prices, maintain full employment, and balance income distribution (e.g., Li, 1995; Kuo, Ranis, and Fei, 1981).

The success of Taiwan's development has attracted attention from both policy makers and researchers on the study of its development model and strategies. For policymakers of developing (and economic-transition) countries, an understanding of Taiwan's development experience is valuable because it may help them prepare or formulate various development policies, programs, and strategies to promote the economic development in their countries. For researchers of economic development, the analysis of Taiwan's development experience provides good opportunities for them to examine the strengths and weaknesses of the development records, test and verify important development theories and models, and draw some lessons and conclusions for further theory advancement.

The study of Taiwan's economic development experience has recently become even more attractive because of the impact of Taiwan's political democratization and the experience of the 1997 Asian financial crisis. Although Taiwan's political democratization process started in the 1970s and accelerated in the 1980s, major political and policy changes occurred after the election of Lee Teng-hui as president in 1990. The process developed included such issues as the power struggle within the Kuomingtang (KMT) factions (the mainstream versus the nonmainstream), the communication and competition between the KMT and the Democratic Progressive party (DPP), the first popular presidential election in 1996 (Lee was elected), and the revision of the constitution in 1997. The political changes further brought the KMT's ruling to an end when the DPP candidate, Chen Shui-Bian, won Taiwan's presidential election in 2000.

On the issue of the Asian financial crisis, Taiwan has experienced relatively fewer negative effects than those of other Asian countries when comparing their economic and financial performance. While showing slowdowns in international trades (especially trades with Asian countries) and depreciation of Taiwan currency, the overall macroeconomic conditions (growth rate, inflation, and unemployment rate) have been rather good, again if we compare the data with those of other Asian countries. It seems that the Taiwan government has achieved another miracle in dealing with the financial crisis. The study of Taiwan's economic development policies and programs may offer information to researchers who are interested in understanding the unique case and experience in Taiwan.

Emphasizing the importance of managing economic development, this chapter examines Taiwan's economic development from the following perspectives. First, the chapter provides an overview of Taiwan's economic development records and an analysis of major economic indicators during the period 1952–1990. Next, the author identifies major policies and factors that contribute to Taiwan's economic development. Third, focusing on recent changes and challenges, the chapter examines Taiwan's economic transformation policies, political reform issues, and the Asian financial crisis. The implications of these changes and challenges are addressed in the concluding section of this chapter.

ECONOMIC DEVELOPMENT RECORD

An examination of Taiwan's economic development record begins with a brief review of its natural setting and related conditions. Taiwan's natural resources are not impressive for a consideration of development. For example, the size of Taiwan, calculated at the time of full tide, is about 36,000 square kilometers (35,961.2 square kilometers of land area and 38.8 square kilometers of reclamation). In addition, within this small land, two-thirds of Taiwan is mountainous, and only about one-fourth of it is considered cultivated land. The nation's natural resources are unimpressive, including few mineral resources, less fertile soil, depleted fishing sources, and limited logging. Closely related to the limitations of the land and its resources, the government of Taiwan also faces the challenging problem of its population size. It was estimated that in 1995 the population was about

Table 5.1
Economic Growth in Taiwan: Growth of Gross National Product,
1952–1990 (selected years)

Year	GNP Amount (U.S.$ million)	GNP Per Capita (U.S.$)	GNP Growth Rate (%)
1952	1,674	196	12.0
1955	1,928	203	8.1
1960	1,717	154	6.4
1965	2,811	217	11.0
1970	5,660	389	11.3
1975	15,429	964	4.4
1980	41,360	2,344	7.1
1985	63,097	3,297	5.6
1990	160,913	8,111	5.0

Source: Li (1995), 269.

21.3 million, with a population density of more than 591 people per square kilometer.[1]

Despite its resource limitations, Taiwan has successfully improved every aspect of economic conditions during the postwar period. The current examination of economic performance focuses on analysis of major economic indicators during the period 1952–1990.[2] The year 1952 was selected as the beginning study year because most researchers recognize 1952 as a benchmark year for Taiwan's economic recovery (after a decade of war and political and economic disorder) (Ho, 1978; Kuo et al., 1981). The economic indicators selected include data representing economic growth, population and unemployment growth rates, consumer prices, economic structures of agriculture, industry, and service, and foreign trade.

First, Table 5.1 provides selected data on Taiwan's gross national product (GNP) during the period 1952–1990, including total GNP, per capita GNP, and real growth rates. The data reveal that during the 38-year period the amount of GNP increased by more than 96 times, from 1,674 million in 1952 to more than 160 billion U.S. dollars in 1990. Per capita GNP figures rose from US$196 in 1952 to more than US$8,000 in 1990, an increase of about 46 times. Most significantly, the calculated annual real growth rate of GNP during this 38-year period achieved an average rate of 8.9 percent. Though not listed in Table 5.1, the real growth rate ranged from the lowest of 1.2 percent in 1974 to the highest of 14.0 percent in 1978. The GNP data indicate that Taiwan's economic growth was indeed very impressive.

Next, along with sustained and strong growth rates, Taiwan's excellent economic performance was also found in the analysis of its population

Table 5.2
Economic Stability in Taiwan: Growth Rate of Population, Unemployment, and
Consumer Prices, 1952–1990 (selected years)

Year	Population Growth (%)	Unemployment Rate (%)	Consumer Price (%)
1952	3.3	4.4	–
1955	3.8	3.8	9.9
1960	3.5	4.0	18.5
1965	3.3	3.3	–0.1
1970	2.4	1.7	3.6
1975	1.9	2.4	5.2
1980	1.9	1.2	19.0
1985	1.3	2.9	–0.2
1990	1.2	1.7	4.1

Source: Li (1995), 269–270.

growth, unemployment, and price rates. The data on these economic indicators are summarized in Table 5.2. During the period 1952–1990, Taiwan's population growth rates maintained an average annual increase of
2.3 percent, reduced from the rate of 3.67 percent in 1952 to a rate of 1.13
percent in 1990. The success of the government's population control policy
is evident in the smaller than 2 percent of annual increase rates after the
mid-1970s. During the same period, Taiwan's unemployment rates maintained an average rate of 2.6 percent, with the rates dropping from 4.4
percent in 1952 to 1.7 percent in 1990. Based on data of the annual increase of consumer prices, the annual increases of the inflation rate in Taiwan, during the period 1953–1990, averaged 6.7 percent. Again, Taiwan's
records on the control of population growth, unemployment, and inflation
rates are very impressive and indicate the success of the government's effort
to maintain economic stability.

In addition to the record of strong economic growth and stable economic
conditions, Taiwan's development experience has also resulted in changes
in its economic structure and sectors. Based on the data for gross domestic
product (GDP), Table 5.3 shows percentage changes in Taiwan's agriculture, industry, and service sectors during the period 1952–1990. The shares
of the agricultural sector in the GDP dropped continuously, from more
than 30 percent in 1952 to about 4 percent in 1990. On the other hand,
the shares of the industry sector in the GDP doubled during this period,
increasing from about 20 percent in 1952 to about 43 percent in 1990.
The shares of the service sector in the GDP showed small increases from
about 48 percent in 1952 to more than 53 percent in 1990. Clearly, the
economic development policy has successfully changed the composition of

Table 5.3
Economic Structure in Taiwan: Changes of Agriculture, Industry, and Service
Sectors, 1952–1990 (selected years)

Year	GDP (NT$ million)	Agriculture (% of GDP)	Industry (% of GDP)	Service (% of GDP)
1952	17,251	32.2	19.7	48.1
1955	29,981	29.1	23.2	47.7
1960	62,507	28.5	26.9	44.6
1965	112,627	23.6	30.2	46.2
1970	226,805	15.5	36.8	47.7
1975	589,651	12.7	39.9	47.4
1980	1,491,059	7.7	45.7	46.6
1985	2,473,786	5.8	46.3	47.9
1990	4,307,043	4.1	42.5	53.4

Source: Li (1995), 271.

Table 5.4
Foreign Trade in Taiwan: Exports, Imports, and Balance, 1952–1990, in U.S.$
million (selected years)

Year	Exports	Imports	Balance
1952	119	205	−86
1955	123	201	−78
1960	164	297	−133
1965	450	556	−106
1970	1,481	1,524	−43
1975	5,309	5,952	−643
1980	19,811	19,733	+78
1985	30,726	20,102	+10,624
1990	67,214	54,716	+12,498

Source: Li (1995), 270.

Taiwan's economic structure, especially in the case of gradually moving
from an agriculture-oriented to a more industry-oriented society.

With regard to Taiwan's external economic condition and relationship,
Table 5.4 lists international trade data of export, import, and balance.
Based on the customs statistics, Taiwan's exports increased from US$119
million in 1952 to more than $67 billion in 1990, an increase of 565 times.
The imports also increased from US$205 million in 1952 to more than $54
billion in 1990, an increase of 367 times. Associated with the increases in

Table 5.5
Equity Indexes of Income Distribution, 1964–1990 (selected years)

Year	Gini Coefficient	The Top 20%/ the Bottom 20%
1964	0.321	5.33
1968	0.326	5.28
1970	0.294	4.58
1980	0.277	4.17
1981	0.281	4.21
1982	0.283	4.29
1983	0.287	4.36
1984	0.287	4.40
1985	0.290	4.50
1986	0.296	4.60
1987	0.299	4.69
1988	0.303	4.85
1989	0.303	4.94
1990	–	5.18

Sources: Lan and Wang (1991), 7; Li (1995), 271.

exports and imports, Taiwan has changed from a trade-deficit situation to a trade-surplus status. In fact, Taiwan continuously enjoyed a trade surplus in the late 1970s and the 1980s. By 1990, the trade surplus reached more than US$12 billion.

Finally, the examination of Taiwan's economic performance records focuses on the issue of income distribution because many researchers indicate that Taiwan's development shows a special pattern of "growth with equity" (Fei et al., 1979). Table 5.5 presents two equity indices of Taiwan's income distribution in selected years: the Gini coefficient and the ratio of the top 20 percent income to the bottom 20 percent. The Gini coefficients dropped from 0.32 in the 1960s to 0.28 in the early 1980s and rose to more than 0.30 in the late 1980s.

The calculated ratios reveal a similar trend of income distribution. The income distribution ratio was 5.33 in 1964 and dropped to 4.17 in 1980, increasing to 5.18 in 1990. The data here indicate that Taiwan indeed achieved a record of sustained growth with improved income distribution during its development years, and that the income gap between rich and poor has gradually increased since the late 1980s.

In sum, the examination of Taiwan's major economic indicators reveals outstanding records of economic development, including strong and sustained growth rates; low and stable unemployment and inflation rates;

changes of economic structure and international trade situations; and an improved income gap in the society.

FACTORS CONTRIBUTING TO ECONOMIC DEVELOPMENT

After examining the past economic performance, this section focuses on identifying the major factors that contribute to Taiwan's outstanding economic development. Researchers of economic development in Taiwan have suggested several factors that are important to Taiwan's postwar development (Dahlman and Sananikone, 1997; Ho, 1978; Kuo et al., 1981; Li, 1995; Lan and Wang, 1991). For the purpose of this book, the present study provides an analysis of these factors based on two categories—general background and supporting conditions—as well as government-related policies and programs. The success of Taiwan's development is based on the combination and interaction of factors in both categories.

General Background and Supporting Conditions

The general background and supporting conditions of Taiwan's postwar economic development include at least four factors: (1) the investment of the Japanese occupation forces during the colonial period 1895–1945; (2) human capital resources in the society; (3) the international economic environment, especially aid from the United States; and (4) the impact of the traditional culture.

First, the investment of the Japanese occupation forces during the colonial period 1895–1945 laid some foundations for later development. To support its own economy at home, the Japanese colonial government established a well-organized infrastructure system for Taiwan, including roads, railroads, airports, harbors, electricity, and water systems. In addition, they provided other services such as public health (e.g., sewage construction, sanitation services, and vaccination programs) and public education systems. Although most of the infrastructure components were destroyed by the Allied bombing during World War II, the education system was critical to Taiwan's development because many of the postwar Taiwanese leaders were educated and influenced by the Japanese system. They learned of Japan's economic development and later adopted many ideas from the Japanese system to establish their own business policies which contributed to Taiwan's development.

The second factor contributing to Taiwan's earlier development has to do with the importance of human resources in Taiwan's society. As explained previously, the legacy of the Japanese colonial education system produced many postwar Taiwanese business entrepreneurs and improved

basic education to the general public, which provided educated human resources for economic development. But it has been generally recognized
and agreed that the influx of refugees from Mainland China during 1949–
1951 provided additional valuable resources for Taiwan's economic recovery. Being defeated by the Communist party, the Nationalist government
retreated to Taiwan and added more than 1.6 million people to Taiwan.
Many of the refugees were trained and experienced professionals, including
government employees, engineers, teachers, technicians, and businessmen.
They brought with them not only the needed administrative skills but also
the financial resources to establish new businesses, and they employed local
workers to contribute to Taiwan's development.

In addition, the international economic environment has been critical to
the success of Taiwan's economic development. This is especially related to
the role U.S. aid played in Taiwan's early development. The outbreak of
the Korean War in June 1950 resulted in the U.S. government's renewed
policy of commitment to military and economic aid to Taiwan. U.S. aid
helped the government rebuild morale and confidence among the public on
the one hand and alleviated the shortage of investment capital (because of
the heavy defense spending) on the other. U.S. aid equaled about 6 percent
of GNP and accounted for more than 40 percent of capital formation in
the 1950s, which not only strengthened Taiwan's economy but also laid
the foundations for implementing several development policies.

Finally, it is important to recognize the impact of traditional Chinese
culture on Taiwan's development. The cultural factor refers to the teachings
of Confucianism, such as loyalty, hard work, thrift, discipline, learning,
and education, which promote positive work values, attitudes, and behavior. The Taiwanese people, including the local Taiwanese and the immigrants from Mainland China, are influenced by the same traditional culture
and share similar social and work ethics. They are eager to learn new
knowledge and skills; they want to work hard to support their family; they
show great respect for the law, public officials, and business owners; and
they emphasize saving for a rainy day or for the development of their own
business. All of these values and ethics have contributed to the overall social
and economic development of Taiwan.

Economic Development Policies and Activities

The existence and support of the generally favorable factors and conditions, as discussed previously, should not be considered a guarantee or
assurance of the success of economic development. Discussion of these factors does not explain the full story of Taiwan's development. For example,
the factors of Japanese investment and U.S. aid are important but are not
limited to Taiwan's situation. Similar factors also existed in the Philippines
during the postwar period, which experienced some problems in its devel-

opment. In addition, the factor of Confucian teachings is shared by the people in Communist China, which suffered economic loss and disasters during the Maoist time.

The successful experience in Taiwan results from the capacity of the Taiwanese government to manage economic development. Four important factors relate to governmental activities: (1) national development policies; (2) the open economic system; (3) the capabilities of public (especially economic) administration; and (4) a stable political and social environment. Whereas the first two factors refer to Taiwan's general economic policy and programs, the last two are related to its political and institutional activities.

First, the Nationalist government formulated and implemented several development policies and programs to promote economic development and to change economic structures. Following the Japanese development experience, the government emphasized the adoption of a model multiyear economic plan to achieve development goals. Between 1952 and 1989, the government implemented eight four-year plans and one six-year plan, which helped transform Taiwan's economic system from colonial agricultural development (before 1950s), import-substitution development (1950–1962), and export promotion development (1962–1980) to accelerated liberalization development (after 1980).[3]

Within these plans, the government had established several development institutions and implemented several policy measures to promote economic development. The development institutions started with the Economic Stabilization Board and Council for U.S. Aid in the 1950s, moved to the Council for International Economic Cooperation and Development in the 1960s, and went to the Economic Planning Council and Council for Economic Planning and Development in the 1970s. The policy measures ranged from land reform to changes of fiscal policy (e.g., tax collection system, investment encouragement programs), to changes of monetary policy (e.g., interest rate policy, foreign exchange management, regulation of banking, insurance, and securities), to reforms of population and manpower policies (e.g., family planning, vocational training) (Li, 1995).

Next, recognizing the country's resource limitations, the government emphasized an open economic system for the purpose of promoting foreign trade to lead to economic development. Immediately after the earlier phase of import restraints for the protection of local industries, the government moved in the direction of export promotion and implemented many policy measures to encourage foreign and overseas Chinese investment. The policy measures introduced included, for example, amendments of the Statute for the Encouragement of Investment, revisions of the income tax law, amendments of customs duties rebate system, and import liberalization and tariff reduction.

One of the key measures emphasized in this export-oriented development policy is the creation of export processing zones. The purposes of export processing zones are (1) to reduce governmental red tape by introducing an integrated and simplified administration to encourage foreign investment and (2) to utilize low-cost labor and duty-free imports (for machinery, parts, and raw materials) by emphasizing production for export to promote employment and earn foreign exchanges (Li, 1995). The first export processing zone was developed at Kaohsiung Harbor in 1966, and two additional zones were developed at Nantze and Taichung in 1971. It is estimated that the cumulative investment in these zones reached more than US$886 million and approximately 6 percent of foreign investment for the period 1966–1991 (Li, 1995, 165). The experience of export processing zones also contributed to the later development of the Hsinchu Science-Based Industrial Park in 1980 when the development policy shifted to high-technology industrialization.

The third government-related factor that contributes to economic development is the capability of Taiwan's administrative system. The contribution of the administrative system, especially the economic administration system, can be analyzed from three aspects: political leaders, economic administrators, and general public employees. Suffering failure in Mainland China after World War II, the political leaders in Taiwan, Chiang Kai-shek and Chian Ching-Kuo, recognized the importance of economic and social stability in their governments. Both leaders relied on experts in economic and financial policy and appointed several loyal administrators to be in charge of economic development activities, with few interventions. The economic administrators, including such talented and diligent people as Chia-kan Yen, Yun-suan Sun, and Kuo-ting Lee, were not only loyal to the political leaders but also very practical in their approach to economic development policies and programs.

In addition to the leadership, the capability and contribution of general public employees cannot be overlooked. As explained earlier, human resources are important to Taiwan's development. The bureaucracy and party organization, brought to Taiwan by the Nationalist government in the late 1950s, and the quality of local people contributed to the establishment of a relatively sophisticated and capable administrative system. These general public employees occupied the middle and low levels of the administrative system and contributed to the implementation of many development policies and programs. The quality and loyalty of government employees remained high later when the government established a civil service system and recruited many talented college graduates through competitive national examinations.

Finally, the success of Taiwan's development has to do with the stable political and social environment of the development period. From 1950 to 1980, there were no major political and social events to challenge the political authority and disrupt the social order. The achievement of a stable environment, however, resulted from the Kuomingtang's (KMT) one-party control. The KMT is modeled on Lenin's Bolshevik party and is responsible for determining policy. In other words, the KMT sets up parallel party organizations at all levels of government and approves all major government decisions on policy and personnel issues. The KMT membership also organized itself in party cells in the government (and the military) organizations and played a supervisory role in policy implementation. Most public employees needed to become KMT members to be able to keep a position or to have opportunities for promotion.

Both Chiang Kai-shek and Chian Ching-Kuo served concurrently as president of the government and as chairman of the KMT, respectively. In addition, they also enjoyed broad powers based on a system of martial law, from a revision of the 1946 Constitution. These powers, enforced by the military under the Taiwan Garrison Command, bestowed the right to restrict freedom of assembly, free expression, and political activities. While achieving political and social stability, control of the KMT has resulted in tension between mainlanders and the Taiwanese. This is because a small group of the mainland political elite dominated the KMT and the political system, excluding the Taiwanese from positions of authority in the government.

RECENT CHANGES AND CHALLENGES

The general environment of Taiwan's economic development has changed significantly since the 1980s. Several new issues have emerged as major concerns for policy makers. This section focuses on three major issues that have dominated the policy-making process and may challenge Taiwan's future development. The three interrelated issues are changes in economic transformation policies, the development of political reforms, and the impact of the Asian financial crisis.

Economic Transformation Policy

Since the 1980s, policy makers in Taiwan have emphasized a "liberalization and internationalization" policy for the goals of transforming the economic system and improving the macroeconomic conditions (Li, 1995). The term *liberalization* represents both the reduction of government control and regulation in economic spheres and the gradual elimination of state subsidies to manufacturers. The term *internationalization* means the opening of the Taiwanese market to foreign businesses without undue restrictions to allow for full foreign competition (Lu, 1985).

The goal of the economic transformation represents Taiwan's intention to replace its labor-intensive industries with technology-intensive or capital-intensive industries. Closely related to the economic transformation, the goal of improving Taiwan's macroeconomic conditions attempts to address economic problems such as the shortage of labor in several industries (e.g., construction and manufacturing), the imbalances between exports and imports (e.g., trade surplus with the United States and trade deficit with Japan), the inflationary pressure in the late 1980s (related to the high savings rate and the overheated stock market), and the declining quality of life (e.g., rising crime rates, environmental problems) (Lan and Wang, 1991).

In the 1990s, the Taiwan government emphasized several policies to cope with changes and set new priorities. The government introduced a Six-Year National Development Plan in 1991 for the purpose of strengthening and upgrading its basic infrastructure. In 1994, the government identified and assigned top priority to the implementation of Twelve Major Construction Projects to cover such issues as transportation, culture and education, and improvement of living conditions. In 1997, the government introduced a Plan for National Development into the Next Century (1997–2000) to cover three areas: strengthening national competitiveness, improving the quality of life, and promoting sustainable development. In addition, the government was also interested in developing Taiwan as an Asia-Pacific Regional Operations Center.

One example of the liberalization aspect of the new economic policy is the privatization of state-owned enterprises (SOEs) (Liou, 1992). The major economic reason for privatizing SOEs is based on the argument that SOEs are inefficient and unprofitable when compared with the private sector. Since the early 1980s, the Ministry of Economic Affairs in Taiwan has decided to merge or shut down several enterprises in the face of continuing losses (e.g., Taiwan Alkali Co., China Coal-Mining Developing Co., and the Taiwan Metal Mining Co.). Similarly, the Taiwanese government has also determined to privatize all commercial and other special-purpose banks to reduce past government or government-dominated (in terms of public-private joint) ownerships and establish private banks and financial institutions to promote the development of the capital industry. The Legislative Yuan of Taiwan finally passed the SOE Privatization Act on June 4, 1991.

One good example of the internationalization aspect of the economic policy has been the increasing foreign (outward) investment since the 1980s. The increases in foreign investment generally include two types: (1) the outflow of capital investment (e.g., in the real estate industry) to developed countries such as the United States, Canada, and Australia and (2) the direct investment in developing countries such as the ASEAN (Association of Southeast Asian Nations) and Mainland China (Lan and Wang, 1991). The second type of direct investment is especially important to Taiwan's economic development because of its policy implications. In the past, the major motive for Taiwan's outward and foreign investment was export facilitation. For example, to facilitate the export of various products, Taiwan's firms were involved in direct investment in the U.S. electrical and electronics industry. But since the mid-1980s, one of the top reasons for outward investments has been the acquisition of cheap labor because of the increased labor cost in Taiwan. In his studies of Taiwan's economic role in East Asia, Chi indicated that the index of Taiwan's unit labor cost almost doubled from 1982 to 1991, which is higher than that of Taiwan's neighboring countries (Japan and South Korea) (Chi, 1995).

One of the outcomes of this outward investment is the increase in Taiwan's investment in the ASEAN countries (and Vietnam) and Mainland China. Investment in the ASEAN focuses on such industries as textiles, electronic and electrical products, rubber, and plastic products. Based on investment data approved by host countries during 1959–1993, Chi showed the importance of Taiwan's investment by ranking Taiwan's investment among all investing countries: first in Vietnam, second in Malaysia (next to Japan), third in Indonesia (next to Japan and Hong Kong), fourth in Thailand (next to Japan, Hong Kong, and the United States), and fifth in the Philippines (next to the United States, Japan, Hong Kong, and the United Kingdom) (Chi, 1995).

Taiwan's investment in Mainland China has been closely related to its cross-strait policy. Before 1979, Taiwan and the mainland engaged in several military and political conflicts, and there were no economic or cultural contacts between the two sides. After China's economic reform and open door policy in the late 1970s, there were indirect business contacts (i.e., small trades through Hong Kong) between the two sides. The economic interaction between Taiwan and Mainland China has grown rapidly since October 1987 when the KMT government lifted a ban on visits by Taiwanese residents to the mainland (Chi, 1995; Deng, 2000; Leng, 1996; Li, 1995). In 1995, China replaced the United States as Taiwan's most important export country. In 1997, the total trade with China reached its highest level to date at $26.36 billion, which was approximately 10.3 percent of Taiwan's total trade. On the investment side, the amount of Taiwanese investment approved by China had reached approximately $41.11 billion by 1998. (The total amount is difficult to estimate due to the indirect nature of the investment.)

Political Reforms and Issues

In addition to changes in economic transformation, Taiwan has also experienced the development of a political democratization movement since the 1980s. A discussion of the political reforms is necessary and important to understand Taiwan's recent economic development because of the close relationship and interaction between the two. On the one hand, the success of economic development has resulted in increased numbers of middle-class citizens in Taiwan's society who are concerned about issues related not only to economic prosperity but also to social justice and political freedom. The development of political democratization, on the other hand, has brought many changes in Taiwan's society, including issues related to different outcomes of resources distribution and arguments about the process and methods of distribution.

As previously discussed in the section on Taiwan's governmental activities, the KMT under Chiang Kai-shek and Chian Ching-kuo totally controlled Taiwan's political and social development for four decades (1945–1985). The total control of the KMT contributed to Taiwan's economic development in terms of providing an effective party-oriented administrative system and a stable political and social environment. The cost of this control was at the expense of social and ideological development as well as the limitation of individual freedom and political participation. The mechanisms of this control are based on the implementation of martial law and the use of propaganda of political and nationalist ideology.

Taiwan's political democratization process started gradually in the 1970s. Democratization activities during this period included the introduction of supplementary national elections for fixed terms on a small quota basis for the Legislative Yuan, the Control Yuan, and the National Assembly (to replace many national representatives who either had died or retired); the succession of Chiang Ching-kuo as president in 1975; the recruitment of many ethnic Taiwanese in the party and government; the appearance of several antigovernment journals (which had been closed frequently); the emergence of young *tang-wai* (outside the ruling party) politicians; and the organization of political demonstration. These earlier democratization activities, however, were considered small and limited in terms of both their scale and impact.

The political democratization process accelerated in the 1980s. Major activities that occurred were the selection of Lee Teng-hui (a Taiwanese technocrat) as vice president in 1984; the KMT scandals (the assassination of Chiang Nan and the bankruptcy of Taipei's Tenth Credit Cooperative) in 1984–1985; the establishment of the Democratic Progressive Party (DPP) in 1986; the lifting of martial law in 1987; the deregulation of the press; the permission for Taiwan citizens to visit their relatives on the mainland (and for specified groups of people from the mainland to visit Taiwan); the legalization of Taiwan-mainland indirect trade, and the death of Chiang Ching-kuo and the succession of Lee Teng-hui in 1988.

The political democratization process continued after the election of Lee as president in 1990. Issues emphasized in the political arena included the power struggle within the KMT factions (the mainstream versus the non-mainstream); the communication between the KMT and the DPP; the conference on political reform; and the official evaluation and apology for the government's actions in the Taiwan Uprising on February 28, 1947; and the first popular presidential election in 1996 (Lee was elected). In 1997, the KMT and DPP worked together to revise the constitution. The major revisions, based on suggestions from the National Development Conference, include, for example, the clarification of the relationship among the president, the premier, and the legislature, and the streamlining of the functions of the Taiwan provincial government.[4] These revisions brought further changes in Taiwan's political arena and power struggles within the KMT.

The political reform and democratization reached the highest point in the March 2000 presidential election. Chen Shui-bina, the DPP candidate and the former mayor of Taipei, won the presidential election by defeating two major candidates: Lien Chan, the KMT candidate and President Lee's vice president, and James Soong, the former governor of Taiwan Province (who became an independent candidate after the KMT expelled him). The victory of President Chen not only ended five decades of KMT rule in Taiwan but also brought many policy changes to Taiwan's future development. Two issues may be especially important to economic development. First, the business relationship between Taiwan and Mainland China needs to be clarified. The KMT regime adopted a patience-over-haste (*jieji yongre*) investment policy to restrict Taiwan's trade with and investment in China for the purpose of protecting Taiwan's own economic growth and national security. This restriction policy, however, has experienced growing resistance and demand for changes over the years due to the changes in Taiwan's economic environment (e.g., the rising labor cost and the appreciation of the New Taiwan dollar). The second issue of concern is President Chen's position on Taiwan's fourth nuclear power plant. The $6 billion power plant has been the subject of controversy for years. The power plant project was supported by the KMT and the state utility Taiwan Power for its importance to Taiwan's energy needs. Concern over power needs became even more serious after the 1999 earthquake when the high-tech industry lost electricity supplies for several weeks. The problem here is that President Chen and his party (DPP) have opposed the nuclear power plant project because of the concern about the safety of nuclear power. President Chen pledged to halt construction during the election campaign, despite the more than $3 billion already spent or contracted. The challenge for the government is to find a balance between the arguments for power needs and environmental concerns and political support.

The Impact of the Asian Financial Crisis

The Asian financial crisis was first noticed in Thailand in June 1997 and later spread quickly to other neighboring countries (especially Indonesia, Malaysia, and South Korea). Currency and equity markets in these countries had experienced huge falls during the second half of 1997 (Goldstein, 1998). For example, exchange rates between U.S. dollars and local currency dropped approximately 49 percent in Thailand, 35 percent in Malaysia, 44 percent in Indonesia, and 48 percent in Korea. The stock markets in these countries also reported huge drops—approximately 29 percent in Thailand, 45 percent in Malaysia, 45 percent in Indonesia, and 50 percent in South Korea. The Asian financial crisis was further spilled over into other vulnerable countries (Russia and Brazil) and affected the financial markets of many developed countries. This section examines the causes of the financial crisis and the impact of the crisis on Taiwan.

Several interrelated domestic and external factors contributed to the financial crisis in Thailand and other countries. For example, some studies (Fisher, 1998; Goldstein, 1998; IMF, 1998) point out that these countries experienced overheating pressures that were related to large external deficits and inflated property and stock market values. The prolonged maintenance of a pegged exchange rate in these countries also encouraged external borrowing, which led to excessive exposure to foreign exchange risk. Moreover, the lack of effective banking and financial sector supervision led to bad lending practices (e.g., lending to bank directors, managers, and their related businesses) and deteriorations in the quality of the banks' loans. These domestic problems worsened because of such external factors as the wide swings of the yen–dollar exchange rate in the mid-1990s and the increase of international investors in these countries due to the weak growth at home and perceived investment opportunities in Asian countries. These investors did not examine the realistic risks involved, for they were blinded by the past strong growth in these countries on the one hand and did not have enough reliable data on the other hand.

The financial crisis has also had some effects on Taiwan's financial markets and economic condition. On the currency and equity market, Taiwan experienced relatively less negative impact when comparing Taiwan's exchange rate and stock market with those of the four countries (Thailand, Indonesia, Malaysia, and South Korea) examined previously. For example, during the second half of 1997, the exchange rate between U.S. dollars and Taiwan dollars underwent a negative change of about 15 percent, while the stock market in Taiwan also fell 9 percent. The major negative effect appeared to be the huge fall in international trade, especially trades with Asian countries. Affected by the 1997 Asian crisis, Taiwan's exports and imports in 1998 had declined by 9.42 percent and 8.53 percent, respectively. The fall of exports was especially high among Asian countries. For example, exports to Southeast Asia dropped by 29.7 percent to Japan (−20 percent), and even Hong Kong and China (−13.4 percent) slumped dramatically.

Many factors contributed to the low or small negative effects of the financial crisis (Chi, 1999). First, a series of financial liberalization policies has been implemented since the late 1970s. These include the implementation of floating an exchange rate regime in 1979, the abolishment of limits on interest rate change in 1989, the lift of the ban on establishing new banks in 1990, the opening of a capital market to foreigners after 1983, and the expansion and improvement of stock and money markets. The outcome of Taiwan's balanced approach and financial liberalization is the small gap between lending and deposit rates and the high ratio of the capital adequacy. In addition, the development of Taiwan's small and medium enterprises (SMEs) has contributed to Taiwan's comparative advantage in terms of high efficiency and flexibility in a competitive market. On the one hand, the large numbers of SMEs has freed Taiwan from the dominance of influential large companies. On the other hand, the SMEs have created an efficient industrial clustering by forming a comprehensive horizontal and vertical networking of industry through cooperation and division of labor among themselves and/or with large enterprises.

Despite these positive factors, the Taiwan government recognized several weaknesses associated with different steps of financial liberalization. For example, the government noticed inadequacy in supervision of financial institutions in high-risk projects and poor investment quality, lack of full investigative authority to examine malpractice in asset management, lack of market information transparency, insufficient liabilities and criminal punishment for violations of fiduciary rules by board directors and supervisors, and inadequate regulations in dealing with such corporate financial problems such as over-rapid expansion, investment concentration on real estates, highly speculative investment, and boosting equity far above the true value (Chi, 1999).

To deal with the financial crisis, the Taiwan government has intervened in the financial market and proposed new domestic development policies ("Chiu Keeps His Ship Steady," 1998). With its huge foreign exchange reserve (approximately $84.5 billion in 1997), Taiwan's central bank has the ability (not just the will) to step in the market to stabilize the currency in cases of speculation or unexpected shocks. On the stock market, the government also formulated policies to stimulate stock prices during the crisis by investing government funds (pension funds, postal savings, social security funds) in the market. To boost the domestic economy, the government has increased its investment for public works to a total of US$5.58 billion for both FY 1999 and FY 2000. These include, for example, the high-speed railway between Taipei and Kaohsiung and the housing construction for war veterans.

In addition, the government has also emphasized financial re-regulations to deal with many problems resulting from the financial liberalization. Several policy measures have been proposed in such areas as (1) bill and bond markets—institutionalizing the governing of bill trading and management, improving credit rating in the bond market; (2) stock market—encouraging investment by institutional investors, increasing financial information disclosure; (3) financial supervision—implementing compulsory deposit insur-

Table 5.6
Major Economic Indicators in Taiwan, 1991–1999

Year	Growth Rate	Per Capita GNP (U.S.$)[1]	Unemployment Rate	Consumer Increase Rate	Price Income Distribution
1991	7.6	8,982	1.5	3.6	4.97
1992	7.5	10,506	1.5	4.5	5.24
1993	7.0	10,956	1.5	2.9	5.42
1994	7.1	11,781	1.6	4.1	5.38
1995	6.4	12,653	1.8	3.7	5.34
1996	6.1	13,225	2.6	3.1	5.38
1997	6.7	13,559	2.7	0.9	5.41
1998	4.6	12,333	2.7	1.7	–
1999	5.7	13,248	2.9	0.2	–

[1]At current prices.
Sources: Selected from DGBAS (1999), *Monthly Bulletin of Statistics of the Republic of China*,
   May 1999, *Statistical Yearbook of the Republic of China, 1998*, and the Web site of
   CEPD.

ance, consolidating financial supervision and examination agencies; and (4) corporate governance—increasing the liability and penalties for violations of fiduciary duty by board members, re-regulating cross shareholdings, and preventing asset diversion (Chi, 1999).

Economic Performance in the 1990s

The changes in economic transformation policies, political reforms, and financial crisis have had some effects on Taiwan's recent economic performance. The tables in this section provide information on Taiwan's macroeconomic condition, international trade, and financial market during the 1990s. First, as revealed in Table 5.6, during the period from 1991 to 1999, Taiwan's economy was quite good despite signs of a slowdown in growth and development. The economic growth rates declined from 7.6 percent in 1991 to 4.6 percent in 1998 (as affected by the 1997 crisis) and went up to 5.7 in 1999. While the per capita GDP had exceeded US$10,000 since 1992 (it declined in 1998 due to the financial crisis), consumer price indices were high between 1991 and 1996 (an average rate of 3.7 percent) and dropped since 1997 (affected by the crisis). The unemployment rates were rising from 1.5 percent in 1991 to 2.9 percent in 1999. The income distribution rates went from 4.97 in 1991 to 5.41 in 1997 and indicated increasing income gaps between the rich and the poor. (The rates were as low as 4.17 in 1980; see Table 5.5).

Next, based on the foreign trade data in Table 5.7, Taiwan performed

Table 5.7
Foreign Trade in Taiwan, 1991–1999

	Amount (in U.S.$ Million)			Annual Rate of Change	
Year	Export	Import	Balance	Export	Import
1991	76,178	62,860	13,318	13.3	14.9
1992	81,470	72,007	9,463	6.9	14.6
1993	85,091	77,061	8,030	4.4	7.0
1994	93,049	85,349	7,700	9.4	10.8
1995	111,659	103,550	8,109	20.0	21.3
1996	115,942	102,371	13,571	3.8	−1.1
1997	122,081	114,425	7,656	5.3	11.8
1998	110,582	104,665	5,917	−9.4	−8.5
1999	121,638	110,698	10,940	10.0	5.8

Sources: Selected from DGBAS (1999), *Monthly Bulletin of Statistics of the Republic of China,* May 1999, *Statistical Yearbook of the Republic of China, 1998,* and the Web site of CEPD.

very well in its international trade and continuously enjoyed trade surpluses during the 1990s. The surpluses reached US$13,571 million in 1996 and were down in 1997 and 1998, $7,656 million and $5,917 million, respectively (because of the financial crisis). The impact of the financial crisis was further evidenced as Taiwan experienced a negative rate of 9.42 in its exports and a negative rate of 8.53 in its imports in 1998. Both exports and imports improved in 1999.

Finally, Table 5.8 offers financial data to examine the impact of the Asian financial crisis. The exchange rate increased approximately 21.8 percent between 1996 and 1998, from US$1:NT 27.49 to US$1:NT 33.46. The money supply (M1B) increased significantly in 1997 (13.9 percent) and was down in 1998 (2.5 percent). The loans and investment annual rates declined from double digits in the first half of the 1990s to single digits in the later half. The rates were 9.1 percent and 7.7 percent in 1997 and 1998, respectively. To boost the market, the central bank continuously lowered its rediscount rates, from 6.25 percent in 1991 to 4.5 percent in 1999.

CONCLUSION: LESSONS AND CHALLENGES

This chapter examined Taiwan's economic development experience by reviewing key economic indicators, identifying major contributors to its development, and discussing recent changes and challenges that may affect its future development. The examinations have led to some general conclusions about the implications of managing economic development in Taiwan.

Table 5.8
Major Financial Indicators in Taiwan, 1991–1998

Year	Exchange Rate (Ave., in U.S. $)	M1B Annual Rate	Loans and Investment Rate	Rediscount Rate
1991	26.81	5.9	22.2	6.25
1992	26.16	15.4	28.6	5.63
1993	26.39	8.2	19.5	5.50
1994	26.46	16.9	15.2	5.50
1995	26.48	4.8	10.5	5.50
1996	27.46	4.1	7.9	5.00
1997	28.71	13.9	9.1	5.25
1998	33.46	2.5	7.7	4.75
1999	32.27	–	–	4.50

Sources: Selected from DGBAS (1999), *Monthly Bulletin of Statistics of the Republic of China*, May 1999, *Statistical Yearbook of the Republic of China, 1998*, and the Web site of CEPD.

First, the analyses of Taiwan's achievements in economic development revealed several important factors that contribute to its development. These factors consist of two categories: general background and supporting conditions and governmental policies and programs. The first category includes factors such as the investment of the Japanese occupation forces during the colonial period, the support of capable human resources in the society (i.e., entrepreneurs and workers of local Taiwanese groups and skilled professionals from Mainland China), the condition of the postwar international economic environment (including U.S. aid), and the impact of traditional culture in Chinese society. The second category refers to the Taiwan government's development policies and programs: the adoption and implementation of a multiyear economic development plan model, the emphasis on an open economic system to promote international trade, the establishment of institutional infrastructures and the capability of public administration (especially economic administration professionals), and the ability to maintain a stable political and social environment. It is important to recognize that the development record results from a combination of factors in both categories.

The important contributions of Taiwan's development policies and programs are directly related to the role of government in managing economic development. Along with other East Asian development countries, several researchers (e.g., Johnson, 1982, 1987; Onis, 1991) have promoted the state-oriented (or -guided) developmental model and emphasized the important role of government in the process of economic development. Two different arguments have been addressed. On the positive side, the outstanding economic growth records resulted from the successful manage-ment and policy performance of the Taiwan government, such as the planned development model, the export-oriented development strategy, the balanced growth approach, and the investment in human resources. On the other hand, the party-dominated government also created some negative effects on Taiwan's development. They are directly or indirectly related to KMT's political and social controls, including, for example, violations of human rights, limitations of political freedom, unfair competition and in-efficient operation of state-owned enterprises, and a decrease in quality of life (environmental and cultural pollution).

Both the positive and negative sides of Taiwan's economic development management were further demonstrated in its reactions during the 1997–1998 Asian financial crisis. Unlike its neighboring countries (especially South Korea, Thailand, and Malaysia), Taiwan has experienced only minor negative effects of the financial crisis. Despite the slowdown in international trades, Taiwan's macroeconomic conditions (i.e., economic growth rate, unemployment rate, and inflation control) were quite good during the pe-riod of crisis (especially when comparing them with those of other Asian countries). While the exchange rate depreciated, the financial and equity markets in general again were better controlled and managed than those of other Asian countries.

The differences of the financial crisis impact (between Taiwan and other Asian countries) may result from various policy measures emphasized by the Taiwan government. For example, before the financial crisis, Taiwan had also experienced similar overheating pressures in domestic economic environment, such as inflated property and stock market values, problems of banking, and financial sector supervision (Kuo et al., 1999). Unlike other Asian countries, the Taiwan government has developed different policy measures to control and stabilize economic and financial conditions because of its unique political environment (i.e., military threats from Mainland China). Based on the political consideration, the Taiwan government fre-quently intervened in the economic and financial markets (e.g., stock, hous-ing, and exchange markets) for the purpose of maintaining social stability. The resources of the intervention are based on Taiwan's huge foreign exchange reserves and various government funds.

The problems of this intervention, however, are related to the question-able institutional arrangements and political operations in Taiwan. As in-dicated by Kuo and his colleagues (1999), Taiwan's financial problems were caused less by external factors than by the oligopolistic alliance among the KMT, local factions, conglomerates, and representatives, with the ad-ministration as a tacit collaborator. The oligopolistic alliance, motivated by self-interests, controlled and manipulated the financial and equity mar-kets through their own banks, holding companies, and joint ventures. The alliance distorted sound market structures and produced unfair competitions and unethical practices. Moreover, the intervention of the alliance was closely related to KMT's political agenda. For example, during the election time, the party-controlled administration formulated policies (e.g., loosening money supply), and the party-controlled investment firms operated in the market to stimulate stock prices for the purpose of creating a positive image of KMT's governance and increasing profits for its campaign expenses.

While being politically effective, the traditional policies and practices of governmental intervention in economic activities have been increasingly challenged by the public. The political reforms introduced since the 1980s have changed Taiwan from a closed and party-dominated society to an open and democratic society. The general public is concerned with the continuing deterioration of political and legal systems and the increasing negative influence of the party and conglomerates on Taiwan's society. Huge social and economic costs are associated with political changes and interventions. The increasing gap between the rich and the poor, as well as the rising concerns of crimes and environments, are good examples of these changes and challenges.

In sum, Taiwan's economic development experiences, both positive and negative, are based on its own political, social, and economic conditions and arrangements. During the past five decades, the Taiwan government was able to produce outstanding economic growth records, change economic structures, and improve the citizen's qualify of life. The KMT-controlled government was quite effective in dealing with many economic crises, such as the energy crisis in the late 1970s and the Asian financial crisis in 1997. The experience of Taiwan development, mixing with both positive and negative outcomes, should be considered a unique case, which resulted from its special political considerations. After the two decades of political reforms, many new issues and concerns (e.g., social justice, environmental protections) have emerged to challenge the past government- and party-controlled development model. The future of Taiwan's development depends on government efforts in such issues as maintaining a peaceful and stable relationship with Mainland China, continuing coordination between political reforms and economic transition policies, establishing a modern and professional legal and political system, as well as making better institutional arrangements and management between public and private sectors. These issues have become more challenging since the election of President Chen Shui-bian and the ending of the KMT's ruling. The changes of political power and party provide a good opportunity to test many lessons that were learned about the experience of Taiwan economic development.

NOTES

1. For more information about Taiwan's natural setting, please refer to sources such as Directorate-General of Budget, Accounting and Statistics (DGBAS) (1996) and Li (1995, ch. 1).

2. The present analysis of Taiwan's economic performance focuses on the postwar development. For information about Taiwan's development before and during World War II, please refer to Ho (1978, especially chs. 2 to 6).

3. The nine four-year development plans covered the following periods: First Four-year Economic Development Plan, 1953–1956; Second Four-year Plan, 1957–1960; Third Four-year Plan, 1961–1964; Fourth Four-year Plan, 1965–1968; Fifth Four-year Plan, 1969–1972; Sixth Four-year Plan, 1973–1976; Six-Year Plans, 1976–1981; New Four-year Plan, 1982–1985; and Ninth Medium-term Economic Development Plan, 1986–1989. For more information about different phases of Taiwan's development, see Li (1995, chs. 2 and 3).

4. For more information about the background and process of political democratization activities, please refer to Chou and Nathan (1987), Wu (1989), Wei (1991), Lee (1991), Chao and Myers (1994), Cheng and Liao (1998).

REFERENCES

Cabestan, Jean-Pierre. (1999). "Taiwan in 1998." *Asian Survey* 39(1): 140–147.

Chao, Linda, and Ramon H. Myers. (1994). "The First Chinese Democracy: Political Development of the Republic of China on Taiwan, 1986–1994." *Asian Survey* 34(3): 213–230.

Cheng, Tun-jen, and Yi-shing Liao. (1998). "Taiwan in 1997." *Asian Survey* 38(1): 53–63.

Chi, Schive. (1995). *Taiwan's Economic Role in East Asia*. Washington, DC: Center for Strategic and International Studies.

Chi, Schive. (1999). *Coping with New Challenges in Taiwan*. http://cepd.kcsoft. com.tw.

"Chiu Keeps His Ship Steady as Other Economies Flounder." *South China Morning Post*, July 6.

Chou, Yangsun, and Andrew J. Nathan. (1987). "Democratizing Transition in Taiwan." *Asian Survey* 27(3): 277–299.

Dahlman, Carl J., and Ousa Sananikone. (1997). "Taiwan, China: Policies and Institutions for Rapid Growth." In Danny M. Leipziger, ed., *Lessons from East Asia*. Ann Arbor: University of Michigan Press.

Deng, Ping. (2000). "Taiwan's Restriction of Investment in China in the 1990s." *Asian Survey* 40(6): 958–980.

Directorate-General of Budget, Accounting and Statistics (DGBAS). (1999a). *Statistical Yearbook of the Republic of China, 1998*. Taipei: DGBAS.

Directorate-General of Budget, Accounting and Statistics (DGBAS). (1999b). *Monthly Bulletin of Statistics of the Republic of China, May 1999*. Taipei: DGBAS.

Directorate-General of Budget, Accounting and Statistics (DGBAS). (1996). *Statistical Yearbook of the Republic of China, 1996*. Taipei: DGBAS.

Fei, John C. H., Gustav Ranis, and Shirley W. Y. Kuo. (1979). *Growth with Equity: The Taiwan Case*. New York: Oxford University Press.

Fisher, Stanley. (1988). *The Asian Crisis: A View from the IMF*. Washington, DC, January 22. www.inf.org/external/np/speeches/1998/012298.htm.

Goldstein, Morris. (1998). *The Asian Financial Crisis: Causes, Cures, and Systemic Implications*. Washington, DC: Institute for International Economics.

Ho, Samuel P. S. (1978). *Economic Development of Taiwan, 1860–1970*. New Haven, CT: Yale University Press.

International Monetary Fund (IMF). (1998). "The Asian Crisis: Causes and Cures." *Finance & Development* 35: 2.

Johnson, Chalmers. (1982). *MITI and the Japanese Miracle*. Stanford, CA: Stanford University Press.

Johnson, Chalmers. (1987). "Political Institutions and Economic Performance: The Government–Business Relationship in Japan, South Korea, and Taiwan." In F. C. Deyo, ed., *The Political Economy of the New Asian Industrialization*. Ithaca, NY: Cornell University Press, pp. 136–164.

Kuo, Chengtian, Shangmao Chen, and Zonghao Huan. (1999). "From Asian Miracle to Asian Debacle: Capital Institutions and Reforms in Taiwan." Paper presented at the Annual Meeting of the American Political Science Association, Atlanta, September 2–5.

Kuo, Shirley W. Y., Gustav Ranis, and John C. H. Fei. (1981). *The Taiwan Success Story: Rapid Growth with Improved Distribution in the Republic of China, 1952–1979*. Boulder, CO: Westview Press.

Lan, Ke-jeng, and Jiann-chyuan Wang. (1991). "The Taiwan Experience in Economic Development." *Issues & Studies* 27(10): 135–157.

Lee, Kuo-Wei. (1991). 'The Road to Democracy: Taiwan Experience." *Asian Profile* 19(6): 489–504.

Leng, Tse-Kang. (1996). *The Taiwan-China Connection: Democracy and Development Across the Taiwan Straits*. Boulder, CO: Westview Press.

Li, Kuo-ting. (1995). *The Evolution of Policy Behind Taiwan's Development Success*, 2nd ed. Singapore: World Scientific Publishing Co.

Liou, K. T. (1992). "Privatizing State-Owned Enterprises: The Taiwan Experience." *International Review of Administrative Sciences* 58: 403–419.

Lu, Alexander Ya-li. (1985). "Future Domestic Developments in the Republic of China on Taiwan." *Asian Survey* 27(9): 1075–1095.

Onis, Z. (1991). "Review Article: The Logic of Developmental State." *Comparative Politics* 24: 109–126.

Wei, Yung. (1991). "Democratization and Institutionalization: Problems, Prospects, and Policy Implications of Political Development in the Republic of China on Taiwan." *Issues and Studies* 27(3): 29–43.

Wu, Yu-Shan. (1989). "Marketization of Politics: The Taiwan Experience." *Asian Survey* 29(4): 382–400.

Chapter 6

From Adversity to Opportunity? Hong Kong's Response to the Asian Economic Crisis

Jermain T. M. Lam and Ahmed Shafiqul Huque

INTRODUCTION

Hong Kong is one of several Asian economies that is suffering from the adverse impact of the financial crisis in Asia. Although the economic turmoil did not originate in Hong Kong, the effects of the financial crisis have been so strong that even strong economies like Hong Kong seriously suffered. Major segments of the Hong Kong economy, including the property market, the stock market, the retail and sales markets, the currency market, and the tourist industry were all affected. Signs of economic recession were obvious, with a record high unemployment rate, continuous negative economic growth rate, high interest rate, a huge government budget deficit, large-scale wage-cutting, and a high number of bankruptcies. The period of 1997–1998 has perhaps been the most difficult time for Hong Kong since its rapid economic takeoff in the 1970s.

This chapter discusses Hong Kong's economic development policies and achievements, analyzes the problems faced by the people of Hong Kong amid the Asian financial crisis, as well as critically evaluates the government's responses to the crisis. The government's adaptability and the ability of crisis management will also be brought out from this discussion. Thus, the role of Hong Kong's leadership in adapting to change and its management of crisis to cope with sudden and future challenges will be analyzed.

ECONOMIC DEVELOPMENT POLICIES AND ACHIEVEMENTS

Hong Kong's economic development policies could best be summed up by two salient economic philosophies: positive nonintervention and prudent fiscal management with a surplus budget. These two economic philosophies have been adopted by the Hong Kong government for almost four decades since the end of World War II. They form the economic framework within which economic policies and social service programs are drafted and planned. Up to the outbreak of the Asian financial turmoil, the Hong Kong government had firmly adhered to these two principles of economic management. As Hong Kong's level of economic development and performance prior to the outbreak of the Asian financial crisis indicate, these two economic management principles worked well and were highly praised by the government, politicians, as well as the general citizens. Yet when Hong Kong was seriously hit by the Asian financial crisis, questions were raised about whether these principles should be strictly followed, reasonably modified, or completely dropped. The Hong Kong government did introduce new measures to alleviate the adverse economic impacts of the Asian financial turmoil, including adjustment of interest rates, injection of large sums of money into the stock market, and strict regulation of the stocks and futures exchanges. The government's measures led to controversial debates and created divisions within the society. Some groups supported government intervention to save the economy, while others saw intervention as a deviation from salient economic management principles. The Hong Kong government has argued on various occasions that the measures were not aimed at intervening in the free economic market and that the measures were positive actions to prevent the economic market from being controlled or manipulated by international speculators. It is important to determine whether the government measures constitute a continuation or deviation from the principles of positive nonintervention and prudent fiscal management. An elaboration of these two key economic management principles in the context of Hong Kong is necessary in order to assess the achievements and inadequacies of these two principles.

The principle of positive nonintervention has long been a directing guideline for the management of the Hong Kong economy and society. This principle basically means a minimum of government regulations and interference in business practices and decisions. The phrase "positive nonintervention" was used by officials to describe the government's role in the economy and the social service sector. Sir Philip Haddon-Cave, the financial secretary during 1971–1981, provided the best explanation of the phrase by saying that "government intervention and involvement would be minimum except under special circumstances," in his speech addressed to the Legislative Council in 1976 (*Hansard*, 1976, 827–830, cited in Miners, 1991, 47). The government proudly attributed the success of the Hong Kong economy to "the consistent economic policies of free enterprise and free trade" (*Hong Kong Yearbook*, 1985, 71). The principal role of the government in the economy, as clearly spelled out in the same document, was "to ensure a stable framework in which commerce and industry can function efficiently and effectively with minimum interference. The government normally intervenes only in response to the pressure of economic and social needs, and neither protects nor subsidizes manufactures" (ibid.). The same economic ideology continued in the 1990s: "The government considers that, except where social considerations are over-riding, the allocation of resources in the economy is best left to market forces with minimal government intervention in the private sector. This basically free-enterprise, market-disciplined system has contributed to Hong Kong's economic success" (*Hong Kong Yearbook*, 1991, 63). As such, the government's primary role is "to provide the necessary infrastructure and a sound legal and administrative framework conducive to economic growth and prosperity" (ibid.).

The second principle of economic management, prudent fiscal management with a surplus budget, is indeed a byproduct of the principle of positive nonintervention. Because the government is determined to restrain its involvement and role in the economy and the social sector, government expenditure would only be made in basic and necessary areas such as law and order, administration, and infrastructure. The idea of prudent fiscal management originated from the Financial Procedures contained in the Colonial Regulations, which stipulated the ultimate fiscal principle of self-support and balanced budget. The objective was to ensure that the British government had no need to financially support the colony. This principle was further refined by successive financial secretaries in Hong Kong to put forward annual surplus budgets. In the 1970s, a set of budgetary guidelines was developed by the then financial secretary Hadden-Cave:

1. Recurrent expenditure should absorb no more than 80 percent of recurrent revenue, and at least 60 percent of capital expenditure should be financed by the surplus on recurrent account. Recurrent expenditure should not be more than 70 percent of total expenditure.

2. The residual deficit on the capital account should at least be financed half by capital revenue and no more than half with debt.

3. Annual debt service charges should not, at any time, exceed income earned on our fiscal reserves.

4. Recurrent revenues should be at least 88 percent of total expenditure.

5. The balance of the fiscal system is defined by the following two ratios: the ratio of direct to indirect taxation targeted at 55:45 and the ratio of direct and indirect taxation taken together to all other recurrent revenue targeted at 70:30.

6. The rate at which total expenditure by the public sector can grow annually in real terms, based on historical experience in the 1970s, can be taken to be about 10 percent.

7. The free fiscal reserves at the beginning of the financial year should be at least 15 percent of estimated expenditure (*Budget*, 1977–78; Tang, 1997, 190).

In the 1980s, the budgetary guidelines were refined, and explicit budget criteria were set with the introduction of the Medium Range Forecast. The most important budgetary criteria were to be found in the following statements:

1. The government aims to maintain adequate reserves in the long term.
2. A substantial element of capital expenditure must be financed from a surplus on the operating account (recurrent revenue in relation to recurrent expenditure). A broad target of at least a 50 percent funding of capital expenditure from the operating surplus is adopted.
3. It is intended that expenditure growth should not exceed the assumption as to the trend growth in GDP.
4. Over a period of time, the aim is to contain capital expenditure growth within overall expenditure guidelines, that is, within the assumption as to the trend GDP growth (*Budget*, 1986–1987; Tang, 1997, 192).

Most of the previous budgetary guidelines were retained in the 1990s. The aim to maintain adequate reserves in the long term has been reiterated in the annual financial budgets.

Until the Asian financial turmoil in 1997, the economic management principles of positive nonintervention and prudent fiscal management with a surplus budget had worked very well in Hong Kong, leading the economy to become one of the most successful economies in the Asia-Pacific Region. In the last three decades, Hong Kong enjoyed steady economic growth, with an average annual growth of 5 percent in per capita GDP (*Hong Kong Annual Digest of Statistics*, various years). Unemployment remained low, with an average of 2 percent of the total working population per year (ibid.). With a stable employment situation, the working population enjoyed real wage increases, and the real wage index recorded a steady increase over the last 30 years with an average annual growth rate of 3 percent (ibid.). In terms of the distribution of income, the size of the middle class expanded, with more people earning the middle-range monthly income of HK$20,000–30,000 (ibid.). With reference to housing tenure, the number of owner-occupiers increased from 23.2 percent of the total population in 1976 to 35.1 percent in 1986 and to 48.2 percent in 1996 (ibid.). As a result of stable economic growth and real wage increase, private consumption grew over 10 times from 1967 to 1997. The stock market, an indicator of the profile of financial investment, also experienced continuous growth and expansion. The Hang Seng Stock Index jumped from 100 points in 1964 to 16,673 in 1997. The admittance of the Stock Exchange of Hong Kong Limited as a member of the Federation Internationale des Bourse de Valeurs further strengthened Hong Kong as an international financial and investment center. Besides, Hong Kong had been successful in transforming itself from a manufacturing-based to a business and financial-service based economy. In the 1970s, the manufacturing industries made the largest contribution to the GDP. Yet its top position was replaced by the wholesale business and financial services in the 1990s. Employment in the financial and wholesale sectors took the largest share (two-thirds) of total employment in the 1990s. With the expansion and consolidation of the financial and banking sector, Hong Kong has been recognized as the third Eurocredit syndication center after London and New York.

Hong Kong's economic success was a result of several factors, including a strategic geographical location, a deep harbor for shipping, an efficient civil service, a sophisticated communication and transport system, a hard-working population, a large Chinese hinterland, and a beneficiary of China's open door policy. Yet it would be equally fair to argue that the economic management policies of the Hong Kong government facilitated, if not contributed to, the continuous growth and prosperity of the economy. The economic management principles at least did not obstruct or create any damage to the free operation of the economy, which was regulating itself through the dynamic interaction of the various economic actors. The government did a good job in restraining itself from over-regulating or intervening in the markets, when the markets were normal without irregularities. Because government intervention in the economy was minimal, economic actors like businessmen, investors, bankers, property developers, and the public made free choices according to various market situations. With a minimum of government regulation and an absence of irregular external influence, the advantages of a free market mechanism were thus fully realized. The operation of the laissez-faire economy was further backed up by the government's restrained role in the social sector. The tax rate remained low, as a result of "prudent" government expenditure on social welfare services. This directly encouraged investment, consumption, and expansion of business operations. The prudent economic management principle certainly lessened society's economic burden and helped boost overall investment confidence and incentive. Under such a favorable economic environment, business investors had ample opportunities for flourishing. However, the Asian financial crisis was a severe test of the effectiveness of these two economic management principles. The impact of the Asian financial turmoil was so strong that people began to question the usefulness of the economic management principles of the government of Hong Kong.

IMPACT OF THE ASIAN FINANCIAL CRISIS ON HONG KONG

The devastating impact of the Asian financial crisis on Hong Kong was first felt in October 1997. When international speculators attempted to break the Hong Kong–U.S. dollar peg by short-selling large amounts of Hong Kong dollars, the Hong Kong government drastically increased the interbank loan interest rate overnight to 300 percent. The stock market dropped quickly, with the Hang Seng Stock Index sliding from 10,000 to 8,000 points within one day after the drastic increase in interest rate. The financial situation further worsened in January 1998 when several financial investment companies went bankrupt with a large number of bad loans and illegal share transactions. Many businesses reported net losses and resorted to cutting workers' wages and sacking employees. Private consumption shrank significantly, resulting in the closing down of large department stores, including the Japanese Matsuzakaya, Daimaru, and Yaohan. The Hong Kong government recognized the depressing economic situation in May 1998 and recorded a 2 percent negative economic growth rate in 1998–1999. The projection was a drastic regression from the financial secretary's earlier projection of a 3.5 percent economic growth rate. In June 1998, the property market suffered a heavy loss with a 50 percent drop in value. Many mortgages turned into bad loans, and buyers had to forfeit their deposits when the banks rejected their mortgage applications. In August, the Hong Kong–U.S. dollar peg again came under attack from international speculators, and this resulted in a record low Hang Seng Stock Index of 6,554 since 1992.

Economic indicators of 1997 and 1998 clearly showed the severity of the impact of the Asian financial turmoil on Hong Kong (*Apple Daily News*, October 26, 1998). The Hang Seng Stock Index dropped from 16,673 points in August 1997 to 6,554 in August 1998, representing a fall of 41 percent. The prime interest rate rose from 8.75 percent in September 1997 to 9.75 percent in October 1998. The GDP growth rate decreased from 6.9 percent in 1997 to negative 5.2 percent, and the rate of unemployment increased from 2.4 percent to 5 percent. The number of unemployed increased from 74,000 in 1997 to 181,000, and the number of vacant posts dropped from 11,390 in 1997 to 10,666. The average wage dropped from HK$10,641 in 1997 to HK$10,000. The number of approved social security subsidy cases increased from 16,462 in 1997 to 26,215 in 1998. The property price decreased from an average of HK$7,500 per square foot in 1997 to HK$3,500 per square foot in 1998. Retail values dropped from HK$204 billion in 1997 to HK$170 billion in 1998, with a 16.7 percent decrease. The annual financial surplus decreased from HK$809 billion in 1997 to HK$214 billion deficit in 1998, as a result of sharp decreases in government revenue from the profit tax, land sales, and stamp duties. The number of tourists dropped from 977,248 in June 1997 to 859,310 in August 1998, implying a decrease in tourist expenditure as a source of income.

Under this unstable economic environment, the confidence of the general citizens dropped to the lowest point, even much lower than the one recorded during the June Fourth incident in 1989. According to Survey Research Hong Kong, the economic confidence index dropped to 69 in July 1998 from the record high of 98 in January 1997 (*South China Morning Post*, October 19, 1998). In June 1989, the economic confidence index was at 81 (ibid.). The A. C. Nielsen Confidence Index Report found that 33 percent of the public rated the performance of the Hong Kong government as either bad or very bad, with only 11 percent giving it a positive mark (ibid.). The same survey, revealed that a large proportion of respondents, 75 percent, thought that the Hong Kong government was not helpful in solving the problem of unemployment. Only a minority of 24 percent of the respondents believed that the Hong Kong government could improve the business environment. Another survey conducted by the Chinese University of Hong Kong confirmed the same observation. The number of respondents who expressed optimism about the economy dropped to 12.9 percent in August 1998 from 43.9 percent in August 1997 (*Apple Daily News*, October 30, 1998). Chief executive Tung Chee-hwa's popularity index also dropped from a record high of 68 in September 1997 to a record low of 51.0 in October 1998 (ibid.). Respondents also gave a failure mark of 45 out of 100 (50 being the pass mark) for the government's performance in improving the economic environment (ibid.). The above survey results show that Hong Kong citizens have lost their confidence in the economy and the leadership of the Tung administration to pull Hong Kong out from the recession. Three significant points emerge from the results of these surveys:

1. The responses and measures taken by the government in handling the financial turmoil were far from satisfactory.
2. Unless the government did something effective to rescue the economy, public confidence in the Hong Kong economy in general and Tung in particular would totally collapse.
3. The status of Hong Kong as an international financial center would be affected.

RESPONSES AND POLICIES OF THE HONG KONG GOVERNMENT

Although the Asian financial crisis started in Thailand in May 1997 and reached Hong Kong in October 1997, the government did nothing until February 1998 to prevent it from affecting Hong Kong or to minimize its impact. The financial secretary announced the 1998 budget in February to reduce various taxes, including the business tax, security stamp duty, rates, airport tax, and property tax. With the concession of taxes, the government estimated that the budget would still be a surplus budget. The objective of these tax concessions was to stimulate consumption, in view of a slow economic growth. However, the government did not give any warning about the Asian financial turmoil. Perhaps the government's attention was too much drawn to the plunging property market, as a result of the introduction of the government's new housing policy. In his 1997 Policy Address, Tung announced that 85,000 new housing units would be provided every year and that a series of measures would be in place to regulate the overheated private property market. This housing policy precipitated a slide in the private property market, and the price of private properties fell 40 percent within six months. Recognizing the serious threat to the economy, the government slightly relaxed the rules for the transaction of private properties in May 1998. It was hoped that this measure would stimulate the ailing property market, while the government still insisted on the target of the annual provision of 85,000 new housing units. Apart from the attempt to revive the property market, the Monetary Authority of Hong Kong also injected more money into the banking system in order to relieve the tight currency circulation. Furthermore, the government was keen to promote tourism by relaxing the visa requirements for visitors from Taiwan and Mainland China.

A second round of rescue bids to save the economy was announced by the government in June 1998. These included:

1. Suspending land sales until March 1999 and freezing grants for sandwich class housing.
2. Providing HK$3.6 billion to double to 12,000 the number of first-time home buyers benefiting from the starter loan scheme, and HK$3.3 billion to increase from 4,500 to 10,000 the number benefiting from the home purchase scheme.
3. Exempting interest earned locally from profits tax, aiming to provide an extra HK$200 billion in liquidity for the banking sector through repatriation of offshore deposits.
4. Setting up a HK$2 billion scheme to help nonexport-related small and medium businesses obtain loans.
5. Rebating rates of HK$3.85 billion for the first quarter.
6. Cutting the duty on diesel by 30 percent.
7. Reducing by HK$200 million annually the charges paid by importers and exporters.
8. Freezing pay increases for 331 directorate officials with monthly salaries of HK$127,900 or above.

The total amount of money involved in the rescue bid was estimated to be HK$44 billion. A public opinion survey conducted by the Chinese University of Hong Kong indicated that the public generally welcomed the rescue bid but expressed doubts about the effectiveness of the measures. The respondents were split in their opinions; 29.9 percent thought the measures "could" save the economy, while 23.3 percent believed the opposite, and 37.8 percent said "half and half" (*Apple Daily News*, June 23, 1998).

Another survey conducted by the University of Hong Kong showed that the rescue bid failed to increase confidence, and support for Tung plunged to a new low in the public support rating (*South China Morning Post*, June 25, 1998).

The third rescue bid, aimed at mapping out long-term strategies for growth, was packaged in Tung's second policy speech delivered in October 1998. Tung alleged that the economic downturn was a result of both external and internal factors. The external factors were attributed to "the intense pressure to short-sell the Hong Kong dollar," "the withdrawal of funds from overseas banks and investors," "the rapid depreciation of Asian currencies," and "the sharp decline in the number of inbound tourists" (*Policy Address*, 1998, 2). These factors were claimed to cause high interest rates, reduction of liquidity in the banking system, steep declines in the property and stock markets, and contraction of consumer and tourist spending. Tung regarded the "bubble economy" and the "narrow economic base" as the main internal factors that made the Hong Kong economy vulnerable. According to Tung, "Hong Kong has become one of the most expensive cities in the world in which to do business, and this has affected our competitiveness. . . . Our economic base has been too narrow, whenever the financial and real estate sectors have encountered problems, the Hong Kong economy has suffered" (ibid.). Based on such analysis, Tung's 1998 Policy Address was tuned to tackle the external challenges and to strengthen the internal economic structures.

Tung proposed a number of major long-term strategies for growth, as summarized here:

1. Strengthen government support for innovation and technological development by setting up an Applied Science and Technology Research Institute.

2. Set up a HK$5 billion Innovation and Technology Fund to provide finance for projects that will contribute to the improved use of innovation and technology in the industrial and commercial sectors.

3. Position Hong Kong as an Internet hub for the Asia Pacific region to help Hong Kong, mainland, and overseas businesses to produce, distribute, and market their goods more effectively both within the region and beyond.

4. Develop a world-class teleport to provide the best possible global satellite links.

5. Enhance Hong Kong's role as an international financial services center by strengthening regulatory systems and developing new products (e.g., the creation of a Venture Board for the trade of shares in smaller and emerging companies).

6. Draw up plans for a new state-of-the-art performance venue to boost Hong Kong's status as Asia's entertainment and events capital.

7. Establish a Heritage Tourism Task Force and a Commissioner for Tourism.

8. Open a Small and Medium Enterprises Office to coordinate services and assistance for smaller businesses.

These measures would require a long time to have a real impact on the economy. Yet the public's immediate response was again skeptical. A survey conducted by the *South China Morning Post* (October 19, 1998) showed that there was a lack of confidence in the effectiveness of the Policy Address to improve the general economic environment. Half of all the respondents said "it would be ineffective," while only 16 percent took a more optimistic view. Respondents were also pessimistic about their personal financial situation over the next 12 months, with 35 percent "expecting matters to worsen," 58 percent "believing there would be no change," and only 7 percent "expecting an improvement." A significant amount, 75 percent, of the respondents thought the Policy Address would not help reduce unemployment. Only 30 percent of the respondents thought the Policy Address would help improve the business environment. These data indicate that Tung's Policy Address had not revived public confidence.

The 1999 and 2000 budgets also did not materially help the economy and public confidence in the government. The government recorded a deficit of HK$322 billion and HK$365 billion in 1999 and 2000, respectively (1999 and 2000 *Budgets*). The Hong Kong government has encountered three deficit budgets (1998, 1999, 2000) in the past 30 years. This phenomenon not only deviated from the salient principle of "setting positive budget" but also violated the principle of the Basic Law, which stated that "The Hong Kong Special Administration Region shall follow the principle of keeping expenditure within the limits of revenues in drawing up its budget, and strive to achieve a fiscal balance, avoid deficits and keep the budget commensurate with the growth rate of its gross domestic product" (*Basic Law*, Article 107). The major reductions of the government income came from the sharp decrease of property tax (-17.4 percent) and the personal income tax (-13.8 percent) in 2000. The fiscal reserves in Hong Kong have been continuously decreasing since 1998, from HK$4,252 billion to HK$3,887 billion in 1999 and subsequently to HK$3,831 billion in 2000. Unemployment climbed to 5 percent, with the economic growth barely reaching a positive figure of 0.5 percent in 1999–2000. Deflation was recorded at 2 percent in the same year. Against these negative figures, the 1999 and 2000 budgets were criticized as ineffective economic management documents by various political parties, including the progovernment parties. For instance, the Democratic party thought that the budgets did not help the lower class to survive through the economic crisis. The Democratic Alliance for the Betterment of Hong Kong believed that the vast majority of the population could not benefit from both the economic rescue policies and long-term developmental strategies. The Federation of Trade Unions echoed that the government's economic policies could not help the unemployed. The Frontiers said that the problem of unemployment was not effectively touched by the Tung administration.

There were some hopes that the Hong Kong economy might revive in late 2000, given the fact that exports surged in May 2000. Exports for the month were up 22.3 percent in the last year, a total of HK$132.8 billion as reported by the Census and Statistics Department (*South China Morning Post*, June 28, 2000). On another front, Hong Kong's gross domestic product (GDP) powered ahead at an inflation-adjusted 14.3 percent in the first quarter compared with the same period of 1999, as a result of the strong export growth of 20.3 percent. Yet economists were cautious about these figures, pointing out that a full recovery of Hong Kong's economy had not been in sight. ABN Amro Asia's regional economist thought that "high interest rates and the possibility of weaker demand in major export markets could dent Hong Kong's export machine" (ibid.). A chief economist from Hong Kong Bank was also not so optimistic: "The property market is still in a slump. People still have not got too much confidence" (ibid.). Similarly, the chief economist at the General Chamber of Commerce was equally cautious, predicting that the pace of growth of Hong Kong exports was likely to slow. The views of these economists might water down the optimistic belief of the recovery of Hong Kong economy. Yet these views could reflect the continuation of the lack of confidence in the performance of the economy and the ability of the administration to deal with the economic hardship.

Lack of public confidence in the Tung administration and the poor economic performance could be attributed to the inconsistent economic policies and the government's low responding capability. It would be fair to say that "the full effect of the government measures to tackle the depressing Hong Kong economy might not be immediately evident" (*Policy Address*, 3) and that "the government has no magic to immediately fix the economy *(Hong Kong Standard*, November 5, 1998). Yet a closer look at the deconomic actions of the government suggests that these activities were inconsistent with the economic management principle of positive nonintervention. The Hong Kong Policy Research Institute found that the index of free market operation in Hong Kong dropped from 100 in 1997 to 94.3 in 1998 (*Apple Daily News*, February 18, 2000). The government's firm commitment to direct the housing market by the annual provision of 85,000 new units was a case in point. Many developers regarded the housing policy as direct intervention into the housing market. It was criticized that the market principles of demand and supply were disrupted by the government directives of building, respectively, 55,000 and 30,000 public and private housing units every year. Private housing in the context of Hong Kong was not only a matter of basic living necessity, but also a tool of investment. As the property market enjoyed rapid growth in the past 10 years, the public regarded property as a reliable source of saving and investment. Yet the drastic change in government policy disturbed this belief and led to the sudden collapse of the private property market. Tung himself advised the general public to delay buying private property when he was the chief executive in designate. When the private property price fell to an average of about HK$4,000 per square foot in 1998, Tung publicly said that, in his view, it was a reasonable price.

Yet on July 5, 2000, Tung suddenly told the public that the 85,000 target had not existed since 1998. Legislators and other experts wondered why they had not been told of the change in 1998 and pointed out that officials had repeatedly insisted since then that the housing policy was still in force (*South China Morning Post*, July 6, 2000). Furthermore, Tung did not clarify whether the housing target had been scrapped, although it did not exist. Tung's housing policy and public speeches confused the public and the developers about the role of government in the property market as well as the direction of the property market. This has certainly affected the confidence of investors.

Another controversial policy was the government's direct injection of HK$1,120 billion into the stock market in August 1998. When the stock market was severely affected by the short-selling activities of the international speculators, the Hong Kong government injected the above amount of money to stabilize the stock market. The society was divided over the government's move and the general implication for the role of government in the stock market. Some took the view that government intervention was necessary to redress the abnormal market operation, while others believed that it would weaken Hong Kong's image as a free international financial market. The government reiterated that "it is not our intention to interfere with market forces, nor is it our intention to broaden the powers of the government. Rather, our aim is to consolidate Hong Kong's ability to manage its monetary affairs, so that we can counter manipulation of our markets and stabilize interest rates" (*Policy Address*, 1998, 3–4). Yet some investors are still skeptical about the role of government in controlling the financial markets in general and the specific timing of government intervention in the markets in particular.

The general public and the investors were further upset by the government's low responding capability in handling crises. This factor affects the government's degree of awareness and alertness to foresee problems and to map out preventive measures to minimize the scope and impact of problems. The chief secretary for administration, Anson Chan, admitted in a Legislative Council meeting that "the government underestimated the scope and impact of the Asian financial turmoil on the economy of Hong Kong" and that "the government would learn from this experience" (*South China Morning Post*, November 5, 1998). The government actions taken during the financial turmoil seemed to be mainly reactive to the actions initiated by international speculators. For instance, the Monetary Authority drastically raised the interbank loan interest to 300 percent overnight after the Hong Kong dollars had been short-sold in October 1997. On another occasion, the government injected HK$1,120 billion into the stock market after the stock and futures markets had been manipulated by international speculators in August 1998. These two incidents showed that the government was not well-equipped with foresight, or the ability to anticipate problems and to discover the inherent weaknesses of the financial system.

The impact of the Asian financial turmoil on Hong Kong and the government's actions in dealing with it exposed a number of problems and weaknesses inherent in the economic management principles of positive nonintervention and prudent fiscal management. First, there are not enough monitoring measures or efforts to oversee the normal functioning of the financial market. The government overemphasizes nonintervention, while underestimating the risk of market manipulation by international speculators. Second, the economic base of Hong Kong is too narrow, with the property and financial sectors as the main economic pillars. Since the government did not invest resources in new areas of growth under the principle of nonintervention" and prudent spending, the Hong Kong economy has become vulnerable to external changes. Third, there are inadequate economic and social security protections for the general citizens due to the government's limited role in social and economic services. Thus, the adverse impact of such crises on the citizens and the economy are magnified. Fourth, the government introduced short-term, piece-meal, and inconsistent policies during the financial turmoil owing to the lack of vision and long-term planning. Fifth, the responding capability of the officials is low, with a low level of awareness and alertness, and this is a result of their prolonged reliance on the principle of nonintervention. These inherent weaknesses further reveal another fundamental problem in the role of leadership in crisis management in the Hong Kong government. If the Hong Kong government could be properly led and guided, perhaps the problems of the Asian financial turmoil and the weaknesses inherent in the economic management principles would not be exposed to such a large extent.

LEADERSHIP AND THE MANAGEMENT OF CRISIS

With the East and Southeast Asian nations coming to terms with reality, various explanations are emerging on the causes and circumstances that resulted in the financial turmoil. The picture is quite different across countries: Japan suffered because of the weakening of currency as well as a steep decline in property prices; and Thailand and Indonesia suffered "because domestic interest rates rose too much" (Ho, 1998, 1). Bad debt had a severe impact in many countries, and there have been demands for reform of financial institutions and strengthening of regulatory mechanisms. However, the case of Hong Kong was quite different from the others. It was natural for Hong Kong to be affected since the problem was spreading in the region, but the small size of the government and a centralized hierarchical structure should have resulted in the advantage of making quick decisions, choosing rational alternatives, and implementing them. However, some recent experiences suggest that it is perhaps a better strategy to dwell on solutions to problems emanating from crises rather than to opt for the first solution that comes to mind.

An extensive review of the financial management process was initiated with the introduction of public sector reform in Hong Kong. This was followed up by the establishment of various methods and mechanisms to ensure that the established activities are efficiently and effectively carried out within a management framework, which includes the application of fiscal guidelines, planning, resource allocation, review of performance, management of public finance, and review of progress (Finance Branch, 1995, 3). The secretary for treasury stated clearly that "The management of public finances is not only about providing the resources necessary to give the community a quality and cost effective public service. It is equally about providing an environment conducive to continued economic growth and success" (Tsang, 1995).

Hong Kong had a long period of economic success, which allowed it to build up a substantial amount of fiscal reserve, and "the objective to make the fiscal system more stable has remained unchanged" (Tang, 1997, 215). It appears that Hong Kong has remained well-prepared for raising revenue and spending them for providing public services. The internal system of managing financial resources is sound. Hong Kong also aspires to remain "a major financial centre through the provision of an appropriate economic and legal environment for an open, fair and efficient market" (*Policy Address*, 1998, 159). With this purpose in view, the chief executive has identified four key areas: to maintain monetary and banking stability in Hong Kong; to further improve the regulatory framework; to strengthen the infrastructure required for a first-class international financial center; and to spearhead further development of the financial market (ibid., 160). These are the areas in which the government's activities have given rise to questions and criticisms, and the issue of violating the principle of nonintervention has emerged. Since Hong Kong's economy is strongly linked with external forces, the government's strategies included ensuring the continuation of the linked exchange rate with the U.S. currency and enhancing the supervision of financial institutions by the Hong Kong Monetary Authority.

If Hong Kong's management of the economic system was sound, why did the financial crisis have such an impact on Hong Kong? The answer is to be found in the fact that Hong Kong was not adequately prepared for the assault on its fiscal system and currency from external sources. Its civil service is generally acclaimed for its efficiency and professionalism, but its performance in dealing with some problems has led to criticism. Analysts are trying to identify the causes behind Hong Kong's reaction to the crisis, and it appears that Hong Kong is suffering from a lack of leadership in crisis management.

Janis highlighted the role of the leader in both "formal" and "informal" aspects (1989). In a community like Hong Kong, the leader has a substantial responsibility and must be seen to participate actively in managing the crisis. The leader helps to set norms, to facilitate the flow and utilization of information, and more importantly, "to engage in vigilant problem solving to the best of his or her own ability and also to function as an informal leader, whenever it seems necessary, to try to help fellow participants avoid giving priority to one or another of the constraints that may be inhibiting them from carrying out to the best of their abilities all the essential steps of vigilant problem solving" (Janis, 1989, 231–234).

In the case of Hong Kong, the locus of leadership is diffused. According to the *Basic Law of the Hong Kong Special Administrative Region of the People's Republic of China*, the chief executive is the head of the region, but senior civil servants appear to be taking the lead in administering it. Because the financial crisis affected Hong Kong, the public felt that the chief executive was not leading them from the front. Combined with some of the chief executive's comments on the state of the economy which proved inaccurate, Hong Kong was being run without a leader in charge. The financial secretary appeared to be leading the battle against speculators and had to make difficult decisions to stave off the crisis. Under the leadership of the financial secretary, a number of short-term measures were initiated to revamp the economy. This demonstrated the government's preference for quick fix solutions that could hurt the economy in the long run. But the emergence of the financial crisis immediately after Hong Kong's reintegration with China added to the pressure on the leaders. The "clumsy handling of the proposed changeover to Chinese-language education last year, the fiasco earlier this year when it tried to kill all Hong Kong's chicken in a scare over avian flu, and the bungled opening of the new airport" (*The Economist*, September 12, 1998) made the government appear less than efficient. The actions taken to minimize the impact of the financial turmoil by injecting massive amounts of funds into the stock market and the later announcement of measures designed to prevent the manipulation of the financial markets did little to enhance confidence.

Effective crisis management entails adequate preparations as well as the management of public relations. There are two aspects of crisis management in the public sector. One can be described as a reflex action that is undertaken when a crisis hits a country. The second approach is to prepare well in advance in anticipation of the crisis. The second strategy involves a series of preparatory moves, including extensive planning and being on constant vigilance. Hong Kong citizens expected to be kept informed of the problems by the leaders, who would also be able to explain the rationale for the choice and methods of implementation of specific measures. These actions indicate that some changes were necessary for the effective operation of the financial system. It is quite pertinent to ask why these had not been implemented earlier. Lane (1993) has pointed out that leaders in the public sector generally emphasize established procedures, are slow to find innovative solutions, and are less sensitive to environmental changes. It has been pointed out that "Hong Kong's financial management during the crisis has been anything but smooth, and financial policy has been marked by a series of sharp reversals, unprecedented intervention in the stock market and a lack of coordination among top officials" (*Far Eastern Economic Review*, September 17, 1998, 53). The government is now left holding an enormous portfolio which, fortunately for the government, has appreciated in value. But there is the specter of another crash that will greatly diminish the fiscal reserve.

CONCLUDING OBSERVATIONS

The process of economic development in Hong Kong has been smooth and successful over the past few decades. As the world economies, particularly those in Asia, continued to grow, Hong Kong reaped benefits as a major center of trading and commercial activities. Genuinely serving as a window to the People's Republic of China, the territory grew and prospered under the able guidance of an efficient and independent civil service. With changes ushered in by Hong Kong's reintegration with China, and an increased level of autonomy of "Hong Kong people ruling Hong Kong," the government was in the process of readjusting priorities and getting over the hype and excitement of the historic handover.

However, the Asian miracle had started to fade away, and a long span of prosperity and uninterrupted growth had made the leaders somewhat complacent about the need to remain alert to the possibility of downturns. Although the financial turmoil spread and most economies were badly affected, Hong Kong has managed to remain relatively less affected by using its huge fiscal reserve. The leaders appeared to have been caught by surprise, and only after the problem surfaced did they embark on plans to salvage the economy. While there are small signs of recovery, the general prognosis is for tougher days ahead. This prognosis underlines the need for the development of an effective, streamlined system of management in order to handle adversity as well as prosperity. The chief executive has expressed optimism to lead Hong Kong to opportunities from the adverse situation. This will require a combination of various factors, including foresight, anticipation, innovation, and efficient execution of administrative principles.

REFERENCES

Apple Daily News (Hong Kong).
Budget (various years). Hong Kong: The Government Printer.
The Economist (London).

Far Eastern Economic Review (Hong Kong).

Finance Branch. (1995). *Practitioner's Guide: Management of Public Finances.* Hong Kong: The Government Printer.

Hansard. (1976). Hong Kong: The Government Printer.

Ho, Lok Sang. (1998). "The Asian Financial Crisis: A Case of Policy Mismanagement." *Newsletter, Centre for Asian Pacific Studies and Centre for Public Policy Studies, Lingnan College* 3(1): 1–2.

Hong Kong Annual Digest of Statistics. (various years). Hong Kong: The Government Printer.

Hong Kong Standard (Hong Kong).

Hong Kong Yearbook. (1985, 1991). Hong Kong: The Government Printer.

Janis, Irving L. (1989). *Crucial Decisions: Leadership in Policymaking and Crisis Management.* New York: Free Press.

Lane, Jan-Erik. (1993). *The Public Sector: Concepts, Models and Approaches.* London: Sage Publications.

Miners, Norman J. (1991). *Government and Politics of Hong Kong*, 5th ed. Hong Kong: Oxford University Press.

Policy Address. (1998). Hong Kong: The Government Printer.

South China Morning Post (Hong Kong).

Tang, Shu-hung. (1997). "The Hong Kong Fiscal Policy: Continuity or Redirection." In Li Pang-Kwong, ed., *Political Order and Power Transition in Hong Kong.* Hong Kong: Chinese University Press, pp. 187–230.

Tsang, D. (1995). Foreword." In Finance Branch, *Practitioner's Guide: Management of Public Finances.* Hong Kong: The Government Printer.

Chapter 7

China Amid the Asian Economic Crisis: Lessons and Experiences

Zhiyong Lan

INTRODUCTION

In early May of 1997, Japan, the nation that had been plagued by economic troubles, hinted that it might raise interest rates to defend the yen. The threat did not materialize but triggered a sell-off of Southeastern country currencies. Immediately following came the precipitous drop in the value of the Thai baht, the Malaysian ringgit, the Philippine peso, and the Indonesian rupiah. Afterward, the Taiwan dollar, South Korean won, Brazilian real, Singaporean dollar, and Hong Kong dollar all came under pressure for devaluation.

And so the Asian stock market fell. By the end of 1997, compared to July 1 in the same year, the stock market in Jakarta had fallen 47.9 percent; Manila, 48.5 percent; Kuala Lumpur, 56.4 percent; Bangkok, 40.7 percent; Singapore, 47.9 percent; Hong Kong, 52.98 percent; Seoul, 21.6 percent; and Tokyo, 18.2 percent (Peng and Zhang, 1998).

Asian currencies dropped massively. Between July 1, 1997 and August 1, 1998, the Indonesian rupiah dropped 79 percent; the Thai baht, 40 percent; the Malaysian ringgit, 40 percent; the Philippine peso, 38 percent; the Korean won, 32 percent; the New Zealand dollar, 27 percent; the Australian dollar, 22 percent; the Japanese yen, 20 percent; the Taiwan dollar, 20 percent; the Singapore dollar, 19 percent; the Indian rupee, 16 percent; and the Sri Lanka rupee, 12 percent (Qi and Guo, 1999, 43).

Large banks in Japan and South Korea closed. Between November 3 and 24, 1997, Japan's largest securities firm (Yamaichi Securities) and the tenth largest banks (Hokkaido Takushoku) collapsed, among the collapse of other financial institutions. On January 31, 1998, South Korea ordered 10 of its 14 ailing merchant banks to close (Nanto, 1998).

Billions of dollars from international financial agencies such as the International Monetary Fund (IMF) poured into the Philippines, Thailand, Korea, Indonesia, and other Asian countries to bail them out of their financial troubles. The Hong Kong government, supported by its large foreign currency reserve (US$96.2 Bn) and China's promised assistance at times of need, aggressively defended its currency. By September 1998, the Hong Kong government had thrown more than HK$120 billion (US$15.5 Bn) into its financial market to prevent the fall of Hong Kong's currency. Consequently, the Hong Kong dollar dropped by only 0.05 percent between July 1, 1997 and August 1, 1998 (Qi and Guo, 1999, 43). Nevertheless, Hong Kong's economy took a heavy blow. The consumer price index dropped, real estate values took a nosedive, and the unemployment rate reached its historical high in subsequent months.[1]

A few years have passed since the beginning of the crisis. While the currencies in the region have by and large been stabilized, and some Asian economies are starting to pick up a little, most of them are still in an economic downturn. For quite a few years, Asian economies were in recession, unemployment rates were high, and stock and real estate markets remained impotent. Amid this sweeping financial crisis, China, a large developing and fast growing economy in the region, managed to avoid financial catastrophe. Its renminbi did not devalue. Instead, by August 1, 1998, its value had actually increased by 0.13 percent (Qi and Guo, 1999, 43). Its GDP continued to grow (9.6 percent in 1997 and 5 percent in 1998) (*China Statistical Yearbook*, 2000). Moreover, China provided as much as US$4 Bn to help bail out the affected Southeast countries (Lu, 1998, 4).

Why was this possible? What were the factors that contributed to China's ability to deal with the epidemic that plagued so many Asian countries and many of their trading partners in the West, especially when China's financial system had as many problems as any of those countries that suffered the crisis (Lardy, 1998)? Were there any lessons to be learned? How did China deal with the situation? What remains as China's challenges? This chapter will look into these questions.

THE CAUSES OF THE ASIAN ECONOMIC CRISIS

Walden Bello, co-author of *Dragons in Distress*, believed that the economies of the Asian countries were victims of "fast-track capitalism," which involved the free flow of short-term high-interest rate investments from foreign countries (1990). These investments created an overvalued real estate market, securities market, and spiraling costs of foreign debt service but did not really help with the growth of industries. When foreign money started to move away, the bubble broke and a chain reaction led to the collapse of the whole system.

Mahatir bin Mohamad of Malaysia, and some other Asian leaders attributed the crisis to the malicious speculative behaviors of international currency speculators such as George Soros, who manipulated Asian monetary markets to make their predatory gains.

Economists, particularly those in the Asian countries, claimed that the practices of the IMF itself had played a role in the downfall of the Asian economies. They argued that the IMF's million dollar bailout plan was the instrument of a new Western economic colonialism. The IMF's austerity policy—the imposition of rigid economic restructuring by Asian governments as a condition for bailout—created rising unemployment and bankruptcies throughout the region. The removal of government subsidies caused the prices of staples like rice and cooking oil to skyrocket. The IMF also insisted that IMF loans to Asian countries be used to repay foreign debt. That was to subsidize the careless loans made by international banking institutions.

The global lender-of-last-resort, the IMF, suggested that the crisis was largely the result of "cronyism," the unhealthy collusion between Asian governments, big business interests, and local banks to keep their markets closed to outsiders. They claimed that Asia's political systems and institutions and the new demands of globalized trade, finance, and media just did not fit with one another. The Asian tiger economies collapsed from within because of unsound banking practices and unfettered expansion.[2]

All these arguments have some elements of truth in them (Hoff, 1998). However, when efforts are made to identify the commonalities that directly caused the crisis, a few of them stand out:

Export-Oriented Development Strategies

The countries in trouble all had an export-oriented economy emphasis. They heavily relied on foreign investment for their high-speed economic growth. Japan adopted its export-oriented development strategy in the 1950s and 1960s; South Korea, Taiwan, and Singapore, in the 1970s. Malaysia and Indonesia also had similar policies. These policies tended to use price subsidies for export-oriented goods, creating a situation where domestic prices were higher than international prices. In order to persuade the domestic consumers to accept higher prices, higher salaries, better fringe, and other welfare benefits, highly valued domestic currencies had to be in place. Highly valued domestic currency and high pay and fringe benefits thus became a heavy burden on productivity. When productivity or exports could not sustain the demand for growth, the currency became an easy target of external forces.

Financial System Loopholes

In most of the Asian countries, finance was tightly controlled by the central government. Their large commercial banks were under strict supervision of the government. This, on the one hand, centralized the financial power of the state to help large-scale economic projects in the process of economic development. However, as times went by, it also created an imbalance between the need for capital and the use of capital. The high savings and controlled low interest rate and controlled loan policy led to inefficient investment or overinvestment. On the other hand, the nonmarket-sensitive low interest rates forced individual or other types of mobile savings to move into alternative financial instruments such as securities, bonds, and real estates. When these sectors were not well managed, as was the case with most developing countries, the financial system became vulnerable to external forces. Also, in state-controlled financial systems, assets mortgages usually consisted of a high proportion of the loan amount. This had been exasperated by the expansionist enterprise strategy. In order to grab for market shares, enterprises mortgaged out their assets for more loans for growth. Since 1990, the assets mortgages in Taiwan, Malaysia, and South Korea had been 40 percent, 32 percent, and 30 percent, respectively. Japan was around 38.8 percent. Fast growth usually led to inflation. High assets mortgage rates made short-term cash needs more compulsory. As a result, the short-term interest rate got boosted up. When debt service pressure became strong, the movements of short interest rates could be surprisingly drastic.

Globalization of International Financial Asset Flows and Lack of International Financial Management Institutions

The ever-growing private assets in various institutions such as hedge funds, mutual funds, foundations, and private enterprises had grown drastically in the last few decades. The adoption of information technology made it easy for them to travel from country to country to seek high returns. In 1996, it was estimated that the volume of privately controlled funds traveling in between nations amounted to US$3,000 billion, equaling three-fourths of the sum of the total budget of G-7 countries in the same year (Chen, 1998, 37). A large corporation in a developed nation easily had a market capitalization larger than the total foreign reserves of a small and midlevel-income country. In addition to the extensive use of financial instruments such as loans, futures, and options by international monetary speculators, these Asian countries virtually had their bank safe wide open to anyone who bothered to stop by and have a grab. China, however, had a somewhat different story.

CHINA BEFORE THE ASIAN FINANCIAL CRISIS

Of the three direct causes of the Asian financial crisis, only one was applicable to China. That was the prevalence of financial system loopholes. In fact, this problem remains a severe one in China. For the other two problems, China's dependency on foreign exports was relevantly low (20 percent of its GDP in 1997), and China's currency was not freely exchangeable in the international market.

Like many other Asian countries, China had a very centralized financial system that revolved around the banks. Before 1978 when it launched its overall economic reform, China was a 100 percent planned economy. Finance, from taxation to expenditure to investment, was under the complete control of the Ministry of Finance. The role of the People's Bank, China's primary bank, was to receive deposits, print money, and provide loans to state and collective enterprises for production activities. The bank's function was no more than a treasury, receiving and distributing funds according to the directives of the Central Government Planning Commission.

In 1983, the People's Bank became China's central bank, governing four specialized banks: the Industrial and Commercial Bank, the Agricultural Bank, the Construction Bank, and the Bank of China that specialized in China's foreign currency management. The four specialized banks were under the policy direction of the central bank, having only a small degree of autonomy in making loans to state-owned enterprises (7 percent of its total loans) (Cao, 1998, 61). They were under the dual management of both the specialized banks' upper management and the state or local government at commensurate levels.

This system was set up for questionable banking management. Under the policy directions of the central bank, all these banks were required to stimulate growth by financing the state-preferred projects. The political pressure of state and local governments for financing the preferred local projects took away even more freedom from the banks in making lending decisions on their own. As a result, overlending was the norm.

To make matters worse, many of the bank loans were bad loans. Because of the policy imperative, the majority of the loans made by the banks were to state-owned enterprises. These state-owned enterprises enjoyed an exceptionally high rate of return on assets (25 percent) before the 1978 economic reform because of the systematic underpricing of agricultural inputs that led to inflated manufacturing profits (e.g., 69 percent of profits in the textile industry in 1980 and 326 percent of profits in tobacco in 1980) (Lardy, 1999). When agricultural prices were liberated after the 1980s for the overall economic reform, the good old days were no more. Manufacturing profits fell (it became about 6 percent in 1996) (Lardy, 1999). In the meantime, the government started to curtail the budget financing of working capital as a result of its enterprise system reform. The contractual system between the state and the enterprises started to take place in the middle of 1983–1984. Enterprises had to borrow significantly from the banks and often could not repay them duly. Poor enterprise management, continued bureaucratic control over enterprise operation, profit embezzlement, or diversion of profit for nonproduction use, underdepreciation of assets in the past for good political image, poor quality of products that resulted in large inventories, and unrecoverable debt from other state-owned enterprises that were business partners, coupled with the rising price of agricultural inputs and more competitive market situation, dragged many state-owned enterprises into financial plight. "Almost half of all state-owned enterprises were at or beyond the brink of insolvency . . . The average debt-to-equity ratio for these firms exceeds that of the highly leveraged Korean chaebol prior to the emergence of the Asian financial crisis (300–400 percent at the end of 1996)" (Lardy, 1999).

A bureaucratically controlled and terribly messed-up financial situation led to rampant inflation and corruption. In fact, rampant inflation and corruption were the primary causes of the massive Tiananmen Student Movement of 1989. In 1993, when China had barely recovered from the 1989 political and economic setback and started to re-focus on economic development, its economy quickly got out of control again. Inflation was up, economic order was chaotic, unjustified loans and overinvestment went wild, international balance of payment was under serious pressure, and economic development was totally off its balance.

These problems did not go unnoticed. When Zhu Rongji, China's current premier, took over the finance sector in the early 1990s, he initiated a series of structural reforms including:

1. *Increasing the macro-management ability of the Central Bank.* In July 1993, the Central Bank removed the flexible authority of provincial banks in loan making (7 percent) and further centralized the power of credit allocation, credit approval, and interest rate adjustment. This alleviated the political pressures for provincial and local level banks to make loans to financially unhealthy enterprises and nonplanned projects from their local governments. It brought the management of the banking industry totally under central control.

2. *Establishing new commercial banks and allowing them to compete with the existing banking system.* In 1994, China added three state-owned commercial banks: the Development Bank, the Agricultural Development Bank, and Imports Bank. These banks did not make any immediate difference. By 1998, one year after the Asian financial crisis, these three banks were making a little less than 6 percent of the total loans outstanding.

3. *Encouraging the growth of various financial institutions in both public and private sectors.* Zhu also made efforts to implement his concept that the risks should be distributed. The government started to withdraw from underwriting all the financial risks.

4. *Emphasizing the use of the "rule of law" to govern China's banking industry.* In 1995, the People's Congress approved "the Law of the People's Bank of China" and "the Law of Commercial Bank." These laws provided legal defense for the bank managers in their dealings with political pressure and inappropriate demands from their counterparts. These laws also helped to regulate the behavior of the banks in their financial activities.

5. *Recognizing and using the control of money supply as a tool to stabilize the economy.* Typical financial management instruments such as reserve requirements, loan/deposit ratio, sale of government bonds, and interest rates started to be openly discussed and frequently used in China's microeconomic management. With these tools and strong executive orders, Zhu successfully brought China's rampant inflation under control (from 24 percent in 1994 to 8 percent in 1997, Zou, 1998) while allowing for continued fast economic growth (8 percent annually). In 1993, the overall investment increased from RMB 550 Bn yuan to RMB 1000 Bn yuan, more than 70 percent. Most of these investments came from bank loans. The bubble economy was ostensible. Pressure for inflation was very high. Zhu considered this an economic crisis and worked hard to tighten bank loans with whatever methods he saw fit. Also, under Zhu's leadership, the central banks started open market operations in foreign currency markets.

Zhu's reform initiatives did not immediately change China's situation of "bad loans." By the time the Asian financial crisis took place, China's financial system was still full of loopholes. The state-owned enterprises' debt-to-assets ratio reached over 570 percent by 1995 (excluding unfunded pension liabilities), over 85 percent of these debts were to the banks, and nonperforming loans as a total share of bank loans were over 25 percent (Lardy, 1999). But the financial sector reform did help tighten central control (under Zhu) over the entire financial system, helped China's economy to have a soft-landing (i.e., to keep growing without runaway inflation), and provided some leverage for the government to combat the problems brought about by the region's sweeping financial crisis.

CHINA DURING THE ASIAN FINANCIAL CRISIS

As mentioned earlier, the immediate impact of the Asian financial crisis on China was not apparent at the time of its happening. China's currency did not devalue, and its GDP growth remained at a relatively high level. Domestically, China's economy immediately after the 1997 crisis was summarized by the statistics shown in Table 7.1.

Foreign direct investment, another important source of growth for China, was reported as stable. It reached RMB 45 billion yuan (US$5.4 Bn) in 1998, compared to RMB 45.3 billion yuan in 1997. While the investment from the 10 Asian countries dropped by 12 percent in the first nine months of 1998, investment from European countries increased by 64 percent, and

Table 7.1
China's Economic Indicators

	1998	1997
GDP Growth percent	7.8	8.8
Industrial Output Growth percent	11.1	8.8
Fixed Assets Investment Growth	10.1	15.0
State Fixed Assets Investment Growth	11.3	22.0
Trade Surplus	40.3	45
Exports (U.S.$ billion)	182.7	182
Imports (U.S.$ billion)	142	137
Retail Price Index percent	.08	–2.6
Consumer Price Index percent	2.8	–.08
Foreign Debt (U.S.$ billion)	130.9	130.9
Foreign Reserve (U.S.$ billion)	139.9	139.9

Note: The 2000 *China Statistical Yearbook* reported a GDP growth of 9.6 percent for 1997
and 5 percent for 1998.
Sources: Qi and Guo (1999), vol. 3; *China Economic Review*, February 1999; 1998 Indian
Express Newspapers, Ltd.

from the United States, 46 percent during the same period (*Outlook Weekly*, January 11, 1999, 4; *China Economic Review*, February 1999, 4). These increases made up for the lost investment from Asian countries.

There were some serious concerns about the estimated 7.8 percent GDP growth for the 1998 fiscal year. The target growth rate for 1998 was originally set for 8.0 percent or more. It was adjusted down to 7.8 percent. To reach this goal, China made various efforts.

First, due to Zhu's reform in the early 1990s, China started using the money supply as a macro-financial management instrument. From May 1996 on, China had many times decreased its loan interest rates and deposit rates to stimulate domestic economy (May and August 1996). When the financial crisis occurred, China reduced its interest rate again on October 1997; March 1998; and July 1998. The People's Bank announced that it would lower the U.S. dollar interest rate to support RMB, after it had lowered its Deutschemark interest rate to 2.625 percent.

Second, the Chinese government made it a policy to stimulate domestic demands through capital injection and implementation of massive governmental projects. In August 1998, the Ministry of Finance sold RMB 270 Bn yuan governmental bonds. The proceeds were used, through its central bank, to support the four major specialized banks to deal with the risky situation during the financial crisis. Moreover, the central government decided to sell an additional RMB 100 Bn yuan long-term bonds to help with infrastructure construction in areas such as agriculture, forestry, hydraulic power and irrigation, environment, transportation, urban infrastructure, and housing. In 1999 and 2000, RMB 110 Bn yuan and RMB 150 Bn yuan were also sold ("The Effect of Three Years' Bound Program," 2001). Over a three-year period of time, 6620 national bonds supported projects got started. The overall planned investment in these bonds-supported projects reached RMB 1510 Bn yuan. That was 63 percent of the total planned investment (RMB 2400 Bn yuan) (ibid.). The massive capital injection was known by some as China's "New Deal." China's high savings rate (based on bank deposits from individuals and institutions) made the bonds program possible. China's savings rate had been consistently reported to be over 30 percent of its GDP (Aaron, 2000; Lardy, 1999).

Third, starting in 1998, conscientious efforts were made to stimulate exports by increasing tax proceeds returns, reduce enterprise investment taxes, adjust fixed assets taxes, and redistribute income allocation among consumers to stimulate consumption. All these were termed a pro-active public finance policy.

Fourth, the central government started to distribute the risk liabilities among the institutions and investors rather than taking them all on its own shoulder. The bankruptcy of the Guangdong International Trust and Investment Company (GITIC) was a case in point. GITIC was a financial enterprise owned by the Guangzhou provincial government. It was approved by the Guangdong government in 1980 and confirmed by the People's Bank of China. It enjoyed privileges of handling foreign currency businesses. Over the years, as a government-supported financial institution, it attracted large amounts of funds and invested widely in various areas of business. In a way, it helped Guangdong Province to attract investment from outside of China proper, particularly from Hong Kong. Its governmental background made many think that it was risk free. However, its internal management was chaotic. Books were not well kept, and unbecoming or even unlawful financial practices were extensive. It aggressively borrowed high-interest short-term funds and invested extensively in foreign securities and bonds. For a while, it made good money. But the Asian economic crisis hit it hard. In the last quarter of 1998, the company was deeply trapped in debt. Auditing revealed that its assets totaled RMB 21.4 Bn yuan, while its total debt was as high as RMB 36.1 Bn yuan, a net of RMB 14.6 Bn yuan losses (exchange rate: 1 U.S. dollar = 8.3 yuan renminbi).

Similar cases of poor management of finance had happened before. For example, in June 1993, the Bank of China's Trust Company built up a debt of RMB 6 Bn yuan and was on the brink of bankruptcy. It was taken over by the central government. In January 1996, the China Agriculture Development and Trust Corporation could not pay its debt; it was closed down. In June 1998, Hainan Development Bank could not clear its debt after having taken over 34 city cooperatives; it was closed. In the same month,

China New Technology Development and Trust Corporation was closed when it accumulated a debt of RMB 6 Bn yuan. In October, 12 city cooperatives were found to have seriously violated banking law and were closed down. The losses were borne by the government, and consequently the economy as a whole bore the brunt of it.

But this time, GITIC was not as lucky. Zhu decided to play for real. Under his directions, the central government and central bank refused to bail it out. GITIC had to declare bankruptcy at the beginning of 1999. It was the very first governmental financial institution that had to go down like this. Soon afterward, it was found that Yue Hai Enterprises, its sister company, which was also owned by the Guangdong government but operated mostly outside of China, was also in a RMB 3 Bn yuan debt. Due to the lessons learned from the GITIC case, which involved an unexpected amount of foreign debt problems yet to be resolved, the central government took it over and started to reorganize the company. The bankruptcy of state-owned large financial enterprises reflected Zhu's determination to get rid of bad financial practices. It was also a serious lesson for the investors who blindly trusted that the Chinese government would always underwrite the risks of their financial corporations regardless of their practices. In the words of Xiang Huaichen, China's minister of finance, when commenting on the bankruptcy of the GITIC, "Be responsible for your own kid. Central government is not going to keep patching up loopholes" (Si, 1999a, 6). The GITIC case started China's history of distributing risks among its financial institutions and the investors. Right after the GITIC incident, a Law on the Closure of Finance Institution was proposed to the State Council (Si, 1999a, 6).

Fifth, Zhu refused to devalue China's exchange rate. Zhu had his reasons not to devalue renminbi in spite of various pressures and speculations from the international community. By the end of 1997, China's foreign debt amounted US$130.9 Bn, 86.1 percent of which was long-term debt and the rest short-term debt. If renminbi were devalued, China's debt burden would increase. Devaluation of currency could also increase the cost of imports. China's imports were mostly raw materials and goods such as oil, steel, chemical fertilizers, paper, planes, ore, machinery, fiber composite, and wool that China had to purchase. The cost of imports could very well offset the export gains by devaluation. Besides, more than 60 percent of China's exports normally went to Asian countries. Now that the currencies in those exporting countries were all devalued and their purchasing power greatly reduced, unless China devalued its renminbi drastically, it would not gain much at all. If it did devalue renminbi, there could be another round of currency devaluation in those countries. Other than these reasons, China had no real pressure to devalue its currency. Its foreign reserve remained at the level of its foreign debt. Zhu's knowledge of economics and of his country's financial situation helped him to stand firm on this promise that renminbi would not devalue.

Sixth, the Chinese government simply wrote off many bad loans made by its banks. As stated before, China's banks had a high percentage of bad loans. According to Dai Xianlong, president of the People's Bank of China, of the US$1,000 Bn loans made by the four major specialized banks, 2.9 percent was scratched off the books after knowing that there was no way they could be repaid. In addition to the amount in the already dead accounts, about 10 percent of the loans were identified as having no chances of recovery (Si, 1999b, 10). If the calculation included accounts that were late in the repayment schedule or had low chances of recovery, the bad accounts were as much as 20 to 25 percent (Zou, 1998). In an open financial market, bad loans would affect the bank's reputation. Citizens would withdraw their deposits. The pressure on the bank would be huge. But all of China's banks were basically governmentally owned. Even their bad loans were as high as 20 to 25 percent, so it did not affect public confidence in its banking system. They would have had no viable alternative either. Savings and deposits increased by 23 percent in 1997, though that was the lowest of the past 10 years. The central government made policies to use central revenue to alleviate the pressure of these loans by about 2 percent a year in the ensuing years from 1997 on. US$3 Bn worth of renminbi were allocated by the central government to help alleviate these bad debts (Zou, 1998).

In spite of all these efforts, China had rough times in both 1998 and 1999. At the outset, cynicism was prevalent regarding the government's goal of a 7.8 percent growth for 1998. In that particular year, there was a popular saying going around among the Chinese cadres. It read: Ceng2 Ceng2 Jia1 Ma3, Ma3 Dao4 Cheng2 Gong1, Ji2 Ji2 You3 Shui3, Shui3 Dao4 Qu2 Cheng2. [The pressure and quota for expanding local investment for infrastructure construction to stimulate the economy keep going up each time they are passed down the bureaucratic hierarchy to a lower level government, and it is a done deal once the quota is imposed down; the data reported back up has been diluted by more water (faked data) each time they got reported to a higher level of the government. Mission accomplished as long as the higher level of the government accepts the cooked data.] These sayings vividly depict the high pressure state and local officials had from the central government for stimulating their economy. When cornered, some had no choice but to report cooked data back to please their superiors. As a result, every provincial authority except Xingjiang reported growth in excess of 8 percent in order to meet the growth target of 8 percent set by Zhu Rongji, China's premier.

This phenomenon did not go unnoticed by Zhu, China's known "Economic Tsa." He openly said that he did not trust the reported figures by the state and local officials. He was hoping that the real growth rate could still stay above 7 percent. The most recently published *China Statistical Yearbook* (2000) revealed that Zhu was overly optimistic. The real growth rate for 1998 and 1999 were 5.4 percent and 4.7 percent, respectively, the lowest ever since the beginning of China's economic reform in 1978.

CHINA AFTER THE ASIAN FINANCIAL CRISIS

Although the 1997 Asian financial crisis did not impact China in any dramatic way, it did slow down China's growth rate and kept China's general price index in the negative territory (see Table 7.2). More importantly, China learned its own lessons from the sweeping financial crisis.

One timely lesson China learned had to do with its strategy to reform large state-owned enterprises. Right before the Asian economic crisis, Zhu and his economic advisors were discussing and exploring the possibilities of establishing large conglomerates like those in Japan and South Korea. They saw it as a viable route for China's large state-owned enterprises which were desperate for a way out. Since 1993, China's foreign trade has accounted for about one fifth of China's economy. The ratio of exports over GDP has fluctuated between 15.3 percent and 22.8 percent (*China Statistical Yearbook*, 2000). For a while, Chinese leaders worked hard to promote its exports, taking it as a fast track to grow China's economy. The Asian economic crisis came in time to cool their heads down. They saw the loopholes of an economy heavily dependent on exports. While efforts have been continuously made to grow its exports to meet the challenges of China's entry into the WTO (World Trade Organization), more efforts are now being made to promote the development of the domestic economy by stimulating domestic spending and expanding internal infrastructure building, including nationally supported housing projects, highway projects, communication projects, and energy projects. Methods are being explored for diversifying its resources and developing multiple economic entities—large and small, state-owned, privately owned, foreign owned, and publicly owned (common shareholding)—and allowing the multiple economic entities to thrive at the same time. China's objective to join the World Trade Organization is now more a strategy to bring in international competition to reform and upgrade its domestic industry and improve China's economic structure than a means to develop its foreign trade.

The financial crisis also warned China early enough (before it totally opened its financial market) of the danger of a poorly managed financial system. China was already in a situation where reforming its financial system was an imperative (Lardy, 1999). The financial crisis set off an alarm and motivated the Chinese leaders to work even harder to establish applicable laws and regulations to govern its financial sector. Zhu is the rare Chinese leader who understands the modern financial system. He wanted

Table 7.2
China's Economic Growth and Foreign Debt Liability

Year	GDP (billion RMB)	GDP Growth Rate**	Price Index***	Price Index Change Rate	Foreign Debt Liability Ratio*	% of Govt. Revenue to GDP	Foreign Debt	Balance of Trade (UDS billion)
1990	1,854.79		102.1		13.5	15.8		257.43
1991	2,161.78	0.161	102.9	0.008	14.9	14.6		339.87
1992	2,663.81	0.220	105.4	0.025	14.4	13.1		444.33
1993	3,463.44	0.265	113.2	0.078	13.9	12.6		598.62
1994	4,675.94	0.288	121.7	0.085	17.1	11.2	92.80	996.01
1995	5,847.81	0.218	114.8	-0.069	15.2	10.7	106.59	1,104.81
1996	6,788.46	0.152	106.1	-0.087	14.2	10.9	116.28	1,155.74
1997	7,446.26	0.096	100.8	-0.053	14.5	11.6	130.96	1,180.65
1998	7,834.52	0.054	97.4	-0.034	15.2	12.6	146.04	1,162.61
1999	8,191.09	0.047	97.0	-0.004	15.3	14.0	151.83	1,373.65

*Liability ratio = the ratio of the balance of foreign debts to the gross national product of the current year.
**Controlled for inflation.
***Preceding year as 100.

the system to be able to: (1) provide a medium of exchange and a "store of value;" (2) furnish a vessel for mobilizing and allocating funds; (3) provide a means of transferring and distributing risk across the economy; and (4) provide a set of policy instruments for stabilizing of economic activities. He first centralized fiscal and financial controls, and then he worked at overall system reform. Commercial banks are growing, in China, as are other financial institutions such as savings banks, insurance companies, pension funds, investment banks, and securities markets. The commercial banks alone make about 15 to 20 percent of the total loans made by Chinese banks and receive 8 to 10 percent of total deposits. By 1999, China had 11 newly established commercial banks, bringing the total number of banks to over 20 by 2000. These banks have broken the oligarchy of the four major specialized banks and have brought life and competition into China's banking industry. Zhu's strategy is to build a financial system outside of the existing one and to let them weed out and exert pressure on the existing one for reform; they are considered too intertwined to be changed from within.

Scholars supporting Zhu's reform have summarized the lessons China learned from its experiences with the crisis as follows: (1) China has to have a reasonable foreign debt/reserve ratio. (2) China needs a better economic structure that is conducive to both the international and domestic markets. (3) China needs to build a highly transparent, highly efficient, and well-regulated financial sector. (4) The government should withdraw from enterprise practices (Lu, 1998). The massive 1998 Chinese administrative reform, also initiated by Zhu Rongji, was directly targeted at changing the role of the government so that state-owned enterprises could be liberated from bureaucratic control and be pushed into the market for competitive operation.

CONCLUSIONS AND FUTURE PROSPECTS

Looking back, we see that the important factors that contributed to China's ability to avoid an economic catastrophe included a controlled foreign currency exchange; a low level of foreign debt (most of which are midterm and long term); a minimal securities market; a large foreign currency reserve; relatively large domestic savings (deposits) which would have had no alternate exits because of the government-controlled banking system; and a responsible leader who understood modern economics and pushed a pro-active financial policy. Some Chinese scholars jokingly refer to these contributing factors as China's many lines of defense to fend off international financial predators.

Some scholars may be tempted to say that foreign exchange control was the only variable that protected China from falling serious victim to the Asian financial crisis. Had China not had a relatively balanced international account, or had China let its domestic economy fall, or had China responded to the crisis situation in a wrong way, the impact of the Asian crisis on the country would not have been at just the current level. Western observers tend to discount the importance of individuals during the financial crisis, for it was really China's governance structure that made it possible for individuals to exert such massive influence. It took only one Mao to launch the Cultural Revolution; similarly, a change of leadership into one Deng's hands gave China an opportunity to embark on a long journey of reform. The leader in between (Hua Guofeng) did not make much of a difference. With regard to Zhu, his talent, economic sensitivity, and decisive personality provided a rare combination of leadership qualities that served China supremely well in its time of need. He was one of the few at China's leadership apex who had real knowledge of economics. And he was supported, or at least tolerated, by the Political Bureau, the highest policy-making body in China. Zhu's leadership steered a chaotic financial system into one that was controllable in a number of new ways, including the rule of law and use of interest rates to control the money supply. His intimate knowledge of modern economics and China's economy helped him to stand firm on the issue of a stable renminbi at a time of great external and internal pressure. His economic policy has thus far worked well for China. His decisiveness and forceful management style also made it possible for him to push for his reform agenda.

Nonetheless, China still faces many serious challenges. As its reform continues, its financial system will be restructured and opened up to the outside world. Many of the lines of defense that worked in China's favor in the 1997 Asian financial crisis may no longer be viable. The problems associated with the three direct causes of the Asian economic crisis—export-oriented development strategy, financial system loopholes, and growing external financial powers—are problems China has yet to deal with. The more China's markets open up, the more acute these problems will become. China is now working on these problems under Premier Zhu Rongji's leadership. Until his structural reform achieves full-range success, the economy will continue to be at high risk.

At present, 90 percent of the profits made by foreign-invested corporations and joint ventures are reinvested in China. According to one estimate, this amount is as much as 1,000 Bn renminbi, equaling the total of China's foreign reserve. If this amount of capital can freely travel in and out after China has opened its financial markets, when a crisis of confidence arises, they could prove a large disturbance to the nation's financial system (Yang, 1999). In addition, in the past 20 years, at least RMB 10,000 Bn yuan worth of public assets have gotten diverted into private hands. When the unregulated fee charges and corrupt behavior of the cadres are also considered, it is estimated that more than RMB 30,000 Bn yuan worth of public assets have gotten into private hands illegally. There is no way of

Figure 7.1
Top Ten Factors to Help Economic Development (a survey of China's executives)

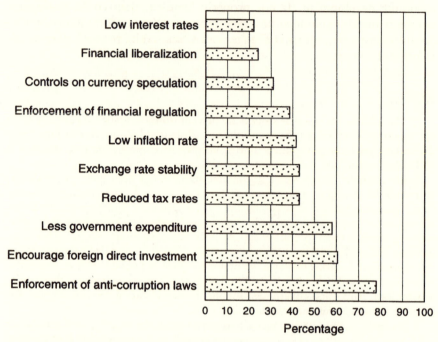

Source: *China Economic Review*, January 1999, 3.

knowing how much public money is deposited in private names. Every year, US$10 to $20 Bn are always unaccounted for in the international balance of payments, signaling that the capital diverted into foreign countries in private names is no less than a few hundred billion US dollars (Yang, 1988). This large amount of unaccounted for financial resources could significantly affect China's financial market once the system opens up fully. The worst prospect is that the trend of illegally diverting public funds into private hands may continue as the reform deepens; bureaucratic power in China has not entirely withdrawn from the market and is still awaiting its chance to take its cut if the situation is not well controlled.[3] Corruption is viewed as a serious problem in China. In a recent economic survey of executives in China (by *China Economic Review*), it was named as the most serious of all economic problems (see Figure 7.1).

Yang Fan, a senior researcher at the Chinese Academy of Social Sciences, warned that while China has successfully dealt with the Asian financial crisis and controlled its economy, the success can only be seen as a one-time deal in a transient problem. More profound problems such as population pressure, environmental deterioration, administrative capacity inadequacy, lack of skilled labor, improper economic institutions and in-frastructure, and sustained political stability, still threaten China's sustained economic development. If not properly handled, they could prove time bombs ready to explode at any time moment (Yang, 1999). Only by suc-cessfully answering all its challenges can China really triumph over its de-velopmental woes.

NOTES

1. The jobless rate stood at around 2.9 percent from December to February 1998 but was over 5 percent by the end of the year. It reached 6.3 percent in June 1999, the highest since the government started keeping its current economic statistics in 1982. About 206,000 people were unemployed.

2. For example, South Korea's economic strength has been built on the success of monolithic business conglomerates known as chaebol. The government's pro-tected domestic market allowed chaebol such as Hyundai and Samsung to thrive. An aggressive marketing strategy by the chaebol backed by the power of the gov-ernment allowed them to quickly expand into the international market. They over-invested and overgrew but did not invest duly in research and development. When the international market turned unfavorable for their exports due to noncompetitive technology, an unfavorable currency exchange rate, and trade barriers, they had to rely on local banks and government support to stay afloat. When this support was not sustained, they fell into trouble.

3. As early as the 1980s, implementation of the contractual system transferred 2 Bn renminbi worth of collectively owned assets into the private hands of the rural cadres who were able to obtain favorable contracts. The next stage involved com-mercial capital transfer. Between 1980 and 1999, an estimated of RMB 200 Bn (10 percent of total retail sales) went into private hands through corruption, commis-sions, retail business sales, tourism, and foreign trade. Following the commercial capital transfer stage was production capital transfer. Between 1985 and 1990, China implemented a double-track system for raw material allocation. State-owned enterprises enjoy governmentally allocated high-quality materials at designated prices, which are normally very low; the collectively owned or private enterprises have to purchase their raw materials from the market at market prices. Through their power to assign state quotas of production material, corrupt officials and people adept at using their connections to power were able to divert public assets into private hands. They could buy low and sell high, often without moving the materials at all; their only trade was a piece of authorization paper. It was estimated that in five years' time, RMB 35 Bn yuan worth of assets (10 percent of the sum of the price differentials between the two systems) went into private hands.

The next finance capital stage came after 1992. The initially offered stocks, the allocated quota of market shares, the manipulation of the securities market, real estate deals, insurance, funds, and property rights exchange, coexistence of state interest rates and black market interest rates, power to authority loans—all pro-vided excellent opportunities for material wealth. Government power and legal in-stitutions have been extensively used to allow debtors not to return loaned money, enabling them to divert funds for purposes of investment and earning bank interests.

In the next five years, assets that are still in government hands will eventually be of turned over to the private sector. These assets include 60,000 square kilometers of land, US$140 billion in foreign reserves, all the publicly owned residential houses, state insurance, and foreign and domestic debts. Already private assets include farmers' contracted land, pensions, medical insurance, and citizens' bank deposits (Yang, 1999).

REFERENCES

Aaron, Henry. (2000). "The Social Security Reform in China: Security and Economic Development." In *Social Security Reform in China*. Beijing: Economic Science Press.

Bello, Walden F., and Stephanie Rosenfeld. (1990). *Dragons in Distress: Asia's Miracle Economies in Crisis*. San Francisco: Institute for Food and Development Policy.

Cao Xin. (1998). "Macro-Economic Adjustment and Zhu Rongji's Economic Thoughts (Hong Guang Tiao Kong He Zhu Rongji Jing Ji Si Xiang)." *Xin Bao* 22(4) (July): 60–62.

Chen, Chaoze. (1998). "Reflections on Asian Financial Crisis." *Xin Bao* 22(4) (July): 35–37.

China Economic Review (1999), pp. 3–4 (a biweekly English magazine published by China's Xinhua News Agency).

China Statistical Yearbook. (2000). Beijing: China Statistical Publishing House.

"The Effect of Three Years' Bond Program: Person-in-Charge of the National Planning Commission's Response to the Correspondent." (2001). *People's Daily*, Overseas Edition, January 4.

Hoff, Gary. (1998). "How the 'Asian Miracle' Became the Asian Economic Crisis." www.ucc.org/global/gl_asecn.htm. pp. 1–4.

Lardy, Nicholas R. (1998). "China and the Asian Contagion." *Foreign Affairs* 77(4): 78–88.

Lardy, Nicholas R. (1999). "The Imperative of Financial Reform." *Orbis* (Spring): 180–191.

Long, Guoqian. (2001). "How to Evaluate the Extent of Foreign Trade Dependency of Our Country." *Issues of International Trade* 11.

Lu, Baipu. (1998). "Asian Financial Crisis and China's Reform and Development." *Economic Management* 11: 4–7.

Nanto, Dick K. (1998). "The 1997–98 Asian Financial Crisis." *CRS Report*, February 6. http://www.fas.org/man/crs/crs-asia2.htm.

Outlook Weekly, January 11, 1999.

Peng, Ge, and Jun Zhang. (1998). "Causes, Impact, and Lessons of the Asian Financial Crisis." *Xin Bao* 22(6) (September): 3–14.

Qi, Ludong, and Guo Shu. (1999). "The Objective Reasons of Why Renminbi Does Not Devalue." *China Potentials* (Zhong1 Guo2 Guo2 Qing2 Guo2 Li4) 3: 43.

Si, Rui. (1999a). "Chinese Communists Are Undertaking a Massive Reform and Restructure of Its Financial Institutions." *Wide Angle* (February): 6–7.

Si, Rui. (1999b). "Who Should Manage the Bad Assets Accounts in the Banks." *Wide Angle* (May): 10–12.

State Development and Planning Commission. (1999). "News Release—Report on the Implementation of the 1988 National Economy and Social Development Plan and Tentative Plan for 1999 National Economy and Social Development," June 16.

Wu, Jianzhong. (2000). "At the Crossroad of the Century, the Economy Is Growing at a Speed Faster Than Expected, Prospects of the Tenth Five Year Plan Could Be Even Better." *Economic Daily*, December 19.

Yang, Fan. (1999). "The Basis of a Stable Renminbi into the Next Century." *Xin Bao* 23 (February): 47–52.

Yi, Mu. (1998). "Chinese Economy and Zhu Rongji's Economic Thoughts (Zhong Guo Jing Ji He Zhu Rongji Jing Ji Si Xiang)." *Xin Bao* 22(4) (July): 55–59.

Zou, Zhizhuang. (1998). "On China's Economic Policy Amid the Asian Economic Crisis." *Xin Bao* 22(9) (December): 8–13.

Chapter 8

Indonesia's Economic Crisis and Dilemma: Contradictions of Two Kinds of Freedom

Yi Feng, Antonio C. Hsiang, and Jaehoon Lee

INTRODUCTION

For the past three decades, the Indonesian economy has grown at an average annual rate of 7 percent. In this broad-based growth period, the percentage of population living below the poverty line dropped from over 60 percent in the early 1970s to around 11 percent in 1996 (Radelet, 1999). The Asian financial crisis of 1997 caught the world by surprise. In a period of months, it wrecked the economies in the fastest growing region in the world. Among nations in Asia, Indonesia suffered the most damaging blow in the crisis, and its recovery has been the slowest (see Table 8.1). From July 1997 to October 1998, the equity market in Indonesia took a mind-boggling nosedive, with a 90 percent loss in its banking sector and 56 percent damage to its composite index. By comparison, Taiwan, Hong Kong, and Japan sustained relatively light damages.

Indonesia has lost nearly 80 percent of its currency value. Many of its banks and corporations have gone bankrupt, and unemployment has risen rapidly, with several million people having lost their jobs. Inflation has been running at an annual rate of 50 to 60 percent. The Indonesian economy has been severely disrupted. Some areas have even experienced serious food shortages. The value of real estate in the metropolitan Jakarta areas has declined by 50 percent. At the height of the crisis, riots erupted across the country, most of which were directed at ethnic Chinese, who make up only 3 percent of the population and yet control approximately 75 percent of the nation's wealth. The world's fourth most populous nation with over 200 million people, Indonesia became the recipient of US$10.1 billion in

Table 8.1
Damage to Asian Financial Markets (percentage change from July 1997 to October 1998)

Economy	Banking	Composite
Hong Kong	–47	–44
Indonesia	**–90**	**–56**
Japan	–46	–30
Malaysia	–75	–66
Philippines	–61	–61
South Korea	–80	–59
Taiwan	–39	–27
Thailand	–87	–68
United States S&P 500	–6	10

Source: Straszheim (1998).

1997, the third largest bailout provided by the International Monetary Fund.[1]

As grim as the initial prognosis was for Indonesia's recovery, Indonesia posted only a mere 0.2 percent of growth in 1999 while some other Asian nations registered far better growth rates, indicating an apparent sign of recovery. South Korea recorded 10.7 percent of growth in 1999 compared to the preceding year, Malaysia 5.4 percent, the Philippines 3.2 percent, and Thailand 4.2 percent, as shown in Figure 8.1.

A long-run perspective shows that economic growth in Indonesia has been anything but smooth. Compared to other nations in the region, its growth trajectory has been marked with unevenness. In the late 1950s and early 1960s, the country suffered from negative growth. After that time, however, economic expansion remained continuous until 1997. While experiencing positive growth rates in later years, the variation of growth rates has been large and the economy has grown unevenly (see Figure 8.2).

In addition to economic determinants, political scientists are interested in investigating the effects of political determinants on economic development in Indonesia. The literature has identified a number of variables responsible for economic growth.[2] However, the majority of the research in this direction has adopted an aggregate, cross-country analysis focused on long-run growth. The objective of this chapter is to study the dynamic change relating these determinants to the development experience of Indonesia. As the following sections argue, the inconsistency and incongruity of political freedom and economic freedom in Indonesia bred the conditions that confine the development of the country and contributed to today's economic debacle. The second section of this chapter evaluates the causal relationships between political freedom and economic freedom. The rest of

Figure 8.1
Real Gross Domestic Product for Selected Asian Economies in 1999 (annual change in percent)

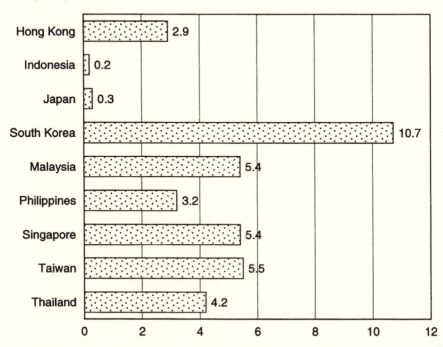

Hong Kong: 2.9
Indonesia: 0.2
Japan: 0.3
South Korea: 10.7
Malaysia: 5.4
Philippines: 3.2
Singapore: 5.4
Taiwan: 5.5
Thailand: 4.2

Source: IMF, *World Economic Outlook: May 2000*.

Figure 8.2
Annual Growth Rates of Indonesian Real GDP per Capita, 1959–1999

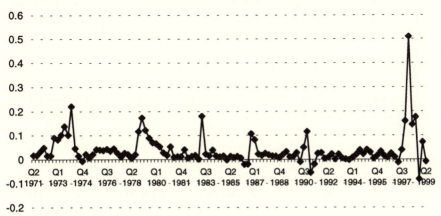

Source: IMF, *International Financial Statistics*, various issues.

the chapter looks at economic freedom and political freedom in Indonesia and their consequences for the country.

RELATIONSHIPS BETWEEN POLITICAL FREEDOM AND ECONOMIC FREEDOM

In Indonesia, the economy has undergone rapid liberalization. The Indonesian market enjoys substantial economic freedom, though this freedom has eroded in recent years. Indonesia ranked 29th among 115 nations in 1995 in terms of economic freedom, down from its place in 1985 (ranked 15th) and in 1990 (ranked 13th) (Gwartney and Lawson, 1997, 116). The potential gains of economic freedom are compromised by the lack of political freedom in the nation. Indonesia is the only nation in the group of countries shown in Table 8.1 that is considered "unfree," as defined by the Freedom House survey (Freedom House, various years). The contradictions between the existence of economic freedom and the paucity of political freedom have distorted the market forces and increased the transaction costs in the marketplace, leading to the recent economic setbacks in the nation. This inconsistency in freedoms is a major reason that Indonesia has metamorphosed from an apparently working market economy into a national economic and political shambles. Political repression in the country has eroded economic freedom and belies conditions needed for economic reforms. The implication for Indonesia is that without securing political freedom in the nation, economic freedom will be eroded and contaminated. In particular, without broad-based support emanating from the political infrastructure, economic freedom only means economic cronyism that favors a small section of the society and therefore cannot be sustained.

In a recent work, Feng (2001) finds that political freedom causes economic freedom, while the noncausality from economic freedom to political freedom cannot be rejected. Overall, the result confirms some of the important arguments and assumptions made in the literature regarding the exogeneity of political institutions (Riker and Weimer, 1993). Political systems do evince a relatively permanent or semipermanent nature, and economic freedom is likely to be endogenous to political freedom. Since Granger causality is a necessary condition for strong exogeneity, we have evidence that political institutions appear to be predetermined and influence economic institutions, though the opposite is not likely to hold universally or in the short run.

Economic freedom depends not only on a tradition of respect for property rights, but also on a political system consistent with economic freedom. While the direct effect of democracy on growth may be ambiguous, its indirect effects on growth can be immensely positive (Feng, 2001). Political freedom may enhance growth by reducing political uncertainty, improving education, increasing investment, or narrowing income inequality. In the

Table 8.2
Economic Freedom Index for Selected Asian Countries, 1975–1995 (selected years)

Country	1975	1980	1985	1990	1995
Hong Kong	9.3 (1)	9.3 (1)	9.3 (1)	9.3 (1)	9.3 (1)
Singapore	6.4 (8)	6.8 (3)	7.7 (2)	8.3 (2)	8.2 (2)
Malaysia	5.4 (18)	5.6 (19)	6.7 (6)	7.1 (5)	7.0 (10)
Indonesia	**5.2 (20)**	**4.7 (29)**	**6.0 (15)**	**6.5 (13)**	**6.3 (29)**
Taiwan	4.8 (28)	5.3 (22)	5.4 (24)	6.2 (20)	6.8 (16)
Thailand	4.8 (28)	4.9 (27)	5.3 (26)	6.2 (20)	7.2 (8)
South Korea	4.4 (38)	4.0 (50)	4.8 (32)	5.0 (39)	6.7 (18)
Philippines	4.1 (50)	4.7 (29)	4.9 (30)	5.8 (25)	7.0 (10)

Note: Figures in parentheses are the ranking of the country.
Source: Gwartney and Lawson (1997).

context of economic freedom, we have some strong evidence that political freedom significantly contributes to economic growth through the channel of developing and maintaining economic freedom (Feng, 2001).

Political elements are factored into economic institutions, which themselves evolve over time. In developing countries, notably the Third World and former communist countries, a democratic system will be instrumental in creating and deepening economic freedom. Political freedom is an important determinant of—if not a necessary condition for—economic freedom. The fundamental implication of the findings for Indonesia is that without political reform and liberalization, economic freedom in that country was fated to be distorted and an economic miracle in this context was destined to fail.

ECONOMIC FREEDOM IN INDONESIA

There was more economic freedom in Indonesia before the financial crisis than in the early years of its economic development. As Table 8.2 indicates, the measure of economic freedom as discussed earlier had been on the rise and then stalled before the outbreak of the financial crisis in 1997. Even though the level of economic freedom in Indonesia is low among the selected countries in the region, it is higher than in Denmark, France, Italy, Spain, Sweden, Greece, India, Bangladesh, and Nepal; it is about the same level as in Belgium, Germany, Peru, Uruguay, and Oman.

Since the 1980s, the country has made significant progress toward economic liberalization. The government has intended to activate its economy through a series of economic reforms. Government programs propelled Indonesia's economic success prior to the emergence of the financial crises.

Figure 8.3
Inflation in Indonesia, Quarter 2, 1971–Quarter 2, 1999

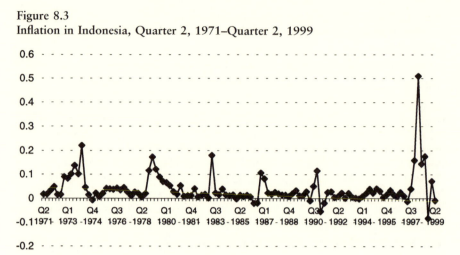

Source: IMF, *International Financial Statistics*, various issues.

Compared with other East Asian economies, due to its large population size and abundant natural resource, "Indonesia has until recently pursued a resource-intensive and home-market-oriented industrialization strategy rather than one based on labor-intensive, export-led production" (Bhatta-charya and Pangestu, 1997, 437). The government vigorously pursued a policy to advance its agricultural sector and succeeded in transforming Indonesia from a rice-importing country to one that is self-reliant in agricultural production. The government pro-agricultural policies included subsidies for inputs such as fertilizer, provision of irrigation and conduit systems, and creation of a domestic food market.

The government was able to install a relatively stable macroeconomic environment. The inflation was mostly low—in single digits—between 1971 and the first three quarters of 1997, despite the cycles of rise in inflation (see Figure 8.3). Although inflation soared to more than 50 percent in the first quarter of 1998, reflecting the impact of the Asian financial crisis, it was contained in a single digit from the fourth quarter of 1998. Inflation represents a set of information for consumers and investors. It affects their decisions on spending, savings, and investment. Frequently, a multitude of factors affect the change in inflation, among which political crises and uncertainty tend to be predominant. Though fluctuating, inflation was under control for most of the years in the data set.

Parallel to a monetary policy that kept inflation low until recently, Indonesia has reformed its fiscal policy to reduce the tax burdens of the nation. Taxation is a key component in measuring economic freedom. "A tax is essentially a government-imposed disincentive to perform the activity being taxed" (Johnson and Sheehy, 1996, 28). The level of taxes in Indonesia has been a moderate one—around 30 percent, down from 35, on high income and only 10 percent on average income. The corporate income tax is topped off at 30 percent. Besides, Indonesia is noted for its low government spending, which is about 10 percent of its gross domestic product.

The government introduced a series of trade and industrial deregulation in the mid-1980s, which encouraged the country to export labor-intensive manufactured products in the world market. Such products included textiles, garments, footwear, toys, furniture, and electronics, "creating millions of jobs in the late 1980s and early 1990s and lifting many Indonesians out of poverty" (Radelet, 1999).

Over the years, the country has cut taxes, lowered barriers to trade, and opened its economy to foreign investment. The protection in Indonesia was considered low, with an average tariff rate at 6 percent, though strict licensing was applied to a number of products such as rice. Figure 8.4 demonstrates the nonoil exports by Indonesia from 1948 to 1998. The dramatic rise in Indonesia's export industries has been an engine for economic growth in the country in the past. Today, the exporting sector will likely lead Indonesia out of its economic woes, taking advantage of currency devaluation.

Indonesia has reformed its foreign investment code to allow 100 percent foreign ownership and to open many sectors that used to be closed to foreign investment, such as electricity, telecommunications, shipping, airlines, railways, roads, and water supply. Since 1969 no foreign banks have been granted a license. This restriction was relaxed in the late 1980s. Though foreign banks are still regulated in Indonesia, they are allowed to participate in the market through a joint venture with Indonesian domestic banks that tend to gain independence from the government (Johnson and Sheehy, 1996).

Along with the relatively open and free structure of the Indonesian economy, "Indonesia's regulatory environment is characterized by bribery, kickbacks, and corruption. Many regulations are applied arbitrarily, and bribes may be necessary to receive an 'exemption' from a government regulation" (Johnson and Sheehy, 1996, 169). In Indonesia, though the market is supposed to determine prices, government regulation has remained high. The government regulates the prices of certain "strategic" items (e.g., rice), setting price ceilings or floors. The government also uses subsidies to promote the agricultural sector. Government enterprises are often protected from market competition. Moreover, Indonesia does not have a modern commercial code system that is compatible with economic activities. "The legal structure provides public officials with too much arbitrary authority. When the discretion of government officials replaces the rule of law, the security of property rights is undermined and corruption (for example, bribes, selective enforcement of regulations, and favoritism) becomes a way of life"

Figure 8.4
Non-Petroleum Export by Indonesia (millions of U.S. dollars), 1948–1998

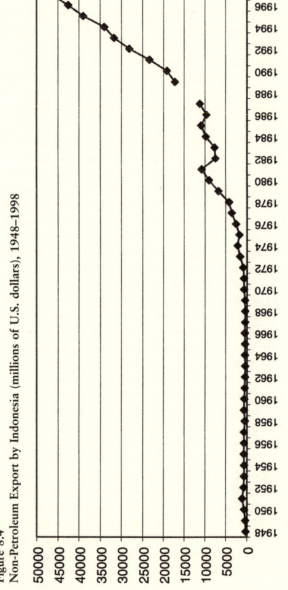

Note: The 1988 datum is missing.
Source: IMF, *International Financial Statistics,* various issues.

(Gwartney and Lawson, 1997, 117). Court rulings leave much for inconsistency and arbitrariness. Finally, Indonesia has a very large black market (Johnson and Sheehy, 1996).

In general, Indonesia has opened its domestic capital market without having established a set of competitive and efficient mechanisms first. Capital liberalization before the establishment of sound domestic financial markets will lead to inefficient allocation of resources. Capital inflows can cause serious consequences for the recipient country because of the market failures in the movement of factors and goods, as well as policy failures in achieving a consistent and credible domestic macroeconomic policy. Both may be associated with the policies of previous nonmarket-oriented economies (Dickinson and Mullineux, 1997; Wihlborg and Dezseri, 1997).

There has been a healthy debate on the sequence of the opening of capital and current accounts (see Feng, 1999). Empirically, some countries (e.g., Chile and Taiwan) liberalized the current account first, followed by the opening or gradual opening of the capital account, while others (e.g., Uruguay and Argentina) prioritized the liberalization of the capital account over that of the current account. In Indonesia, the liberalization of the two accounts seems to be simultaneous. As certain sectors benefit from state protection or regulation, the inflow of foreign capital tends to be allocated to these protected, yet inefficient sectors, causing distortion of the economy.

The economic arguments in favor of liberalizing the current account before the capital account "depend generally on distortions in goods and factor markets, adjustment costs, the need for macroeconomic stabilization, and domestic financial market distortions" (Wihlborg and Willett, 1997, 118). Large capital inflows could lead to substantial appreciation of the real exchange rate, "either directly under flexible exchange rates, or by inducing monetary expansion and inflation under a pegged exchange rate," causing a reduction in export expansion (Wihlborg and Willett, 1997, 115). In the case of Indonesia, the inflow of foreign capital creates financial instability, which is underlined by the lack of sound market mechanisms, despite the appearance of an open economy. The liberalization of Indonesia's capital market was premature and out of pace with its development. Indonesia opened its capital markets too fast and too early, particularly considering the lack of sound regulatory and supervisory institutions and rampant corruption associated with the Suharto family and close friends.

As Figure 8.5 indicates, since the 1980s, domestic credit has been on the rise. A series of financial reforms aiming at liberalization was launched in the late 1980s. The number of banks more than doubled from 108 to 232 between 1988 and 1993 (Radelet, 1999). The ill-regulated and ill-supervised expansion of the financial sector resulted in a tremendous increase in nonperforming loans. Up to the financial crisis, the increase in lending had become dramatic in the 1990s. Taking into consideration the lack of sound market mechanisms discussed earlier, such huge amounts of

Figure 8.5
Domestic Credit (in billions of rupiah), 1965–1999

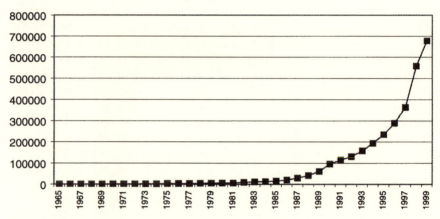

Source: IMF, *International Financial Statistics*, various issues.

lending implies that the degree of inefficiency and distortion in the market worsened in the 1990s. The seeds of financial disaster had already been sown.

During this period, the families of the political elite benefited from the liberalization reforms. The Suharto family and its close circle of friends controlled a large portion of economic activities. The cronyism and favoritism relating to the first family multiplied as the ruler's children came of age in the late 1980s and early 1990s when economic reforms enhanced lucrative opportunities and imposed few constraints on their greedy enterprises. "Foreign financiers, fully aware of the growing weakness of the financial sector and the corruption associated with the Suharto family businesses, were more than happy to finance these activities. After all, they earned high profits on these loans, and presumed (along with everyone else) that these protected enterprises could not fail and would be able to make all their debt payments" (Radelet, 1999). After Suharto's 32-year rule, most Indonesians feel robbed. While the Indonesian people are suffering economic catastrophe, Suharto and his family are believed to have enriched themselves tremendously. The Indonesia Business Data Center, a consulting firm in Jakarta, estimates the family assets at 200 trillion rupiah which is about $17.5 billion at the exchange rate of June 1998, or $80 billion at 1997 ("Settling Accounts," 1998).

When the financial crisis started in 1997, countries with relatively open economies but lacking sound economic policies were hit hardest. The creditors quickly withdrew their lending, and borrowers with huge foreign debts tried to cover their positions. Figure 8.6 indicates sharp devaluation of the rupiah in the third quarter of 1997. The value of the U.S. dollar to

Figure 8.6
Indonesia Rupiah Exchange Rate (rupiah/U.S.$), Quarter 1, 1967–Quarter 2, 2000

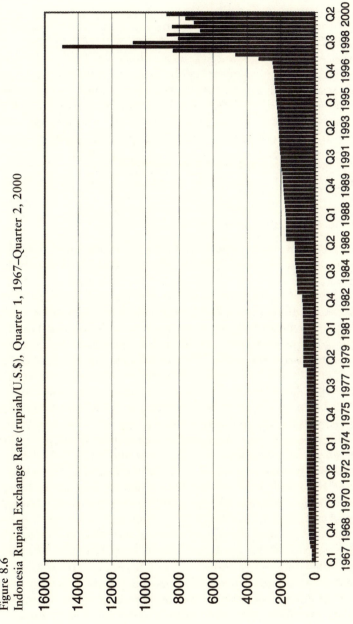

Source: IMF, *International Financial Statistics,* various issues.

the rupiah increased from 2,450 rupiah to one dollar in the second quarter of 1997 to 3,275 in the third quarter. By the second quarter of 1998, it reached 14,000. Indonesian currency has fallen faster than the dollar did in the Great Depression (Lamb, 1999). Although the rupiah's massive slide stopped at the end of 1999, it has not regained its pre-crisis value.

After the financial crisis hit Thailand in July 1997, Indonesia, unlike neighboring Malaysia, adopted the classical liberalized policy. It floated the rupiah, eased foreign investment regulations, and refrained from spending its foreign reserves. All this had no effect on preventing the outbreak of the crisis in Indonesia. The question was not whether or not the crisis management measures based on the classical liberalized policy were appropriate to cope with the symptoms at the incipiency of the crisis. Indeed, what many failed to understand was that investors who took advantage of the weak economic system and strong political clout now started to exit the market because they anticipated the worst was about to begin.

POLITICAL FREEDOM IN INDONESIA

A fundamental answer to the deterioration of Indonesia's economy lies in the contradiction between the country's liberalized economic policy and its fossilized political system. Indonesia has been enmeshed in an incongruity of fast economic liberalization and stalled political freedom. Economic liberalization favored the *nouveau riche* and the family members of the political elite. Helped by speculative investors at home and abroad, they have taken advantage of the lack of a democratic legal system in order to get rich fast, thus contributing to the bubble economy that finally burst in 1997.

As Figure 8.7 demonstrates, Indonesia's economic freedom stalled in the mid-1990s, following an ascendance in the preceding decade. Without being bolstered by political freedom, economic liberalization reached its limit and soon became distorted. As aptly pointed out by McBeth, "[w]hen the forces of reform hit up against the immovable object of political interests, reform makes a detour . . . the reason for the foot-dragging is that reform has reached the point where the only interests left unchallenged are those close to the hearts of some very powerful people" (1998, 128–129). As time passed, political monopoly and the subsequent political repression were on the increase in the nation. Indonesia has been left as the only fully autocratic country in the group of nations with which it was normally associated—the four newly industrializing countries (Hong Kong, Singapore, South Korea, and Taiwan) and the four newly exporting countries (Indonesia, Malaysia, the Philippines, and Thailand). The rest of this section explores the rise of political autocracy in Indonesia and its implications for economic development. In this context, we argue that rising political monopoly and repression that ultimately led to the distortion of economic

Figure 8.7
Economic Freedom and Political Repression in Indonesia, 1975–1995

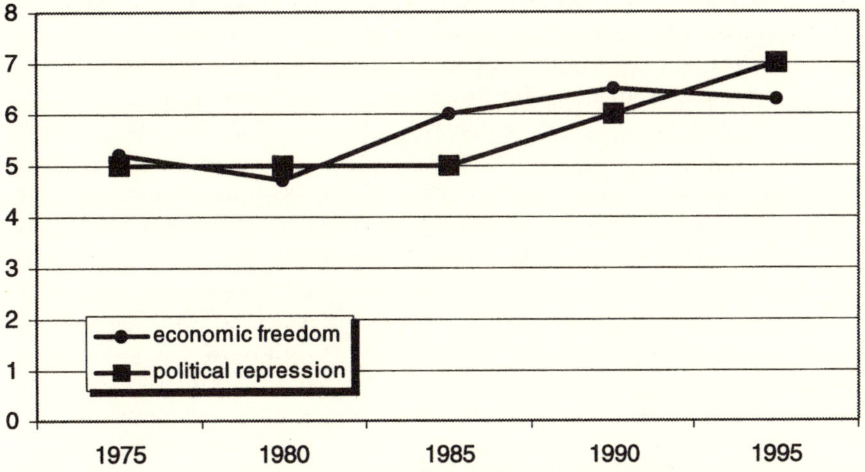

Sources: Gwartney and Lawson (1997); Freedom House/Gastil (various years).

liberalization in Indonesia have been responsible for Indonesia's crisis to-day.[3]

Emerging from the Gestapu (*Gerakan September Tiga Puluh*, the pro-Communist coup of September 30, 1965), General Suharto quickly crushed the coup, becoming a leader of the "New Order." Lacking Sukarno's pop-ularity and the legitimate popular consent of parliamentary democracy be-tween 1949 and 1957, Suharto's New Order sought its legitimacy elsewhere. Suharto and his supporters soon introduced *Pancasila* for their regime legitimacy. Originally conceived by Sukarno in 1945, *Pancasila* is based on five principles: belief in the one supreme god; just and civilized humanity; the unity of Indonesia; democracy led by the wisdom of *musy-awarah* (deliberations) and *mufakat* (consensus) among representatives; and social justice for all the peoples of Indonesia. The development of this political ideology culminated in 1985, when all social and political organ-izations were required to adopt *Pancasila*. Consequently, the abstract prin-ciples under *Pancasila* evolved into a comprehensive ideology with the government as the ultimate authority for formulation and interpretation. *Pancasila* prescribed a society modeled on the traditional family in which parental authority was respected and maintained and to which the interest of an individual family member was subordinate. Emphasizing authority, *Pancasila* reinforced Suharto's personal power, making him comparable to a traditional Javanese king (Demaine with Cribb, 1998).

Fencing themselves off with *Pancasila* from potential challenges, Suharto and his supporters turned their focus on political stability and economic development for their legitimacy to rule. However, political stability was maintained through political repression, while economic development was associated with serious economic distortions that encouraged "discretionary control in fixing prices, controlling supplies of fertilizer and kerosene, setting licensing arrangements for imported goods and imposing arbitrary ceilings on bank credits" (Pabottingi, 1995, 250). MacIntyre (1991) characterizes the New Order as one managed by the bureaucratic elite and military in which Golkar (*Sekretariat Bersama Golongan Karya*, also known as *Sekker Golkar*, the government-backed functional group) and ABRI (*Angatan Bersendjata Republik Indonesia*, Armed Forces of the Republic of Indonesia) were main pillars to sustain the regime.

Golkar's monopoly in Indonesian politics became an established fact in 1971.[4] In order to meet domestic and international expectations and the demands of a reversion to democracy, Suharto allowed elections in July 1971. Nonetheless, the government promulgated a doctrine of "monoloyalty" under which government officials were supposed to support the government only. Other political parties thus lost the support they had received from government apparatuses (Demaine with Cribb, 1998). To further the dominance by Golkar, in 1973 the government combined various opposition parties into two parties rife with internal conflict: the *Partai Persatuan Pembangunan* (PPP, United Development party), comprising the four Muslim parties, and the *Partai Demokrasi Indonesia* (PDI, Indonesian Democratic party), composed of the remaining parties.[5] Golkar's monopoly of Indonesian politics severely retarded political freedom and civil liberty in the country. It also facilitated the family influence of the political elite in business and economic affairs. As McBeth (1998) states, "the business activities of the Suharto family blanket everything from cars, telecoms, petrochemicals, and toll roads to power plants, airlines, taxi cabs–and even birds' nests" (1998, 128–129). The political monopoly prevented true economic liberalization that was supposed to benefit the whole country rather than only a handful of the most powerful people and their families.

Golkar's political domination was made possible by the power wielded by ABRI which ruthlessly silenced and neutralized the opposition. Interethnic, interreligious, or interclass issues were banned from public discussion. Frequent and arbitrary applications of the notorious Antisubversion Law muted any voices that might destabilize Suharto's regime. The law was so obscure that anyone could be arrested and detained without trial if one was barely "suspected of trying to topple the government or merely distorting a vague state ideology known as Pancasila" (Higgins, 1998, 2). Rooted in the 1959 State of Emergency Law in the Sukarno era, the Antisubversion Law[6] allowed imprisonment without trial and, as quoted from the *Amnesty International Special Report on Indonesia*, alleged offenders of the law were often "convicted on the basis of their own confession written after torture" ("Poor Human Rights Record," 1995, 16). Despite an improvement of press freedom following Suharto's implementation of a new policy of openness in 1990, mysterious disappearances of activists and political detentions were on the rise (Higgins, 1998, 2).

All these unjust activities and irregularities were justified on the pretext of forging and preserving the unity of the Republic. As such, any attempts to destabilize the unity of the Republic—in reality, the Suharto regime's stability—were not tolerated. The Indonesian armed forces stood as a vanguard of the Suharto regime. ABRI's involvement in civilian politics was justified by the doctrine of *dwifungsi* (dual function), which stretched its conventional role as a defender of the nation from foreign threats to a guardian of the nation from "domestic dangers of any kind, military, political, socioeconomic, cultural, or ideological" (Liddle, 1999, 44). Based on the doctrine of *dwifungsi*, ABRI placed "active and retired military personnel in the assembly, parliament, and provincial and district legislatures; in executive and staff positions in central, provincial, and district administration; in positions of formal and informal authority over Golkar; and by keeping the population under surveillance through territorial commands that covered the country from Jakarta to the outermost islands and down to every village" (Liddle, 1999, 44–45). Although it was reduced to 38 after the Suharto regime's debacle, the appointment of a military contingent in the 1,000-member MPR (*Majelis Permusyawaratan Rakyat*, People's Consultative Assembly) reached 100 before 1997.[7]

Despite the regime's pursuit of the preservation of the "unity of the Republic" at the expense of civil rights and political freedom, sociopolitical polarization in Indonesia often led to political and economic crises in the Republic. Indeed, Indonesia, an archipelago of some 17,000 islands with more than 300 ethnic groups with different religions, has never been short of the potential rifts caused by sociopolitical polarization. Tensions that emanate from race, religion, class, and the center-periphery relationship have haunted ruling regimes since independence. Rather than dealing with them in an institutionalized framework, Indonesian leaders often ruled through ruthless political suppression accompanied by military brutality.

The seemingly stable appearance of the political autocracy of the New Order notwithstanding, the Suharto regime was fundamentally enmeshed in a dilemma. As Pabottingi points out, the "New Order's [legitimacy] dilemma [was] underscored by its violation of key elements of the national consensus and ideals" (1995, 224). The façade of political stability built on the basis of military brutality and political repression as well as the borrowed economic prosperity started to erode, as accumulated economic distortions undermined development. When the economy takes a downturn, the legitimacy of the political system evaporates and a change in political regime is in the offing (Feng, 1997). The seemingly stable Suharto regime collapsed as its legitimacy disappeared. This led to political uncertainty, social chaos, and a decline of confidence in Indonesia's economy. At the end of May 1998, the Indonesian government pumped 8 trillion rupiah (about $760 million), or twice the capital of the Bank of Central

Asia, into this troubled institution to cover huge withdrawals by panicked citizens (Iritani, 1998). Nonetheless, capital infusion was not enough to reassure depositors who were concerned about how the future of Suharto's political career and that of the New Order regime would unfold.

The consequences of economic liberalization in the absence of compatible political freedom mandate that at this juncture Indonesia needs to firmly establish a political system that is based on the rule of law rather than the rule of a person. True democratic institutions would lead to solid regime legitimacy and make political predictions possible, thus minimizing political uncertainty and enhancing investor's confidence. The nation's economy can be furthered if the Indonesian government institutionalizes a structure of a politically free society and respects the democratic rule of law under which *every* citizen has equal political, civil, and social rights. Indonesia, unlike the Indonesia of the colonial period or of the nation-building period, now possesses a well-educated populace that could function as good citizenry of any democracy. Considering such changes in the vital social and economic foundations for democracy, initiating and consolidating political freedom for everyone will obviously help the country to solve its political and economic issues.[8] Indeed, "guns alone cannot stop violence. Only respect for humanity and submission to rule of law can protect people. [However, both] were lacking in the Suharto administration" (Pekerti, 1998, 9).

In this perspective, we note a series of reconciliatory steps initiated by the new Indonesian government in the aftermath of the Suharto dynasty's debacle in May 1998. B. J. Habibie, who was sworn in as the third president of Indonesia following Suharto's resignation, vowed to initiate a wide range of reforms, including the release of political prisoners and the repeal of the notorious Antisubversion Law (Lamb, 1999, A8). Furthermore, he agreed to East Timor's referendum on independence. In the United Nations-sponsored referendum held in East Timor on August 30, 1999, 78.5 percent of East Timorese voted for independence (DeVoss, 2000).

Jakarta and the representatives of Aceh separatists in May 2000 agreed on a truce for the first time since the violent clash between the Aceh insurgencies and ABRI began 25 years before. President Abdurrahman Wahid visited West Papua (Iryan Jaya) in December 1999 and held extensive dialogues with representatives of the province. Although he empathized that he would not accept any discussion regarding the independence of West Papua (Iryan Jaya), he promised to permit the province greater autonomy (Lamb, 2000, A4).

This series of reconciliatory steps taken by Jakarta should not be regarded merely as temporal appeasement gestures. Rather, they should be understood as Jakarta's effort to renew legitimacy based on national consensus and ideals and to sever ties with the New Order that was laden with political repression and economic distortions.

Indonesia stands at an important juncture in its history. Although it cannot yet entirely eliminate remnants of the New Order era, we have still witnessed Indonesia's fresh start in 1999. (See Appendix 8.1 for the results of the recent parliamentary election.) Given that Indonesia plays a significant role in regional and international politics and economic affairs, it would be in everyone's interest to "make Indonesia, the world's fourth most populous country, the world's third largest democracy" (Bresnan, 1998, 7).

CONCLUSION

This chapter focuses on the contradiction between political freedom and economic liberalization in Indonesia as a source of economic crisis in the nation. We argue that one fundamental source of Indonesia's economic crisis today has been the incompatibility of liberalization programs and the repressive political system in the country. Furthermore, we empirically test the causal relationship between economic liberalization and political freedom. The finding that political democratization causes economic freedom has important implications for Indonesia or any development-oriented autocracies. The double goals of political stability and economic growth in Indonesia were shortlived and crisis-ridden because of the incongruity and incompatibility of the two kinds of freedom we have described in this chapter. Without political liberalization, economic liberalization may lead to premature development and economic stillbirth.

Expressing his perspectives on the Asian economic crisis, Robin Cook, British foreign secretary, offers the following observation: "Real development has as much to do with building an open society as with orthodox market economics. Liberty and open government are not a brake on growth but the basic conditions for genuine and sustainable development. Politics and economics, human rights and fiscal discipline, democracy and competitiveness are no longer worlds apart but essential ingredients to success in the modern world" (1998, 9). Similarly, as argued elsewhere, what Indonesia needs "is to put in place a political system that places value on accountability and transparency, that controls corruption and sets up an administrative and regulatory system that is suited to the age of globalization" (Chanda, 1998, 15).

The lessons that Indonesia learned from the past and the challenge and opportunity for the future lie in the institutionalization of a government of liberal democracy that checks the ruling class and its access to political and economic prerogatives. The political system based on liberal democracy will ensure the basic human value of equality and justice for all, and will foster economic freedom that existed but was stunted in Indonesia under a repressive government. Only by doing so will Indonesia be able to attain social development and sustained growth in the long run.

Appendix 8.1
Results of the 1999 Parliamentary Election

Party	% of Valid Vote	Seats
PDI-P *Partai Demokrasi Indonesia-Perjuangan* (Indonesian Democratic Party-Struggle)	33.74	154
Golkar	22.44	120
PKB *Partai Kebangkitan Bangsa* (National Awakening Party)	12.61	51
PPP *Partai Persatuan Pembangunan* (United Development Party)	10.71	39
PAN *Partai Amanat Nasional* (National Mandate Party)	7.12	35
PKP *Partai Keadilan dan Persatuan* (Justice and Unity Party)	1.01	6
PDI *Partai Demokrasi Indonesia* (Indonesian Democratic Party)	0.62	3
PBB *Partai Bulan Bintang* (Crescent Star Party)	1.94	2
PDR *Partai Daulat Rakyat* (People's Rule, or Sovereignty, Party)	0.40	2
Others	9.35	50

Source: The International Foundation for Election Systems (2000).

NOTES

This work is partially supported by a grant from the National Science Foundation (SBR-9730474).

1. South Korea received an IMF bailout package of US$21 billion in 1997 and Mexico was rescued by an IMF package of US$17.6 billion in 1996.

2. For instance, see Barro (1991, 1997).

3. For a theoretical framework, see Chen and Feng (1996) who demonstrate that political stability, political polarization, and government repression all condition and constrain an individual's economic decision to invest in reproducible capital in the marketplace. Economic growth, which is a function of the accumulation of reproducible capital, will be increased or decreased as a function of regime instability, political polarization, and government repression.

4. Paradoxically, Golkar is not a political party, with no individual membership and virtually no identity except during the election period. Therefore, it is exempt from many restrictions on political parties. More importantly, it enjoys the support of the bureaucracy and the armed forces.

5. Golkar received 62.8 percent of the vote in the 1971 elections, and its share of the vote remained largely unchanged until it was surpassed by Megawati's PDI-P

in the 1999 election. Golkar's share of the vote was 62.1 percent in 1977, 64.3 percent in 1982, 73.2 percent in 1987, 68.1 percent in 1992, 74.5 percent in 1997, and 22.4 percent in 1999. (See Appendix 1.)

6. The Antisubversion Law was repealed in early 1999. However, the Security Bill that purported to replace the law sparked nationwide demonstrations in which numerous students were shot and killed in clashes with the Security Forces.

7. The appointment of a military contingent was reduced to 75 from 100 in 1997. The total number of MPRs was also reduced to 700 from 1,000 as mandated by the 1999 election law.

8. Some scholars attribute such variables as poverty and the lack of democratic experience to the collapse of short-lived parliamentary democracy that the Indonesian elite, such as Sukarno and Hatta, installed right after independence. See, for instance, Bandyopadhyaya (1983) and Vasil (1997).

REFERENCES

Amnesty International. (1977). *Indonesia: An Amnesty International Report.* London: Amnesty International Publications.

Bandyopadhyaya, K. (1983). *Burma and Indonesia.* Atlantic Highlands, NJ: Humanities Press.

Barro, R. J. (1991). "Economic Growth in a Cross-Section of Countries." *Quarterly Journal of Economics* 106: 408–443.

Barro, R. J. (1997). *Determinants of Economic Growth: A Cross-Country Empirical Study.* Cambridge, MA: MIT Press.

Berfiled, S. (1998). "Looking for Social Justice: The Dynamics behind Ethnic Tensions." *AsiaWeek*, March 20, p. 26.

Berndt, E. R. (1991). *The Practice of Econometrics: Classic and Contemporary.* New York: Addison-Wesley.

Bhattacharya, A., and M. Pangestu. (1997). "Indonesia: Development Transformation and the Role of Public Policy." In Danny M. Leipsiger, ed., *Lessons from East Asia.* Ann Arbor: University of Michigan Press, pp. 387–442.

Borsuk, R., and R. Chua. (1998). "Habibie Says He Wants Chinese to Return." *Wall Street Journal*, August 4, p. A14.

Bresnan, J. (1998). "Act Now on Indonesia." *Washington Post*, July 5, p. C7.

Chanda, N. (1998). "Rebuilding Asia." In Dan Biers, ed., *Crash of '97: How the Financial Crisis Is Reshaping Asia.* Hong Kong: Review Publishing Company, pp. 8–17.

Chen, B., and Y. Feng. (1996). "Some Political Determinants of Economic Growth." *European Journal of Political Economy* 12: 609–627.

Ching, F. (1998). "Building a Better Indonesia." *Far Eastern Economic Review*, September 3, p. 31.

Cook, R. (1998). "The Need for Transparency Is Clear." *Los Angeles Times*, May 15, p. B9.

Demaine, H., with R. Cribb. (1998). "Indonesia: Physical and Social Geography." In *The Far East and Australasia Yearbook.* London: Europa Publications, pp. 389–415.

DeVoss, D. (2000). "The World/East Timor: U.N.'s Last Chance to Build a Nation." *Los Angeles Times*, September 17, p. M2.

Dickinson, D., and A. Mullineux. (1997). "Currency Convertibility, Policy Credibility and Capital Flight in Poland and the Czech and Slovak Federal Republic." In C. Ries and R. Sweeney, eds., *Capital Controls in Emerging Economies*. Boulder, CO: Westview Press, pp. 64–88.

Far Eastern Economic Review. (1961). "Indonesia: Politics and Social Affairs." *Asia Yearbook*, Hong Kong.

Feng, Y. (1997). "Democracy, Political Stability and Economic Growth." *British Journal of Political Science* 27: 491–418.

Feng, Y. (1999). "Capital Account Liberalization: Sequencing and Implications." In B. Chen et al., eds., *Financial Market Reform in China: Progress, Problems and Prospect*. Boulder, CO: Westview Press.

Feng, Y. (2001). *Democracy, Governance and Economic Performance*. Unpublished manuscript, Claremont Graduate University, Claremont, CA.

Feng, Y., and A. Hsiang. (1998). "Economic Development in Latin America: A Comparative Analysis." In Kuotsai Tom Liou, ed., *Handbook of Economic Development*. New York: Marcel Dekker, pp. 523–549.

Feng, Y., and J. P. Zak. (1999). "Determinants of Democratic Transitions." *Journal of Conflict Resolution* 42: 162–177.

Freedom House. (1990). "Tables of Independent States: Comparative Measures of Freedom." *Freedom at Issue* 112: 18–19.

Freedom House. (1995). "Tables of Independent States: Comparative Measures of Freedom." *Freedom Review* 26: 15–16.

Gastil, R. D. (1978–1989). *Freedom in the World*. Westport, CT: Greenwood Press.

Gastil, R. D. (1985). "Table of Independent Nations: Comparative Measures of Freedom." *Freedom at Issue* 8: 8–9.

Gwartney, J., and R. Lawson (1997). *Economic Freedom of the World 1997: Annual Report*. Vancouver, B.C.: The Fraser Institute.

Gwartney, J. D., R. Lawson, and W. Block. (1996). *Economic Freedom of the World: 1975–1995*. Vancouver, B.C.: The Fraser Institute.

Helliwell, J. F. (1994). "Empirical Linkages Between Democracy and Economic Growth." *British Journal of Political Science* 24: 225–248.

Higgins, A. (1998). "Vanishing Dissidents Pay for Economic Turmoil in Indonesia; The Beleaguered Regime Denies It Is to Blame. But, Reports Andrew Higgins in Jakarta, Activists Are Disappearing." *The Guardian* (London), April 6, p. 2.

"Indonesia's Anguish." (1998). *New York Times*, October 16, p. A24.

International Foundation for Election Systems. (2000). "Results Summary; Indonesia: June 7, 1999, Parliamentary Election." http://www.ifes.org/eguide/resultsum/indonesiares.htm (October 2).

International Monetary Fund. (1999). *International Financial Statistics CD-ROM* (February). Washington, DC: International Monetary Fund.

International Monetary Fund. (2000). *International Financial Statistics* (August).

International Monetary Fund. (2000). *World Economic Outlook: May 2000*. Washington, DC: International Monetary Fund.

Iritani, E. (1998). "Indonesia Vows '99 Election Will Take over Key Bank." *Los Angeles Times*, May 29, p. A4.

Johnson, B. T., and T. P. Sheehy. (1996). *1996 Index of Economic Freedom*. Washington, DC: The Heritage Foundation.

Kormendi, R. C., and P. G. Meguire. (1985). "Macroeconomic Determinants of Growth: Cross-Country Evidence." *Journal of Monetary Economics* 16: 141–163.

Lamb, D. (1999). "Economic Meltdown Boosts Democracy Movements in Asia; Rights: Drumbeat of Dissent in Region's Southeast Marks Shift from Traditional Acquiescence to Authority." *Los Angeles Times*, February 10, p. A8.

Lamb, D. (2000). "Delegates Issue Independence Call for Irian Jaya." *Los Angeles Times*, June 5, p. A4.

Liddle, R. W. (1999). "Regime: The New Order." In Donald K. Emmerson, ed., *Indonesia Beyond Suharto: Polity, Economy, Society, Transition*. New York: Asia Society.

Lipset, S. M. (1959). "Some Social Requisites of Democracy: Economic Development and Political Development." *American Political Science Review* 53: 69–105.

MacIntyre, A. (1991). *Business and Politics in Indonesia*. Sydney: Allen and Unwin.

Mally, M. (1999). "Regions: Centralization and Resistance." In Donald K. Emmerson, ed., *Indonesia Beyond Suharto: Polity, Economy, Society, Transition*. New York: Asia Society.

McBeth, J. (1998). "Dept. of Connections." In Dan Biers, ed., *Crash of '97: How the Financial Crisis Is Reshaping Asia*. Hong Kong: Review Publishing Company, pp. 128–134.

McCawley, T. (2000). "On Neutral Ground, Rebels Face Indonesian Government." *The Christian Science Monitor*, May 12, p. 7.

Mydans, S. (1998). "Role of Military: A Potential Unifier Split by Conflicting Goals." *New York Times*, May 15, p. A6.

Napier, C. (1999). "The Fragile Archipelago." *BBC Online Network*. http://news 6.thdo.bbc.co.uk/hi/english/events/indonesia/specialreport/newsid270000/270462.stm (September 30).

Pabottingi, M. (1995). "Indonesia: Historicizing the New Order's Legitimacy Dilemma." In Muthiah Alagappa, ed., *Political Legitimacy in Southeast Asia: The Quest for Moral Authority*. Stanford, CA: Stanford University Press, pp. 244–256.

Pekerti, A. (1998). "Power Alone Isn't Enough in Indonesia." *Los Angeles Times*, June 25, p. B9.

"Poor Human Rights Record." (1995). *South China Morning Post*, August 17, p. 16.

Radelet, S. (1998/1999). "From Boom to Bust: Indonesia's Implosion." *Harvard Asian Pacific Review* 3: 62–66.

Richburg, K. B. (1998). "Ethnic Chinese: Indonesia's Scapegoats."*Washington Post*, December 23, p. A01.

Riker, W. H., and D. L. Weimer. (1993). "The Economic and Political Liberalization of Socialism: The Fundamental Problem of Property Rights." *Social Philosophy and Policy* 10: 79–102.

"Settling Accounts." (1998). *The Economist*, June 6, p. 39.

Solomon, J. (1998a). "New Jakarta Plan Favors Ethnic Indonesians." *Wall Street Journal*, November 11, p. A14.

Solomon, J. (1998b). "New Muslim Political Parties Sow Unease among Some Indonesians."*Wall Street Journal*, August 13, p. A10.

"Still Living Dangerously." (2000). *Financial Times Asia Intelligent Wire/Bangkok Post*, October 15.

Straszheim, D. (1998). "The Realities of Global Competition." Paper presented at the International Studies Association West Annual Meeting, Claremont, CA, October.

Vasil, R. (1997). *Governing Indonesia: National Development and Democracy.* Singapore: Butterworth-Heinemann Asia.

Wihlborg, C., and K. Dezseri. (1997). "Precondition for Liberalization of Capital Flows: A Review and Interpretation." In C. P. Ries and R. J. Sweeney, eds., *Capital Controls in Emerging Economies.* Boulder, CO: Westview Press, pp. 33–44.

Wihlborg, C., and T. Willett. (1997). "Capital Account Liberalization and Policy Incentives: An Endogenous Policy View." In C. P. Ries and R. J. Sweeney, eds., *Capital Controls in Emerging Economies.* Boulder, CO: Westview Press, pp. 111–136.

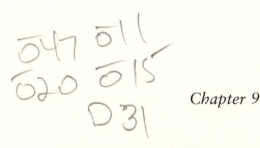

Chapter 9

Managing Economic Development in the Presence of Ethnic Diversity: The Malaysian Experience

Yi Feng, Ismene Gizelis, and Jaehoon Lee

INTRODUCTION

In 1994, *The Handbook of Country and Political Risk Analysis* forecast that during the period 1994–1998 political stability would prevail in Malaysia. It also predicted that Malaysia would have one of the strongest economies in the world and that a political transition to Anwar Ibrahim would occur by 1996 without any disruptive effect on the country's economic growth. Finally, the report forecast that a global economic downturn in 1997–1998 would have minimal effect on the country's development because of the Asia Pacific region's strong economic trends (Coplin and O'Leary, 1994, 50–51). Unfortunately every single prediction in the report failed, given the outbreak of the Asian financial crisis and the arrest of Anwar on September 20, 1998.[1]

The Asian financial crisis in September 1997 hit Southeast Asian countries one by one. They started falling like dominoes, with Thailand, Malaysia, the Philippines, and Indonesia all experiencing currency tumbles and stock market crashes. At the end of October, the crash of Hong Kong's stock market seemed to threaten global financial security. Indonesia had to be rescued by the IMF and other donors with a relief package of $40 billion. South Korea soon followed, requiring almost a $60 billion bailout of the formerly miraculous economy that now teetered on the edge of bankruptcy. Political inertia before the runoff elections created panic among the investors, and the living standards of average Koreans fell ("The IMF and Asia," 1997, 20; "A Fatal Resolve," 1997, 83). As a result of this unprecedented crisis, not only has the structure of income distribution deteriorated, but the middle class has also been significantly reduced in the region.

Moreover, this new development persisted in spite of rebounding economies in the region. In Korea after the crisis, for example, the rate of earnings of the top quintile has increased, while those of the rest have diminished as shown in Table 9.1.

The Gini coefficient and the top-bottom quintile earnings ratio have increased, as shown in Table 9.1. This indicates that a widening gap in earnings has become a new post-crisis social phenomenon in Korea. The earnings of the top quintile in 1998, according to the National Statistical Office of Korea, showed an increase of 2.3 percent, while those of the other 80 percent realized diminished earnings from 5.5 percent to 14.9 percent. This unequal trend in earnings is due, in part, to mass layoffs and bankruptcies that directly victimized lower quintile groups. On the contrary, the top quintile, having possessed relatively larger financial assets than any other groups, greatly benefited from various crisis management measures, such as deferred taxes on interest income, in addition to already large interest gains from soaring market interest rates. Consequently, the structure of income distribution was inevitably distorted and polarized as unequal earnings were exacerbated. This, in turn, resulted in the collapse of the middle class, leading to sociopolitical instability in Korea (Koh, 1998).

In Malaysia, political confrontations ensued as a result of the crisis and ended with the purge and arrest of Deputy Premier Anwar Ibrahim. Then, why did the forecast of Malaysia's political and economic future fail to detect any potential problems in the Malaysian political and economic systems? Were political events related to the economic crisis that swept Pacific Asia? This chapter explores political aspects of long-term economic development in Malaysia. The main argument is that political development and economic growth are intertwined and mutually reinforcing. Political stability and policy consensus enhance economic growth, while higher levels of economic growth reduce the level of polarization and enhance national unity. Malaysia, among other developing countries, is a good example in which a mutually reinforcing relationship between political institutions and economic development has been well recognized by and clearly reflected in various governmental policies.

This chapter does not focus solely on the immediate causes of the financial and economic turbulence Malaysia has just encountered. Rather, this chapter aims at charting the genesis and course of Malaysia's long-term economic growth and the interaction between growth and political institutions. This perspective has a few important implications. First, it enables us to understand what benefits economic growth has brought to Malaysia's multiethnic society. Second, an examination of the interaction between the economy and political institutions sheds light on the political underpinnings of Malaysia's growth trajectory. Finally, the historical approach in this chapter helps reveal Malaysia's future path of growth.

Table 9.1
Household Income Distribution of Urban Working Families in Korea by Quintile, 1995–1999

| Year | Income Distribution by Quintile (%) | | | | | Ratio (Top/Bottom) | Gini Coefficient |
	Bottom	Second	Middle	Fourth	Top		
1995	8.5	13.5	17.5	23.0	37.5	4.42	0.284
1996	8.2	13.3	17.5	23.1	37.9	4.63	0.291
1997	8.3	13.6	17.7	23.2	37.2	4.49	0.283
1998	7.4	12.8	17.1	22.9	39.8	5.41	0.316
1999	7.3	12.6	16.9	22.9	40.2	5.49	0.320

Source: "Table 19: Income Distribution by Quintile," *The Trends of Annual and Fourth Quarter 1999 Household Income and Expenditure of Urban Working Families* (Seoul, Korea: National Statistical Office, March 2000).

PATTERNS OF DEVELOPMENT IN MALAYSIA

Understanding the patterns of economic development in Malaysia requires a comprehension of the fundamental economic and political divisions among the three ethnic groups that comprise almost 95 percent of the total population: the Malays, the Chinese, and the Indians. Malaysia was part of the United Kingdom's empire until it became independent in 1957. Since its independence, Malaysia has become a federation of two Borneo states in Indonesia and eleven states on the Malaya peninsula.[2] The population consists primarily of Malays (55 percent of the population), Chinese (35 percent), and Indians (10 percent).[3] Most Malays live in rural areas, predominantly in the four northern states of the peninsula. Chinese are typically urban dwellers, with an income level twice as high as that of the Malays. They tend to reside in the state of Selangor surrounding the capital Kuala Lumpur, the most highly developed region in the country. Financially, Indians fall in between the Chinese and the Malays, many of them working as rubber tappers. Although the Chinese are by far the wealthiest group, the Malays are politically the most powerful (Hammer et al., 1995).

Unlike neighboring Indonesia, the transition from Britain's colonial rule to independence was peaceful in Malaysia, occurring with no major transformation of political and economic structures. Nonetheless, ethnic polarization was the primary threat to Malaysia's economic development. Malaysia's political and economic stability hinged on a balance among the three ethnic groups, particularly between the Chinese and the indigenous Malays (Bumiputera). After independence, an elite consensus was reached through bargaining among the three major political groups—the United Malay National Organization (UMNO), the Malayan Chinese Association (MCA), and the Malayan Indian Congress (MIC). Malays would have control of the government in exchange for full citizenship status for the Chinese and the Indians. Nevertheless, the Chinese soon dominated commerce and business (Root, 1996, 70–71). The growing economic gap between the Chinese and the Malays was one of the leading causes of the ethnic conflict that culminated in a violent riot following the May 10, 1969 election, killing 196 people.

From 1966, the year after Singapore seceded, to 1992, the real GDP per capita increased from 1,728 to 5,729 international dollars, moving the country ahead of all Latin American countries except Mexico and Venezuela.[4]

For this period, real GDP per capita in Malaysia—based on purchasing power parity—grew at an average annual rate of 4.8 percent, which is lower than South Korea (7.7 percent), Singapore (7.5 percent), and Taiwan (6.7 percent), similar to Indonesia (4.9 percent) and Thailand (4.6 percent), but significantly higher than the Philippines (1.2 percent) (see Figure 9.1).

Figure 9.1
Real GDP per Capita for Selected Pacific Asian Economies, 1960–1995 (in international dollars)

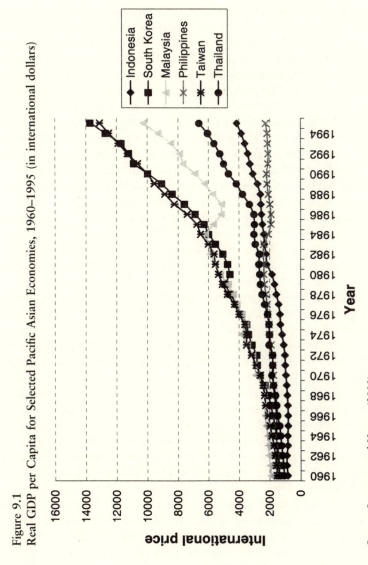

Source: Summers and Heston (2000).

The temporal variation in annual growth rates in Malaysia, as discussed in detail below, is related to the political and policy decisions of the Malaysian government. Prior to the racial riots of 1969, the growth rate was merely an average of 2.6 percent in Malaysia. However, with an ambitious launching of a series of national development plans, the growth rates increased to 5.4 percent and 4.5 percent on average during the phase of the First Malaysia Plan (1MP, 1966–1970) and the Second Malaysia Plan (2MP, 1971–1975) respectively. As the Malaysian government devised and implemented a long-term development plan called the First Outline Perspective Plan (OPP1, 1971–1990), the growth rate continued to rise and the average growth rate reached 7.6 percent during the phase of the Third Malaysia Plan (3MP, 1976–1980). From the 1980s through the early 1990s, Malaysia's growth rate leveled off at 4.1 percent, reflecting the mid-1980s recession when the Malaysian economy drastically shrank to −6.2 percent and −6.9 percent in 1985 and 1986, respectively (Summers and Heston, various years). The Malaysian economy successfully rode out the recession in 1987 and continued its high growth until it was hit by the unprecedented regional crisis. Nonetheless, the economy again demonstrated its resilience as growth bounced back to 5.4 percent in 1999 (IMF, 2000).

Many empirical studies have indicated that the primary economic determinants of economic growth are investment, human capital, international trade, and inflation. For instance, Levine and Renelt (1992) and Barro (1997) all identify trade and investment as major inputs for growth. Discussing Mexico's financial crisis that occurred at the end of 1994, Summers points out that one important lesson with long-term implications is that "high rates of domestic savings are essential for healthy development (Summers, 1995–1996, 46). Romer (1990) concludes that human capital is the major input to research and development which innovates technologies. Finally, Kormendi and Meguire (1985) find that inflation has generally been regarded as having a negative impact on economic growth.

The main characteristic of the Malaysian economy has been its strong trade position due to its historical dependency on richly endowed mineral reserves. Indeed, its high concentration of primary commodities led Malaysia to intensively engage in international trade. In 1986, Malaysia had about 35 percent of the world's production of rubber, approximately 60 percent of palm oil, and about 35 percent of tin ("Malaysia," 1986). In 1970, its primary exports—rubber, tin, timber, palm oil, petroleum, and the like—already constituted 31.6 percent of the country's GDP (Kasper, 1974, 9). In the same year, exports accounted for about 46 percent of Malaysia's GDP. The dependency on exports gradually increased to 58 percent in 1980 and has exceeded 90 percent since 1994, as shown in Figure 9.2.

Malaysia's export-led growth was made possible not only by the country's rich factor endowments, but also by its physical infrastructure and

Figure 9.2
Growth of Malaysia's Exports Compared to GDP (in billions of ringgit)

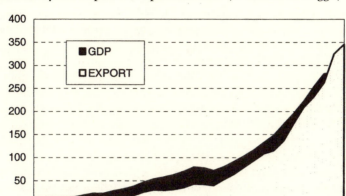

Source: IMF, *International Financial Statistics*, various years.

human capital development. Malaysia had inherited a fairly conditioned infrastructure when it became independent from British rule (Kasper, 1974, 6), as substantial investments in transport, communication facilities, and public utilities had been made during the 1950s. Thus, the physical infrastructure "has never represented a serious bottleneck for private development" (Anand, 1983, 5).

Human capital development is also salient in Malaysia. The secondary school enrollment rate rose from 34.2 percent in 1970 to 56.3 percent in 1990 and continued to rise to 64 percent in 1998, as shown in Table 9.2, while the illiteracy rate dropped from 41.5 percent in 1970 to 16.5 percent in 1995 and to 13.6 percent in 1998. Malaysia's human capital is constantly improving because the government emphasizes and promotes this sector. Primary school enrollment was low during the 1960s and early 1970s, a period fraught with ethnic conflict that peaked in 1969. Since then, primary enrollment has increased dramatically (99.9 percent in 1998) as the Malaysian government endeavored to expand education to all segments of the population and to reduce lifelong inequalities between rural and urban populations and among the three ethnic groups.

To ensure universal primary education and to expand secondary education, the Malaysian government has earmarked over 16 percent of national economic resources to education. In terms of overall gross enrollment in secondary education, Malaysia (62 percent) is now similar to China (61 percent), but ahead of India (49 percent) and Thailand (55 percent), and is catching up with the Philippines (79 percent) (World Bank, 1998).

Malaysia has had quite a high savings rate—about 35 percent of its

Table 9.2
Indicators for Human Capital Development in Malaysia

	1970	1985	1990	1995	1998
Secondary school enrollment rate[a]	34.2	52.9	56.3	58.7	64.0[c]
Illiteracy rate[b]	41.7	23.5	19.1	15.6	13.6

[a]Percentage gross.
[b]Percentage of people age 15 and up.
[c]1997 figure.
Source: World Bank (2000).

GDP—but even this level of savings is insufficient to satisfy the people's needs for imports and investment. About 42 percent of Malaysian imports are capital goods and about 41 percent are raw materials. These are necessary imports for Malaysia to become an industrialized country with state-of-the-art technology ("States of Denial," 1996).[5]

Inflation rates are relatively low in Malaysia, compared to those of other developing countries, particularly Latin American countries during the late 1970s and early 1980s. The inflation rate in Malaysia rose from 2.56 percent in 1989 to 4.72 percent in 1992, a rise due largely to the increase in import prices, as imports account for 30 percent of the consumer price index. Although the inflation rate soared to 5.28 percent in 1998, it was well contained at a rate of 2.77 percent in 1999. Meanwhile, domestic credit growth rates reached about 21.2 percent a year on average between 1990 and 1997, whereas the average growth rate was only 5.3 percent for the period 1975–1982. The credit growth peaked at 31.2 percent in 1996 and plummeted to −2.7 percent in 1998, reflecting the severe impact of the Asian financial crisis (see Table 9.3).

Examining the path of Malaysia's growth, we may conclude, despite the recent setbacks, that rich factor endowments, good physical infrastructure, excellent human capital development, well-contained inflation, a high rate of domestic savings, and the availability of domestic credits have all accommodated Malaysia's economic development. Its strong export growth accelerated economic growth as a whole at a speed that Malaysia has never witnessed in the post-independence era.

Malaysia's remarkable economic achievement can be attributed to political institutions that affect some fundamental economic variables. Increases in private savings and investment, as well as a decline in income inequality, are critical in affecting economic growth. Political institutions within a country reflect levels of political and economic freedom as well as determine levels of political stability and consensus. A stable political environment attracts both foreign and domestic investment (Alesina and Sachs, 1988;

Table 9.3

Inflation, Savings, and Domestic Credit Growth in Malaysia, 1975–1999

	Inflation[a]	Savings[b]	Credit Growth[c]
1975–1982	5.33	21.6	5.3
1983–1989	2.02	29.4	19.9
1990	2.81	29.1	18.0
1991	4.40	28.4	18.5
1992	4.72	31.3	16.2
1993	3.54	33.0	12.3
1994	3.73	32.7	14.8
1995	3.40	33.5	29.5
1996	3.48	36.7	31.2
1997	2.71	37.3	29.3
1998	5.28	38.8	–2.7
1999	2.77	N/A	0.3

[a]Figures obtained from IMF (2000b).

[b]Annual percentage change. The 1998 figure is preliminary. Compiled from "Table A1: Selected Asian Economies: Basic Economic Data," IMF, *World Economic Outlook: Interim Assessment*, December 1997 and "Table 5: Malaysia: Composition of Investment and Saving in Current Prices, 1994–98," IMF, *Malaysia: Recent Economic Development*, 1999.

[c]Annual percentage change (end of year). Computed from IMF (2000a).

Cukierman et al., 1992; Feng, 1997). The next section examines the political determinants of economic development and explores their impact on economic growth in Malaysia.

POLITICAL DETERMINANTS OF GROWTH

Alesina, Roubini, Özler, and Swagel start their article with the statement "Economic growth and political stability are deeply interconnected" (1992, 1). This statement is corroborated to a certain extent by the public choice literature on institutions, property rights, and economic growth (e.g., Knack and Keefer, 1995; North, 1990; Scully, 1988, 1991). Moreover, studies have indicated that political instability affects such critical economic variables as inflation and investment, and external borrowing (Alesina, Roubini, Özler, and Swagel, 1992; Barro, 1991; Cukierman, Edwards, and Tabellini, 1992).

Chen and Feng (1996) discuss three fundamental political conditions for economic growth—political instability, political polarization and government repression. These constitute the basic political environment for economic growth and socioeconomic development, conditioning and constraining an individual's economic decision to invest in reproducible capital in the marketplace. Economic growth, a function of the accumulation of reproducible capital, will increase or decrease as a function of instability, polarization, and repression. In sum, political instability, policy polarization, and government repression all decrease growth. The following subsections explore the political implications for Malaysia's economic development.

Maintaining Political Stability

Under the current political system, the dominant political party, the United Malaysia National Organization (UMNO), controls a coalition of 14 parties under the banner of the Barisan Nasional (BN, National Front). The Malayan Chinese Association (MCA) and the Malayan Indian Congress (MIC) have also been major members of the coalition since the days of the Alliance (see Appendix 9.1).

The major opposition parties are the Parti Islam SeMalaysia (PAS) and the Democratic Action party (DAP). Coalescing with Parti Keadilan Nasional (National Justice party), headed by Wan Azizah Wan Ismail, the wife of the former deputy premier, Anwar, PAS and DAP formed an opposing coalition called Barisan Alternatif (BA, Alternative Front). The rise of the BA as a successful political coalition became clear at Malaysia's tenth election held in November 1999. PAS captured 27 of 42 seats contested and reasserted its role as a leading opposition party. DAP won 10 seats, while newly formed Keadilan (National Justice party, led by Wan Azizah) seized 5 seats in the parliament. Nonetheless, the opposition failed to penetrate the BN's majority in Dewan Rakyat (House of Representatives). Seizing more than two-thirds of the 193-member parliament (148 seats) in the election, BN still secured a sufficient number of seats to control the parliament (see Appendix 9.1). Although the current political and economic situation casts doubt on whether this coalition will remain vibrant in the future, it has in the past provided the nation with political stability.

Despite the recent rise of the opposition parties, especially that of PAS, removal of the ruling Barisan Nasional from office is highly unlikely. The BN's preponderance of power, as demonstrated in Appendix 9.1, seems incontestable as yet. Consequently, the probability of the opposition parties capturing the central government through elections is low. Instead, business communities, as well as the public in general, have been more concerned about the change in the power structure of the BN—especially within the UMNO, the senior partner in the coalition.

Radical policy changes have not been unprecedented in Malaysia. Although the BN has dominated the Malaysian government and politics since independence, occasional policy shifts have not been rare incidents. The policy shift in 1986, moving the industrial development emphasis from import substitution to export promotion, is an example. Mahathir initiated

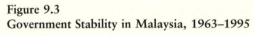

Figure 9.3
Government Stability in Malaysia, 1963–1995

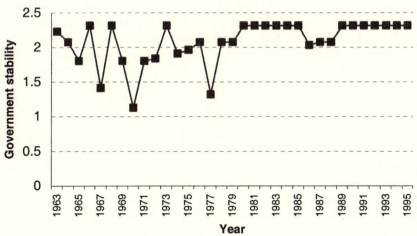

Source: Le (1998).

the shift immediately after he captured the top post in the government. Thus, we could conclude that economic actors would be interested in predicting who, or which group, would control the Malaysian government.

Despite the prevalence of political stability, government crises have occasionally erupted even under the condition of dominant party rule, resulting in a slowdown of economic growth. A major government crisis is defined as any rapidly developing situation that threatens to bring down the present regime—excluding situations of revolt aimed at such overthrow (Banks, 1979). Given that Malaysia lacks other forms of political instability such as revolutions, military coups d'état, and assassinations, government crises are perhaps the best indicator of political instability in the country. Figure 9.3 plots the likelihood of major government crises in Malaysia from 1963 through 1995. The measure of government crises we use here as developed by Le (1998) is based on a function of government crises determined by other political acts. In Figure 9.3 we reverse the government crisis index so that a higher number represents a higher degree of government stability. It turns out that the propensity of government crises was relatively high in the early years and eventually leveled out in the last 10 years, a trend that is consistent with the relatively slow growth in the 1960s and fast growth from 1984 through 1996.

Government crises and the rate of growth, in general, move in opposite directions. This pattern is especially conspicuous for the periods 1974–1978 and 1984–1987, consistent with the argument that growth declines when government stability is low and, conversely, growth gains when government stability is high. Between 1972 and 1981, the business communities watched with great anxiety the return and the subsequent ascension of Mahathir bin Mohamad, who had been banished to the political wilderness mainly because of his anti-Chinese position ("Dr. Mahathir," 1986). Mahathir's rise to power was rapid. He was readmitted to the UMNO in 1972 and became a member of the Supreme Council that had expelled him. He served in the Dewan Negara (Senate) in 1973 and in Dewan Rakyat (House of Representatives) in 1974. He was the minister of education from 1976 to 1981 before he was sworn in as prime minister in July 1981 ("Dr. Mahathir," 1986).

Mahathir's return to the Malaysian political arena first instilled great uncertainty in the business community. The traditional liberal economic policies pursued by previous regimes were gradually abandoned as he rose to the top post in the Malaysian government. As shown in Figure 9.1, the Malaysian economy began to rebound after 1975. The uncertainties in the business community were perhaps removed as Mahathir consolidated his power and ascended as the next premier.

A similar pattern can be seen between 1984 and 1986 when the UMNO and the government were on the verge of a split as the power struggle between Mahathir and his then-lieutenant Musa Hitam intensified. Consequently, government crises increased in 1984 and growth slowed down until Musa resigned and Mahathir successfully strengthened his position.

The pattern of prolonged harmony and stability was again disrupted in 1997 when differences in economic policies arose following a series of economic jolts that shook Malaysian society. Deputy Premier and Finance Minister Anwar, who had been building up a liberal economic system, collided with Prime Minister Mahathir, mainly over issues of how to ride out the crisis. Anwar and Bank Negara (the central bank) "preferred high interest rates and austerity measures to control Malaysia's sliding currency," while Mahathir was determined to push through a "policy of greater government spending and lower [interest] rates to boost the economy" (BBC News Online Network, 1998a). Anwar proposed an austerity plan that included more than a 20 percent cutback in the government budget. However, the plan did not deter Mahathir from authorizing multibillion-dollar government projects. Upon the arrest of Anwar, who accused Prime Minister Mahathir of "paranoia and resisting urgently-needed political reform" (BBC News Online Network, 1998b), thousands of protesters headed into the streets of Kuala Lumpur and clashed with riot police. The sign of a split, both in the government and the ruling UMNO, became obvious. Malaysia's hard-sought harmony and stability seemed to be evaporating. In a sense, this was more like a repetition of the 1986 incident. In the aftermath of the 1985 recession, then-Deputy Premier and Home Affairs Minister Musa Hitam, resigned from his posts due to "irreconcilable" differences with Mahathir over the industrial policy ("Malaysia," 1986).

In January 1999, Abdullah Ahmad Badawi, a Mahathir loyalist, assumed office as deputy premier, filling the political vacuum created by Anwar's sacking in September 1998. He also took control of the Home Ministry from Mahathir amid a public outcry over the beating of Anwar while in police custody. It was expected that this appointment would be conducive to political stability, stimulating the market ("Malaysia Will Reduce Capital Restriction," 1999).

In sum, empirical evidence suggests that growth is affected by political stability in Malaysia. Although the country's long-run political stability has provided a relatively stable environment for economic development, occasional political turbulence has disrupted its transcendent growth trajectory. What provoked this change in Malaysia's political stability? As illustrated earlier, growing tensions among political actors over policy outcomes have at times threatened the political and economic order of the country. This, in turn, leads us to consider polarization in Malaysian politics and economic development.

Minimizing Polarization

The Malaysian economy is a mixture of private enterprise and public management, whose primary goal has been the achievement of both political and economic stability among the three major ethnic groups. The critical socioeconomic element in Malaysia is the disparity in political and economic status among the three ethnic groups. The genesis of political polarization in Malaysia lies in the nature of the Malaysian ethnic mosaic. One would always find racial texture when dissecting Malaysian society by the urban-rural or wealth–indigence dichotomy. Indeed, as it is often claimed, everything in Malaysia has an ethnic character. The extremely slow process of income distribution in the early years led to racial riots in May 1969 when the preexisting formula for peaceful cohabitation among the three ethnic groups collapsed. Riots broke out in Kuala Lumpur when Malays demanded the expulsion of non-Malays.[6] The Malay political leaders (including the current prime minister Mahathir) argued that economic and political equity among the three ethnic groups was necessary for harmony to be reestablished. In other words, Malays demanded to become active economic actors as well as political actors (Root, 1996, 71–72).

After the riot, the Malaysian government tried to restructure the economic and political foundations of the country, focusing on the alleviation of ethnic tensions. Hence, it created an economic doctrine called the New Economic Policy (NEP). The NEP, quickly adopted from the initial phase of the Second Malaysia Plan, was the fundamental framework of the First Outline Perspective Plan and led Malaysian economic and social re-

Table 9.4
Mean Household Income of the Major Ethnic Groups, 1970–1997 (selected years)

	1970	1979	1984	1995	1997	Average Annual Growth Rate (%) 1970–1984	1995–1997
Urban	428	587	695	2,593	3,205	4.5	11.2
Rural	200	331	372	1,307	1,570	6.1	9.6
Malays	172	296	384	1,604	1,917	8.8	9.3
Chinese	394	565	678	2,890	3,516	5.1	10.3
Indian	304	455	494	2,140	2,725	4.5	12.8

Note: Unit in constant 1970 M$/ringgit for 1970, 1979, and 1984; unit in constant 1995 ringgit (RM) for 1995 and 1997.
Sources: "Table 4.10: Household Income by Ethnic Group, 1970, 1979, and 1984," Jesudason (1989), 114; "Table 3–3: Mean Monthly Gross Household Income by Ethnic Group, 1995 and 1997," *Mid-Term Review of the Seventh Malaysia Plan 1996–2000*, 68.

structuring for the period from 1971 through 1990. The programs outlined in the NEP are, as manifested in the Second Malaysia Plan, "[t]he measures to raise incomes in rural areas, where Malays and other indigenous people predominate, will not only help to eradicate poverty, but also serve the objective of correcting racial economic imbalance" (Kasper, 1974, 54). The policy had a dual goal: to eradicate poverty among all Malays[7] and to correct the economic disparities among all ethnic groups so that levels of income would not be associated with ethnicity.

As noted, the NEP had important economic and political implications. Economically, it aimed to eradicate widespread poverty in rural areas. "Pioneer" industries in rural areas were encouraged, thereby absorbing growing labor forces and improving income for the local Malays. The national leaders were convinced that this would eventually alleviate inequalities in wealth. Indeed, the mean household income in rural areas was far behind that in urban areas in 1970, as shown in Table 9.4. The mean income of the Malays was about half that of the Chinese. The NEP helped create a momentum of growth for the rural and Malay sectors such that the mean annual growth rate for rural areas reached 6.1 percent between 1970 and 1984 compared to 4.5 percent for urban areas. The growth rate was 8.8 percent for the Malays compared to 5.1 percent and 4.5 percent for the Chinese and Indians, respectively, for the same period. Obviously, the Malays' upward mobility was made possible, by funds that had been redirected to rural areas (see Table 9.5), along with other preferential policies in licensing, employment, education, and the like. Until the initial phase of

Table 9.5
Economic Development Plans, 1966–2000

	1MP (1966–1970)	OPP1 (1971–1990)				OPP2 (1991–2000)	
		2MP (1971–1975)	3MP (1976–1980)	4MP (1981–1985)	5MP (1986–1990)	6MP (1991–1995)	7MP (1996–2000)
Agriculture and Rural Development	1,000	2,129	7,585	8,359	9,265	9,019	8,301
Commerce and Industry		1,618	3,205	5,433	9,739	5,752	8,583
Transport		1,781	5,017	4,116	8,990	10,759	19,684
Utilities and Energy [a]		931	3,444	3,249	9,814	4,878	5,098
Other Services [b]	2,010	641	2,251	1,607	6,297	828	1,472
Social Services	800	1,348	5,561	6,388	9,866	13,468	27,630
General Administration		349	1,229	805	1,096	1,888	7,261
Defense and Security	740	1,024	3,784	9,372	2,445	8,408	11,470
Total [c]	4,550	9,821	32,076	39,330	57,512	55,000	89,500

Notes: Unit in millions M$/ringgits. Figures for 2MP and 4MP are estimates; for the 6MP and the 7MP, revised allocations are used. OPP1 refers to the First Outline Perspective Plan, OPP2 the Second Outline Perspective Plan.

[a] Figures for this item in the 6MP and the 7MP include mineral resources development, communications, energy, and water resources.
[b] Figures for this item in the 6MP and the 7MP include feasibility study and research and development.
[c] Some differences are due to rounding.

Sources: Data for 1MP–5MP taken from various issues of the Europa World Yearbook. Data for 6MP and 7MP are reconstructed from "Table 2–3: Federal Development Allocation and Expenditure by Sector, 1986–1995," Sixth Malaysia Plan 1991–1995, 1991 and "Table 5–1: Federal Development Allocation and Expenditure by Sector, 1996–2000," Mid-Term Review of the Seventh Malaysia Plan 1996–2000, 1999.

the Fifth Malaysia Plan (5MP), a major portion of the budget for these national development plans had been directed to agriculture and rural development. This momentum leveled off at the Sixth Malaysia Plan (6MP, 1991–1995), in which approximately 9,020 million Malaysian ringgit at the current prices, or 16.4 percent of the total budget, were allocated to agriculture and rural development. This budget was surpassed only by the budget devoted to transportation (10,759 ringgit, or 19.6 percent of the total budget allocation) (Government of Malaysia, 1991b, 76, Table 2.9).

The Malaysian government has followed three primary channels of redistribution: education, health, and welfare transfers. The combined federal expenditures per capita on education, health, and pensions were highest in rural regions where most Malays lived and lowest in the area of Selangor where most Chinese resided. Malays received per capita benefits that exceeded the mean by 22 percent, while benefits for the Chinese were 30 percent lower than the mean (Meerman, 1979, p. 7).

Although in other areas such as public utilities, the Chinese urban dwellers tended to benefit more than the rural residents did, Malaysia still had a far more equal distribution of resources between rural and urban populations than other middle-income developing countries. In fact, Malaysia's Gini coefficient is one of the lowest in the region (33.7), even lower than that of South Korea (33.9) or China (34.5). The percentage of the Malaysian population below the poverty line is 15.5, ahead of Indonesia (17.9), India (40.9), and the Philippines (52.0).[8] Income inequality is critical for economic development; many empirical studies on growth indicate that higher levels of inequality reduce the rate of economic growth (e.g., Perotti, 1996).

The NEP programs have been most successful in the area of medical care. In 1974, the poorest quintile income group received 19 percent of all public expenditures on patients' visits and the richest quintile group, 20 percent. In 1984, the poorest quintile received 25 percent of the expenditures, while the richest quintile received 16 percent (Hammer et al., 1995, 530–532). These results imply that poor people increasingly used public medical facilities more than richer segments of the population after implementation of the NEP. Nevertheless, the decline in the use of medical facilities by the wealthiest segments of the population can be explained by an increase in their use of private facilities. (The richest quintile accounted for 30 percent of private facilities visits in 1974, while in 1984 the percentage rose to 34.) The role of the private sector is critical in providing services and resources to the richest segments of the population, thereby releasing public resources for the poorest segments of the population (Hammer et al., 1995, 548). The preference of the richest segment of the population for private practice allows government expenditures to be better-targeted (Hammer et al., 1995, 530–532). In a cross-country setting, 88 percent of the Malaysian population have had access to health care, compared to only 43 percent in

Indonesia and 59 percent in Thailand. South Korea boasts the best medical access in the region—100 percent (World Bank, 1998).

Overall, the NEP was effective in redistributing resources through health expenditures and education. This improved the quality of human capital, which had significant ramifications for the whole economy (Hammer et al., 1995, 540–541).

Aside from the tangible and direct effects of this policy on economic and social development, positive externalities were created by maintaining political stability. The NEP allowed the UMNO to reestablish its leadership among the Malays. By transforming the national income structure, the NEP permitted the UMNO to solidify its legitimate domination of Malay politics (Jesudason, 1989, 109–117). This development strategy seemed to have been successful as the BN, with the UMNO as its senior partner, has swept all national elections since 1974. Indeed, to the UMNO, the 1969 election was, in a sense, a sheer "disaster" in which it lost 40 seats out of 114 to newly emerging oppositions—the PAS, the DAP and the UNSO. The PAS widened its support among poor Malays in rural areas. Hence, correction of the income imbalance between the rural and urban sectors, as a sociopolitical imperative, was desperately needed, so that it could be translated into an improvement in interracial wealth polarization and a reduction in social division. This strategy has worked remarkably well, enabling the UMNO to regain its support in rural areas mainly at the expense of the Chinese in the short run. It is because the NEP initiatives favored bumiputera (indigenous Malays) through the provision of the 30 percent bumiputera corporate equity ownership in addition to the mandatory bumiputera employment quota.

The Chinese, as well as other nonbumiputeras (nonindigenous Malays), had to adjust to the unfavorable environment that emerged.[9] Some Chinese announced that "[t]he marriage between Chinese economic power and Malay political power broke up" (Milne and Mauzy, 1980, 346). However, in the long run, all social and ethnic groups have been able to benefit from the NEP as it reduced the social and racial tensions that disrupted economic development in earlier years. This is the assumption of "shared growth," the rationale behind the NEP, pursued by the government. The assumption is that shared growth allows every ethnic group to be satisfied so that no intense grievances expressed in the future would jeopardize the stability of the political system (see Root, 1996).

As seen in Table 9.4, however, the Malay mean household income again fell to about half of that of the Chinese in 1995 and 1997. The Malay average annual growth rate also lagged behind that of other major ethnic groups. More importantly, the average annual growth rate in the urban area exceeded the rate in the rural area during the period 1995–1997. This new development may also be related to a reduction in the direct budget allocations for agriculture and rural development, as noted in Table 9.5, which fell behind those of other areas during the 6MP (1991–1995) and the 7MP (1996–2000). Nonetheless, no serious resentment emanated from the rural Malays. Indeed, as proudly proclaimed by a government official, Malaysia has experienced no such ethnic clashes since 1969 (Hassan, 1994). It seemed that the "enlarged pie" they shared satisfied everyone. Enjoying the social harmony and stability that the NEP has brought about, Malaysian elites, despite some setbacks as a result of the mid-1980s recession, do not seem anxious to retire the policy any time soon. On the contrary, at the expiration of the NEP in 1990 they were encouraged to reemphasize and reinforce the basic tenets of the plan as reflected in the initiatives of the New Development Policy (NDP). Hence, the NEP, Malaysia's own solution for its inherent sociopolitical and socioeconomic problems, would still shape Malaysian society for years to come. (See Malaysia, Government of, 1991a).

In sum, ethnic polarization is inherently potent in Malaysia, but it has been relatively well contained by political consensus and particularly by rapid economic growth. Malaysia could redistribute its national income among major ethnic groups through rapid growth without aggravating interracial hostilities. Growth not only gained strong support for the Malaysian government, but it also gave legitimacy to the UMNO's domination of Malaysian politics. Conversely, the contracting economy would likely turn "shared growth" into a zero-sum game. This would perhaps be the phase where Malaysian society would experience the reemergence of sociopolitical polarity.

Governing the Market and Polity

Until the racial riots of 1969, the Malaysian economic policy consisted of a laissez-faire capitalist framework. Some scholars sought the root of the laissez-faire tradition in the country's historical heritage (Kasper, 1974, 47–50). In the past, the ethnic Malays did not interfere with the economic activities of the British or Chinese in exchange for Malay dominance in the political sphere. "This separation of spheres was inherited by independent Malaysia" (Kasper, 1974, 47), and this historical heritage later became the basis of the laissez-faire capitalistic development model for post-independence Malaysia.

The racial riots of 1969 marked an important juncture at which Malaysia began to depart from the old laissez-faire model. By the mid-1970s, the government began to expand its role in the economy by introducing new controls and regulations. When the government enacted the Petroleum Development Act (PDA) in 1974, its determination to increase control in the economy became an established fact (Jesudason, 1989, 130). The government formulated and enacted the Industrial Coordination Act (ICA) in 1975. If the PDA was directed at foreign companies, the ICA aimed at domestic ones. It was clear that the government attempted to fulfill the objectives spelled out in the Second Malaysia Plan (2MP), especially in the reduction of the unemployment rate among ethnic Malays, through regulating and controlling business licenses. The role of the state was thus enlarged in order to push through the NEP objectives. The policy, as Mahathir so aptly described it, was "as much a political instrument as a social and economic engineering programme" (Bandara, 2000).

This radical socioeconomic "engineering program" raised the level of uncertainty about the future within nonethnic Malay communities, particularly the Chinese. This, in turn, led to a failure in mobilizing sufficient domestic private investment crucial to implementing the NEP, forcing the government to rely on foreign capital inflows to bolster the shortfalls in this area (Jesudason, 1989, 146).

Nonetheless, the increased state power reflected by the new regulations and controls should not be confused with the socialist model attempted in India, Pakistan, or Indonesia. As stipulated in 2MP, "private investment is necessarily a dominant element in the dynamic growth of the economy" (Kasper, 1974, 49). The government's expanding role in the economic sphere notwithstanding, the private sector was still a key player in the economy. The rationale behind Malaysia's development model was "in no way socialist-inspired" in spite of extensive government controls and the emergence of large quasi-government corporations (Milne and Mauzy, 1980, 351). In fact, Malaysian national elites have never pushed forward a wide range of nationalization. They have never resorted to socialist or communist tenets to solve their social, political, and economic problems. Large quasi-government enterprises were "intended to serve as effective and symbolic institutions of indigenous economic nationalism" (Milne and Mauzy, 1980, 351).

An important change of government policy came in the wake of the 1985 recession. The relaxation of the NEP's tight grip became obvious. Various changes in policies began to be implemented in order to stimulate private investment. These changes included privatization programs and incentive packages to attract foreign investment. For instance, foreign firms, though constrained by a 20 percent export requirement, did not have to abide by a provision of a 30 percent maximum holding by indigenous Malays (*Asia Yearbook*, 1987).

The recent Asian crisis has also led to an easing of the main policy provisions. The Malaysian government announced that it would allow "100 per cent ownership of new projects in the manufacturing sector [until] the end of 2000" (Toh, 1998). According to this temporary suspension of the NEP mandates, the foreign high-tech producers or the foreign producers who provide "other priority products for the domestic market," for instance, would now be able to own up to 100 percent of corporate equity,

Table 9.6
Economic Freedom Index for Selected Asian Countries, 1975–1997 (selected years)

Country	1975	1980	1985	1990	1995	1997
Hong Kong	9.3 (1)	9.3 (1)	9.3 (1)	9.3 (1)	9.3 (1)	9.4 (1)
Singapore	6.4 (8)	6.8 (3)	7.7 (2)	8.3 (2)	8.2 (2)	9.4 (1)
Malaysia	**5.4 (18)**	**5.6 (19)**	**6.7 (6)**	**7.1 (5)**	**7.0 (10)**	**7.5 (39)**
Indonesia	5.2 (20)	4.7 (29)	6.0 (15)	6.5 (13)	6.3 (29)	7.2 (49)
Taiwan	4.8 (28)	5.3 (22)	5.4 (24)	6.2 (20)	6.8 (16)	7.1 (51)
Thailand	4.8 (28)	4.9 (27)	5.3 (26)	6.2 (20)	7.2 (8)	8.2 (18)
S. Korea	4.4 (38)	4.0 (50)	4.8 (32)	5.0 (39)	6.7 (18)	7.3 (47)
Philippines	4.1 (50)	4.7 (29)	4.9 (30)	5.8 (25)	7.0 (10)	7.9 (31)

Notes: Figures in parentheses are the ranking of the country. Data for 1997 were quoted from
    Gwartney, Lawson, and Samida (2000); the1998/1999 data were used for the other years.
Source: Gwartney and Lawson, various years.

being free from the provision of the 30 percent bumiputera equity ownership (IMF, August 1999, 106).

Such changes in the economic environment are well reflected in an index
of economic freedom provided by Gwartney, Lawson, and Block (1996).
They define the basic components of economic freedom as the protection
of private property and freedom of exchange. Individuals are said to have
economic freedom if two conditions hold. First, property they acquire without the use of force, fraud, or theft is protected from physical invasion by
others. Second, they are free to use, exchange, or give their property to
another as long as their actions do not violate the identical rights of others.
For 1975, this index placed Malaysia as the 18th highest country in terms
of economic freedom, higher than Indonesia, Korea, Taiwan, the Philippines, and Thailand, as shown in Table 9.6. The level of Malaysian economic freedom has been rising since 1975.

In 1998, Malaysia deviated from market economy principles by imposing
currency controls with a view to reducing its exposure to financial turbulence in East Asia.[10] These restrictions led to problems of pricing, trading,
and settlement for international investors and domestic banks and traders
alike. It further reduced their confidence in Malaysia's economy. It was
predicted that "Mr. Mahathir's move to tighten his grip on his troubled
nation could take Malaysia completely off the path of economic liberalization" ("Malaysian Currency Controls Roil Asia Markets," 1998).

Meanwhile, from the political perspective, Malaysia is often viewed as a
country with a "democratic, federal government, which is run by tough-
minded centralists" (Sherwell, 1986, 3). Somewhat ambiguous as Malay-

sian democracy may be, its political freedom, contrary to the continued improvement in economic freedom and rapid economic growth, has been deteriorating with the BN's protested domination of Malaysian politics.[11] Figure 9.4 shows deteriorating conditions of political rights and civil liberties in Malaysia as reflected in the indices developed by Raymond Gastil (various years). Having muted the local media, directly controlling the police, and frequently resorting to the notorious age-old Internal Security Act (ISA), Mahathir often blames "excessive democracy" for the economic decline and social malaise (Nadel, 1995). Indeed, he has never been shy to disclose his skeptical views of democracy. In a conference of Asian historians held in Sabah on July 2000, Mahathir "warned that too much democracy [could] lead to violence and instability" and that the "pursuit of democracy could lead to hardship and anarchy, destroying an otherwise stable and prosperous society" (BBC News Online Network, 2000).

One may assert that growth and democracy are inversely related in the Malaysian setting. However, such an assertion is premature, for it neglects the indirect effects that democracy brings into an economy. Democracy may have its indirect effects on economic growth through other channels such as political stability, private investment, rule of law, and education (Feng, 1998). In addition, this assertion also neglects the effects of economic development on democratization. In fact, those who took to the streets of Kuala Lumpur on September 20, 1998, chanting *Reformasi* (Reform) included the "new" middle class and all ethnic backgrounds (Donald, 1998). As noted, the logic of the second pillar of the NEP intended to "eventually eliminate the identification of race with economic function" (Milne and Mauzy, 1980, 326). In this respect, the state elites may have been correct that economic functions could at least dilute ethnic identity. But they have neglected the demands that the "future" middle class would bring forth. Perhaps the Anwar incidents indeed were "merely the flashpoint for a mounting feeling of frustration" against the present political system in Malaysia (Montagnon and McNulty, 1998). Recent developments in Malaysia seem to be a litmus test for whether or not the linkage thesis of growth and democracy—that is, economic growth leads to an emergence of a middle class, which contributes to a democratic transition—will be applicable in Malaysia.

IMPLICATIONS AND CONCLUDING REMARKS

Growth and political development are interrelated. Growth is greatly constrained by the perceptions of investors and consumers who carefully assess the effects of political changes on the marketplace, calling for an examination of the three dimensions of the political fundamentals that affect growth: political stability, political polarization, and political repres-

Figure 9.4
Indices for Political Rights and Civil Liberty in Malaysia, 1973–1996

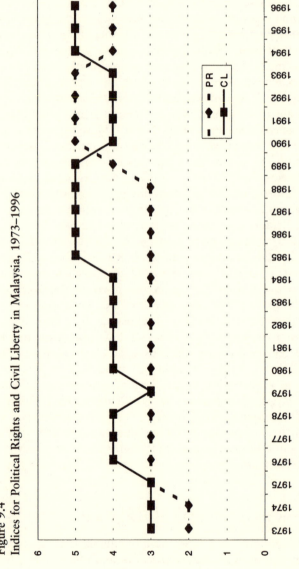

Notes: 6 being least free, 1 being freest. PR refers to political rights, while CL indicates civil liberties.
Source: Gastil/Freedom House, various years.

sion. They shape the political environment for economic development in Malaysia.

Malaysia's rapid economic development was largely attributable to the tradition of yielding political consensus, which created a stable political environment, paving the way for the ethnic accords among the three major ethnic groups.[12] This, in turn, reduced the likelihood of political polarization along ethnic or geographical lines. Moreover, the active government policies targeting income inequality among the three ethnic groups bolstered the "shared gains" from rapid economic growth while minimizing ethnic resentment. Hence, the rapid ascension of the Malaysian economy was a product of the political institutions that created and fostered an environment attractive to investment and dynamic economic activities.

With the onset of the Asian financial crisis in July 1997, Malaysia lost 61 percent of its equities (Straszheim, 1998). The country once again found itself in the painful process of restructuring. The conflict between Mahathir and Anwar indicated an inevitable rift between two different philosophies of economic management. Anwar supported the economic policies that the International Monetary Fund recommended as the cure for the crisis. However, Mahathir was unwilling to follow them for fear that those policies would send the Malaysian living standard plummeting as it did in neighboring Indonesia ("Malaysia's Nasty Bruising," 1998, 43; "Malice in Wonderland," 1998, 41). Mahathir perhaps knew only too well the potential consequences of the drastic contraction of Malaysia's economy.

Numerous protests broke out against Anwar's arrest and the subsequent sentences that followed. The economic future of Malaysia still remains unclear, casting doubts on its political future as well. Although the country is still far from experiencing an extremely disruptive political change, the stability of the political system remains questionable given continued political oppression.

In the face of growing challenges engendered by the economic crisis, Malaysia seems to have responded with past strategies. It is not surprising that Mahathir was determined to enlarge the role of the state and to get rid of his political opponents. However, the opposition parties to the BN are no longer in disarray, having solidified their support over the years. The series of changes taking place in the political arena suggests that Malaysia stands at an important juncture as evidenced by the results of the 1999 election. The source of polarization no longer lies only in ethnic division. The emergence of the new middle class as a consequence of economic growth has changed the fundamental structure of Malaysia's politics. Indeed, the middle class began to wield its power, exerting pressures on the ruling coalition with its demands for a more open society.

As noted, the legitimacy of the ruling coalition has largely hinged on rapid economic growth. However, the source of legitimacy seems to have shifted. A significant indicator of this trend could be detected in numerous protests. The seeds of Malaysia's current political situation reside in the very nature of the political system which lacks political rights and civil liberties. As personal wealth increases and people become subject to the economic forces that affect their standards of living, so does their desire to participate in the political and economic decision making of the government. This growth-driven political evolution toward democracy has occurred in South Korea and Taiwan (see Feng, 1999). As this chapter implies, political stability cannot be a panacea for economic development if it is not followed by extended political liberties, particularly in times when economic conditions are uncertain.

Economic growth may sustain authoritarian regimes for a short period of time. In the long run, however, more democratic institutions are required when the people develop new needs and increase their demands on and expectations from the political system (Feng, 1998; Feng and Hsiang, 1998). Economic development and political development are intertconnected and mutually reinforcing. In Malaysia, political stability and economic growth were not followed by more mature and democratic political institutions. The threat for the country's future path of growth may therefore lie in the very nature of its political system.

NOTES

This work is partially supported by a grant from the National Science Foundation (SBR-9730474).

1. Mr. Anwar was fired from his job and expelled from the ruling UMNO (The United Malay National Organization) party on September 2, 1998. He was arrested on September 20 on charges, alleged by the Malaysian police, of corruption and "illegal sexual misconduct."

2. In 1948, the states of Peninsular Malaya became the Federation of Malaya, with its defense and foreign affairs still under British control. In 1957, Malaya won its independence, while Singapore, North Borneo, and Sarawak remained as British colonies. In 1963, Malaysia, consisting of 11 states of Malaya, Singapore, Sarawak, and Sabah, was founded. In 1965, Singapore left Malaysia to become an independent state.

3. The remainder of the population (less than 1 percent) consists of various ethnic groups. The British policy of immigration encouraged the explosive mixture of Chinese, Indians, and Malays.

4. The real GDP per capita data are from Summers and Heston (1995), who adjust national income levels according to the purchasing power parity standard, thus avoiding the complications caused by foreign currency exchange rates.

5. Although the import of capital goods is critical for industrialization, not all of them are necessary for Malaysia's needs, but rather satisfy the ambitious plans of Prime Minister Mahathir ("States of Denial," 1996).

6. At that time, the Malays controlled only 1.5 percent of businesses, compared to 22.5 percent held by the Chinese, while the rest of the corporate equity was under foreigners (Root, 1996, 71).

Appendix 9.1
Results of Parliamentary Election, 1955–1999 (selected years)

Year	1955[a]	1959	1964	1969	1974	1978	1982	1986	1990	1995	1999
Alliance	51	74	89	74							
BN[b]					135	130	132	148	127	163	148
PAS[c,e]	1	13	9	12		5	5	1	7	7	27
KeADILan[e]											5
DAP[e]				13	9	16	9	24	20	8	10
Socialist Front		8	2								
PPP		4	2	4							
Parti Negara		1									
Malayan Party		1									
UDP			1								
PAP			1								
Gerakan[d]				8							
USNO				13							
SCA				3							
SNAP				9	9	1					
SUPP				5							
Pesaka				2							
Semangat 46									8	6	
Pekemas					1						
PBS									14	8	3
Independent									4		
Total	52	104	104	114	154	154	154	177	180	192	193

[a]Pre-independence Federal Legislative Council; [b]Barisan Nasional (BN) replaced Alliance as the enlarged coalition; [c]PAS was in BN in the 1974 general election; [d]Gerakan joined BN in the 1974 general election; [e]PAS, KEADILan, and DAP were members of Barisan Alternatif (BA, Alternative Front) in the 1999 election.

Source: Barisan Nasional, "Results of Parliamentary Election 1955–1999," http://www.bn.org.my/about/election.html (June 15, 2000).

7. Part of the aggressive policy of political and economic equality was the re-affirmation of equal citizenship, political participation, and office holding, as well as tolerance of religion, language, and other institutions of the minority coalitions (Root, 1996, 72).

8. The year for Malaysia is 1989, Indonesia, 1987, India, 1992, and the Philippines, 1985.

9. See Jesudason (1989) for details.

10. Under the controls, foreign investors cannot withdraw their investment within one year, and ringgit is fixed to the U.S. dollar at the rate of 3.80 ringgit.

11. The Alliance/BN coalition has remained in power since independence. Please refer to Appendix 9.1.

12. The Constitution of Malaysia is often regarded as an outstanding example of political and ethnic accord.

REFERENCES

Alesina, Alberto, and Jeffrey Sachs. (1988). "Political Parties and the Business Cycle in the United States, 1948–1984." *Journal of Money, Credit, and Banking* 20(1): 63–82.

Alesina, Alberto, Nouriel Roubini, Sule Özler, and Philip Swagel. (1992). *Political Instability and Economic Growth.* Working paper no. 4173. Cambridge, MA: National Bureau of Economic Research.

Anand, Sudhir. (1983). *Inequality and Poverty in Malaysia: Measurement and Decomposition.* New York: Oxford University Press.

"Anwar Welcomes Successor But Slams Appointment of Finance Minister." Agence France-Presse/*New Straits Times*, January 11.

Far Eastern Economic Review. (1981, 1987). "Malaysia: Politics and Social Affairs." *Asia Yearbook*, Hong Kong.

Bandara, Kapila. (2000). *South China Morning Post*, August 31, p. 10.

Banks, Arthur S. (1979). *Cross-National Time-Series Data Archive User's Manual.* Binghamton: State University of New York at Binghamton.

Banks, Arthur S. (1996). *Cross-National Time-Series Data.* Binghamton: State University of New York at Binghamton.

Barisan Nasional. (1998). "Component Parties." http://www.bn.my/static.html (November 16).

Barisan Nasional. (2000). "Results of Parliamentary Election 1955–1999." http://www.bn.org.my/about/election.html (June 15).

Barro, Robert. (1991). "Economic Growth in a Cross-section of Countries." *Quarterly Journal of Economics* (106): 408–443.

Barro, Robert. (1997). *Determinants of Economic Growth: A Cross-Country Empirical Study.* Cambridge, MA: MIT Press.

BBC Online Network. (1998a). "Malaysian PM 'Paranoid.' " *World: Asia Pacific*, September 2. http://news.bbc.co.uk/hi/english/world/asia-pacific/newsid 164000/164503.stm (November 17).

BBC Online Network. (1998b). "Malaysia's Deputy Prime Minister Fired." *World: Asia Pacific*, September 2. http://news.bbc.co.uk/hi/english/world/asia-pacific/newsid163000/163200.stm (November 17).

BBC Online Network. (2000). "Mahathir Warns Against Too Much Democracy." *World: Asia Pacific*, July 27. http://news.bbc.co.uk/low/english/world/asia-pacific/newsid853000/863873.stm (September 22).

Chen, Baizhu, and Yi Feng. (1996). "Some Political Determinants of Economic Growth." *European Journal of Political Economy* 12: 609–627.

Coplin, William D., and Michael O' Leary, eds. (1994). *The Handbook of Country and Political Risk Analysis*. New York: Political Risk Services.

Cukierman, Alex, Sebastian Edwards, and Guido Tabellini. (1992). "Seignorage and Political Instability." *The American Economic Review* 82: 537–555.

"Dr. Mahathir Bin Mohamed, Prime Minister/Minister of Defense, Malaysia." (1986). *Defense and Foreign Affairs* (May): 48.

Donald, Alice. (1998). "Malaysia Sails in Uncharted Political Water." *World: Asia-Pacific* (BBC Online Network), September 4. http://news.bbc.co.uk./hi/english/worldasia-pacific/ newsid176000/ 176571.stm (November 17).

"A Fatal Resolve Not to Bulge." (1997). *The Economist*, November 22, pp. 83–87.

Feng, Yi. (1997). "Democracy, Political Stability, and Economic Growth." *British Journal of Political Science* 27: 391–418.

Feng, Yi. (1998). "Democracy, Governments, and Economic Performance: Theory, Data Analysis, and Case Studies." Unpublished manuscript, Claremont Graduate University.

Feng, Yi. (1999). "Political Institutions, Economic Growth, and Democratic Evolution: The Pacific Asian Scenario." In Bruce Bueno de Mesquita, ed., *Governing for Prosperity*. New Haven, CT: Yale University Press.

Feng, Yi, and Antonio C. Hsiang. (1998). "Economic Development in Latin America: A Comparative Analysis." In Kuotsai Tom Liou, ed., *Handbook of Economic Development*. New York: Marcel Dekker, pp. 523–551.

Gastil, Ramond. (1978–1989). *Freedom in the World*. Westport, CT: Greenwood Press.

Gwartney, James, and Robert Lawson. (1998–1999). *Economic Freedom of the World: Interim Report*. http://fraserinstitute.ca/books/econfree/countries/malaysia.htm (March 28).

Gwartney, James D., Robert Lawson, and Walter Block. (1996). *Economic Freedom of the World: 1975–1995*. Vancouver, B.C.: Fraser Institute.

Gwartney, James, Robert Lawson, and Dexter Samida. (2000). *Economic Freedom of the World: 2000 Annual Report*. http://www.freetheworld.com/efwPDF/EFWCrprt.pdf (October 2).

Hammer, Jeffrey S., Ijaz Nabi, and James Cercone. (1995). "Distributional Effects of Social Sector Expenditures in Malaysia, 1974 to 1989." In Dominique van de Walle and Kimberly Nead, eds., *Public Spending and the Poor*. Baltimore, MD: Johns Hopkins University Press, pp. 522–554.

Hassan, Kalimullah. (1994). "Umno Attributes Success to NEP and National Front." *The Straits Times* (Singapore), August 30, p. 17.

"The IMF and Asia." (1997). *The Economist*, November 22, pp. 20–21.

International Monetary Fund (IMF). (1998). *International Financial Statistics Yearbook 1997*. Washington, DC: IMF.

International Monetary Fund (IMF). (1999). *Malaysia: Selected Issues*. IMF Staff Country Report No. 99/66. Washington, DC: IMF, August.

International Monetary Fund (IMF). (2000a). *International Financial Statistics*. Washington, DC: IMF.

International Monetary Fund (IMF). (2000b). *World Economic Outlook May 2000*. Washington, DC: IMF.

Jesudason, James V. (1989). *Ethnicity and the Economy: The State, Chinese Business, and Multinationals in Malaysia*. New York: Oxford University Press.

Kasper, Wolfgang. (1974). *Malaysia: A Study in Successful Economic Development*. Washington, DC: American Enterprise Institute for Public Policy Research.

Knack, Stephen, and Philip Keefer. (1995) "Institutions and Economic Performance: Cross-Country Tests Using Alternative Institutional Measures." *Economics and Politics* 7: 207–227.

Ko, Se-wook. (1998). "A Year under the IMF: The Social Image of the Rich-Gets-Richer-and-the-Poor-Gets-Poorer." *The Kumminilbo Daily*, November 17, 1998, p. 3.

Korea, Government of. (2000). *The Trends of Annual and Fourth Quarter of 1999 Household Income and Expenditure of Urban Working Families*. Seoul: National Statistical Office, March.

Kormendi, Roger C., and Philip G. Meguire. (1985). "Macroeconomic Determinants of Growth: Cross Country Evidence." *Journal of Monetary Economics* 16: 141–163.

Le, Quan Vu. (1998). *Political Instability Index*. Claremont, CA: Department of Economics, Claremont Graduate School.

Levine, Ross, and David Renelt. (1992). "A Sensitivity Analysis of Cross-Country Growth Regression." *The American Economic Review* 82: 942–963.

Lipton, Michael. (1998). "Urban Bias and Inequality." In Mitchell A. Seligson and John T. Passé-Smith, eds., *Development and Underdevelopment*. Boulder, CO: Lynne Rienner, pp. 389–395.

"Mahathir Shifts into Reverse." (1997). *Asiaweek*, December 20, p. 24.

Malaysia, Government of. (1991a). *The Second Outline Perspective Plan 1991–2000*. Kuala Lumpur: National Printing Department.

Malaysia, Government of. (1991b). *Sixth Malaysia Plan 1991–1995*. Kuala Lumpur: National Printing Department.

Malaysia, Government of. (1999). *Mid-Term Review of the Seventh Malaysia Plan 1996–2000*. Kuala Lumpur: Economic Planning Unit, Prime Minister's Department.

"Malaysia: Elementary, My Dear Mahathir." (1986). *The Economist*, March 15, p. 59.

"Malaysia Will Reduce Capital Restriction." (1999). *International Daily*, January 11, p. C5.

"Malaysian Currency Controls Roil Asia Markets." (1998). *Wall Street Journal*, September 3, p. A14.

"Malaysian Party Chief Quits after Election Loss." (1990). *Journal of Commerce*, October 25, p. 5A.

"Malaysia's Nasty Bruising." (1998). *The Economist*, October 3, pp. 43–44.

"Malice in Wonderland." (1998). *The Economist*, September 12, pp. 41–42.

Meerman, Jacob. (1979). *Public Expenditure in Malaysia: Who Benefits and Why*. New York: published for the World Bank by Oxford University Press.

Milne, R. S., and Diane K. Mauzy. (1980). *Politics and Government in Malaysia.* Vancouver: University of British Columbia Press.

Montagnon, Peter, and Sheila McNulty. (1998). "Another Asian Casualty? Malaysia's Political Game Has Changed." *The Financial Times* (London), October 3, p. 11.

Nadel, Alice. (1995). "Vision of Mahathir." *South China Morning Post*, April 16, p. 13.

National Statistical Office. (2000). *The Trends of Annual and Fourth Quarter 1999 Household Income and Expenditure of Urban Working Families.* Seoul: National Statistical Office.

North, Douglass C. (1990). *Institutions, Institutional Change and Economic Performance.* Cambridge: Cambridge University Press.

Perotti, Roberto. (1996). "Growth, Income Distribution, and Democracy: What the Data Say." *Journal of Economic Growth* 1: 149–187.

Romer, Paul M. (1990). "Endogenous Technological Change." *Journal of Political Economy* 98: S71–S102.

Root, Hilton. (1996). *Small Countries, Big Lessons: Governance and the Rise of East Asia.* Oxford: published for the Asian Development Bank by Oxford University Press.

Sarel, Michael. (1998). "Growth in East Asia: What We Can and What We Cannot Infer." In Mitchell A. Seligson and John T. Passé-Smith, eds., *Development and Underdevelopment.* Boulder, CO: Lynne Rienner, pp. 407–421.

Scully, Gerald W. (1988). "The Institutional Framework and Economic Development." *Journal of Political Economy* 98: 652–662.

Scully, Gerald W. (1991). "Rights, Equity, and Economic Efficiency." *Public Choice* 68: 195–215.

Sherwell, Chris. (1986). "Malaysia Faces Crisis of Maturity." *Financial Times*, March 29, p. 3.

"States of Denial." (1996). *The Economist*, August 10, pp. 56–57.

Straszheim, Donald. (1998). "The Realities of Global Competition." Paper presented at the International Studies Association West Annual Meeting, Claremont, CA, October.

Summers, L. (1995–1996). "Summers on Mexico: Ten Lessons to Learn." *The Economist*, December 23–January 5, pp. 46–48.

Summers, Robert, and Alan Heston. (1995). *The Penn World Table* (Mark 5.6). Cambridge, MA: National Bureau of Economic Research.

Toh, Eddie. (1998). "KL to Allow 100% Foreign Equity in Manufacturing Till End–2000." *Business Times* (Singapore), August 6, p. 4.

Van de Walle, Dominique, and Kimberly Nead, eds. (1995). *Public Spending and the Poor.* Baltimore, MD: Johns Hopkins University Press.

World Bank. (1998/2000). *World Development Indicators CD-ROM.* Washington, DC: World Bank.

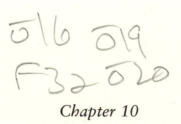

Chapter 10

Financial Reform, Capital Flows, and Macroeconomic Management: The Case of Thailand

Ng Beoy Kui

INTRODUCTION

Thailand started to lick its wounds when it finally agreed to float its baht on July 2, 1997 as a means of preventing further loss of its external reserves in its fight against speculative attacks. A month later, Thailand also came under the International Monetary Fund (IMF) assistance program through which total financial support of US$17.2 billion was initially pledged and a series of economic reforms and corporate restructuring were initiated. Unfortunately, the crisis that erupted in Thailand eventually spread throughout the entire East Asian region. The contagion effect was so strong and virulent that it brought the downfall of a number of prominent politicians and changes in central bank governors in the region. It even had a rippling effect on Russia a year later. The financial turmoil brought the ongoing financial reform in Thailand to a standstill.

Financial reform started in Thailand as early as 1979–1980 when it introduced a number of policy measures. Among others, Thailand enacted laws empowering the minster of finance to vary the ceilings on interest rates offered by financial institutions and introduced a repurchase market for government securities as well as the amendment of the Commercial Banking Act to broaden the ownership of commercial banks. The reform gained momentum in the early 1990s when the Bank of Thailand (BOT) concurrently liberalized interest rates and exchange control. Initially, the reform started smoothly, but from 1992 onward, it was somewhat disrupted by massive capital inflows. These capital inflows finally caused financial collapses in 1996 and the abandonment of the pegging exchange rate system in July 1997.

A number of hypotheses have been advanced in the academic literature to explain the financial crisis. However, not many of these hypotheses have touched on the issue of reform sequencing and policy mistakes and mismanagement on the part of the Thai authorities. This chapter seeks to fill this gap and examines the two issues in detail. The objective is to draw experiences and important lessons from this unfortunate episode.

This chapter is therefore confined to a discussion of issues involving financial reform, especially reform sequencing in Thailand as well as policy mistakes and mismanagement by the Thai authorities in their macroeconomic management. Specifically, the chapter attempts to document the objectives and phases of financial reform in Thailand prior to the financial crisis; examines the impact of capital flows on financial reform and macroeconomic management, as well as the Thai government's policy responses; studies the issue of sequencing problems in financial reform and policy mistakes and mismanagement by the Thai authorities as the main cause of the financial crisis; and summarizes the major issues discussed and the lessons to be learned from the financial crisis.

PHASES OF FINANCIAL REFORM

Financial reform in Thailand started in the late 1970s. For the next decade, reform measures were introduced mainly in response to specific problems rather than as part of an overall reform strategy (Robinson et al., 1991). Only after 1990 did the reform measures follow a more comprehensive approach, with the ultimate objective of developing Bangkok as a regional financial centre.

Background, Objectives, and Initial Reform Measures

Prior to the financial reform of the 1980s, the financial system in Thailand, like its counterparts in other Southeast Asian countries, was characterized by financial repression, including financial dualistic structure, underdeveloped money and capital markets, restrictions on interest rate and foreign ownership of domestic financial institutions, direct credit control, and exchange restrictions (Ng, 1985). As a result, the phenomenon of negative real interest rates was prevalent in the formal banking sector (Ng, 1995, 20, Table 2), and financial disintermediation to the informal financial sector was equally rampant. According to the 1980 Household Saving Survey conducted by the Bank of Thailand (BOT), about 16 percent of total household savings and 40 percent of total household borrowings came from this informal sector (Kirakul et al., 1993). With the onset of the Second Oil Crisis in 1979–1980, Thailand's structural weakness began to emerge with severe current account deficits, mounting external debt, fiscal imbalances, and rapid inflation. Subsequently, Thailand underwent a series of structural adjustment programs, with an emphasis on fiscal adjustment. The adjustments were so successful that by the second half of the 1980s, Thailand began to enjoy fiscal surpluses and a fall of current account deficits from an average of 5.4 percent of GDP between 1976–1985 to only 0.6 percent in 1986. During this period of adjustment, financial reform played an insignificant role mainly because the private savings and investment gap had not been widened to a crisis level. This was so as Thailand's financial repression was still characterized by low private savings and equally low private investment, with a consequently insignificant gap.

Events in the second half of the 1980s took a drastic turn, however. The private savings-investment gap began to widen after 1988 when domestic investment increased rapidly. By 1990, the current account deficit as a percentage of GDP reached a peak of 8.5 percent, while the public sector had already closed its savings-investment gap with fiscal surpluses in 1989 and 1990. This signaled to the Thai government that it could no longer delay its financial reform. In the meantime, the Thai government had already been seriously considering promoting Bangkok as a regional financial hub as far back as the mid-1980s (The Commission [hereafter cited as *Nukul Commission Report*], 1998, 13). Of no less importance was the Bank of Thailand's desire to move away from using direct controls such as interest rate ceilings, credit controls, and exchange restrictions as instruments for monetary management. All these controls called for an urgent implementation of financial reform.

Against this background, beginning in 1979 Thailand introduced a number of policy measures to launch the financial reform, as follows:

- Thailand amended the Civil and Commercial Code s654 in 1979 to empower the minster of finance to vary ceilings on interest rates offered by domestic financial institutions.
- Thai authorities in 1987 and 1988 allowed financial institutions, in particular commercial banks, finance companies, and securities companies to expand their scope of banking business to include leasing, and investment banking business.
- Thai government amended the Commercial Banking Act in December 1988 to broaden the ownership of commercial banks and also eased restrictions on opening branches by foreign banks in Thailand.
- A repurchase market was developed for government securities in 1979.
- The government tightened laws and regulations relating to prudential supervision of financial institutions.

Financial System Development Plan, 1990–1998

These reform measures, introduced in the 1980s, were ad hoc in nature. Only after 1990 did the financial reform become more systematic and comprehensive. This was evident in the formulation and implementation of the

Financial System Development Plans, 1990–1998, prior to the financial crisis. The first plan covered the period 1990–1992 in order to enhance the efficiency of the financial system and financial resource allocation. The second plan, ranging from 1993 to 1995, was more ambitious, aimed at raising the efficiency of the financial markets, mobilizing domestic savings, and developing Bangkok as a regional financial hub. The third Financial System Development Plan (1996–1998) had more objectives, namely to support the economy's growth potential and to ensure the stability of the economic and financial system; to broaden, deepen, and strengthen the financial system; to enhance the efficiency of supervision and examination; and to develop financial infrastructures, including information technology and human resource development (Duriyaprapan and Supapongse, 1996).

The reform measures for these three plans as a whole can be summarized as follows:

- Financial deregulation and liberalization, including interest rate liberalization completed in 1992, relaxation of portfolio management, removal of exchange control in 1993, and expansion of scope of business.
- Strengthening of prudential supervision such as the capital adequacy ratio, the reserve requirement for doubtful debts (June 1994 and December 1995), and the separation of securities companies under the Securities and Exchange Commission (SEC).
- Development of new financial instruments and facilities such as the establishment of the Securities and Exchange Commission, the Export-Import Bank of Thailand, the Thai Rating and Information Services (1993), the Bond Dealers' Club (1994), and so on.
- Development in the payment and settlement system such as BAHNET (May 1995) and THAICLEAR (mid-1996).
- The planned establishment of the Government Pension Fund for civil servants and provident funds of public and private enterprises.
- Development of Bangkok as a regional financial center with the establishment of the Bangkok International Banking Facilities (BIBF).

CAPITAL INFLOWS, MACROECONOMIC IMPACT, AND FINANCIAL CRISIS

Financial reform measures were implemented smoothly in the 1980s without much disruption from capital flows. Therefore, capital flow was not an important issue in the implementation of financial reform in Thailand prior to 1987. This was because the amount of capital inflows then was insignificant (about 2 percent of its GDP between 1982 and 1986), and most of the inflows were of direct foreign investment. Short-term private inflows were insignificant as Thailand still imposed a strict exchange control regime until 1990.

Nature and Types of Capital Inflows

With the liberalization of exchange restrictions between 1991 and 1993 and the setup of the Bangkok International Banking Facility (BIBF) in 1993, the nature and types of private capital inflows changed drastically (see Table 10.1). In the second half of the 1980s, most of the private capital inflows were of direct foreign investment (DFI), of which Japan accounted for more than 50 percent by 1988. After Japan went into recession in the early 1990s, DFI as a form of private capital inflows declined rapidly. The situation worsened further partly because of keen competition for DFI from neighboring countries and China. Portfolio investment, on the other hand, rose rapidly in 1989 as mutual and pension funds in developed countries looked to emergent markets in Asia as investment alternatives and as a means to portfolio diversification. Of importance was the pull factor for these capital inflows into Thailand, which had recorded impressive economic growth since 1989. Net private capital inflows for Thailand as a whole went up from 2 percent of GDP to 8 percent by 1989. Surges of private capital flows became more massive so that for the first half of the 1990s, private capital inflows averaged about 10 percent of GDP. By then, the components of these inflows changed again from portfolio investment to foreign borrowings by the private sector, in particular domestic commercial banks. The sharp rise in bank borrowings was prompted in part by the introduction of the BIBF in Thailand in 1993. Such an offshore facility provides domestic borrowers with a convenient and easier access to the international money and capital market.

Macroeconomic Impact and Policy Responses

As noted by Chew and Ng (1994), persistent and massive capital inflows are associated with sharp exchange rate appreciation, accumulation of external reserves, excess bank liquidity, investment boom, consumer and asset price inflation, overheating, and buildup of a bubble economy. Capital inflows in the form of short-term types is also particularly dangerous to developing economies, for any reversal of the flows would result in capital flight, volatility in exchange rate, and loss of confidence among foreign investors. These observations were prevalent in Thailand when it encountered surges of capital inflows in the first half of the 1990s.

The nominal exchange rate remained almost unchanged during the first half of the 1990s as Thailand had adopted a pegging exchange rate system in 1961. The real exchange rate (see Table 10.2), however, had appreciated since 1991 to the extent that exports began to decline in the second quarter of 1996, as compared with an average of 10 percent growth for the past decade. As a consequence, the current account deficit in Thailand widened

Table 10.1

Composition of Total Net Private Capital Flows in Thailand, 1987–1997

	1987–1991 (% share)	1992–1996 (% share)	1997 (U.S.$ billion)
Banks[1]	6.5	55.6	–6.5
Non-banks	93.5	44.4	–1.8
Direct Investment	22.0	10.9	3.6
Other Loans	35.2	1.5	–10.0
Portfolio Investment	9.1	20.4	4.6
Non-resident Baht Account	17.5	20.2	N/A

[1]Includes Bangkok International Banking Facility (BIBF) since 1993.
Source: Bank of Thailand.

to an unsustainable level (more than 5 percent of GDP during the period 1995–1996), which sparked off the later financial crisis.

In the meantime, external reserves built up rapidly—from US$13.2 billion in 1990 to US$37.2 billion in 1996. Despite the sharp increase in the external reserves, the amount was not adequate to cover short-term external debt after 1994 when short-term external debt was 107 percent of the external reserves. This precarious situation worsened as the percentage went up to 122 percent in 1995 and 1996. Bank loans also expanded at a steady rate of over 20 percent for the period 1990–1995 and recorded a slowdown in 1996 as property and stock markets showed signs of severe stress. The expansion in bank loans financed largely by short-term borrowings from the offshore market arose mainly from public investment in infrastructure and private investment in property and real estate. As a result, investment as a percentage of GDP rose from an average of 33 percent in the second half of the 1980s to an average of 41.5 percent in the first half of the 1990s. The investment ratio thus far exceeded the savings ratio (an average of 34.8 percent for the first half of the 1990s), resulting in a widening of the current account deficit. The investment boom did not cause consumer inflation as tight monetary policy and a balanced budget were able to dampen inflationary pressure, with inflation rates for the first half of the 1990s not exceeding 6 percent on average. However, the heavy investment in the property market caused the property price index to rise threefold over a five-year period beginning in 1990. In 1996, the property market collapsed, coincident with a sharp downturn in the stock market. The financial system began to feel severe stress when nonperforming loans as a percentage of total loans rose sharply from 7.7 percent to about 19 percent in 1996 (Corsetti et al., 1998).

As early as 1992, the Bank of Thailand had already noted the potential

Table 10.2
Key Economic Indicators of Thailand, 1985–1999

Year	GDP Growth (%)	Inflation (%)	Current Account (% of GDP)	GNS/GDP (%)	GDI/GDP (%)	External Reserves (U.S.$ billion)	Debt Service Ratio (%)	Real Exchange Rate[1]
1985	4.6	2.4	-4.0	24.4	28.2	3.0	22.7	N/A
1986	5.5	1.9	0.5	26.5	25.9	3.8	20.6	N/A
1987	9.5	2.5	-0.7	27.3	27.9	5.2	17.1	N/A
1988	13.3	3.8	-2.6	30.0	32.6	7.1	12.9	102
1989	12.2	5.4	-3.5	31.6	35.1	10.5	10.6	98
1990	11.2	5.9	-8.5	32.8	41.3	14.3	9.1	100
1991	8.5	5.7	-7.7	34.4	42.7	18.4	9.8	97
1992	8.1	4.1	-5.7	33.7	40.0	21.2	10.5	90
1993	8.3	3.3	-5.1	34.1	39.9	25.4	10.8	88
1994	8.9	5.0	-5.6	34.8	40.3	30.3	11.3	89
1995	8.8	5.8	-8.0	34.9	41.6	37.0	11.4	87
1996	5.9	5.9	-7.9	33.2	41.7	38.7	12.2	80
1997	-0.4	5.6	-2.0	32.9	35.0	27.0	15.8	124
1998	-10.2	8.1	12.8	33.1	20.3	29.5	20.8	N/A
1999	4.2	0.3	10.2	30.2	19.9	34.8	20.5	N/A

[1]Refers to the end-of-period exchange rate and an increase means depreciation.
Sources: Bank of Thailand, Quarterly Bulletin, various issues; Radelet and Sachs (1998).

danger of short-term capital inflows. However, only in August 1995 did the bank impose an exchange control measure, requesting banks and finance companies to place deposits with the central bank up to 7 percent of the total short-term capital inflows with no interest. When export declined in 1996 for the first time in 10 years, the policy measures undertaken included maintaining a tight monetary policy and balanced budget, resolving problems encountered by exporters, reviewing strategies of export promotion, and speeding up export credit provided by the Exim-Bank.

Despite these policy measures, the Thai banking system was already under severe stress. The stress began to surface when the problems of the Finance One Company and the Bangkok Bank of Commerce turned into financial panic in mid-1996. Together with a sharp decline in exports since the second quarter of 1996, a rumor in Hong Kong about devaluating the baht ignited speculative attacks on the baht on July 29, 1996. While the attacks were temporarily fended off, they recurred in earnest in the first half of 1997. As a consequence, the Bank of Thailand earmarked a total of US$23.4 billion out of US$39 billion of its total external reserves to defend the pegging exchange rate system. The final countdown came when Thailand decided to float its baht in July 1997 and the currency was devalued by more than 50 percent.

CAUSES OF THE FINANCIAL CRISIS AND REFORM SEQUENCING

A number of causes have been suggested to explain the origin of the Thai financial crisis, including "unproductive investment financed by short-term capital flows, overvalued exchange rates, overlending and asset price bubbles, inadequate supervision and moral hazard in the financial sector, herd behaviour, panic and self-fulfilling speculative attacks" (Nidhiprabha, 1998b, 309). However, there has not been much discussion on the sequencing issue of financial reforms and policy mistakes and mismanagement by the Thai authorities as a major cause of the current financial crisis. This section deals with the sequencing issue, while the next section focuses on policy mistakes and mismanagement.

Issue of Reform Sequencing

The sequencing literature (Mathieson and Rojas-Suarez, 1993; McKinnon, 1993; Villanueva and Mirakhor, 1990) emphasizes the importance of ordering economic reforms and meeting the preconditions for each reform stage in order to ensure the overall success of economic reform. Although there is no general consensus on the ordering and proper sequence, the literature generally agrees that the order should be macroeconomic stabilization, strengthening the safety and soundness of the domestic financial system, financial liberalization, trade liberalization, and finally capital account liberalization.

The Bank of Thailand apparently noted the importance of sequencing economic reform as evidenced by the two articles written by Wibulswasdi (1995, 1996), the then deputy governor of the Bank of Thailand. As such, Thailand's financial reforms since 1979 had generally conformed to such a general ordering of economic reforms. As noted by Wibulswasdi (1995), financial reform in Thailand prior to the financial crisis was characterized by correct timing, proper sequencing, and an appropriate approach. The timing was correct in the sense that Thailand implemented its interest rate liberalization at a time when the economy was near the trough of the business cycle amidst low inflation in the second half of 1992. Such timing was crucial, for it automatically preempted Thailand from a real interest rate hike and subsequent loan defaults by borrowers, as experienced by Indonesia in its financial reforms in the 1980s. In terms of sequencing, capital account liberalization was undertaken more or less in tandem with domestic liberalization. As such, interest rate ceilings were removed after 1989 and completely eliminated by 1992, while exchange restrictions were progressively liberalized from 1990 to 1991 and 1993. As to the approach, financial reform measures were introduced concurrent with wide-ranging economic reform, including fiscal reform, tariff reform, price deregulation, and industrial reform.

The simultaneous interest rate and exchange control liberalization adopted by Thailand caused surges of capital inflows, thereby infringing the usual sequence of economic reform as recommended by the sequencing literature: that is, a country should not liberalize its capital account until its domestic liberalization process is completed. Wibulswasdi (1995) did not give an explanation for this need to adopt external deregulation concurrently with domestic liberalization. Thailand undertook such a reform approach in a hurry, possibly because of its eagerness to develop Bangkok as a regional financial hub, and it also wanted to exploit the opportunity to replace Hong Kong in part as a financial center that might arise when Hong Kong finally reverted to China's rule in July 1997. Second, Bangkok also wanted to exploit geographical proximity and cultural closeness with Indochina and Myanmar to provide financial services to this region. This venture seemed to be viable as Vietnam and Myanmar had already carried out economic reforms and had opened up to the outside world, while peace was also in sight in Cambodia. In the transition, these countries required substantial capital funds for economic development, especially for infrastructure projects. At one stage, Thailand was even more ambitious to make the Thai baht the regional currency (*Nukul Commission Report*, 1998, 15). Only when the countries of Southeast Asia rejected the suggestion did Thailand finally drop the idea.

In hindsight, developing Bangkok as a regional financial hub was a premature idea. First, the return of Hong Kong to China's rule has not resulted in massive capital outflow from the island as was widely anticipated. Hong Kong, which has been well established as an international financial center, remains a formidable competitor to Thailand. Second, Bangkok also does not enjoy any comparative advantage in its endeavor as compared with Singapore, another financial center in the region. In fact, Singapore with its formidable foreign exchange and futures markets is "too near for comfort" for Thailand (Ng, 1998). Third, geographic proximity and cultural closeness to Indochina, as is often cited in official documents, does not materially help to promote Bangkok as a financial center because capital is internationally mobile and sensitive only to changes in economic and political factors rather than geography, culture, and language. Finally, economic reforms in Indochina and Myanmar did not take off fast enough to stimulate substantial demand for loanable funds and thus provide a viable hinterland for Bangkok as a regional financial center. This explains why "out-out" loan activities in the BIBF with neighboring countries such as Vietnam and Myanmar did not materialize, and "out-in" lending activities by domestic commercial banks became dominant in offshore banking activities.

Of importance was the fact that Thailand had not met all the preconditions for establishing capital account convertibility. According to Mathieson and Rojas-Suarez (1993, 30), the preconditions are (1) minimizing differences between domestic and external financial markets; (2) maintaining flexibility in prices and wages; (3) removing taxes on financial income and wealth, and transactions; and (4) strengthening the safety and soundness of the domestic financial market. In the case of Thailand, it had only met preconditions (1) and (3) partly. Although Thailand had completely liberalized the interest rate by 1992, there were still restrictions on foreign participation in banking activities such that keen competition between domestic and foreign financial institutions did not prevail. Once capital accounts become fully convertible, domestic financial institutions may not be able to withstand severe competition in the international market. Prices and wages in Thailand were also not flexible enough to absorb and fuse off any unexpected shocks. In particular, Thailand still had its minimum wage legislation, which imposes rigidity in the wage system. Finally, Thailand also failed to meet precondition (4). As noted by the *Nukul Commission Report* (1998, 14), the Bank of Thailand had relaxed rather than tightened prudential supervision, which would have strengthened local financial institutions. For instance, in 1993 the central bank allowed all financial institutions to maintain capital adequacy ratios below BIS requirements. In addition, the definition for nonperforming loans for prudential supervision purpose was also well below international standard requirements. The report also noted that the central bank did not come up with stringent guidelines for the supervision of BIBF operations.

The Thai authorities were responsible for yet another area of wrong sequencing of financial reform. Although the Thai authorities had managed to maintain price stability prior to its interest rate liberalization, it had failed to maintain its external balance (current account balance) before it liberalized its capital account. Thailand had achieved its current account balance in 1986 after its successful structural adjustment in the first half of the 1980s. However, the current account deficit as a percentage of GDP widened to 8.5 percent in 1990, which far exceeded 5 percent, the benchmark used by the International Monetary Fund (IMF) in its annual consultation with members. Afterward, the current account deficit narrowed but still hovered around 5 percent until 1994. However, the deficit again reached a peak of 8.0 percent in 1995 and 8.1 percent in 1996. By then, foreign investors already knew that the current account deficit which had been financed by short-term capital inflows would not be sustainable any longer and decided to withdraw funds from Thailand. Capital account convertibility thus provided a ready avenue for such capital flight.

Related to the current account deficit was the failure of the Thai authorities to mobilize adequate domestic saving through financial reform to keep up with investment growth. This was in part due to yet another wrong sequencing in its financial reform plan. Mobilization of domestic savings, which was scheduled only in the second and third plans, should have been given top priority in the first plan in 1990–1992 before the liberalization of current accounts and the development of Bangkok as a regional financial center. This sequence was important in two respects. First, such a mobilization effort would have helped reduce the savings-investment gap, which would promote the confidence of foreign investors. Such confidence was crucial for the development of Bangkok as a financial center. Second, given a fixed exchange rate as maintained by Thailand, higher savings would help lower the domestic interest rate so as to prevent interest-sensitive capital inflows, especially foreign borrowings by local entities.

POLICY MISTAKES AND MISMANAGEMENT

Apart from the wrong sequencing of financial reform, the Thai authorities made several policy mistakes and management errors, which culminated in the financial crisis in 1997. The most important policy mistakes included maintaining a fixed exchange rate in an era of globalization, a wrong policy mix, a wrong emphasis on price stability to promote competitiveness, failure to upgrade and restructure the economy, and ineffective management of capital flows.

Maintaining and Defending the Pegging Exchange Rate System

As far back as 1994, the IMF had advised BOT to abandon the basket pegging exchange rate system, which placed an enormous weight on the

U.S. dollar (more than 80 percent). Thailand did not heed the advice because it worried that abandonment of this system would lead to a sharp appreciation of the exchange rate, which might adversely affect Thai exports. In fact, exports had been growing comfortably at more than 20 percent annually. Moreover, Thailand had a vested interest in maintaining the pegging exchange rate system for three reasons. First, a stable exchange rate would be able to attract foreign investment and capital, which were needed to sustain high economic growth after 1989. Second, a stable exchange rate would inject confidence among foreign investors and was a crucial factor in developing Bangkok as a regional financial center. Lastly, a stable exchange rate had been a key factor in economic success in the past.

When Thai exports suffered a severe slowdown in the second quarter of 1996, BOT misjudged, certain that the sharp fall in exports was only temporary and cyclical in (*Nukul Commission Report*, 1998) rather than due to a loss in competitiveness arising from exchange rate misalignment. When the Thai baht came under speculative attack in July 1996, BOT still maintained and defended the pegging system. By September 1996, the market was already much concerned about the unsustainability of the system based on the following information:

- A widening current account deficit might lead to devaluation of the baht.
- The property sector in 1996 was facing a severe crisis.
- The persistent decline in the stock market since early 1996 was a leading indicator forewarning economic slowdown.
- The fall in government revenue continued.
- Financial institutions were facing growing bad debt problems (Nukul Commission Report, 1998: 43–44).

With the appreciation of the U.S. dollar against the yen in early 1997, the Thai baht was again under severe speculative attacks and BOT defended the baht with much determination. The speculative attacks were so fierce that finally Thailand had no alternative but to abandon the pegging system in July 1997, as its external reserves had been dwindling rapidly. The total cost of the defense was US$23.4 billion out of a total of US$37 billion in its external reserves.

This policy mistake arose mainly from the BOT's complacency which had developed from its past success in defending the exchange rate system against foreign speculators. However, circumstances had changed considerably due both to globalization and to the rapid developments in computer technology and telecommunication since the early 1990s. With the change in circumstances, market overreaction and herding behavior became common phenomena, especially in a situation where information was not readily available or the system was not transparent enough to the investing public. This was particularly so where funds could move across borders electronically at lightning speed. Such phenomena often cause massive and disruptive capital flows. The flows can be extremely huge and more often than not, in each case, larger than the GDP of many developing countries. As such, a fixed exchange rate system can be sustainable only in the presence of sound economic fundamentals, a huge amount of external reserves, and noninternationalization of domestic currency.

Wrong Policy Mix

Another policy error was the wrong policy mix that caused capital inflows in the first place. In the 1980s, price stability and a pegging exchange rate system had been the two key factors for achieving high economic growth in Thailand. When the investment boom started in 1990, inflation pressures began to mount. However, the Thai authorities determined to wipe out the inflationary pressure by maintaining a balanced budget and a tight monetary policy under the pegging exchange rate system. Such a policy mix, however, caused a widening of interest differentials between domestic and foreign financial markets (offshore markets), as shown in Table 10.3. The differentials allowed banks to exploit profit opportunities by arbitraging between the two separate markets. The explanation is simple.

Under the pegging exchange system as practiced by Thailand prior to July 1997 and then under uncovered interest parity conditions, the value of x will be zero and there will not be any exchange risk in cross-border transactions, as follows:

$$i = i^* + x \qquad\qquad (10.1)$$

where

   i = domestic interest rate

   i^* = foreign interest rate

   x = expected depreciation of domestic currency

When Thailand maintained a balanced budget and a tight monetary policy, the domestic interest rate rose rapidly and exceeded international interest rates such as London Interbarik Borrowing Rates (LIBOR) (see Table 10.3). As long as $i > i^*$ there will be capital inflows—provided that the differential is more than enough to cover the transactions cost and default risk in arbitrage activities. In the Thai case, the interest differentials had encouraged foreign borrowings by domestic banks and private corporations from BIBF, especially when the domestic cost of funds also increased rap-

Table 10.3
Interest Rate Differentials between Thailand and Abroad, 1992–1999 (percent per annum)

Year		MLR	LIBOR	Fixed Deposit 12-Month Deposit Rate	MLR – LIBOR	MLR – Fixed Deposit Rate
1992	Q1	12.50	4.20	9.83	8.30	2.76
	Q2	12.00	3.90	8.67	8.10	3.33
	Q3	12.00	3.10	9.00	8.90	3.00
	Q4	11.50	3.00	8.67	8.50	2.83
1993	Q1	11.25	3.10	8.50	8.15	2.75
	Q2	11.25	3.10	8.50	8.15	2.75
	Q3	11.25	3.10	8.50	8.15	2.75
	Q4	10.50	3.00	7.33	7.50	3.17
1994	Q1	10.00	3.70	6.67	6.30	3.33
	Q2	11.00	4.60	7.17	6.40	3.83
	Q3	11.50	5.10	7.75	6.40	3.75
	Q4	11.75	6.00	8.17	5.75	3.58
1995	Q1	13.00	6.10	9.08	6.90	3.92
	Q2	13.50	6.10	10.25	7.40	3.25
	Q3	13.50	5.90	10.25	7.60	3.25
	Q4	13.75	5.90	10.25	7.85	3.50
1996	Q1	13.75	5.38	10.00	8.37	3.75
	Q2	13.25	5.52	9.33	7.73	3.92
	Q3	13.25	5.63	8.81	7.63	4.44
	Q4	13.25	5.50	8.00	7.75	5.25
1997	Q4	15.25	4.25	10.00–13.00	11.00	2.25–5.25
1998	Q4	11.50–12.00	3.75	6.00	5.50–6.00	5.50–6.00
1999	Q4	8.25–8.50	2.31	4.00–4.25	5.94–6.19	4.25–4.25

MLR = Minimum lending rate; LIBOR = London Interbank Borrowing Rate.
Source: Bank of Thailand, *Quarterly Bulletin*, various issues.

idly (widening the differentials between the minimum lending rate and the rising fixed deposit rate as shown in Table 10.3). As noted earlier, such a policy mix was a mistake because the package invited short-term capital inflows, which carried adverse consequences such as real exchange rate appreciation, asset inflation, and a buildup of a bubble economy. In addition, any reversal of such flows would eventually result in a loss of confidence among foreign investors.

Price Stability, Flexible Wage, and Competitiveness

The Thai authorities also failed to implement measures fast enough to introduce a flexible wage system as a strategy to promote international competitiveness. Moreover, the Thai authorities had emphasized the fact that price stability and a fixed exchange rate would be adequate to maintain international competitiveness (*Nukul Commission Report*, 1998). However, international competitiveness involves more than just a real exchange rate, as indicated by equation (10.2), as follows:

$$REER = \frac{eP^*}{P} \qquad (10.2)$$

where

> e = exchange rate expressed as currency price of a unit of
>   foreign currency
> P^* = foreign price level
> P = domestic price level

Using equation (10.2), given no change in exchange rate, the fiscal balance and tight monetary policy as implemented by the Thai authorities may be able to ensure price stability and, therefore, seemingly export competitiveness. However, this measure of export competitiveness has a flaw. Although price stability will not lead to a demand for a substantial wage increase by trade unions, any increase in nominal wage by employers arising from a tight labor market will also lead to a rise in real wage (W/P) and thus an increase in labor cost in real terms. Thailand encountered precisely such a situation when the investment boom arose from expansion in the real estate and property sector (nontraded sector), sustained by overseas borrowings started in 1990. The situation worsened as China, a new competitor to Thailand, decided to devaluate its currency by 30 percent in 1994. The tight labor market finally caused the nominal wage to rise rapidly. According to the Thailand Development Research Institute, the average annual real wage for the period 1982–1990 recorded only a 2 percent increase. However, from 1991 to 1994, the compound growth rate of real wages rose above 9 percent. Therefore, a better measure of export competitiveness is equation (10.3) which uses the relative unit labor cost as a basis for measuring international competitiveness, as follows:

$$REER = \frac{eULC^*}{ULC} \qquad (10.3)$$

$$REER = \frac{P_T}{P_N} \qquad (10.4)$$

where

$ULC^* =$ foreign unit labor cost
$ULC =$ domestic unit labor cost
$P_T =$ price level of traded goods
$P_N =$ price level of nontraded goods

Cost competitiveness, especially in terms of labor cost, was crucial to Thailand in two respects. First, most of the export industries were highly labor intensive, and second, these export industries encountered a highly competitive international market. As noted by Warr (1998), export industries in Thailand were especially vulnerable to a rise in real wage as the era of cheap labor was coming to an end by the early 1990s.

Of no less importance was the appropriate resource allocation between two competing sectors; that is, the traded and nontraded sector. However, equation (10.3) does not reveal such information, while equation (10.4) does. As the prices of the nontraded sector rise more rapidly than those of the traded sector, resources will tend to move from the traded to the non-traded sector. In order to bid for scarce resources, the traded sector has to raise factor prices, resulting in higher cost and becoming less competitive. In Thailand, high economic growth coupled with massive capital inflows in the first half of the 1990s led to a rapid expansion of the nontraded sector such as the real estate and property sector. This raised the factor prices of the nontraded sector vis-à-vis those of the traded sector. As scarce resources (financial and labor resources), especially those borrowed from abroad, moved to the nontrade sector at the expense of the traded sector, especially the export sector, Thailand suffered a loss of competitiveness and subsequently a widening of the current account deficit.

Based on the preceding discussion, price stability alone would not ensure competitiveness. The ability to contain sharp increases in nominal wage and labor costs is equally important in maintaining competitiveness. Of no less importance is the need to contain nontraded goods prices from rising too fast as to exceed prices of traded goods. This is to prevent adverse resource allocation against the traded sector. The Thai authorities were obviously complacent about these issues. After exports showed a sharp slowdown in 1996, following a consecutive real appreciation of the Thai baht in 1991, the Thai authorities did not undertake any immediate policy measure to prevent the loss of international competitiveness.

Upgrading and Restructuring of the Economy

Over the long term, the sustainability of the external balance depends on the continuous upgrading and restructuring of the economy. Surprisingly, the Thai authorities paid little attention to this area, especially when Thailand had already entered a new era of high labor cost. Thailand should have prepared for the next stage of development and moved away from cost competitiveness toward competitiveness based on core competencies as Singapore has done. However, past success had bred complacency, which had led to the Thai authorities' failure to design in a long-term strategy for sustaining economic development.

Management of Capital Flows

The Thai authorities also failed to take immediate action against capital inflows, and the measures it did undertake later were too late to alter the already deteriorating situation. As far back as August 1992, BOT had already noticed the seriousness of the capital inflows through foreign borrowings by local entities (*Nukul Commission Report*, 1998). But BOT did not take immediate action as Malaysia had done in 1993 (Ng, 1994). Only in August 1995, when the number of BIBF borrowers had risen to a much higher level than the BOT expected, did BOT immediately introduce measures to restrict capital inflows. By then, the central bank's action use too late to tackle the problem.

In addition, the August 1995 measure was inadequate, for it only required banks to deposit with BOT, without interest, no less than 7 percent of total money borrowed from offshore. Such a measure paled in comparison to the requirement of a 30 percent deposit imposed in Chile (*Nukul Commission Report*, 1998, 33). The measure was also considered half-hearted as compared with the more drastic measures undertaken by Malaysia in 1993 when it encountered the same problem of massive capital inflows. Among the measures undertaken by Malaysia were restrictions on swap transactions by banks, prepayment of external debt, persuasion of the DFI to flow in at a later period, and implementation of several sterilization measures, including the issue of savings bonds and a transfer of funds from the Employee Provident Fund to the central bank (Ng, 1994).

POLICY RESPONSES AND IMPACT

The immediate policy response was to abandon the pegging system on July 2, 1997. The other policy strategy was to restore both internal and external stability under the International Monetary Fund (IMF) economic adjustment program. Under the program, a standby package of US$17.2 billion was granted on August 20, 1997. The adjustment program included the use of both monetary and fiscal policy to strengthen macroeconomic fundamentals. Monetary policy was aimed at stabilizing the baht and inflation. A high interest rate policy was adopted in the earlier part of the crisis. The policy stance shifted to a more relaxed monetary policy in May and August 1998, when the exchange rate and prices were more stable and the Thai economy was already in deep recession.

On the fiscal front, the original IMF program required the Thai government to operate an overall public sector surplus of 1 percent of fiscal year GDP to improve the current account. However, the deep recession forced the IMF to move its fiscal target from a 1 percent surplus to a deficit of 2 percent of GDP, in the wake of higher unemployment and adverse social implications.

In addition, the Thai government also took various measures to facilitate financial sector restructuring such as closure of insolvent finance companies and setup of three important institutions to deal with practical matters and issues of financial restructuring process. The institutions were the Financial Institutions Development Fund, the Financial Sector Restructuring Authority, and the Asset Management Corporation. As for the remaining financial institutions, their capital bases were also strengthened through a more realistic loan classification and provision and private sector-led recapitalization. Of no less importance was the modernization of the legal, institutional, and regulatory system to facilitate corporate and financial restructuring as well as the acceleration of the process of foreclosure.

By June 2000, Thailand had completed a 34-month IMF program under which a total of US$14.1 billion out of US$17.2 billion was utilized (IMF, December 2000). The economy at first went into deep recession, with a sharp decline of 10.8 percent in real GDP, but the current account improved from a deficit of 3.2 percent of GDP in 1997 to a surplus of 14.3 percent in 1998. During the same period, inflation also declined from 7.7 percent to 4.3 percent. With a shift in policy stance from May 1998, the Thai economy recovered to a positive GDP growth of 4.2 percent and 4.3 percent in 1999 and 2000, respectively. A sharp reversal of fixed investment from a severe decline of 45.1 percent in 1998 to a slower fall of 4.1 percent in 1999 reflected the investor's confidence. Such confidence is expected to sustain in 2001 with a positive growth of 4.3 percent. The current account improved further in 1999 and 2000 with respective surpluses of 10.2 percent and 7.5 percent of GDP.

CONCLUDING REMARKS

Thailand was successful in its structural adjustment in the first half of the 1980s because fiscal adjustment alone was more than adequate to resolve the macroeconomic imbalances, as the source of the problem arose mainly from fiscal deficits. The private sector savings-investment gap was also never an issue even as late as 1989 as direct foreign investment continued to flow in to fill the gap. Only in early 1990 when foreign direct investment, especially from Japan, dwindled drastically did the need for financial reform become more apparent and urgent. This was particularly so when Thailand decided to develop Bangkok as a regional financial center. As a consequence, the three plans were scheduled to be implemented between 1990 and 1998. However, the massive capital inflows in the form of foreign borrowings by domestic commercial banks and accompanying problems such as overvaluation of the exchange rate and overheating of the economy left the financial reform in disarray. Specifically, the financial crisis in 1997 had crippled the financial reform with financial collapses and the eventual abandonment of the pegging exchange rate system.

In its effort to implement financial reform, the Thai authorities made several policy mistakes, including inappropriate sequencing of financial reform, a wrong policy mix, laxness in promoting cost competitiveness, failure to upgrade and restructure the economy, and ineffectiveness in its attempt to manage capital flows. Misjudgment, complacency, and overconfidence by Thai officials in their management of the Thai economy also played a part in bringing about financial turmoil. All these mistakes have been well documented in the *Nukul Commission Report* of 1998.

The key lessons from this unfortunate episode are as follows:

1. A proper sequencing of economic reform as suggested in the academic literature has practical relevance for the successful implementation of economic reform.
2. Macroeconomic stability in the form of internal and external balance is of paramount importance to inject foreign investors' confidence. Ignoring this critical factor will leave financial reform in disarray.
3. Complacency and overconfidence bred on past success can be a serious hindrance in successfully managing a country's economic development.

REFERENCES

Chew, Soon Beng, and Beoy Kui Ng. (1994). "The Role of Private Capital Flows in the Development of Asia." Paper presented at the Asian Development Bank Seventh Workshop on Asian Economic Outlook, Manila, October 24–28.

The Commission Tasked with Making Recommendations to Improve the Efficiency and Management of Thailand's Financial System. (1998). *Nukul Commission Report: Analysis and Evaluation on Facts Behind Thailand's Economic Crisis*. Bangkok: The Nation, March.

Corsetti, G., P. Pesenti, and N. Roubini. (1998). *What Caused the Asian Currency and Financial Crisis?* www.Stern.nyu.edu/nroubini/asia/AsiaHomepage.html.

Duriyaprapan, Chittima, and Mathee Supapongse. (1996). "Financial Liberalisation: Case Study of Thailand." *Bank of Thailand Quarterly Bulletin* 36(3) (September): 35–52.

International Monetary Fund (IMF). (2000). "IMF Concludes Post-Program Monitoring Discussion on Thailand." Public Information Notice (PIN) No. 00/110, December.

Khan, Mohsin S., and Carmen M. Reinhart. (1995). "Macroeconomic Management in APEC Economies: The Response to Capital Inflows." In Mohsin Khan and C. M. Reinhart, eds., *Capital Flows in the APEC Region*. Washington, DC: International Monetary Fund, Occasional Paper 122, pp. 15–30.

Kirakul, Suchada, Jaturong Jantarangs, and Parisun Chantinahom. (1993). "Economic Development and the Role of Financial Deepening in Thailand." Bangkok: Bank of Thailand, *Papers on Policy Analysis and Assessment*, pp. 39–54.

Mathieson, D. J., and Liliana Rojas-Suarez. (1993). *Liberalisation of the Capital Account: Experiences and Issues*. Washington, DC: International Monetary Fund, Occasional Paper 103.

McKinnon, R. I. (1993). *The Order of Economic Liberalisation: Financial Control in the Transition to a Market Economy*. Baltimore, MD: Johns Hopkins University Press.

Ng, Beoy Kui. (1985). *Some Aspects of the Informal Financial Sector in the SEACEN Countries*. The SEACEN Centre Staff Paper No. 28. Kuala Lumpur: South East Asian Central Banks (SEACEN) Research and Training Centre.

Ng, Beoy Kui. (1994). "Central Bank Management of Bank Liquidity: The Case of Malaysia." Singapore: *Economic Quarterly* 1(1) (new series): 40–43.

Ng, Beoy Kui. (1995). *Financial Reforms in the ASEAN Countries: Approach, Focus and Assessment*. Sabre Centre Working Paper Series No. 10–95. Singapore: Sabre Centre.

Ng, Beoy Kui. (1998). *Hong Kong and Singapore as International Financial Centres: A Comparative Functional Perspective*. Sabre Centre Working Paper Series No. 6–98. Singapore: Sabre Centre.

Nidhiprabha, Bhanupong. (1998a). "Adverse Consequences of Capital Flows and Thailand's Optimal Policy Mix." In C. H. Kwan et al., eds., *Coping with Capital Flow in East Asia*. Singapore: Nomura Research Institute and Institute of Southeast Asia Studies, pp. 192–219.

Nidhiprabha, Bhanupong. (1998b). "Economic Crises and the Debt-Deflation Episode in Thailand." *ASEAN Economic Bulletin* 15(3) (December): 309–318.

Nijahthaworn, B. (1993). "Managing Foreign Capital in a Rapidly-Growing Economy: Thailand's Experience and Policy Issues." *Bank of Thailand Quarterly Bulletin* 33(2) (June): 19–38.

Nijahthaworn, B. (1995). "Capital Flows, Policy Response, and the Role of Fiscal Adjustment: The Thai Experience." *Bank of Thailand Quarterly Bulletin* 35(3) (September): 37–50.

Nijahthaworn, B., and Thanisom Dethamrong. (1994). "Capital Flows, Exchange Rate and Monetary Policy: Thailand's Recent Experience." *Bank of Thailand Quarterly Bulletin* 34(3) (September): 35–49.

Radelet, S., and Jeffrey Sachs. (1998). "The Onset of the East Asian Financial Crisis." Paper presented at the National Bureau of Economic Research (NBER) Currency Conference, February 6–7.

Robinson, D. et al. (1991). *Thailand: Adjusting to Success: Current Policy Issues*. Washington, DC: International Monetary Fund, Occasional Paper 85.

Tseng, Wanda, and Robert Corker. (1991). *Financial Liberalisation, Monetary Demand, and Monetary Policy in Asian Countries*. Washington, DC: International Monetary Fund, Occasional Paper 84.

Villanueva, D., and Mirakhor. (1990). "Strategies for Financial Reforms: Interest

Rate Policies, Stabilization, and Bank Supervision in Developing Countries." *IMF Staff Papers* 37(3) (September): 509–536.

Warr, Peter G. (1998). "Thailand." In Ross H. McLeod and Ross Garnaut, eds., *East Asia in Crisis: From Being a Miracle to Needing One?* London and New York: Routledge, pp. 49–65.

Warr, Peter G., and Bhanupong Nidhiprabha. (1995). *Thailand's Macroeconomic Miracle: Stable Adjustment and Sustained Growth*. Washington, DC: World Bank.

Wibulswasdi, Chaiyawat. (1995). "Strengthening the Domestic Financial System." Bangkok: Bank of Thailand, *Papers on Policy Analysis and Assessment*, pp. 1–11.

Wibulswasdi, Chaiyawat. (1996). "How Should Central Banks Respond to the Challenges Posed by the Global Integration of Capital Markets?" Speech given at the MAS 25th Anniversary Symposium, May 10. *Bank of Thailand Quarterly Bulletin* 36.

Chapter 11

The East Asian Crisis and Recovery: A Reappraisal

F. Gerard Adams

Many observers have been surprised by the rapid turnaround of the East Asian economies after the 1997 crisis. The signals of recovery are now sufficiently clear in most of the countries of the region to permit a post-mortem. As economic trends have changed direction, thinking about the causes of the crisis has also evolved. What some analysts saw principally as an episode of international exchange rate contagion is being attributed to more fundamental causes, such as domestic imbalances and cyclical forces, collapse of an asset bubble, lack of international competitiveness, improvident foreign financial flows, and prudential failures. Ultimately, almost all the East Asian countries suffered a cyclical swing in demand—for exports, consumer durables, fixed investment, and inventories—that amplified the decline and, more recently, helped to fuel the recovery. The impact of the crisis on the viability of the banks and finance companies caused a severe shortage of domestic credit, a credit crunch, which continues in some East Asian countries to this day. International contagion has also been a factor. Its impact depends greatly on the economic fundamentals of the country exposed to a potential loss of investor confidence. To interpret what happened in East Asia, it is necessary to look more closely at the relationships between the domestic real economy, financial structure and behavior, and monetary and fiscal policy, and international exchange rate regimes and financial and capital flows. A reinterpretation is an important first step in devising strategy and institutions to avoid further crisis episodes and to deal with the evolving world economic slowdown.

In this chapter, we begin by updating the information about the crisis. After a statistical overview, we focus first on the sequence of events in Thailand, generally seen as the country where the crisis began and where

Figure 11.1
GDP Growth during the Asian Crisis

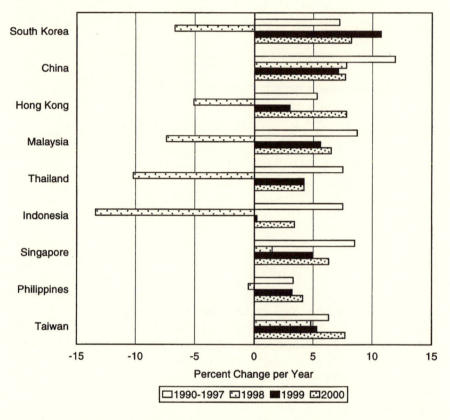

moderate recovery is under way. We consider to what extent other East Asian countries faced similar conditions and whether these led to similar outcomes. Then, we evaluate various economists' views about the crisis. We do so in a framework that involves the real economy as well as domestic and international financial considerations. Then we consider the role of the IMF in achieving policy and structural adjustments. Finally, we ask what challenges must be met to permit the East Asian countries to return to a sustained rapid growth path.

UPDATE ON THE EAST ASIAN CRISIS

Although the crisis has had a general impact on most, if not all, East Asian countries, the specifics of their experience have varied considerably (see Figure 11.1). Throughout most of the 1990s (until 1997), many of the East Asian countries[1] maintained boom rates of GDP growth, supported in large part by an expansion of exports and extraordinary levels of domestic demand. The accompanying boom in asset prices, stocks, and land prices had already faded as growth slowed perceptibly in some countries—Indonesia and Korea—and turned negative in Thailand in 1997. After the crisis, GDP growth fell sharply to double-digit negative values in Thailand and Indonesia and to more modest declines elsewhere. Taiwan and China continued to show substantial positive growth, though somewhat slower than in the past, and Singapore and the Philippines were also less affected than other countries. As we discuss further, this reflected the somewhat different position of China and the less serious imbalances in Taiwan, Singapore, and the Philippines than in other countries. Since the crisis, Indonesia continues to experience serious difficulty and has shown some recovery only in the past year. Others like South Korea, Malaysia, and Thailand have recovered strongly. As we have noted, still others like China and Taiwan were only marginally affected by the crisis. Even so, looking across the region, it is apparent that a serious decline in GDP growth took place. Although there has been considerable recovery, even four years after the crisis, the region has not achieved the GDP it would have had the crisis not occurred and had earlier trends continued. It is welcome to see substantial recovery in 1999 and 2000, suggesting that the real demand and production aspects of the crisis may be on the mend.

Extremely high rates of capital accumulation supported the 1990s expansion (see Figure 11.2). These reflected high domestic saving rates and capital inflow. The high rate of investment is noteworthy because it appears to have led to a decline in the marginal return to capital. In Korea, the investment boom led to excessive broadening and deepening of industrial capital (Baily and Zitzewitz, 1998). In Thailand, it accounted for a wasteful allocation of funds to golf clubs and residential, hotel, and office development, substantially in excess of likely future requirements.

The importance of export markets in these developments is shown by the growth rate of exports (see Figure 11.3). The path of exports is somewhat different from that of GDP. We note, first, that the decline of exports occurred earlier than the decline in GDP; in 1996 in Thailand, in 1997 in Singapore and Malaysia. There was practically a universal drop in 1998, except in the Philippines where export growth remained high.

Along with the decline in exports in 1996 and 1997 there was a substantial swing of imports, first to high growth rates, resulting in negative trade balances, except notably in China and Taiwan (see Table 11.1).

The region's current account deficits (as a percentage of GDP) and its debt service ratios (debt service/exports of goods and services), shown in Figure 11.3 and Table 11.2, point clearly to the vulnerability of the balance-of-payments situation to which some countries were exposed in 1996, Thailand, in particular.

Debt service ratios had risen to spectacular levels in Indonesia and Thai-

Figure 11.2
Investments in Southeast Asia as a Percentage of GDP

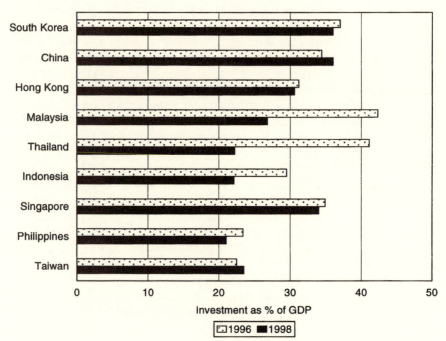

land. The implications of even a moderate slowdown of exports vis-à-vis the ability of these countries to meet their external obligations are apparent in the figures for 1998 when the debt service ratio for Indonesia was almost 100 percent. Other East Asian debtor countries, notably Korea and Malaysia, had more favorable debt service ratios.

The risks become particularly serious when a large share of the capital inflow takes the form of short-term liabilities, either portfolio investment or bank lending. Ito (1999) comments on the rapid expansion of capital flows in the 1990s and notes that growth was predominantly in the form of potentially volatile short-term finance rather than more stable foreign direct investment. His calculation shows that for several of the East Asian countries—Thailand, Indonesia, and South Korea—short-term bank liabilities exceeded available foreign reserves (see Figure 11.4). The trade balance situation turned around more quickly than had been anticipated. Massive changes in trade, both exports and imports, meant that by 1998 current account deficits had been turned into large surpluses. These changes mirror the movements of international capital flows into the region, prior to the crisis, and out of the region, thereafter.

The years 1999 and 2000 showed substantial cyclical recovery in export

Figure 11.3
Growth Rate of Exports in Southeast Asia (U.S.$)

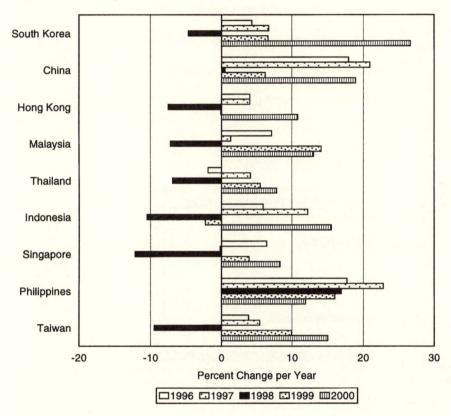

Table 11.1
Trade Balance, 1996–2000 (U.S.$ billion)

	1996	1997	1998	1999	2000
South Korea	−14	−3	41	29	22
China	20	46	49	27	23
Hong Kong	−16	−20	−10	−3	−6
Malaysia	4	4	17	23	22
Thailand	−9	2	16	14	12
Indonesia	6	10	18	17	16
Singapore	2	1	17	13	11
Philippines	−11	−11	0	3	1
Taiwan	18	14	11	15	16

Table 11.2
Debt Service Ratios (debt service/exports of goods and services), 1996–2000

	1996	1997	1998	1999	2000
South Korea	5.8	6.7	6.3	6.2	6.1
China	21.3	20.0	21.2	21.0	18.4
Malaysia	15.9	14.4	18.8	13.9	9.8
Thailand	35.8	37.6	66.4	49.4	30.6
Indonesia	75.5	76.1	97.4	74.0	60.7
Philippines	24.0	19.9	14.5	14.4	N/A

Figure 11.4
Short-Term Liabilities over Foreign Reserves

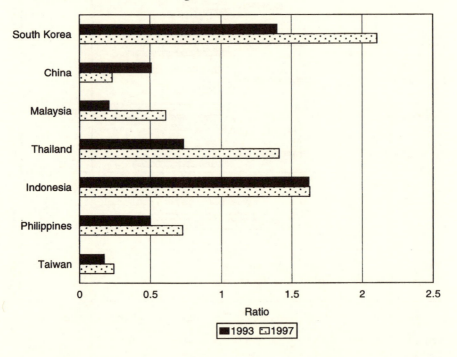

trade throughout the area, probably accounting for a large part of the rapid economic recovery. Undoubtedly, the adjustment of exchange rates has much to do with changes in trade patterns. Exchange rate indices (1996=100) are shown on a US$ per unit of foreign currency basis in Figure 11.5. Substantial readjustment in exchange rates is apparent. Although the rate for China remained stable, other countries showed significant declines, ranging from 20 percent in Taiwan and Vietnam to over 50

Figure 11.5
Exchange Rate Indices, 1996–1999 (1996 = 100)

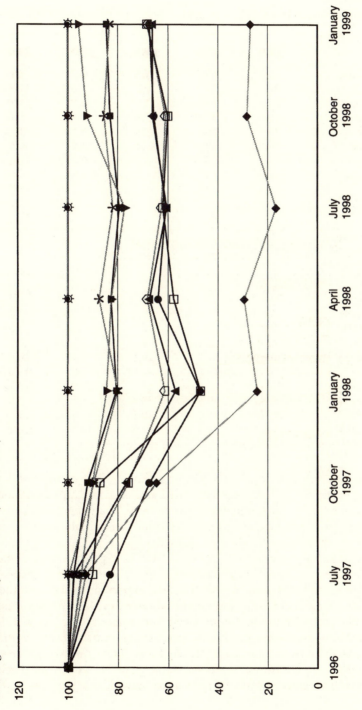

Table 11.3
Inflation (percent change CPI), 1996–2000

	1996	1997	1998	1999	2000
South Korea	5.0	4.4	7.5	0.8	1.1
China	8.3	2.8	−0.8	−1.4	1.0
Hong Kong	6.0	5.7	2.6	−3.3	−3.3
Malaysia	3.5	2.7	5.3	2.7	1.4
Thailand	5.8	5.6	8.1	0.3	3.3
Indonesia	7.0	6.2	58.4	20.5	6.5
Singapore	1.4	2.0	−0.3	0.4	1.4
Philippines	5.2	6.6	10.4	4.6	5.5
Taiwan	2.3	1.8	1.7	0.4	1.3

Table 11.4
Money Supply Growth (M2) per Year, 1996–2000 (percent)

	1996	1997	1998	1999	2000
South Korea	16.2	19.2	19.0	27.9	22.4
China (M1)	19.8	25.0	12.7	17.5	8.3
Hong Kong	10.9	8.3	11.8	8.1	8.7
Malaysia (M1)	16.6	11.7	−29.4	29.2	20.0
Thailand	13.5	15.8	−4.5	11.0	13.2
Indonesia	29.6	23.2	62.3	11.9	18.7
Singapore	9.8	10.5	30.2	8.5	7.0
Philippines	20.5	8.0	19.3	13.9	12.7
Taiwan (M1)	4.3	13.7	2.5	10.4	16.1

percent in South Korea and Thailand to almost 75 percent in Indonesia. The readjustment of exchange rates has altered competitive relationships between the East Asian countries, favoring those whose currencies appeared to have been overvalued relative to the Chinese renminbi yuan before the crisis. That there was overshooting is evident from the recovery in some of the exchange rates from their 1997 or 1998 low points, even in the case of Indonesia where political uncertainties are still affecting confidence.

It is important, however, to note that the expansion and devaluation did not lead to significant swings in overall inflation rates, except in Indonesia (see Table 11.3).[2] In the Indonesian case, inflationary pressures in 1998 are associated not only with decline in the exchange rate but also with rapid growth of the money supply (see Table 11.4). This contrasts sharply with other East Asian countries where monetary growth was kept in check and, in fact, went negative as in Malaysia and Thailand.

Numerous attempts have been made to look for other financial variables that would measure risks or indicate the probability of financial crisis (Agenor et al., 2000). The size and composition of borrowing in international markets is clearly relevant. Studies of risk of crisis and of early warning signals have also pointed to other variables like the ones considered above—such as current account deficits, overvalued exchange rate, weak banking system financing a boom in asset values, and fiscal deficits. We consider some of these factors in the following country-specific summaries.

Country Specifics—Thailand

We focus first on the Thai situation because this country appears to have been the leader of the crisis.[3] Table 11.5 presents a chronology.

Even before the crisis, the Thai economy faced a number of serious cyclical problems. A surging investment boom had created growing excess capacity and declining investment returns (IMF, 2000c). Much of this expenditure had gone into nontraded sectors, especially residential and office real estate. By 1996, vacancy rates were mounting. An asset bubble that had greatly increased stock and real property prices had burst. At the same time, Thailand was losing competitiveness in export markets so that export growth turned negative in 1996. A cyclical slowdown was likely even in the absence of broader financial crisis.

The expansion was greatly augmented by the massive inflow of foreign capital and the resulting credit availability. The Bangkok International Banking Facility established in 1993 opened the Thai capital market to large inflows of foreign capital, much of it short-term bank lending channeled through banks and finance companies. (Note the mismatch between short-term borrowing and long-term investments.)

As foreign investor sentiment about the Thai economy changed in late 1996, the problem of managing excessive capital inflows turned into one of dealing with massive outflow. The Bank of Thailand used its foreign exchange reserve holdings in a vain effort to maintain its 25 baht to the U.S. dollar exchange rate peg. At the same time, difficulties in domestic banks and finance companies caused the suspension of most finance companies and led to bank runs at the weaker commercial banks. Unable to maintain the exchange rate and faced with a serious banking crisis, the Thai government turned to the IMF for assistance. Funding from the IMF, other international institutions, and private sources was provided, subject to strict conditions about bank closures and reconstruction, and a turn of the government budget from deficit to a modest surplus.

At this point, the Thai economy slumped into a classic recession pattern. Investment fell drastically as firms faced vastly increased foreign debt obligations, higher interest rates, and a decline in credit availability. Firms sought to minimize their holdings of inventories. There was also a signifi-

Table 11.5
Chronology of the Thai Crisis

1993	Creation of Bangkok International Banking Facility
	Opening of Thai financial markets to foreign short-term capital flows
1994–1995	Investment boom
	Stock market and property value bubble
	Current account deficit, inflow of foreign capital
	Accumulation of private foreign debt (60% of GDP)
1996	Loss of trade competitiveness, export slowdown
	Current account deficit at 8% of GDP
	Large domestic fiscal deficit
Late 1996	Attack on the baht
	Intervention of Bank of Thailand to maintain the 25 baht/U.S.$
Early 1997	Collapse of finance companies and bank runs
June 1997	16 finance companies suspended
July 1997	Crash of the baht
August 1997	42 more finance companies suspended
Late 1997	Intervention of the IMF, $17.2 billion credit
	High interest rates, credit crunch
	Increase in taxes, reduction in deficit
	Drop in final demand: consumption, investment, etc.
1998	Deep recession, fiscal stimulus
	10 percent decline in GDP
	20 percent decline in industrial production
	Change of government
	Modification of policy agreements with IMF
1999	Rapid export growth
	Low interest rate policy
	Moderate recovery GDP growth at 5 percent

cant downward swing of consumption, particularly of cars, as incomes diminished, unemployment rates rose, and credit became difficult to obtain. The business cycle swing was far larger than anyone, including the experts at the IMF, had anticipated.

The beginnings of recovery date from late 1998. Improvement in trade competitiveness and a recovery of domestic consumption helped to generate a gradual resumption of production activity. In agreement with the IMF, the new Chuan Leekpai government eased fiscal policy with tax cuts and some increases in social welfare expenditures. At the same time, there was a substantial reduction of interest rates.

A survey carried out at the Sasin Graduate School of Business Administration in Bangkok, Thailand, demonstrates how drastically anticipations

Table 11.6
Results of the Sasin Survey Before and After the Crisis

	Evaluation of the Business Environment				
	Before the Crisis	**After the Crisis**			
	1995–1996 (%)	**1998 (%)**	**1999 (%)**	**2000 (%)**	**2001 (%)**
Very optimistic	28.6	2.4	1.5	1.1	3.6
Moderately optimistic	45.2	4.9	24.7	27.2	25.0
Uncertain	11.9	11.0	34.5	25.0	31.3
Worried	13.1	37.8	36.1	41.3	34.8
Very pessimistic	10.2	43.9	3.1	5.4	5.9

	Evaluation of Return to Rapid Growth			
	1998 (%)	**1999 (%)**	**2000 (%)**	**2001 (%)**
Very optimistic	10.4	5.3	2.5	9.1
Moderately optimistic	31.2	43.3	34.1	29.8
Uncertain	13.0	23.5	27.0	23.1
Worried	33.8	25.1	28.7	31.4
Very pessimistic	11.6	2.8	7.8	6.6

changed as a result of the crisis (see Table 11.6). In response to a question on current business conditions, before the crisis in 1995–1996, two-thirds of the respondents were moderately or highly optimistic. After the crisis, the situation had changed dramatically. In August 1998, two-thirds of the respondents were moderately or highly pessimistic. Repeats of the survey in 1999 and 2000 showed some recovery, with fewer very pessimistic but more than two-thirds still pessimistic or uncertain.

A forward-looking question, asking whether the respondents expected a return to rapid growth after the crisis, showed a continuation of moderate optimism in the period from 1998 to 2000. More than 40 percent of the respondents were optimistic, though a similar number were pessimistic. By 2000, the number of optimists had declined somewhat and more were uncertain or pessimistic. Probing questions about the reasons for uncertainty revealed that insecurity about political developments was the dominant consideration, though fear of a recurrence of the economic/financial crisis remains.

In late 2000, Thailand was still only partway through the process of restructuring financial institutions and corporations (Claessens et al., 1999). Nevertheless, the economy has been rebalanced, away from excessive expansion in nontraded sectors, and has had a relative price adjustment and shift toward traded goods sectors which appear to be favorable for recovery (IMF, 2000c). The economy was recovering, but the business outlook remained insecure. Export performance had declined, a critical factor. Domestic demand remained weak. Although GDP growth was still above 4 percent, it was being marked down. In 2001, it is not clear how quickly Thailand will return to its pre-crisis rapid growth path, in view of slowing demand in Thailand's trade partner countries.

Country Specifics—Indonesia

In mid-1997, the macroeconomic situation of Indonesia was more favorable than that of Thailand, though Indonesia's foreign debt was more serious. Export growth had not fallen as seriously, and the fiscal balance had remained positive. But Indonesia's short-term external debt had been rising, though in contrast to other East Asian countries, largely in terms of corporate borrowing rather than intermediation through the banks.

In November 1997, following an over 30 percent currency depreciation, the IMF organized an agreement providing lines of credit from the IMF, the World Bank, and private sources amounting to $36 billion. This agreement contained the usual elements intended to improve confidence, including tight monetary policy, fiscal restriction, plans for financial sector restructuring, and structural reforms for the corporate sector. After some initial success, the rupiah began to slide sharply once again. The main factors contributing to the sharp deterioration of the rupiah, much sharper than elsewhere in the region, included vacillating monetary and exchange rate policies, failure to fully implement structural reforms, and, particularly, political uncertainty. The central bank's liquidity support for financial institutions accounted for the rapid monetary growth noted above. As a result, in contrast to other countries in the region, depreciation of the exchange rate has been accompanied with rapid inflation, a process that represents a vicious circle. A repeated series of negotiations and renegotiations with the IMF took place in a highly uncertain political environment, with widespread civil unrest.[4]

Toward the end of 1998, market sentiment improved, and the exchange rate stabilized. Modest GDP growth resumed in 1999. Political uncertainties continue to dominate the Indonesian situation and suggest that it may be a long time before foreign investors will find Indonesia an attractive destination.

Country Specifics—Malaysia

Following a period of extremely rapid growth during the first half of the 1990s, Malaysia's economic fundamentals appear to have been somewhat stronger in 1997 than those of other East Asian countries. There were, however, risks in connection with rapid credit expansion and declining asset quality and a collapse of asset prices. The ringgit came under significant downward pressure in mid-1997, along with other regional currencies. Malaysia dealt with the crisis differently from other countries by refusing IMF assistance and imposing, in September 1998, capital controls on outward capital movements and pegging the ringgit. These controls were replaced by an "exit levy" in 1999 permitting withdrawal of funds but at a cost. The controls were wide ranging and were apparently effective. Their main impact was the elimination of the offshore ringgit market. Their effectiveness may be attributed to the fact that Malaysia had substantial foreign exchange reserves and to the undervaluation of the ringgit at 3.8 per U.S. dollar compared to other currencies which were recovering from their post-crisis lows (IMF, 1999a). Somewhat surprisingly, the controls appear to have had little impact on direct foreign investment inflows.

Other dimensions of macroeconomic policy in Malaysia have been quite similar to those customarily recommended by the IMF. Tight monetary policy and restrictions on lending, designed to slow the property market expansion and to stabilize the exchange rate in 1996 and 1997, were followed by a loosening of monetary policy and more expansive fiscal policy to strengthen the economy in 1999. Malaysia moved ahead—it appears more rapidly than other countries—with structural reform of its corporate and banking systems. Malaysia's economic performance since the crisis has been comparable to, or even a little better than that of, other countries in the region. An IMF evaluation concludes (IMF, 1999b) that although currency controls appear to have been effective in limiting capital outflows, it is difficult to disentangle their impact from that of other forces that were operating.

The Malaysian economy has been expanding more rapidly than that of its neighbors and has benefited from high oil prices. Its outlook is, however, closely tied to the situation in the electronics industry and in its market economies, particularly Japan.

Country Specifics—South Korea

Despite its strong macroeconomic performance and solid fundamentals, by early 1997 South Korea presented a picture of a greatly overextended economy with a weak financial sector and excessively leveraged industry.[5] Like Thailand, South Korea had relied heavily on inflows of short-term foreign capital, near 5 percent of GDP in 1996 and early 1997, to support its chaebol's investment boom. Investments had gone heavily into industrial capacity, seeking ever larger market shares at the cost of declining marginal productivity (Baily and Zitzewitz, 1999; Pormeleano, 1998). These investments were largely financed by banks closely linked to the industrial conglomerates to whom they were lending. There was insufficient prudential supervision of the banking system and a lack of transparency in the data, some of which may have been misreported.

Adverse external shocks like the declining competitiveness of exports, which were partly a result of the strengthening dollar and of weak semiconductor prices, complicated the situation. The year 1997 was marked by a decline in the stock market, as well as a downgrading of South Korea's debt rating and serious financial problems in banks and the corporate combines. In December 1997, the won depreciated about 70 percent. External and internal financial collapse resulted in a sharp drop in domestic consumption and investment during 1998.

In December 1997, the Bank of Korea sharply increased interest rates and sought foreign assistance. A $58 billion loan package was put together by the IMF, the World Bank, the ADB, and bilateral donors including the United States. This assistance was conditional on an IMF adjustment program intended "first and foremost to restore market confidence and to stabilize financial markets" (IMF, 2000a, 9). Monetary policy was tightened to produce higher interest rates, but fiscal measures were loosened to offset the impact of the expected slump in the economy as well as to provide a social safety net. After a period of stabilization, monetary policy was eased to substantially reduce interest rates, though it is not clear whether business financing is available at lower rates. The adjustment program included wide-ranging structural reforms as well as macroeconomic policies. Financial sector reforms sought to increase bank supervision and to restructure banks and nonbank financial institutions.

Corporate sector reforms were aimed at improved competition and changes in corporate organization. An objective has been to resolve the insolvent position of several industrial groups. Corporate reforms have gone much more slowly than anticipated and remain largely unfinished (Claessens et al., 1999). Despite the economic recovery, bankruptcies and foreign takeovers of large industrial groups like Kia were still unsettled at the end of 2000. Nevertheless, as export demand has increased and as domestic demand has recovered, Korea has shown more rapid economic recovery than other countries. The recovery has followed a V-shaped pattern with 9 to 10 percent GDP growth in 1999 and 2000, returning to Korea's crisis level of GDP and reducing unemployment to less than 5 percent. The Korean adjustment appears to have been far sharper and the recovery quicker than in other such episodes (Lee and Rhee, 2000).

Country Specifics—Philippines

After a long period of ups and downs, during the first half of the 1990s the Philippines had several years of good growth up to 6 percent in 1996 under the reform and economic opening strategy of the Ramos regime. As in other East Asian countries, there remained substantial vulnerabilities: rapid credit expansion, an investment boom, inflow of foreign capital, and an overvalued exchange rate linked to the U.S. dollar. The Philippines also had much lower savings and investment rates than those elsewhere in the region. On the other hand, the risks were probably less than in other countries, since the period of credit expansion had been much shorter and the economy was somewhat more open and market-oriented than elsewhere.

The Philippines suffered substantial currency depreciation following the floating of the peso in July 1997. Thereafter, economic activity slowed but to only a small (0.5 percent) reduction in 1998, reflecting a fall in agricultural and industrial output but continued growth in services. Export growth continued very strong, in contrast to some of the other countries in the region. Moderate recovery began in 1999. The Philippines weathered the crisis better than other countries, but it has not shared their rapid recovery. Today, political uncertainties stand in the way of a return to rapid expansion.

Country Specifics—China

The Chinese economy was already showing signs of a slowdown at the time of the Asian crisis. The statistics show slower, though still very high, growth rates, ranging from 10 percent and declining to 7 percent per year. The slowing down reflects the decline in demand in the East Asian region as well as the impact of uncertainty on consumer spending domestically. But in view of its strong external balance, high level of reserves, and controlled exchange market, China escaped the worst effects of the crisis. Domestic fiscal stimulus, amounting to 2.5 percent of GDP, as well as eased monetary policy, helped offset the weakness of demand. Since mid-1999, China has been recovering rapidly, and GDP growth has accelerated as a result of buoyant exports, recovery of consumption, and continued fiscal stimulus.

The Chinese have begun to address the problems of their publicly owned banks and state-owned enterprises, but much remains to be done. There are also serious social problems as workers leave the slow-growing provinces in the inland and western parts of the country to move to rapidly growing eastern urban centers. These problems pose challenges somewhat different from those encountered in the more private enterprise-based economies of East Asia.

Country Specifics—Hong Kong

The East Asian crisis affected the Hong Kong economy severely, with a sharp fall in external demand and a consequent sharp decline in GDP (5.1 percent) in 1998. Interest rates rose sharply and asset prices declined. The

Hong Kong dollar was able to resist a speculative attack in August 1998, in view of Hong Kong's substantial reserve position and close links to the rest of China. To maintain confidence, the authorities intervened by buying stock on the stock exchange and eased fiscal policy. Adjustment proceeded rapidly, with domestic price declines and layoffs. Moderate recovery, reflecting a return to more rapid growth in China and recovery in other crisis-hit East Asian economies, began in 1999.

Country Specifics—Taiwan

Taiwan largely escaped the crisis. With a continued strong trade balance and large reserves, Taiwan is a net exporter of capital to the region. The Taiwan economy showed continued growth based on an export boom for electronics and communication equipment. A weakening of domestic demand and continued foreign direct investment helped Taiwan avoid the vulnerabilities that accentuated the crisis elsewhere in the region. In 1999 and 2000, increasing demand caused modest acceleration of exports and growth.

Country Specifics—Vietnam

More than China, Vietnam remains a highly controlled economy with a large, though relatively declining, state-owned sector. Vietnam's economic growth slowed markedly in 1998 and 1999, but the slowdown cannot be attributed to the Asian crisis. "The country is too isolated from the world economy to have caught the Asian flu" (Pierre, 2000). Vietnam's key problems are domestic, poor management of state-owned enterprises and the banking sector which is largely government owned, excessive bureaucratic regulation and licensing rules, and so on. Lacking flexibility and transparency, Vietnam experienced a sharp decline in foreign direct investment which reached a peak in 1996.

Country Specifics—Singapore

Strong fundamentals allowed the Singapore economy to weather the crisis better than neighboring countries. In 1998 Singapore slipped to the edge of recession—a positive GDP growth rate of just 0.4 percent in 1998—as a result of the crisis in the region and the slowdown in the electronics market. But Singapore's strong external balance, stable banks, and policy enabled it to avoid capital flight and accounted for the fact that the crisis was not serious. Surging exports of electronics and regional demand for services have caused rapid growth to resume. In view of Singapore's limited space and already heavy capital intensity, the Singapore government is promoting a private sector, knowledge-based approach to future development (IMF, 2000b).

Table 11.7
Alternative Explanations for the East Asian Crisis

Domestic Considerations	International Considerations
Bubble economy speculation	Overvaluation of exchange rate
Cost and capacity pressures	Loss of trade competitiveness
Unsustainable investment boom	Excessive short-term capital inflows
Moral hazard	Mismatch between short-term liabilities and reserve
Weakness of banks and bank regulation	Exchange rate expectations and contagion
Crony capitalism	International speculative attack
	International capital flow liberalization

Country Characteristics—Summary

There were clearly significant differences between the various East Asian countries, but there are also common elements and linkages that caused them to go into the crisis together. Thailand, Indonesia, and South Korea shared domestic imbalances as well as international forces. Although the details were different, all three had experienced an unsustainable boom, an asset bubble, and an overleveraged banking system. All three had seen a decline in their export performance. And all three were greatly exposed by excessive short-term international capital inflows. These elements provide some basis for the crisis. Its timing and the involvement of other countries in the area may well reflect the phenomenon of international contagion. We evaluate these elements in greater detail in the next section.

CHANGING PERSPECTIVES ON THE CAUSES OF THE CRISIS

A variety of explanations related to international and to domestic factors have been offered to account for the 1997 East Asian crisis (see Table 11.7).

It is useful to distinguish between the proximate causes of the pattern of growth and collapse in East Asia and the vulnerabilities that turned what might have been a slowdown into a crash. We note, for example, that a downward shift of an unsustainable investment boom, cost and capacity pressures, or loss of trade competitiveness may *cause* a cyclical swing. Inadequate bank regulation or international capital flow liberalization may make a country *vulnerable* when other forces turn unfavorable. In the East Asian case, it was ultimately the vulnerability of the region that turned a slowdown into a crash.

From a "headline" perspective, the crisis began on July 2, 1997, with the collapse of the Thai baht. It spread gradually to other East Asian currencies—the Indonesian rupiah in September, the Malaysian ringitt in October, and the Korean won in December. Ultimately, currencies of countries as far away as Brazil and Russia were affected, and for a while in 1998, there was fear that the entire world financial system might be engulfed.

Early evaluations of the crisis naturally focused on *exchange rate expectations and contagion* (Krugman, 1979), a financial panic interpretation (Radelet and Sachs, 1998). Since late 1996, Thai authorities had intervened in an attempt to support the longstanding 25 baht to the U.S. dollar exchange rate.[6] When this costly effort failed, the crash of the baht caused expectations of collapse in other East Asian countries, apparently augmented by speculative attacks. Malaysia's Mahathir placed the blame squarely on a cabal of *international hedge fund* operators, arguing that underlying economic conditions in the East Asian countries did not justify the exchange rate depreciation that occurred. Some economists put great emphasis on the contagion theme. Sachs (1998) added the position that the IMF's suggested remedial measures only made things worse by further undermining investor confidence.

At about the same time, reports that finance companies and banks in the region held massive quantities of nonperforming loans that could not be repaid raised questions about *banking behavior and supervision* (Claessens et al., 1998). Some argued that extending loans to business friends without adequate evaluation of the creditors' prospects and ability to repay was characteristic of East Asian business culture, sometimes summarized under the pejorative term, *crony capitalism. Moral hazard* arose as investors felt they had implicit public sector guarantees for their assets and for stability of the exchange rate. Some experts have argued that this explained excessively leveraged investments which were typical in the region. At the same time, *failures of prudential bank supervision* aggravated the situation by failing to recognize the problem and to avert it before it was too late. This represents a dimension of the structural interpretation of the crisis (Corsetti et al., 1998). It is the responsibility of bank regulatory authorities to rein in banks and finance companies when (and preferably before) they engage in unsound lending practices. But this supervision calls for a degree of accounting accuracy and transparency that was not prevalent in East Asia. Moreover, it is not certain that East Asian banks and finance companies would normally have near enough reserves to meet their obligations should creditors want to withdraw their funds.[7]

Capital flow liberalization linked the loose practices of domestic banks with the broader international financial market. In Thailand, as we have noted, this phenomenon can be traced back to 1993 with the development of offshore banking, the Bangkok International Banking Facility (BIBF). The idea was to create a regional financial center. Thai banks would borrow funds abroad and re-lend to borrowers in neighboring East Asian countries. These would be so-called out, out transactions. The problem was that many of them turned out to be out, in transactions bringing foreign short-term funds into Thailand at low world interest rates. These funds were borrowed in dollars at 7 percent and lent out locally in baht at approximately 14 percent, a very large margin given the widely held assumption that the baht exchange was fixed. Concurrently, the Bank of Thailand sought to maintain high minimum interest rates domestically in an effort to moderate the economic boom, to attract foreign capital, and to stimulate saving. Moreover, this policy had the support of domestic banks who sought to control domestic interest rates. Thus, even though there was a large inflow of funds, domestic interest rates did not fall. The large interest rate differential between foreign and domestic rates was maintained. This differential provided great incentive for banks to intermediate such transactions, often without adequate supervision. Surprisingly, foreign lenders also do not appear to have looked too closely at the viability of their loans. Before one attributes full responsibility for the failures to local banks, it is important to ask whether foreign lenders should not also bear some prudential responsibility.

The Thai experience with capital flow liberalization is a reminder of the so-called impossible trinity: the inability to reconcile fixed exchange rates, open capital markets, and an independent monetary policy.

It was only in retrospect, as the East Asian economies dropped into recession, that the *business cycle aspects* of the crisis were recognized. Macroeconomic statistics for the period preceding the 1997 crisis suggest that some of the countries, particularly Thailand and South Korea, were heading into a business cycle swing. In Thailand, as we have noted, a construction boom produced office buildings, hotels, and residences far in excess of foreseeable needs. A large government deficit also provided stimulus. Boom conditions sharply increased imports. The financial crisis quickly led business firms to cut back inventories and to stop investment. Consumer purchasing declined sharply, with auto sales in Thailand in early 1998 running at less than 20 percent of their level the year before. Government spending was also held in check, in part in response to IMF pressures. The result was a general recession.

Economic fundamentals bringing on the crisis may be considered from three directions:

• Trade competitiveness
• Return on investment
• Asset values

As we note, the stability of the exchange rate was a critical consideration in maintaining capital inflows. By 1996, boom conditions in Thailand caused the baht to become *overvalued*. *Thai exports lost competitiveness*, particularly against East Asian supplier countries. This, along with depressed markets in Japan and the growing productive potential of China, interrupted the rapid growth path of Thai exports in 1996,[8] while imports continued to grow rapidly. The resulting current account deficit amounted to 8 percent of GDP, a large enough figure to represent a danger signal. A similar lack of competitiveness and depressed markets appears to have affected South Korea, Indonesia, and Malaysia, though the current account deficits remained relatively smaller.

Declining returns on investment were the result of a long period of intensive investment growth. As has been documented for Korea (Baily and Zitzewitz, 1998) and as is evident from surpluses of investment in housing, offices, and hotels in Thailand, the investment boom of the 1990s was not only unsustainable but probably also unrealistic. Declining returns and/or losses resulted. Many of the projects begun in the boom period remain unfinished (at last count over 400 unfinished projects in Bangkok alone).

Finally, we note an early contributor, the collapse of East Asian financial and land asset values. Stock markets in East Asia tanked in 1995–1996, and land values began to fall as the construction boom faded. The drop in asset values contributed in no small measure to the failure of banks and finance companies that had invested or provided security loans. The degree of nonperforming loans reflects not simply failure to evaluate the prospects of particular projects, but also failure to appreciate the great degree of risk involved in excessively bubbling security and property markets. Whether this represents a result of moral hazard, assuming explicit or implied government guarantees, is a matter of some debate.

Can one choose one or another of the explanations for the crisis? In retrospect, it is clear that all of the various approaches have some validity and that they interacted in important ways. Separately, some might have caused a smaller localized swing. Others simply amplified the vulnerabilities of the situation. Together they account for the widespread crisis.

There is little doubt, however, that the combination of circumstances represented an explosion waiting to happen. The combination of insufficient foreign exchange reserves, a pegged but insecure exchange rate, and excessive optimism can quickly lead to a reversal of sentiment; capital inflows can quickly turn into capital flight. Such a change in perspective can be the result of a business cycle or a financial crisis in the banking system, basically local phenomena. It may also reflect what is happening internationally, for example, a loss of export competitiveness. And finally contagion or panic hypotheses may have some validity if a crisis occurs, particularly in neighboring countries.

This raises a challenging question: Do the growing internationalization of the world economy and the increasing flexibility of international capital flows threaten to make financial crises a more likely and more serious occurrence?

THE ROLE OF THE IMF AND THE WORLD BANK

With the benefit of hindsight, experts at the IMF recognize that:

the Asian crisis differs from other crises [faced by the IMF] in key respects . . . Unlike the typical case in which the IMF's assistance is requested, these crises did not result mainly from the monetization of fiscal imbalances and only in Thailand were there substantial external current-account imbalances. Instead, they were rooted mainly in financial sector fragilities . . . which made these economies increasingly vulnerable to changes in market sentiment, a deteriorating external situation, and contagion. (Lane et al., 1999, 1)

In the IMF expert's words, "the crises were made in the private sector . . . rather than the more conventional situation of monetization of public sector deficits" (Lane et al., 1999, 56). This influenced the IMF's programs and accounts. More than usually, financial support was made conditional on extensive programs of structural reform.

The traditional role of the IMF has been to assist countries faced with balance-of-payments disequilibrium (Bordo and James, 2000). In most cases, the IMF was dealing with problems at the level of one country alone, though on several occasions during the 1980s and the 1990s there have been regionwide difficulties and cases of contagion from one country to another, the *tequila effect* in Latin America, for example. Typically, the problems had been the result of fiscal and external account imbalances and called for rigorous macroeconomic stabilization policy.

The currency crises in East Asia were significantly different. With the exception of Thailand, Korea, and, to a lesser extent, Indonesia, the fiscal and trade deficits in the region were not considered serious. The economies of the region had been growing very rapidly for some time, but there was little inflationary pressure. The international institutions were aware of and warned of some strains and imbalances but did not anticipate either the severity or the timing of the crisis.

The seriousness of the situation reflected the vulnerabilities of the banking and corporate sectors aggravated by volatile short-term capital flows. As a result, the IMF's programs called for a broader approach than past IMF operations. Macroeconomic policies were adjusted to build confidence and stanch capital outflows. These policies involved fiscal restrictions buttressed by tightened monetary policies. In addition, the IMF made its assistance conditional on structural reforms that were aimed at fixing the underlying long-term problems of banking and corporate governance and, in some cases at providing social safety nets.

In practice, the policy approach became a cause for considerable dispute both internally, in the countries themselves, and between the countries and international institutions. In response, the IMF administered its proposals with considerable flexibility. The initial fiscal policy recommendations, particularly for Thailand, appeared to be quite restrictive. Recommending tax increases and expenditure reductions, the IMF sought to persuade the Thai government to eliminate the budget deficit, even to run a small surplus. This was clearly not possible in the face of the drastic decline in business activity. Moreover, it would have aggravated the already serious social situation. Subsequently, the IMF was forced to adjust its fiscal policy advice in line with the realities of the situation, accepting deficits in later "letters of intent." In other East Asian countries, where the fiscal imbalance was less serious, IMF programs continued to recommend fiscal adjustment, arguing that an improvement in the fiscal balance and national savings rate would help to improve confidence on the international level. It was also necessary to take domestic considerations into account: the domestic credit picture and the very heavy fiscal burden of rebuilding the banking system. Here, also, the IMF adjusted its recommendations in the face of changing conditions. As the crisis deepened, positions were reversed; the need for fiscal stimulus was recognized.

In their evaluation, Lane et al. (1999) point out that reports that the IMF imposed harsh fiscal austerity exaggerate the reality. Admittedly, the IMF initially underestimated the seriousness of the situation. But headline reports compared IMF programs with pre-crisis national projections and exaggerated the amount of adjustment the IMF sought. As the situation developed, the IMF experts altered their recommendations accordingly. Nevertheless, it can be argued that IMF fiscal policy recommendations should have been less stringent at the beginning and more supportive later when the severity of the situation was fully apparent. It can also be said that had the IMF been able to intervene in the period of excessively rapid growth that preceded the crisis the situation might have been eased, if not avoided altogether. On the other hand, it is understandable that before the crisis, when balances of payments were in surplus because of capital inflows and currencies tended to appreciate, the IMF was not in a position to exercise much influence.

The initial monetary policy stance was largely driven by market conditions. The loss of confidence by the market participants, domestic as well as international, would inevitably have led to rapidly rising interest rates at the same time as the exchange rate was depreciating. A tight monetary position with high interest rates would tend to improve confidence and at the same time prevent further deterioration of the exchange rate. The latter was a particular concern because of fears that depreciation in the exchange rate would result in rapidly rising inflation. The IMF did not suggest pegging exchange rates but suggested reliance on a floating exchange rate regime. Rapid inflation did not occur in Thailand and South Korea, but it turned out to be a major problem in Indonesia, as we have noted. After the exchange rates had stabilized, central banks made efforts to lower interest rates.

An important question with regard to the effectiveness of monetary policy concerns the availability of credit at the prevailing interest rate. There are widespread perceptions of a serious credit crunch in the East Asian crisis countries. Anecdotal evidence indicates that firms are unable to obtain funds. There is also reason to think that with high proportions of non-performing loans (NPLs) and under pressure to improve their balance sheets to Bank for International Settlements (BIS) standards, banks extend loans only to the most qualified borrowers. The empirical evidence is quite mixed. On this matter, the data for Thailand support a credit crunch (Agenor et al., 2000), but indications are less clear in other countries. While monetary indicators do not point to a sudden tightening of the money supply, they might not be expected to measure a change in access to credit, particularly for smaller and less financially qualified firms. The survey work of Claessens et al. (1998) suggests that considerations other than credit availability were also important in determining the decline of credit use. We may conclude that low interest rates were not effective in stimulating investment because in many cases credit was not available at these rates and because at that time there were few financially viable investment opportunities. We note that a credit crunch may not be so much the result of the central bank's monetary policies as a consequence of the balance sheet problems of the financial sector.

The structural reform aspects of the IMF program proved to be the most controversial and most difficult to implement. In view of the perception that the structural and balance sheet difficulties of the financial system and corporations were the result of underlying systemic problems, the IMF programs ranged more broadly than they might have otherwise. According to the IMF, "a comprehensive strategy was needed principally because of the interdependence of reforms in different areas" (Lane et al., 1999, 18). The structural reforms proposed aimed not only at restructuring insolvent or illiquid financial institutions but also at broader structural problems that were thought to be at the root of the crisis. These included deficiencies and financial and corporate governance, prudential regulation of the banking system, promotion of competition, opening up of markets to foreign capital and entrepreneurship, and dealing with social problems. The World Bank and the Asian Development Bank were heavily involved in the development and financing of the structural reform programs and also supported social safety net measures. It is not surprising that many of these measures became a focus for political controversy. Foreigners as well as locals have seen these measures as intervention in local affairs. Enactment of these proposals has been difficult and much more time consuming than expected.

Financial system reforms, the cornerstone of restructuring programs, faced the dual challenges of the immediate crisis, still largely evolving, and the longer run interest in assuring the stability of the financial system. Measures needed to be taken to deal with illiquid or insolvent institutions, to close them down, and to strengthen the balance sheets of the banks that would continue to operate. Unfortunately, in Thailand and Indonesia, the closing down of finance companies provoked the very insecurity and bank runs that the authorities were trying to avoid. The consolidation steps were to be followed by improvements in bank prudential regulation. This turned out to be particularly difficult in a system where much banking had been done on the basis of "relationships" and where there had been much government intervention in the allocation of credit. The lack of an appropriate institutional and legal framework delayed these tasks considerably.

As the restructuring of the financial system proceeded, it quickly became apparent that significant changes in a corporate operation would be necessary. A high level of nonperforming loans, particularly from corporations, must be dealt with before finance companies and banks could be put back in order. But the lack of adequate laws to govern corporate restructuring and bankruptcies represented a significant barrier. Financial and corporate restructuring, always a lengthy process, took longer than anticipated to get going and is still under way.

Corporate restructuring and regulation also sought to achieve other objectives. These included improving accounting transparency, promoting competition, privatizing state-owned enterprises, and dismantling intercorporate relationships, like the chaebol in South Korea. Steps were also taken to increase trade and capital account liberalization. This approach is controversial since liberalization of the capital account has been seen as one source of the area's vulnerability to financial crisis.

Finally, as the effects of the crisis on the unemployment and real incomes of the poor became increasingly apparent, efforts were made to develop or improve social safety nets. These measures included some income transfers and programs to provide employment and training, efforts to reduce the impact of rising prices on poor consumers, and measures to maintain access to education and health care.

Not only were the programs wide ranging, but they were also extremely detailed. An argument can be made that many of the reforms were necessary in order to maintain confidence and to prevent a relapse or continuation of the crisis. But one may also take the position that they were overly complex and detailed (Goldstein, 2000). As we have noted, many of the IMF and World Bank proposals are seen as interference with the cultural tradition of business and government in Southeast Asia. It is not clear to what extent the reliance of the IMF and its sister institutions on Anglo-American business culture was appropriate to the East Asian region. Only recently many people were arguing that some of the characteristics of East Asian business, the relationships between government and business, for example, were responsible for the rapid economic expansion in the region. Although it is a matter of judgment whether the IMF's extension of its programs into such cultural/social issues was beneficial, in most cases the IMF did not have other options. Financial relief could only be provided on the assurance that systemic problems would be remedied and that funds would be managed properly.

CHALLENGES OF THE EAST ASIAN EXPERIENCE

Now that the immediate effects of the crisis are past and that growth has resumed, the situation can be reappraised. The crisis resulted from the interaction of a number of forces, some internal, some external, some more present in some countries than in others. The immediate cause of the crisis may be attributed to cyclical factors such as an unsustainable investment boom, an asset bubble, and a slowdown in exports. In the absence of significant vulnerabilities, these developments might not have caused a massive regionwide financial crisis.

The challenges of preventing crises in the rapidly growing open economies of East Asia are illustrated by the following contradictions:

- Maintaining sustained high rates of investment and growth calls for macro stability, as is demonstrated by a comparison between the East Asian and Latin American experience (Adams and Davis, 1994). But it is not possible to fully smooth out the business cycle. This means that the economic system and the policy strategy must be sufficiently forward-looking, robust, and transparent to prevent crisis reactions. Fluctuations in domestic demand or in exports should not cause capital movements that could drive the region into financial crisis.

- International capital movements and foreign direct investment make important contributions to capital formation and technical change in developing countries. Free movement of capital is an important priority. It is not optimal to close down international financial movements or to impose capital controls. The challenge is to maintain a degree of confidence domestically and in the region so that open economies are not subject to speculative attacks.

- Exchange rate stability has advantages from the perspective of trade and financing. On the other hand, efforts to maintain fixed rates have frequently resulted in overvaluation and speculative attack. The challenge is to maintain a degree of stability that will meet the needs of investors and traders and at the same time permit gradual adjustment in accord with market conditions.

- Domestic credit allocation should be managed largely by private market forces. Yet it is important to prevent speculative excesses and overleveraging that represent a basis for internal financial crisis. This may be difficult to do in a world where business relationships are based as much on "trust" as on formal business plans, contracts, and prudential supervision. It may be desirable to move Asian business practices more in the direction of Western business culture and regulatory control with greater transparency, greater attention to financial calculations, better legal structures, and greater competition. But it is not clear that these objectives can be achieved in the near term future or that they will guarantee stable, crisis-free development.

- The international financial institutions play an important role as a source of emergency financing and policy advice. They must continue to serve this function without being seen as intervening in domestic political affairs. It is not clear whether changes in IMF and World Bank practices will be sufficient or whether the present structure of the international financial institutions needs to be amended.

It may be a long time before all the lessons of this crisis experience can be sorted out and before preventive measures can be put in place. Many things need to be done at the level of the individual developing country and at the level of the international economy.[9]

NOTES

1. We exclude Japan in this discussion. Unless otherwise indicated, our data source is WEFA Group, 2000.

2. However, it is not certain that the general inflation rate data, generally used for this purpose, reflect the magnitude of the price cycle. Prices of building materials and construction costs rose rapidly during the boom period prior to the collapse.

3. For a discussion, see Thailand Ministry of Finance (1999).

4. For a discussion of some of the political issues that have affected the Indonesian situation, see Nasution (1999).

5. For a detailed discussion, see Patrick (1999) and other papers in the same volume.

6. Chinn and Dooley, (1999, 362) say that *"highly managed exchange rate systems—such as those prevailing for the Thai baht and the Indonesian Rupiah—have been and will continue to become more vulnerable to speculative attack."*

7. Fane and McLeod (1999) argue that even the Basle Accord's 8 percent capital adequacy ratio is inadequate in developing countries.

8. In Thailand, the 25 baht to the U.S. dollar exchange rate goes back to the 1980s, following a period of exchange rate instability that was widely seen by the local business community as damaging. The Bank of Thailand maintained that the baht was floating against a market basket of other currencies. But in fact the rate was kept fixed within a narrow band in relationship to the U.S. dollar. In the 1993–1995 period, as a result of large capital inflows, the Bank of Thailand was forced to intervene to keep the baht from appreciating. But by 1996 the 25 baht to the dollar exchange rate meant that the baht was overvalued from a competitive point of view.

9. There is a growing literature about policies and institutions for crisis prevention. See, for example, Summers (2000).

REFERENCES

Adams, F. G., and I.-M. Davis. (1994). "The Role of Policy in Economic Development: Comparisons of the East and Southeast Asian and Latin American Experience." *Asia Pacific Economic Literature* 8(1) (May): 8–26.

Agenor, P. R., J. Aizenman, and A. Hoffmeister. (2000). *The Credit Crunch in East Asia: What Can Bank Excess Liquid Assets Tell Us?* NBER Working Paper

7951, October. Cambridge, MA: National Bureau of Economic Research (NBER).

"The Asian Financial Crisis: An Evaluation of Monetary and Exchange Rate Policy Responses by Thai Regulators." (2000). Unpublished paper.

Baily, M. N., and E. Zitzewitz. (1998). "The East Asian Miracle and Crisis: Microeconomic Evidence from Korea." *Brookings Papers in Economic Activity* (1995): 249.

Bordo, M. D., and Harold James. (2000). *The International Monetary Fund: Its Present Role in Historical Perspective.* NBER Working Paper 7724, June. Cambridge, MA: NBER.

Claessens, S., S. Djankov, and L. Lang. (1998). *Corporate Growth, Financing, and Risks in the Decade before East Asia's Financial Crisis.* World Bank Policy Research Working Paper 2017, November. Washington, DC: World Bank.

Claessens, S., S. Djankov, and D. Klingebiel. (1999). *Financial Restructuring in East Asia: Halfway There?* World Bank Financial Sector Discussion Paper No. 3, September. Washington, DC: World Bank.

Corsetti, G., P. Pesenti, and N. Roubini. (1998). *What Caused the Asian Currency and Financial Crisis?* NBER Working Papers 6833 and 6844; also *Banca d'Italia Temi di Discussione* (343) (December). Cambridge, MA: NBER.

Chinn, M. D., and M. P. Dooley. (1999). "International Monetary Arrangements in the Asia-Pacific: Before and After." *Journal of Asian Economics* 10(3) (Fall): 361–384.

Fane, George, and Ross H. McLeod. (1999). "Lessons for Monetary and Banking Policies from the 1997–98 Economic Crises in Indonesia and Thailand." *Journal of Asian Economics* 10: 395–413.

Goldstein, M. (2000). "IMF Structural Programs." Paper presented at the NBER Conference on Economic and Financial Crises in Emerging Market Economies, Woodstock, VT, October.

International Monetary Fund (IMF). (1999a). *Malaysia: Recent Economic Developments.* IMF Staff Country Report No. 99/85. Washington, DC: IMF.

International Monetary Fund (IMF). (1999b). *Malaysia: Selected Issues.* IMF Staff Country Report No. 99/86. Washington, DC: IMF.

International Monetary Fund (IMF). (1999c). *Philippines: Selected Issues.* IMF Staff Country Report No. 99/92. Washington, DC: IMF.

International Monetary Fund (IMF). (2000a). *Republic of Korea, Economic and Policy Developments.* IMF Staff Country Report No. 00/11. Washington, DC: IMF.

International Monetary Fund (IMF). (2000b). *Singapore: Selected Issues.* IMF Staff Country Report No. 99/35, also 00/83m. Washington, DC: IMF.

International Monetary Fund (IMF). (2000c). *Thailand: Selected Issues.* IMF Staff Country Report No. 00/21. Washington, DC: IMF.

Ito, T. (1999). *Capital Flows in Asia.* NBER Working Paper 7134, May. Cambridge, MA: NBER.

Krugman, Paul. (1979). "A Model of Balance of Payments Crises." *Journal of Money, Credit and Banking* 2(3): 312–325.

Lane, T., A. Ghosh, J. Hamann, S. Phillips, M. Schulze-Ghattas, and T. Tsikata. (1999). *IMF-Supported Programs in Indonesia, Korea, and Thailand: A Preliminary Assessment.* IMF Occasional Paper 1978. Washington, DC: IMF.

Lee, J.-W., and C. Rhe. (2000). "Macroeconomic Impacts for the Korean Financial Crisis: Comparison with the Cross-Country Patterns." Unpublished paper, University of Rochester.

Mishkin, F. S. (1999). *Lessons from the Asian Crisis*. NBER Working Paper No. 7012, April. Cambridge, MA: NBER.

Nasution, A. (1999). "A Long and Bumpy Road to Economic Recovery: The Case of Indonesia." *Journal of Asian Economics* 10.

Patrick, Hugh. (1999). "A Summation of the Conference." Korea and the Asian Economic Crisis: One Year Later (Special Issue). *Joint U.S.–Korea Academic Studies* 9: 1–7.

Pierre, Andrew J. (2000). "Vietnam's Contradictions." *Foreign Affairs* 79(6) (November–December): 69–86.

Pormeleano, M. (1998). *The East Asia Crisis and Corporate Finances*. World Bank Policy Research Working Paper 1990, October. Washington, DC: World Bank.

Radelet, S., and J. Sachs. (1998). "The East Asian Financial Crisis: Diagnosis, Remedies, Prospects." *Brookings Papers on Economic Activity* 1: 1–90.

Sachs, J. D. (1998). "The IMF and the Asian Flu." *The American Prospect* 9(37) (March). http://www.prospect.org/print/v9.

Summers, L. H. (2000). "International Financial Crises: Causes, Prevention, and Cures." *AEA Papers and Proceedings* (May): 1–16.

Thailand Ministry of Finance. (1999). *Thailand's Economic Reform* (October). Bangkok: Official Publication of the Ministry of Finance.

WEFA Group. (2000). *Asian Economic Outlook* (3rd Quarter). Eddystone, PA: The WEFA Group.

Index

About the Contributors

F. GERARD ADAMS is McDonald Professor at Northeastern University in Boston. He moved there recently from the University of Pennsylvania in Philadelphia, where he is emeritus professor. For many years he has also been visiting professor at the Sasin Graduate Institute of Business Administration of Chulalongkorn University in Bangkok. His career has spanned the petroleum industry, government service at the Council of Economic Advisers and the Organization for Economic Cooperation and Development, and the academic world. He has specialized largely in applied econometric studies and forecasting, particularly the relationships between trade, firms, and markets and the macroeconomy. In recent years, much of his work has been concerned with the "Miracle and Meltdown" in East Asia. He has written and edited numerous books and articles, including *The Business Forecasting Revolution* (1986) and, most recently, *East Asian Development* (with Shinichi Ichimura) (Praeger, 1998) and *Public Policies in East Asian Development* (with William E. James) (Praeger, 1999).

ROSALIND CHEW is Head of the Employment Studies Unit in the Nanyang Business School at the Nanyang Technological Univerisity, Singapore. She is currently a senior lecturer in the Division of Human Resource and Industrial Relations of the School of Accountancy and Business at Nanyang Technological University. She is the author of *Worker's Perceptions on Wage Determination in Singapore* (1990), *The Singapore Worker: A Profile* (1992), *Employment-Driven Industrial Relations Regimes* (with Chew Soon Beng, 1995), and *Wage Policies in Singapore: A Key to Competitiveness* (1996). She has also published in various journals, including *Computational Economics* and the *Journal of Manpower*. Her research interests include the study of industrial relations, wages, wage determination and wage systems, and characteristics of the labor force.

CHEW SOON BENG is Professor of Economics and Industrial Relations and Program Director of Master of Science (Managerial Economics) in the Nanyang Business School at Nanyang Technological University, Singapore. He is the author of *Small Firms in Singapore* (1988), *Trade Unionism in Singapore* (1991), *Employment-Driven Industrial Relations Regimes* (with Rosalind Chew, 1995), and *Values and Lifestyles of Young Singaporeans* (1998). He has also published in journals such as the *Singapore Economic Review*, the *China Economic Review*, and the *Journal of Advances in Pacific Basin Business Economics and Finance*. His current research interests include the economics of industrial relations regimes, issues of collective bargaining, and entrepreneurship.

CAL CLARK is an Alumni Professor of Political Science at Auburn University. His recent books include *Women in Taiwan Politics* (with Chou Bih-er and Janet Clark, 1990), *The Evolving Pacific Basin in the Global Political Economy* (with Steve Chan, 1992), *Flexibility, Foresight, and Fortune in Taiwan's Development* (with Steve Chan, 1992), *Comparative Development Patterns in Asia* (with K. C. Roy, 1997), and *The ROC on the Threshold of the 21st Century* (with Chien-Min Chao, 1999). He has also been the special editor or co-editor of issues of *Governance* (1994), *Business & the Contemporary World* (1995), *American Asian Review* (1996), and *Policy Studies Review* (2000). His research and teaching specialty is East Asian political economy.

YI FENG is Associate Professor at the School of Politics and Economics at Claremont Graduate University. He has published on the topics of political economy of growth, development, and political transformation. He is co-editor with Jacek Kugler of *The Applied Expected Utility Model* (1997) and, with Baizhu Chen and Kim Dietrich, of *Financial Market Reform in China: Problems, Progress, and Prospects* (2000). His current research interests include regional integration, labor markets, and endogenous trade policy in developing countries. He is also a co-principal investigator in a project on political development, demographic change, and sustainable growth, which is sponsored by the National Science Foundation.

ISMENE GIZELIS is Visiting Assistant Professor at La Verne University. Her primary research interests are conflict resolution in secessionist ethnic conflict, economic and political development in middle-income countries, and income distribution and welfare transfers, and her current research project explores the impact of socioeconomic conditions, particularly the status of women on the intensity of ethnic conflict. She also worked as a research associate and faculty member for the 2000 State of the World Conference at the University of Missouri–St. Louis.

YEON-SEOB HA is Associate Professor of Public Budgeting and Public Finance in the Department of Public Administration at Yonsei University in Korea. His research and teaching interests center on a broad area of public finance and financial management with a special focus on taxation.

ANTONIO C. HSIANG is an Assistant Professor of the Graduate Institute for Latin American Studies at Tamkang University. His research and teaching interests are in international relations, international political economy, comparative politics in Latin America, and political economy of Latin American development. He has published on those topics in English, Spanish, and Chinese.

AHMED SHAFIQUL HUQUE is an Associate Professor of Public and Social Administration at the City University of Hong Kong. His recent publications include *Public Administration in the NICs* (1996), *Social Policy in Hong Kong* (1997), and *The Civil Service in Hong Kong* (1998). Dr. Huque is editor-in-chief of *Public Administration and Policy* and a former vice president of the Hong Kong Public Administration Association. He is currently conducting research on the management of crisis in public services.

JERMAIN T. M. LAM is Associate Professor in the Department of Public and Social Administration, City University of Hong Kong. He specializes in political and administrative changes in traditional politics. He has conducted a number of funded researches and published extensively in refereed journals of politics, public administration, management, and Asian studies. He has also written and edited books on politics and public administration in Hong Kong and Newly Industrialized Countries. His current funded research is titled "Essentials and Tools of Democratic Governance in Asia."

ZHIYONG LAN is Associate Professor of Public Administration in the School of Public Affairs at Arizona State University. His research interests include public administration theory and reform, comparative public administration, and public finance in the People's Republic of China. He was a Research Fellow at the University of Hong Kong between 1997 and 1999.

JAEHOON LEE is a doctoral candidate in Political Science at Claremont Graduate University. He is Vice President and Senior Researcher at the International Management Research Institute, a Los Angeles-based business consulting firm specializing in Korea and other East Asian countries. His research interests include contemporary politico-economic transformation in Asia, and he has conducted various seminars on Korean affairs.

KUOTSAI TOM LIOU is Professor and Chair of Public Administration at the University of Central Florida. He has published four books and more than 50 refereed journal articles and book chapters in the areas of administrative reform, economic development, organizational management, and public budgeting and finance. He is currently serving as co-editor of two journals (*Policy Studies Review* and the *International Journal of Economic Development*) and is on the editorial board of seven journals. He has also served as a consultant for many public and nonprofit organizations on policy and managerial issues. In 2000, he received the honorary appointment of Visiting Professor from Zhongshan University (Guangshong, China) and Anhui University (Hefei, China).

NG BEOY KUI is Associate Professor in the School of Accountancy and Business, Nanyang Technological University. His research interest includes macroeconomic management and economic reforms in the Southeast Asian countries, including Thailand. He has published research papers on foreign exchange markets, capital markets, capital flows, as well as financial reforms in Southeast Asia. Thailand has been one of the key countries for these studies. At the moment, he is conducting research on the financial crisis in Thailand and Malaysia.

EDWARD W. SCHWERIN is an Associate Professor of Political Science at Florida Atlantic University. He is the author of *Mediation, Citizen Empowerment, and Transformational Politics* (Praeger, 1995), which was awarded Best Book in Transformational Politics by the American Political Science Association in 1995. He has also published articles on political economy and dispute resolution. He teaches courses in Asia and Political Rim Politics, International Political Economy, World Politics, War and Peace, and Comparative Politics.

ROY W. SHIN is Professor of Public Policy and Political Economy in the School of Public and Environmental Affairs at Indiana University–Bloomington. His current research interests focus on technology policy and environmental management. He is editor of *Policy and Management Review*.